Software Specification
and Design

WILEY SERIES IN
SOFTWARE ENGINEERING PRACTICE

Series Editors:

Patrick A. V. Hall, The Open University, UK
Martyn A. Ould, Praxis Systems pic, UK
William E. Riddle, Software Design & Analysis, Inc., USA

Software Specification and Design

A Disciplined Approach for Real-Time Systems

Marilyn Keller Visicom
Ken Shumate Hughes Aircraft Company

John Wiley & Sons, Inc.
New York / Chichester / Brisbane / Toronto / Singapore

Copyright ©1992 by John Wiley & Sons, Inc.
Portions of this work are based on material developed by Telesoft.
Copyright ©Telesoft, 1990. Adapted with permission.

Library of Congress Cataloging in Publication Data
Shumate, Kenneth C.
    Software specification and design : a disciplined approach for
real-time systems / Kenneth C. Shumate, Marilyn M. Keller.
      p. cm. – (Wiley series in software engineering practice)
    Includes bibliographical references (p. 395) and index.
    ISBN 0-471-53296-7 (cloth)
    1. Computer software–Development. 2. Real-time data processing.
I. Keller, Marilyn M., 1956- . II. Title. III. Series.
QA76.76.D47S54   1992
004'.33–dc20   91-28911

Printed in the United States of America

10 9 8 7 6 5 4 3 2 1

Printed and bound by Courier Companies, Inc.

CONTENTS

This book shows how to specify and design complex software systems, providing the technical basis for a repeatable, defined, managed, and potentially optimized process for systems and software development. It addresses three aspects of system development. First is specification of requirements: what the software is to do. Second is design: how the software is to accomplish its function. The third topic is perhaps the most difficult: the transition from requirements to design. This book deals with all three aspects, with special emphasis on the transition from software requirements to design.

In order to set the stage for software specification, methods, techniques, and notations are also presented for the pre-software systems engineering phases: system requirements analysis and system design. This is a vital issue for the design of large systems. Such systems always involve the concurrent development of hardware and software; the software—which we call *systems software*—must be developed in the context of the overall system development. The five key developmental phases of such software are:

- System requirements specification
- System design
- Software requirements specification
- Software top-level design
- Software detailed design

Although the methods presented are language-independent, the software design methods are best illustrated with specific language-oriented design examples; it is important to give specific illustrations of the approaches, techniques, heuristics, rules, and guidelines provided for the transition from requirements to design, and for the complete design itself. The programming language Ada is used for such examples. You need not know Ada to read this book successfully.

WHAT THIS BOOK DOES

This book, first of all, shows you how to specify software requirements, starting with the system requirements and system design phases. There is a concise, but thorough, presentation of the systems analysis methods needed to determine what the requirements are and how to successfully document and communicate them to others. The presentation is accomplished in the context of the first three phases of the development cycle, the last being the analysis and specification of software requirements.

In addition, this book will show you how to use information hiding principles, abstract data types, stepwise refinement, and object-oriented design to identify and document the significant components that establish the architecture of a software system. It will show how to identify and document the algorithms and data structures that actually solve the problem stated in the software requirements specification. For concurrent systems, it will show you how to identify concurrent processes and their interrelationships, and how to package and document the overall system architecture.

The methods presented focus on what is commonly called *top-level* and *detailed* design, although they are also applicable to design styles that repeatedly apply the methods in a manner known as *iterative* or *recursive*. Two important aspects of the design methods presented are (1) the balance between functional decomposition and modularization and (2) the use of the notion of layers of abstraction. In order to address these aspects of design in detail and in specific terms, the detailed design phase of software development is included.

Perhaps most important, the book addresses the transition from the software requirements specification to the software design. One of the most difficult jobs of the software designer is the transition from a problem specification to the initial software architecture—and the satisfactory demonstration that the software design satisfies, and can be mapped or traced back to, the software requirements specification. This book shows how to do that job.

Without being tied to a specific scheme or set of documents, the book also shows how to document the requirements specification and the design and how to demonstrate traceability from both the major design modules and specific algorithms back to the software requirements. There is a strong emphasis on graphics as products of analysis and design in order to ease the task of communicating information to others and to facilitate engineering reviews.

The methods presented in this book have been successfully used to specify, design, and implement real systems in Ada and other languages.

FIVE IMPORTANT CHARACTERISTICS OF THIS BOOK

1. It deals with *both* software specification and design.
2. It provides graphics, guidelines, and a step-by-step methodology.
3. It ties the methodology to a rational development process.
4. It addresses the transition from specification to design.
5. It uses a single large case study to illustrate all aspects of specification and design.

It deals with both software specification and design. It is important not to treat requirements specification and design as isolated and independent issues. This book provides a single, unified treatment of these related topics, and hence necessarily addresses the transition from specification to design. It does so in the context of large "systems" development (including both hardware and software specification), addressing the traditional phases (or sets of activities) of large projects. That is, it addresses the *methodology* of specification and design in the context of a *defined and repeatable process* of system development. This book is much more software-oriented than traditional texts about requirements specification, but much more systems-oriented than traditional software design books. The approach is consistent with and supports the philosophy of *concurrent engineering*, which encourages a philosophy of multi-discipline teams.

It provides graphics, guidelines, and a step-by-step methodology. A set of graphic notations alone does not make a methodology: It does not provide for effective use of the notation. In addition to a consistent set of graphic notations for specification and design, this book provides guidelines for their use (hints, heuristics, rules, tips, and so on), and a step-by-step process—including a realistic example—to explain and illustrate the methodology. It is not a cookbook—design is inherently a creative process—but it does provide ample guidance for those who wish it, or for implementing common and standard approaches across all teams in a large project or company.

It ties the methodology to a rational development process. The set of methods described for software specification and design are closely tied to a set of "rational" development activities, as in Parnas' "A Rational Design Process: How and Why to Fake It" [PAR86]. The point is that although we do not wish to have a document-driven lockstep development process, it *is useful* to have a *nominal* standard—a rational process. The design methods of this book are closely tied to such a rational process; they both *are based on* such a process and *enhance* the process to support repeatable activities and measure progress against standard goals and milestones. The methods provide the technical basis for *Managing the Software Process* [HUM89] and improving an organization's level of process maturity.

It addresses the transition from specification to design. Since the book addresses both software specification and design, it must necessarily address the transition. It does so explicitly, by providing a large set of guidelines and hints to guide the designer from the products of analysis and requirements specification to both the logical and physical representation of the software architecture—the top-level design. In fact, each of the transitions from one phase of the rational development process to the next are addressed; the software specification-to-design transition being given special emphasis, as it is not much addressed in current literature.

It uses a single large case study to illustrate all aspects of specification and design. The case study is an example of a classic real-time, multiprocessor, multi-tasking, process control application dealing with issues such as

communications interfaces and protocols, hardware/software interactions, and real-time feedback control loops. It deals with a specific application domain (automation of certain aspects of a steel mill), but with lessons that are widely applicable to all real-time systems. The case study illustrates in considerable detail those aspects of system requirements and system design that are of special importance to software engineers, then deals specifically with software specification and design. The systems requirements and design issues deal with the entire factory, while the software parts of the case study focus on a smaller subset/prototype in order to address the software requirements-to-design topic in greater
detail.

OVERVIEW OF THE BOOK

The book has three parts, including a major case study as an intrinsic part of the text of the chapters. The case study permeates the book; portions of it are used to make concrete the guidelines recommended to the designer.

Part One, "Introduction," overviews the book, and the software development process. Discussion of various software development activities, documents, and reviews is intended to establish a context for the rather formal set of requirements and design methods to follow. It also discusses the problems frequently seen in the system development process.

Part Two, "Software Specification," provides a basic knowledge of the various methods of systems analysis and engineering that are the starting point for the design methods presented later. There is a strong presentation of how to represent the analytical effort of the first three phases of system development, culminating in the software requirements specification.

Part Three, "Software Design," presents a method of making the transition from requirements to a top-level design. The emphasis is on concurrent or real-time software (being most typical of the sort of systems software which is the subject of this book), but it addresses sequential software design as a subset of the design of concurrent software. A number of important design principles and methods are reviewed, discussed, and then integrated into a single consistent approach, culminating in the complete software design. The way the method relates to the software specification developed in Part Two is presented, with an emphasis on the transition from requirements to design.

Appendix A, "Software Design Concepts," addresses general software design issues that are important throughout Part Three and are most effectively addressed together. The topics addressed are:

- Software design approach
- Information hiding and data abstraction
- Object-oriented design
- Modular real-time design
- Modular structured design

A single large case study is used throughout the book. Part One introduces the full case study in terms of an initial problem statement and a set of exercises. As the exercises are solved throughout the chapters of Parts Two and Three, and the text's solutions are presented, more and more of the problem details are revealed. The case study covers all five phases of system development addressed by this book and illustrates allocation, traceability and documentation; as usual, there is a special emphasis on the transition from requirements to design.

GRAPHICS

The software requirements specification and the design methods for both the sequential and concurrent approaches are strongly graphics-oriented. The graphics methods draw heavily from those commonly used in requirements analysis and design today, but they integrate the wide variety of approaches into a single consistent set of graphics. The graphics are intended and suitable for the development of large software systems in a highly ordered and structured development process with documentation, traceability, and formal design reviews. Since they draw largely from existing graphics notations, the graphics are generally supported by widely available computer-aided software engineering (CASE) tools.

USE OF THE BOOK

The book is suitable for university courses in software engineering having a design emphasis, for intensive seminars dealing with software specification or design, or for individual study by engineers involved with specifying or designing software systems. It should also be useful as either a primary or supplemental text in systems engineering courses that contain a software component. It can provide the technical basis for a repeatable, defined, managed, and potentially optimized process for systems and software development.

ACKNOWLEDGMENTS

Hundreds of people have made a contribution to the ideas in this book, based on reviews of early drafts, comments on related material we have published, and — most of all–interactive classroom discussion as we have repeatedly taught this material. We thank them all, but reserve special thanks for Carol Filbeck; she did the majority of the graphic material and helped us prepare the manuscript in innumerable other ways. Much of this material was developed while the authors were employed at TeleSoft, and we gratefully acknowledge TeleSoft support and permission to use the material we developed and taught during that period.

LIST OF FIGURES

Software Specification
and Design

PART I

INTRODUCTION

Part One is the foundation material for the book. It discusses the contents of the book and how to use it effectively; then it establishes the context for the sort of software specification and design that is the subject of the book—systems software. It discusses classical systems and software engineering, explains why an integrated approach is necessary, and notes that much of the classical approach is still valid and retained. The final chapter presents an overview of the methods of the rest of the book and introduces the problem statement for the case study that is used to illustrate the methods of software specification and design. The problem statement, essentially a customer's operational requirement, has to do with a complex process control application for a steel furnace. The system to be developed, based on the customer requirements, is called the Furnace Monitoring System (FMS).

CHAPTER 1

Overview

Objective: to provide an introduction to the issues addressed by the book and present its overall organization

The purpose of this chapter is to provide you with an overall viewpoint of the subject and structure of the book. The topics covered are:

- The challenge of software specification and design
- Issues addressed by the book
- Organization of the book

1.1 THE CHALLENGE OF SOFTWARE SPECIFICATION AND DESIGN

The most difficult challenge to software engineering—especially to software specification and design—is the development of software in the context of large combined hardware/software systems development. Examples of such systems are air traffic control at the national level, military command and control systems, automated oil refineries or steel processing plants, and so on. Increasingly, mechanisms such as automobiles, copiers, and printers have similar characteristics. Such systems need not be physically large; they need only be complex and involve a number of components that are not identified at the beginning of the development. In other words, the system, and not just the software, needs to be designed. If we develop effective processes and methods for dealing with such systems, they can effectively scale down either to smaller systems developments or to software-only projects.

1.2 ISSUES ADDRESSED BY THE BOOK

This book provides a process and methodology for software specification and design in the context of systems, such as those addressed above, that are characterized by a multi-phase, multi-year development, in which the discipline of *systems engineering* plays an important role. Systems engineering and systems engineering methods will be discussed in Chapter 2. For now, it is sufficient to say that systems engineering is the discipline that transforms user needs or operational requirements into system performance requirements and an overall system design. Systems engineering also plays a management role during hardware and software design and coordinates specialty engineering disciplines, such as safety, reliability, maintainability, availability, integrated logistics support, man–machine interface, and so on. Systems engineering plays less of a role in development as the design grows more detailed, but it becomes particularly important again during system integration and delivery to the customer. These characteristics of systems engineering and the multi-phase aspects of systems development are expressed in Figure 1-1. (We will see in Chapter 2 that this is only a notional process—an "ideal" or "rational" set of phases—but is a useful model nonetheless. It is equivalent to think of the phases as activities to be accomplished, rather than a strict step-by-step set of phases.)

The Process   Figure 1-1 illustrates the various phases or activities in large systems development, with particular emphasis on software and hardware development. The shading illustrates the subject matter of this book, with system requirements and system design being addressed primarily from the aspects that are important to software development.

> The *system requirements analysis* phase addresses the overall system requirements —the job the system must do to satisfy the customer's operational need or requirement. This is the *what* of the system.
>
> The *system design* phase is concerned with the establishment of the overall system design—as hardware and software subsystems—and the allocation of the system requirements, defined during the earlier phase, to hardware and software components. This is the *how* of the system.
>
> The *software requirements analysis* phase addresses the software subsystems on a subsystem-by-subsystem basis to further define *what* is to be done—what problem is to be solved—by the software of each subsystem. The *software specification* is the product, or documentation, resulting from this phase.
>
> The *software design* phases are analogous to the system design phase in the sense that they define components (now pieces of software) that satisfy the requirements: the *how* of the software. The *software design* is the product, or documentation, resulting from this phase.

The phases, their relationship, and the transitions among them will be addressed further in Chapters 2 and 3 and then in detail in the remainder of the book. *Systems engineering* is the discipline that oversees the entire process and is explicitly concerned with system design and system and software requirements specification.

The reason we show this entire process is that it is vital to understand that the software requirements and the transition to a software top-level design—at least for the sort of systems we are discussing—are not developed independently; they are derived from the system requirements and system design.

The Methodology   Software developed in such a context is called *systems software,* and hence the methods are collectively referred to as "Systems Software

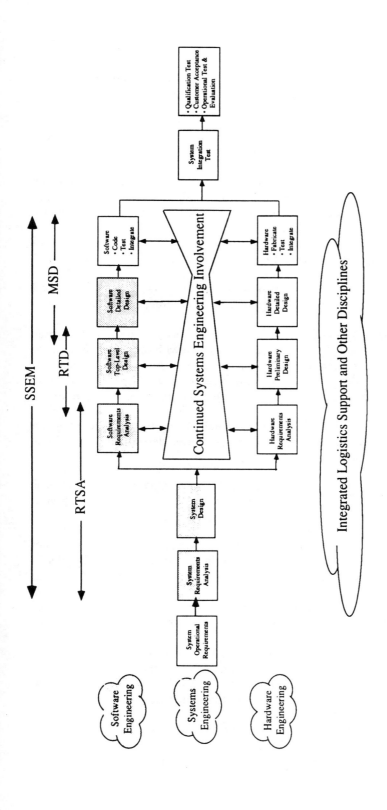

Figure 1-1 The Systems Development Process

Indicates scope of this book

SSEM: Systems Software Engineering Method
RTSA: Real-Time Structured Analysis
RTD: Real-Time Design Method
MSD: Modular Structured Design

Engineering Methodology" (SSEM). The component methods of SSEM, as shown in Figure 1-1, are:

- Real-Time Structured Analysis (RTSA)
- Real-Time Design (RTD)
- Modular Structured Design (MSD)

RTSA is the approach toward structured analysis that incorporates those elements needed for real-time software design. It goes considerably beyond traditional structured analysis, however, by incorporating timing and control issues and generally addressing methods for system design.

RTD is the approach for making the transition from software requirements to software design, ending with a complete top-level design (architecture) of the software system. (Since sequential systems — software not exhibiting concurrency — are a subset of real-time systems, they are also dealt with by RTD.) RTD is developed in sufficient detail to show exactly how requirements are grouped and allocated to software components.

MSD is the method that picks up at the late stages of top-level design and carries into detailed design and resulting code. It deals primarily with sequential systems or with the parts of real-time software that are executed as a single thread of control.

All aspects of the methods have a strong emphasis on traceability from one phase to another, tracing ultimately back to the user or customer operational requirements or needs.

Since this is a book on *software* specification and design, why is there so much emphasis on the entire *system* development process and understanding of methods for system requirements and design?

> It is a central thesis of this book that it is necessary to understand the overall systems development process and methodology in order to specify and design software components of such larger systems effectively.

It is beneficial, of course, for *any* software engineer to understand these issues, but it is *mandatory* for those who wish to participate in the construction of large systems. Once the issues are understood for large systems, the approach and methods scale down nicely for smaller systems or software-only projects. Equivalently, it is necessary for systems engineers involved with the specification of software systems to understand something of software design and the nature of the requirements-to-design transition.

This book meets the needs of both software engineers involved with large systems and systems engineers who specify software requirements. It also meets the needs of those organizations wishing to improve the *maturity* of their software development process, particularly in the sense of [HUM 90]; it provides the technical foundation for a process that is repeatable, defined, managed, and potentially optimized.

It is not the intent of this book or of SSEM to "break new ground." In fact, all of the individual methods are currently in use in the aerospace/electronics industry in the United States and Europe; SSEM is simply an *integrated view*

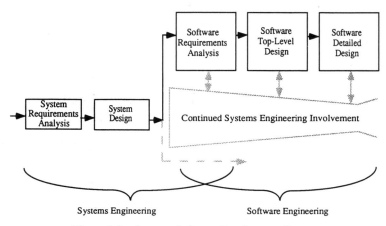

Figure 1-2   Systems Software Development Process

of the overall approach and the flow of events throughout the development process. Figure 1-2 illustrates the portions of the overall development process that are the immediate concern of SSEM. The half-size boxes for the systems portions of the development indicate that SSEM is concerned with, and provides techniques for, software-related portions of such activities. SSEM does not address the systems engineering effort in detail, but unlike most software-oriented methodologies, it *is* concerned with systems engineering and the consequences for systems software development.

1.3 ORGANIZATION OF THE BOOK

The book has three parts, including a major case study as an intrinsic part of the text of the chapters. The case study permeates the book; portions of it are used to make concrete the guidelines, hints, rules, and heuristics recommended to the designer.

The Parts and Chapters   Part One, Introduction, overviews the book and the software development process. Chapter 2 deals in a broad sense with the issues of large system development, while Chapter 3 is an overview of SSEM.

Parts Two and Three have many similarities. Each of their chapters is organized around the idealized development model of Figures 1-1 and 1-2. They address the phases of development called:

- System Requirements Analysis
- System Design
- Software Requirements Analysis
- Software Top-Level Design
- Software Detailed Design

Figure 1-2 is repeated at the beginning of each of the remaining chapters as a marker and reminder of where we are in the process. Each of the chapters has a similar format:

- *Transition* from previous phase.
- *Graphic* notation used during the chapter.
- *Guidelines* that are generally applicable to the subject of the chapter, either specification or design.
- *Methodology—Step by Step* detailed and highly organized description of how to accomplish the phase of system development being discussed. It addresses how to use the graphic notation, tells where general guidelines are applicable, and introduces additional guidelines. Each set of steps involves iteration and gives criteria for deciding when the steps are complete.
- *Example* of an application of the step-by-step process to the case study developed throughout the five chapters—from system requirements through detailed design.
- *Traceability* is not a separate section of any of the chapters, but it is a component of each of the five sections from "Transition" through "Example." Tracing backwards from phase to phase—ultimately to the user or customer requirements—is an important aspect of SSEM.
- *Keys to understanding* the things you need to have grasped from the discussion and example. (If you don't understand the key ideas, you should reread applicable portions of the chapter.)

Part Two, Software Specification, provides a basic knowledge of the various methods of systems analysis and engineering that form the starting point for the design methods presented later. There is a strong presentation of how to represent the analytical effort of the first three phases of system development—culminating in the software requirements specification. Chapters 4, 5, and 6 deal, respectively, with the first three phases of development shown in Figure 1-2. Chapters 4 and 6 can be read as a single chapter on requirements specification. Indeed, that is how most texts present the material. We feel that breaking the material into two parts in accordance with the phases of development is important because that is the way systems are really built; it clarifies the issues to be addressed and brings out the role of systems design and systems engineering.

Part Three, Software Design, presents a method of transitioning from requirements to a top-level design. The emphasis is on concurrent, or real-time, software (which is most typical of the sort of systems software that is the subject of this book), but sequential software design as a subset of the design of concurrent software is also addressed. A number of important design principles and methods are reviewed and discussed, then integrated into a single consistent approach. The way this method of transitioning relates to the software specification developed in Chapter 6 is presented, with an emphasis on the transition from requirements to design. There is substantial discussion of traceability back to the requirements. Chapters 7 and 8 deal, respectively, with the final two phases of development shown in Figure 1-2.

The Case Study   A case study is introduced at the end of Chapter 3 and is used as an illustration and example throughout the remaining chapters. The case study is an example of a classic real-time, multi-processor, multi-tasking process control application, dealing with issues such as communications interfaces and protocols, hardware/software interactions, and real-time feedback control loops. The case study is called the "Furnace Monitoring System (FMS)." It deals with a specific application domain (automation of certain aspects of a steel mill), but with lessons that are widely applicable to all real-time systems. The problem concerns the information gathering and control of a large number of blast furnaces in a hostile physical environment, with data required and control exercised by two physically distant locations.

The FMS illustrates in considerable detail those aspects of system requirements and system design that are of special importance to software engineers, then deals specifically with software specification and design. The system requirements and design issues deal with the entire set of furnaces and their control, while the software parts of the case study focus on a smaller subset/prototype in order to address the software requirements-to-design topic in greater detail.

The FMS is a very realistic problem, with the level of detail and specification typical of what an engineer might initially receive from a customer as part of what has been called a "Mission Needs Statement" (MNS) or a "Required Operational Capability" (ROC). We usually call this an *Operational Requirement* or simply a *Customer Need*. It is the problem statement for which the engineering staff is to design and implement a solution.

Part One introduces the full case study in terms of an initial problem statement and a set of exercises. As the exercises are solved throughout the chapters of Parts Two and Three, and the text's solutions are presented, more and more of the problem details are revealed. The case study covers all five phases of system development addressed by this book and illustrates allocation, traceability, and documentation; as usual, there is a special emphasis on the transition from requirements to design.

The Appendix   Appendix A, "Software Design Concepts," addresses general software design issues that are important throughout Part Three and are most effectively addressed together. The topics addressed are:

- A.1 Software Design Approach
- A.2 Information Hiding/Data Abstraction
- A.3 Object-Oriented Design
- A.4 Modular Real-Time Design
- A.5 Modular Structured Design

The Software Design Approach discussion is relatively brief, since the subject is so widely known; we simply state the main principles and refer to earlier works.

The discussion of Data Abstraction and Information Hiding principles is more extensive, since, although the general ideas are known, the methods are not in common practice.

The discussion of Object-Oriented Design (or Development, known in either case as OOD) is intended to introduce the topic and the importance of its viewpoint, to point out some possible disadvantages, and to focus on the aspects of OOD important to SSEM. Not all aspects of OOD are incorporated.

Modular Real-Time Design is a summary discussion of the requirements-to-design transition in the real-time case, using principles of concurrency, modularity, and the portions of OOD adopted by SSEM. It makes the point that for real-time systems, it is important to address tasking issues early in the top-level design.

Modular Structured Design is the approach that integrates notions of Structured Design with information hiding, data abstraction, and OOD. The main point is that software design calls for a balanced approach between functional decomposition (the "Structured Design" part) and information hiding (the "Modular" part).

Graphics   The software requirements specification and the design methods for both the sequential and concurrent approaches are strongly graphics-oriented. The methods draw heavily from those commonly used in requirements analysis and design today, but they integrate the wide variety of approaches into a single consistent set of graphics. The graphics are intended and suitable for the development of large software systems in a highly ordered and structured development process with documentation, traceability, and formal design reviews. Since the graphics approach draws from current practice, there are generally extensive Computer Aided Software Engineering (CASE) tools available to support development.

Reading the Book   If you are unfamiliar with a formal systems development process, you will want to read Chapter 2 with some care. Otherwise, it can be skimmed lightly—but it should be at least skimmed, since it explains the importance of process (and the fact that the seemingly orderly process is only an idealized view) and the viewpoint of SSEM. Chapter 3 is an intentionally short overview of SSEM, intended to be read by all.

Systems engineers need to read Part Two with considerable care to understand the viewpoint and methods of SSEM, while looking at Part Three as an overview of what is done with the products of their effort. Many systems engineers will have their own, and different, methods for the systems-oriented phases (Chapters 4 and 5), but they are still likely to be consistent with the software specification methods of Chapter 6 and hence compatible with SSEM.

Software engineers working closely with the systems engineering function also need to read Part Two carefully, perhaps skipping over some of the alternate designs of Chapter 5. It is important to recognize early that Chapters 4 and 6 work together to provide the notation and guidelines for requirements specification. All software engineers need at least to go through the steps of Part Two, perhaps only skimming Chapter 5. Part Three goes to the heart of the software engineering function and is the payoff from the earlier sections of the book.

All readers will find that some of their favorite topics or specialty viewpoints are not included. Many of these are briefly discussed in Chapter 2. There is for example, no specific documentation standard. Nor is there an explanation of such topics as how to conduct reviews or use checklists. Such techniques surrounding the basic methods are properly a part of organizational culture; each organization—in some organizations, each project —will have to add these extra factors to define a complete project handbook. This book is long enough as it is!

The material can be covered in a five-day intensive seminar, with lecture in the morning and a good bit of laboratory minds-on case study work in the afternoon.

1.4 KEYS TO UNDERSTANDING

- In order to build software in the context of large systems development, it is necessary to understand more than just the software development methods and process.
- Similarly, successful systems engineering for software requirements specification requires considerable understanding of software design methods and process, especially the requirements-to-design transition.
- Figure 1-1 illustrates the overall system development process. (We will see in Chapter 2 that this is only an "ideal" or "rational" process, but is a useful model nonetheless.)
- Figure 1-2 illustrates the portions of the process that are addressed by this book. The book is structured around this idealized development process. The associated set of methods is called *Systems Software Engineering Methodology* (SSEM).
- A single large real-time case study will be used for illustration and exercises throughout the book.

CHAPTER 2

Systems Engineering and the System Development Process

Objective: to establish a foundation of the current system development process and methods, in order to provide a basis for integration of various methods into a coherent scheme of software specification and design

The purpose of this chapter is to summarize classical systems development issues, discuss why new methods are needed, and point out how the old and the new may be usefully integrated. The methods and graphics discussed are general in nature, and not those of the Systems Software Engineering Methodology (SSEM)—although it uses many of the same methods and graphics. The topics covered are the following.

- Large systems development
- Systems engineering
- Software engineering
- Relationships among phases
- Integration of ideas

The rationale and foundation for SSEM will be introduced along the way.

2.1 LARGE SYSTEMS DEVELOPMENT

This section deals with the general process and methodology of systems development and with models of system development—including a pessimistic real-world viewpoint. The section presents a broader perspective, which allays some of the problems of the pessimistic model, and then it introduces the notion of "faking" a rational model in order to justify the nominal step-by-step phased model of Chapter 1.

General: Process and Methodology In order to provide for the orderly development of large systems, it is necessary to define a *methodology:* a set of procedures, graphics, and guidelines that explains how to accomplish systems and software engineering. It is important that the methodology be embedded within a *process:* the set of steps that must be accomplished to complete a task. Paraphrasing Boehm [BOE88], a process model performs two primary functions:

1. It determines the *order of the stages* involved in development and evolution.
2. It establishes the *transition criteria* for progressing from one stage to the next, which consist of *completion* criteria for the current phase and *entrance* criteria for the next phase.

The process model addresses two questions vital to the system developer:

1. What shall we do next?
2. When do we stop doing it?

Boehm's discussion is about software development, but it is exactly applicable to the full systems development process. Process is distinct from methodology in that while process deals with order of the stages and transition criteria, methodology deals with *how to accomplish each phase.* The emphasis of methodology is on:

- *How to navigate through a phase*—determining and allocating requirements, defining system and software architecture, partitioning criteria, creation of data structures and algorithms
- *How to represent phase products*—data flow diagrams, state transition diagrams, structure charts, information hiding modules, program design language

Models of the System Development Process   There are many different potential models of system development, ranging from an informal continuous "cut and try" process (for the software development phase, known as "code and fix") to a formal method that insists upon completion of one step (never to return or redo) before start of another.

The code-and-fix model seems natural to many developers, because that is how they create individual programs, by themselves or in teams of two or three. The approach does not scale up to large systems, however, and the early history of systems development is littered with examples of failed code-and-fix projects.

In response to the failures of the cut-and-try or code-and-fix models of development, a formal process, commonly called the *waterfall model* [ROY70], was instituted by many developers, especially for work performed for the U.S. Department of Defense (DOD). It is viewed by some as being characterized by a relatively rigid and document-driven set of steps. (This had surely not been the intent of Royce in the cited paper; in fact, he advocates a build-it-twice philosophy, using an early prototype or "simulation" in order to determine trouble spots.)

The basic steps are essentially those of Figure 1-1, but the usual illustration shows the "steps" leading downward, hence allowing "water" to "fall or flow" down the steps. The implication of the waterfall is that there is no going back, although most practitioners of the waterfall allow each phase to influence the immediately preceding phase (and ultimately all preceding phases). Some experienced developers simply use the waterfall as a model for tracking status and reporting both technical and management issues to customers—as a nominal or idealized model—without attempting to force the actual engineering effort into rigid phases. We will see that this is a wise approach.

The waterfall model has been widely criticized, for example in the *Defense Science Board Task Force Report on Military Software* [DOD87]. The strongest criticism has been that it is vitally reliant on complete and unambiguous specification prior to design.

The Real-World Development Model   Of course, if the user's needs were constant and fully specified, and if the developers were perfect at each stage, the nominal model would fit reality; the development would proceed in an orderly fashion from one phase to the next. However, that's not how the real world works. All experienced systems and software development professionals know that the development process is iterative and prone to error, backtracking, reworking—perhaps "chaotic" is not too strong a word. A pessimist might even characterize the development process as being more like Figure 2-1—chaotic indeed! Figure 2-1 does not illustrate a model of development that we should *strive for,* but one that is likely to occur if we do not explicitly introduce order. However, we must not impose order in the form of a straitjacket, or we will fall prey to problems related to difficulty of changing development products. Let's first look at the issues raised by Figure 2-1 and then see how we can address the problems.

The primary driver of potential chaos has to do with specification of requirements. Brooks, in "No Silver Bullet: Essence and Accidents of Software Engineering" [BRO87a] first asserts that

> I believe the hard part of building software to be the specification, design, and testing of this conceptual construct, not the labor of representing it and testing the fidelity of the representation.

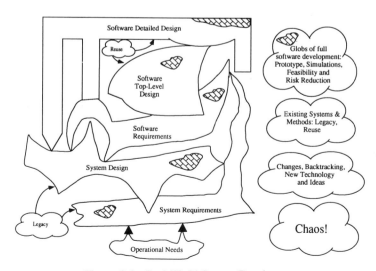

Figure 2-1   Real-World System Development

He then goes on to emphasize the point that the very most difficult part is the specification:

> The hardest single part of building a software system is deciding precisely what to build. No other part of the conceptual work is as difficult as establishing the detailed technical requirements, including all the interfaces to people, to machines, and to other software systems. No other part of the work so cripples the resulting system if done wrong. No other part is more difficult to rectify later.

Of course, this goes double for the specification of *system* requirements! Brooks then makes an eloquent case for the need for iteration between analyst and customer to define the requirements:

> Therefore, the most important function that the software builder performs for the client is the iterative extraction and refinement of the product requirements.

He finishes with:

> I would go a step further and assert that it is really impossible for a client, even working with a software engineer, to specify completely, precisely, and correctly the exact requirements of a modern software product before trying some versions of the product.

The conclusion is the need for some sort of prototyping or iterative development, even causing Brooks to advocate "growing" software rather than "building" a software product.

The second important driver of potential chaos is simply that developers are not perfect. As the system development proceeds, we may discover that some aspect of the requirements cannot be met with current or readily developed technology, or some technology in the design proves to be faulty, or whatever. Such issues will often cause at least a partial revisit of earlier phases.

The final major driver of potential chaos is that of *legacy*—that which exists when we start development, either in the form of an existing system that is to be modified, software available for reuse, organization methods and biases, existing documentation, and so on. Actually, systems are less often built completely from scratch than as modifications of existing systems. Such issues both affect the overall development style and, particularly when legacy enters part way through development, cause the revisit and modification of earlier-phase products. Now this is not all bad; much of the legacy issue is the factor of *taking advantage* of what has gone before. However, it sure can make a mockery of a rational step-by-careful-step development process.

Figure 2-1 also shows some of the attempts to cope with change and inability to specify requirements, showing that there are likely to be prototypes, simulations, and so on—including software development going on throughout the development process! This is important to recognize; software development is not an isolated event that occurs only during the last two phases of Figure 1-1.

In the following two sections, we will see how both systems engineering and software engineering use iterative development methods to cope with the issues raised by Figure 2-1. First, however, it is useful to take an even broader perspective of development to understand the framework for requirements–design iteration.

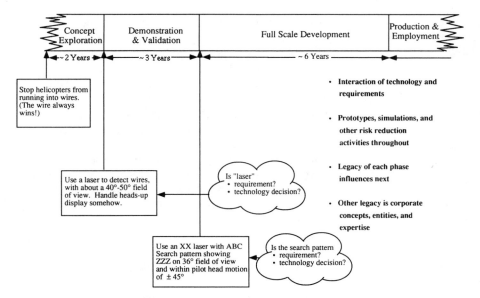

Figure 2-2 "Full" System Development Cycle: A Broader Viewpoint

A Broader Perspective of the System Development Process   Figure 2-2 shows major stages in the development of a system ("stages" being larger than, and potentially containing, phases such as shown in Figures 1-1 and 1-2). The initial, basic user need is to stop helicopters from running into wires when they are flying nap-of-the-earth (nominally zero altitude) at high speeds, including at night. The Concept Exploration stage addresses at least parts of the first two phases of Figure 1-2 and may address them all; that is, it can be a complete system development, including software implementation. This would be done, however, in a relatively informal manner, with the entire cycle of development expected to repeat during later stages. Notice that at the end of Concept Exploration there is a new, more refined, requirement—but one that is still somewhat mushy (note the use of "somehow"). That's OK for this stage of development.

Demonstration & Validation (DemVal) surely incorporates or revisits system requirements analysis and system design and, more likely than not, involves all five of the phases in Figure 1-2. At the end of the DemVal stage, the requirements are much more precise (although still susceptible to change later as everyone learns more and technology advances), and the "real" development, often called Full-Scale Development, can begin. This third stage incorporates all five phases, although most of the effort of the two systems phases may have been essentially completed during DemVal.

The primary activity of the first two stages (Concept Exploration and DemVal) is the clarification and partial firming of the original requirements, stated in documents with titles such as "Mission Needs Statement" (MNS) or "Operational

Requirements." There is constant iteration between system requirements and system design; there often must be tradeoffs between what the customer believes is necessary and what is actually technically possible and financially feasible. In order to accomplish this (virtually combined) requirements definition and system design, there is a whole sequence of partial and trial designs—often including significant software development—combined with tradeoff studies to assess technical and financial feasibility. There are simulations, sizing and timing studies, hardware and software tool selection, prototypes, and other activities; all can be basically considered risk reduction for the later full-scale development effort.

Now, what's important about all this is the intrinsic iteration and refinement built into the process. There is extensive interaction of technology and requirements with consequent requirements–design iteration; there are prototypes, simulations, and other risk reduction activities; there is ample time for legacy to influence the development; and all of this occurs before the "formal" development process starts.

We have seen a notional rational and orderly—ideal—process (Figure 1-1). We've seen the potential for chaos in the real world (Figure 2-1). And we've just seen a broader viewpoint that accommodates iteration and backtracking. Does the backtracking, chaos, and so on, combined with the criticism of the orderly waterfall, lead us to abandon order? How do we reconcile these views?

A Rational and Orderly Development Process: The Idealized Model

David Parnas and Paul Clements have done a marvelous job for us in the paper—you have to watch the title carefully; it tells the story in a single phrase—"A Rational Design Process: How and Why to Fake It" [PAR86]. The answer is in defining an ideal or rational process (Figure 1-1), trying as best we can to follow the rational process, and, even if we can't quite do so, *making it look to the world outside the project as though* we are following the ideal process—even if the development really looks like Figure 2-1. Therefore, a rational, even idealized, process model is useful, and even if we cannot follow it completely, we can follow it as closely as possible and produce the work products associated with the ideal process.

This is what is meant by "faking" the process. We might think of it as "pretending" to follow the ideal process. Why would we want to do this? Paraphrasing and building on Parnas's five reasons, faking the process:

- Provides guidance to designers. Even inexperienced designers can at least get a start on the process and work on the steps in the right order.
- Allows us to come closer to a rational design than if we proceed on an ad hoc basis. The effort to follow the ideal process will focus activity and direct attention to proper areas of concern.
- Establishes a *standard* process. This is particularly valuable for a large organization that undertakes many different projects by different components and people.
- Provides a mechanism for measuring progress. It is possible to compare progress to that of the ideal process and see where corrective action needs to be taken.

- Simplifies review of the project by outsiders. Such outside review is essential for success and is often mandated by the customer of the final system to be constructed.

The paper contains further arguments for faking the rational process and how to do so. We conclude—and this is the viewpoint of SSEM—that a rational process is necessary as an ideal or nominal model. The ideal model—the one we should strive for while knowing we cannot attain it—is represented by Figures 1-1 and 1-2; this model will be used to structure the presentation of methods of software specification and design.

Finally, remember again that these steps are not conducted in linear order. There is constant feedback to and modification of system requirements during the design process. There are prototypes, simulations, "chunks" of software development, and so on, that give us the insight we need to make requirements modifications. But don't get lost in the chaos; it is our job to plan the development so as to place as much order on the chaos as we can—to make the process rational.

One way we do so is to assume (even "pretend" is not too strong) that the requirements are *essential requirements*, in the sense that they are the *pure specification* of customer needs that must be satisfied. Of course, we strip away the pretense whenever necessary, but between the necessary times we treat the requirements as essential.

The next two sections take a more detailed look at the methods used during the five phases of Figure 1-2. There tends to be more discussion of the software aspects of specification and design (of course), except where the systems discussion is generally applicable to both systems and software; then it is discussed as part of systems issues.

2.2 SYSTEMS ENGINEERING

Paraphrasing [BLA90], systems engineering consists of the application of efforts to:

- Transform an operational need into a description of system performance parameters
- Determine a preferred system configuration through an iterative process of:
  Functional analysis
  Synthesis
  Optimization
  Definition
  Design
  Test
  Evaluation
- Incorporate related technical parameters and ensure compatibility of all physical, functional, and program interfaces
- Integrate all specialty engineering efforts into the overall project activities

Another way to look at it is that systems engineering is the process used to transform an operational need into a working system that satisfies the requirement.

Having said all that, let's look at the way systems engineering works and incorporates the iteration we have been discussing. The two major efforts more or less completely under the control of systems engineering are system specification and system design. We will discuss each of these phases and then the important interaction between them, which helps cope with the complexity of Figure 2-1.

For each of the phases, and for the phases of software engineering as well, we will discuss the:

- Process
- Products
- Transition to the following phase

It turns out to be useful to separate the process from the products. Davis [DAV90, page 21] points out that what he calls "problem analysis" (which we call the process) and "product description" are quite different activities.

He states the distinction as: "During problem analysis, analysts spend their time brainstorming, interviewing people who have the most knowledge about the problem at hand, and identifying all possible constraints on the problem's solution." It is a time of information gathering and organization.

On the other hand, "During product description it is time to take pen in hand, to make some difficult decisions and prepare a document that describes the expected external behavior of the product to be built to solve the now-understood problem." Notice that it is not just a documentation phase; rather, the process of documentation helps clarify and organize ideas. This is the period to resolve conflicting ideas and eliminate inconsistencies.

These are not, however, sequential and mutually exclusive activities. What actually goes on is some analysis, some description, further analysis, and so on in iteration. But the process finally must result in some readable product that describes what has gone on. Davis presented the issue in the context of the analysis phase, but each of the concepts is largely applicable to the design phases as well.

2.2.1 System Requirements Analysis

System specification, the statement of system requirements, occurs during the first phase of Figure 1-1, "System Requirements Analysis." We will discuss the process, products, and transition to the next phase of system design.

System specification and design are so tightly coupled that the most important description of the interaction will actually come during the discussion of iteration between the phases, in Section 2.2.3. The discussion below is necessarily summary in nature; for a more extended discussion, the Thayer and Dorfman IEEE Tutorial *System and Software Requirements Engineering* [DOR90] is excellent.

Process The activities are those described by Davis as being part of the analysis phase (brainstorming, interviewing, and so on), generally with the following steps in the process:

- Establish system objectives
- Identify functions and function interactions
- Specify performance for each function
- Define an overall operational concept
- Iterate for various levels of concern

The concept of iteration is important; it incorporates the notion of hierarchical decomposition of requirements in order to assist in controlling complexity.

Some authors, notably McMenamin & Palmer [MCM84], regard the resulting requirements as "essential" in the sense of reflecting the "true" or "pure" customer requirements. They even make an assumption of *perfect technology,* even to the point of assuming arbitrarily fast ("infinitely fast") processors. Hatley & Pirbhai [HAT87] talk about the "technology-independent" requirements. It turns out that these ideas are often extraordinarily powerful for clarifying one's viewpoint and for avoiding design during the requirements definition statement. However, they are not quite the way things must really happen, at least for the sort of systems that are the main concern of SSEM.

To carry the notion of "essential" or "technology-independent" through to its conclusion would be overly likely to result in unrealistic requirements (e.g., a customer need to shuttle to the moon and back on an hourly basis while . . . and so on). What really happens is a back-and-forth iterative process that allows technology to influence requirements.

The reason the notions of "essential" and "technology-independent" are important is that it allows one to separate the concerns, at least temporarily, of requirements and design. For example, when specifying timing requirements for some algorithm for aircraft collision avoidance, one should not (at least for the moment) be worrying about processor *and* inter-center/interprocessor communication speeds (or even if there are interprocessor communications). But it is vital to address these issues later, going back to modify the requirements (and perhaps the system concept) if necessary.

These notions of "essential" and "technology-independent" are so useful that they are adopted by SSEM, but always with the realization of the actual iterative bouncing between requirements and design. There is an analogy here to the whole notion of a rational (in the Parnas sense) development process. The viewpoint of "essential" is an idealized world view that is helpful in stating requirements, even if we can only strive for it without ever really attaining a complete specification before doing some system design.

Products   Each organization has its own specialized graphics methods and tools, but some products that have been found to be widely applicable are the following:

- Functional Flow Block Diagrams (FFBD) are used to structure requirements in functional terms. They show the various things to be accomplished (first in general and then in more detail using hierarchical decomposition), and the flows of information, material, equipment, people, and so on between system functions.

- Time Line Sheets show what sorts of activities occur at given times and how long the activities take.
- Process Flow and Sequence Diagrams are similar to time line sheets, but add decision blocks (including time for decision making) and alternate flows.
- Data flow diagrams (DFD) and associated techniques can be used as an alternative to FFBD.

Developers also use a wide variety of other specific documents, such as end-item maintenance sheets, failure mode effect and criticality analysis, fault tree analysis, and operator task analysis. Most of these products are discussed in detail in [DOA79].

Transition to Next Phase   The two most difficult transitions are those from analysis to design. (The similarity of the two transitions is discussed further in Section 2.4). The transition from system requirements analysis to system design involves a fundamentally creative element in the determination of alternate system designs, their evaluation and comparison in trade studies, and the choice of the "best" system design. The graphics of SSEM are an important component of describing the alternative system designs and hence, of making the choice of the final design. The other aspect of the transition is the allocation of requirements to the components of the system design. The allocation is not done after the fact, but in an iterative fashion as an integral part of the system design process. This is discussed in considerable detail in Chapter 5.

2.2.2 System Design

System design—the determination and representation of system components and their interaction—occurs during the second phase of Figure 1-1. We will discuss the process, products, and transition to the next phase of system design.

Process   The steps of system design can be considered in many ways, but always involve at least:

- Determination of alternative designs, including components and interfaces
- Allocation of requirements to components of the design
- Tradeoff analysis of the value of alternating designs and the degree to which they satisfy requirements
- Iteration with requirements analysis
- Determination and documentation of chosen design

Products   Typical products include:

- Schematic Block Diagram (SBD) to show the actual system components, both hardware and software, and the characteristics of their interconnections such as voltage levels, type of data bus, width of a runaway

- Architecture Flow Diagram (AFD) and associated graphics (essentially an alternative to the SBD), chosen by SSEM and shown in Chapter 5
- Requirements Allocation Sheets (RAS), which show the relationship between requirements and the components of the design
- Requirements Traceability Matrix (RTM), shown in Chapter 5 as an alternative to RAS
- Message catalogs, showing the bit-level detail and meaning of data communication messages

Most of these products are discussed in detail in [DOA79].

The hardware and software components are often considered to be important components of configuration control; they are therefore called *hardware configuration items* (HWCI) and *computer software configuration items* (CSCI). We will use these names throughout the book. They are shown in either the SBD or the AFD.

Transition to Next Phase   The transition from system design to software requirements analysis is logically straightforward, being simply a change of focus from the overall system to the set of individual software components, their interfaces among each other, and their interfaces with the remainder of the system. The creation of additional requirements to satisfy the system design—the *derived* requirements—illustrates how system design drives the software requirements. This is the point of transition from systems to software engineering. The right approach in regard to those two disciplines is for the work to be done with a blend of expertise, with the systems engineering function retaining overall control in order to cater to continued hardware–software tradeoffs and potential design changes as a consequence of design–requirements iteration.

In some companies, this transition is organizationally complex, since different organizations are responsible for systems engineering and software engineering, but the transition is not technically complex—at least not using SSEM.

2.2.3   Requirements-to-Design Iteration

Figure 2-3 is taken from [DOA79, page 2-1], a guiding document for systems engineering efforts for the U.S. Government. This basically encompasses both the

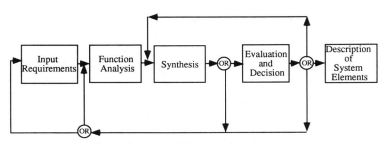

Figure 2-3   The System Engineering Process

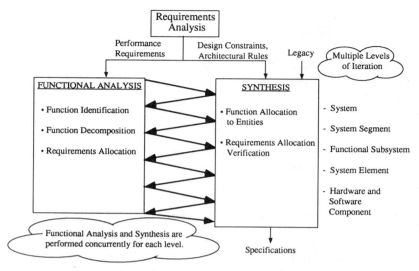

Figure 2-4   System Design and Requirements Iteration

system requirements analysis (Function Analysis) and system design (Synthesis, or determination of alternate designs, and Evaluation and Decision, determination of which design is to be implemented). What is important to note is the extensive feedback between the phases; this is what occurs during the Concept Exploration and DemVal stages discussed earlier and (as necessary) even during Full-Scale Development. Figure 2-4 is another viewpoint of this iteration, showing a "bouncing" back and forth between requirements and design at many different levels of system and software development.

Two other important characteristics of the system requirements and design phases are the use of hierarchical decomposition and a functional viewpoint. The "divide and conquer" philosophy of decomposition is the only real way to cope with the complexity of large systems. The decomposition occurs along the lines of the functions of the system—what it is intended to do, perform, or accomplish.

The same document that provided Figure 2-3 also states [DOA79, page 2-5]: "The first step in the system engineering process is function analysis." A more tutorial document, also providing guidance for U.S. Government systems engineering, defines functional analysis as [DSM86, page 6-1], "a method for analyzing performance requirements and dividing them into discrete tasks or activities. It involves the identification and decomposition of the primary system functions into subfunctions at ever-increasing levels of detail." Both documents also emphasize the importance of the functional approach to systems engineering.

A standard systems engineering text also stresses the importance of this process [BLA90, page 55]: "An essential element of preliminary design is the employment of a functional approach as a basis for the identification of design requirements for each hierarchical level of the system." The point of this discussion has been that the hierarchical approach based on functional decomposition is (and long has been) the foundation of systems engineering requirements specification and, hence, the basis for the software requirements for large system developments.

This is an important issue to understand in regard to its consequences for software development. The primary representation of the software architecture is not functional; rather it is based on the representation of a set of modules that hide design decisions and often represent entities in the actual system outside the software. We won't be discussing this in detail until Chapter 7, but the modular design representation is distinctly different from a functional representation of the software. (Actually, SSEM in its Real-Time Design (RTD) and especially its Modular Structure Design (MSD) components, provides for a dual representation—both functional and modular—of the software architecture but the modular approach dominates.)

Systems engineers and systems users are highly satisfied with the functional/hierarchical approach, and are unlikely to change. It is important that the software portion of the system development process take this into consideration and be prepared to make the transition from functional to modular representations.

The next phase of development is software requirements analysis. Although, as Figure 1-2 indicates, systems engineering is still quite important during this phase, we will discuss it in the context of software engineering.

2.3 SOFTWARE ENGINEERING

Paraphrasing Pressman [PRE87, page 19], the essential elements of software engineering are the following:

- Use of sound engineering principles to obtain, in an economical manner, software that is reliable and efficient when executing on real machines
- Use of *methods, tools,* and *procedures,* which simultaneously allow development of high-quality software and managerial control of the development process

"Methods" refers to the technical "how to's," often including special graphics notation. "Tools" denotes automated support for design, code, and test. "Procedures" refers to the sequence in which methods are applied; description of deliverables; reviews; and controls and milestones that allow assessment of progress.

Davis [DAV90, page 16] makes the useful distinction between "software only" developments and "systems" developments, which the hardware specification and design phases occur in parallel, and are later integrated, with the software development. Figure 2-5, adapted from Davis, illustrates the differences. The viewpoint of SSEM is that of Figure 2-5b. The importance of the distinction is that a software-only project may start with little legacy of the sort created during the lengthy process of Figure 2-2, and it often has a hardware suite already specified. The systems developments, on the other hand, must deal with all the complexity of the full systems engineering process.

While making the point that the difficult problems we deal with are primarily those shown in Figure 2-5b, Davis also makes the important point that it is vital to differentiate requirements analysis from design for two reasons [DAV90, through-

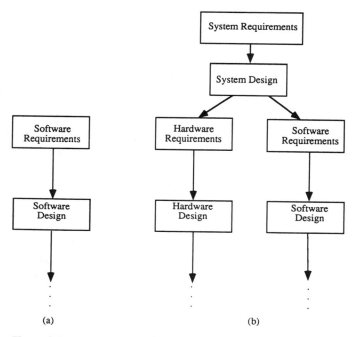

Figure 2-5 Development Life Cycles: (*a*) Software; (*b*) Systems (Software and Hardware)

out pages 55 to 56]. The first reason is that they have different goals: The goal of requirements analysis is understanding of the problem (*what* the system is to do), whereas the purpose of design is largely concerned with implementation (*how* things are to be accomplished). The second reason is cost: Design is much more expensive than analysis, involving many costly efforts such as tradeoff studies among different design alternatives. One will not be allowed to spend such money—and should not attempt to do so—before knowing what problem is to be solved.

Having said all that, let's look at the way software engineering works and incorporates the iteration we have been discussing to make some sense out of the chaos of Figure 2-1. The two major products more or less directly related to software engineering are software specification (the result of software requirements analysis) and software design. We will discuss each of these phases and the important interaction between them that helps cope with the complexity of Figure 2-1.

2.3.1 Software Requirements Analysis

Software specification—the statement of software requirements for a single computer software configuration item (CSCI) and its interfaces—occurs during the third phase of Figure 1-1, "Software Requirements Analysis". We will discuss the process, products, and transition to the next phase of software top-level design.

The discussion of process and products in this section is quite short; it only addresses the few things that are different from *system* requirements specification. All the lessons, graphics, guidelines, and so on from system requirements specification are applicable to the specific issues of software requirements specification.

Process   The specification of software requirements begins where the system design has left off: with the requirements allocated to a CSCI and its interfaces. Remembering that the system requirements analysis is functional in nature, with the requirements allocation being in terms of either functional flow block diagrams (FFBDs) or data flow diagrams (DFDs), and associated products in each case, it is best to continue the functional description of requirements. (There are those who disagree with this and favor an object-oriented approach for requirements, as explained in the Appendix A section "Modular Real-Time Design". The discussion explains why we advocate the functional approach.)

The most important part of the process is integrating the allocated requirements with the derived requirements that result from the specific technology adapted during system design. It is otherwise similar to, but perhaps more detailed than, system requirements analysis.

One viewpoint of system requirements analysis that is specifically adopted is that of the notion of *essential* or *technology-independent* requirements specification. This seems a strange viewpoint at this time, since, of course, the software is technology-specific, based on the decisions that have been made during system design. Nonetheless, it is useful for the software requirements specification to treat the combination of allocated (customer) and derived (system design– and technology-specific) as now being "essential" as far as the software is concerned.

The "technology" that is now considered to be perfect is that of the internal software interaction. For example, in the earlier example of specifying timing requirements for some algorithm for aircraft collision avoidance, one should not (during software requirements analysis) be worrying about factors such as time taken for a subprogram call or for a task context switch (or even if there *are* subprogram calls or task context switches). Of course, it is vital to address such issues later, but that will be accomplished by a similar sort of back-and-forth requirements-to-design iteration as earlier described for the systems case. In the software development arena, it has become fashionable to call such interaction *prototyping* or *iterative/recursive* development.

While we fully support such requirements–design iteration (and prototyping and iterative/recursive development), the notions of essential requirements and technology-independent viewpoint are so powerful that we frequently take such a viewpoint—realizing, just as in the systems case, that this is an idealized view, as is the whole notion of a rational development.

Products   As with system requirements analysis, each organization has its own specialized graphics methods and tools, but some products that have been found to be widely applicable are:

- Data Flow Diagrams (DFD), used to represent the logical activities or processes that take place in the system, in terms of the data flows they operate on and transform. We will occasionally use "DFD" to stand for the entire range of techniques that include:

    Context diagram, showing the interfaces to the world outside the CSCI being specified

    DFDs themselves, giving a multi-layered hierarchical decomposition of the software requirements and containing data flows, data stores (where data reside over time in a static sense, at least logically), and the processes that transform the data

    Process Specifications (PSpecs), which define the exact processing that occurs by the lowest-level or primitive processes (those processes that are not further decomposed into lower-level processes)in a DFD

    Data dictionary, which defines the elements of the DFD and associated processes

- Control Flow Diagrams (CFD), which show the logic behind when processes are activated and deactivated. They have similar elements to DFDs (a significant difference being the frequent use of state transition diagrams) and are often combined on the same diagram.

- Entity-Relationship Diagrams (ERD) [CHE76], which group together the data stores from all the DFD/CFD diagrams and show the relationships between the data. A more recent and more elaborate version is the Object Diagram [RUM91].

The use of ERDs and related products and techniques has commonly become known as *information modeling* [FLA81]. A recent outgrowth of information-modeling efforts that has an even greater—nearly exclusive—emphasis on data relationships, in place of top-level focus on data flows, processes, and control issues, is called variously Object-Oriented Requirements Analysis (OORA, sometimes pronounced "oooh-raaaah") or just Object-Oriented Analysis (OOA).

Transition to Next Phase   This is another potentially difficult transition, with characteristics that are similar to the system requirements-to-design transition, particularly the fact that the software design is a fundamentally creative activity. The whole point of the Real-Time Design (RTD) methods advocated in this book is to control and minimize the complexity by providing a concrete set of guidelines; but the job is still by no means easy. Usually, the various software design alternatives are not analyzed and 'traded off' in quite as formal a manner as for the earlier transition, but the creative process is quite similar.

In addition, there are four differences between requirements representation and software architecture:

- Processes vs. tasks
- Functional vs. modular

- Flat vs. hierarchical
- Logical vs. physical

For each of the differences, there is an aspect of transition. In SSEM, a large number of guidelines will be provided, but many alternatives exist and the process is fundamentally creative in nature. The differences are discussed in detail in the following:

Processes vs. tasks. The potentially concurrent elements represented by processes on the DFD must be grouped into concurrent pieces of software that will either actually operate concurrently (in a multi-processor system) or appear to do so (in a single-processor multi-tasking system). Attention must begin to be paid to issues such as external interrupts, timing, and mutually exclusive access to data structures.

Functional vs. modular. The requirements analysis presents a model that is fundamentally functional in nature: its architecture is based on, and defines, the functions (or actions, or processes, or activities) that the system is to accomplish. It provides a step-by-step description of what the system must do to satisfy the customer.

On the other hand, effective software engineering principles demand that the major software modules—the ones that define the architecture of the software system—be based not on functional step-by-step considerations, but instead on information-hiding and modularization. The modules hide design decisions, often about data structures, in order to make the software piecewise separable. This characteristic of hiding information—each module making visible only that information necessary to use the module—leads to software that is easier to assign to separate teams, to create and test, to modify. Information hiding applied to data structures leads to the use of data abstraction methods: a set of design principles that use definition of modules that hide data structures as the primary modularization and decomposition method.

The first two differences lead to the initial transition steps of RTD—(1) determining the software tasks, based on the processes and data stores of the data flow diagram, and (2) determining the modules, based on design information-hiding criteria. The two steps are performed iteratively and interactively—not in a sequential, mutually exclusive fashion. The RTD presentation begins with the processes-to-tasks transition first, because, in practice, we have found that to be most useful; but the transition from functions to modules is at least as important (some would say more so). Perhaps its very importance is why experience has proven that it is useful to wait until the initial tasking decisions have been made before commiting to modularization decisions. In any event, the main guideline here is not that it either one must be considered before the other, but that both must be considered in tandem.

Flat vs. hierarchical. The requirements, expressed as data flows, are a "flat" structure. (Although DFDs are nominally hierarchical, they are truly flat in the sense that all requirements are expressed in the primitive transforms, which contain PSpecs.) The actual software, however, must be organized in a hierarchical fashion, illustrating the calling or invoking relationships among the modules. The transition mechanism is initially almost mechanical, but it then calls for significant analysis and trading off of alternative approaches, using software-oriented coupling and cohesion as the primary criteria. This part of the transition transforms the data flow diagram into a traditional structure chart.

Logical vs. physical. The fourth aspect is in some sense simply a summary and reaffirmation of the first three: the other differences or transitions are the mechanism for developing the actual physical architecture—the tasks, subprograms, and modules as actual code. For tasks we mean this in a literal sense, as schedulable and dispatchable pieces of code. Similarly, for subprograms we mean named and callable code segments. For modules, the organization will be simply logical in many languages (although perhaps reflected in the library structure), while in languages such as Modula-2 (modules), Ada (packages), and C++ (classes) the information hiding can be explicitly expressed in coded form.

Each of the four aspects is influenced by the process and the products of the previous phase. The products of methods involving DFDs and CFDs have a direct relationship to software design; changing DFDs or CFDs will affect the software architecture, including task determination and module structure.

The direct relationship is not so clear in the case of products that deal exclusively with data entities and their relationships (such as "receives," "purchases," or "is composed of,"). The most widely used graphical product is the Entity-Relationship Diagram (ERD). While the ERD approach is important, and the data relationships clearly influence data structure design within modules—and have a strong influence on data structure for database-oriented systems, in which data intensiveness overwhelms process and control issues—their actual direct impact on the software design is less clear. Certainly, the literature does not discuss the ERD-to-software design issue in terms of effects on the software architecture. What they are clearly useful for, in certain classes of systems, is improving understanding about data stores and objects. As Chen notes, as the lead-off rationale for the approach [CHE90], "The entity-relationship (ER) model has been used successfully worldwide as a tool for communication between the system analysts/designers and the end user . . . "

SSEM has as its primary focus the process and control models (largely associated with DFDs, CFDs, and related products) and the related transition to the software design. There is significant attention to data relationships in terms of use of the data by actions during event–action analysis—the primary attention being paid to coupling and cohesion issues—but there is no explicit use of the ERD notation or of information modeling or its recent offspring, object-oriented analysis.

2.3.2 Software Top-Level Design

Software top-level design, the determination and representation of software components and their interaction, occurs during the fourth phase of Figure 1-1, "Software

Top-Level Design." We will discuss the process, products, and transition to the next phase, software detailed design.

Process The process of software design can be conducted in many different ways. For example, Nielsen & Shumate have the following steps, including initial consideration of requirements analysis [NIE88, page 211] (skipping or modifying Ada-specific steps):

- Determine hardware interfaces (Context Diagram).
- Assign a task to each hardware interface (at least as a "first cut").
- Decompose the middle part of the software—what is left after hardware inter-actions are taken care of—using DFDs, if not already provided.
- Determine concurrency, identifying tasks from the DFDs and any associated control.
- Determine process interfaces, addressing issues of synchronization and mutual exclusion as you go along.
- Encapsulate tasks into modules, using data abstraction and information-hiding principles.
- Translate the design into graphics and Program Design Language (PDL).
- Decompose large tasks, using a balanced functional decomposition and data abstraction viewpoint.
- Conduct design reviews, using the criteria given as design guidelines.

Other methods have different steps. SSEM is similar to the above but is explicitly language-independent and offers additional guidelines for the requirements-to-design transition. Instead of discussing process further, it is important at this time to introduce some issues of software design that have strongly influenced the SSEM approach.

There have been three important developments in the design of software that have not been common practice. Although not really new, they are part of what has become known as "modern software practice": information hiding; data abstraction; and object-oriented development. The three developments are explained in the following:

Information hiding: Parnas [PAR72b] introduced the concept of "information hiding," the idea that we should decompose software into modules such that each is "characterized by its knowledge of a design decision which it hides from all others." The design decision might relate to either an algorithm or a data structure. This is literally intended as design guidance. That is, we make a list of difficult design decisions and build the software architecture by creating modules that hide or encapsulate the decisions.

Data abstraction: The idea of abstract data types is that we can use data structures abstractly by reference to operations on the data (such as "push" to a stack), rather than direct reference to a data structure (such as "add to front of the linked list"). In this context, the data structure is often referred to as an "object". The idea has been discussed in the literature for many years. Liskov and Guttag [LIS86] recently integrated and clarified the construction and use of abstract data types. They define a data abstraction as " . . . a set of objects and a set of operations characterizing the behavior of the objects." Their book largely concerns concepts of design, " . . . how to do program decomposition based on abstraction."

Object-oriented development (OOD): Object-oriented development has been popularized by Booch [BOO86]. He draws on earlier design literature, including work of Liskov, Guttag, and Parnas. The method involves designing software around abstractions of "objects" in some real world problem. (Here an object is an "entity" or "thing," such as a ship, car, operator, or communication line, rather than simply a data structure as described above. However, OOD sometimes uses the word "object" in virtually the same way that we discussed earlier as "data abstraction.") The development model of OOD is that it " . . . lets us map solutions directly to our view of the problem." It allows software objects to both provide operations and use the operations provided by other objects. The operations are visible as subprograms exported by modules of the software. Such modules are, themselves, called objects.

Booch [BOO87] also introduced an important graphic aid to visualizing program components and their interactions: the *architecture diagram*. It shows the objects in a software system and their relationship to one another.

(Note: Depending on the author or the viewpoint, OOD can entail much more than those issues discussed, including inheritance (with a child module "inheriting" operations from a parent), run-time binding of data to operations, and many implications of these issues. The degree to which OOD has influenced SSEM is only in regard to the issues addressed in the previous paragraphs, and not in regard to inheritance and so on.)

Each of the three issues will be dealt with at length in Appendix A. The point is that there are some new (or at least not-in-common-practice) software design ideas that must be dealt with; SSEM—RTD and MSD—deals with the issues.

Products   There are a wide variety of documentation representations of software designs, with little standardization or agreement on terminology. We will focus on the main products of SSEM:

- Task Communication Graph (TCG) identifies the tasks and their interactions.
- Software Architecture Diagram (SAD) identifies the major modules (the ones that hide design decisions) in the system.
- Structure Chart shows all the subprograms and their calling relationship.

Transition to Next Phase   The "transition" from top-level design to detailed design is straightforward, simply being the continued refinement of the top-level design, involving refinement of algorithmic detail and substantial additional modularization. The SSEM/MSD detailed design methodology balances functional decomposition and data abstraction in such a way as to take advantage of the best of both approaches. There are correspondingly two representations of the design: structure charts for the step-by-step processing of functional decomposition and a software architecture diagram to show the modularization using information hiding and data abstraction.

2.3.3 Requirements-to-Design Iteration

Virtually all the discussion of requirements-to-design iteration related to systems is relevant for software as well. Traditionally the iteration has not been as strong, or as formalized, but perhaps that's why there have been some problems with software development, changing requirements, and so on. It can be at least partially viewed as a problem with software aspects of the waterfall model—or at least with an overly strict interpretation of the process of going from step to step.

In addition to the iteration "forward" from requirements to design, there is iteration "backward" with the system design. Both the iterations may be accomplished in any of a number of ways. For example, there may already be preliminary designs existing from an earlier Demonstration and Validation stage. Alternatively, there may be explicit efforts for "trial" designs, as risk reduction efforts, much in the same way alternate system designs were developed and "traded off" with regard to the requirements. Such trial designs are likely to be evaluated with analytical tools, simulations, prototypes, and so on. These activities are all legitimately part of the software requirements specification phase.

The most widely known response to criticism of the waterfall model has been Barry Boehm's "spiral" model, presented in *A Spiral Model of Software Development and Enhancement* [BOE88]. Figure 2-6 illustrates the model, with the process starting in the center and proceeding as cycles of the spiral. The figure is largely self-explanatory for our purposes, with the major point to be made being that the exact actions to be taken at each cycle around the spiral are *risk-driven,* based on the analysis and prototype activity that takes place before commitment to further development. SSEM is consistent with such a development approach.

2.4 RELATIONSHIPS AMONG PHASES

This section points out that the systems development cycle can be viewed as alternating phases of requirements analysis followed by design. The two requirements phases are quite similar to each other; the two design phases are quite similar to each other. The analysis phases differ in quite distinct and important ways from the design phases.

Figure 2-7 is an alternative viewpoint of the phases of the development cycle and the resulting products. It graphically illustrates the two-step process of analysis-design for each of system- and software-oriented phases. (For simplicity, the figure combines preliminary and detailed design as a single software-specific phase called design.)

Each of the phases has a corresponding product, namely:

- System requirements
- System architecture
- Software requirements
- Software architecture

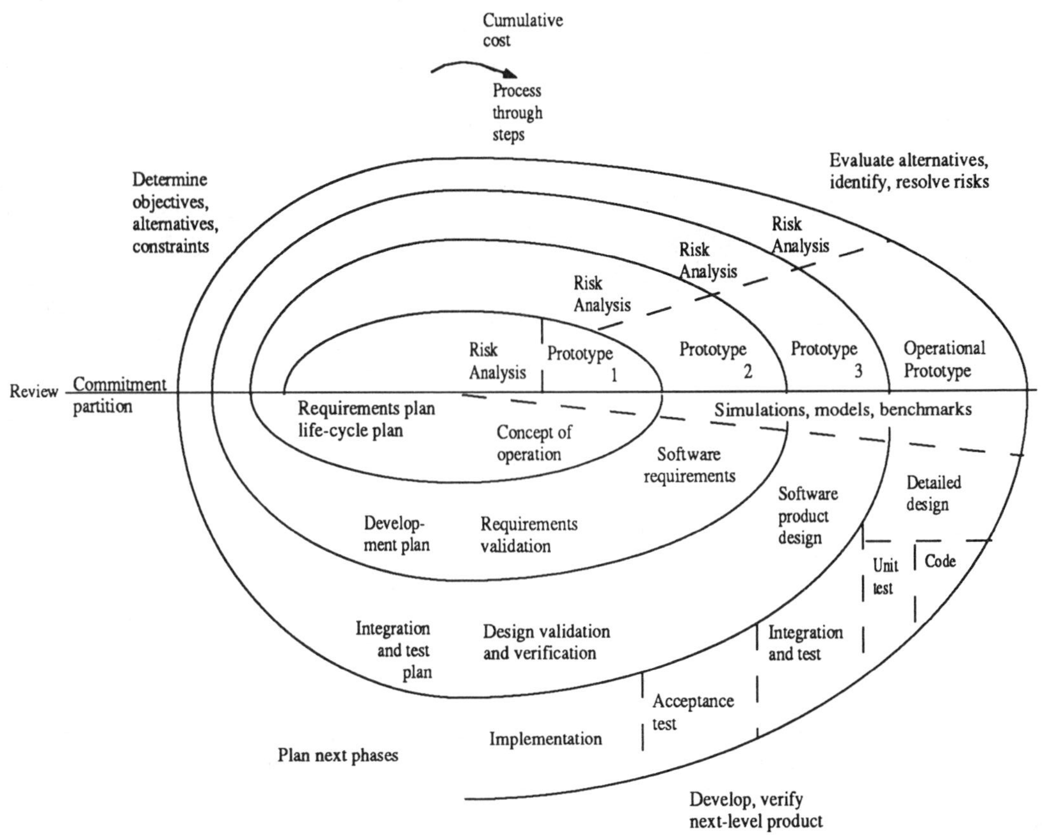

Figure 2-6 Sprial Model of the Software Process

Adapted from Boehm, Barry W., "A Spiral Model of Software Development and Enhancement," *IEEE Computer*, May 1988

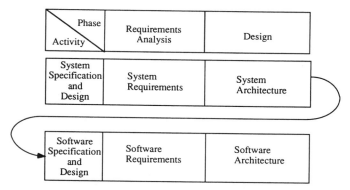

Figure 2-7   Similar Nature of System and Software Phases

Figure 2-7 makes it clear that the set of phases in the development cycle are actually two sets of similar activities, each consisting of two subphases. The activity of *system* specification and design consists of analysis, followed by design. Similarly, indeed virtually identically, the activity of *software* specification and design consists of analysis, followed by design.

It should not be surprising that there is a fundamental similarity in the activities of the two analysis phases and a similarity in the activities of the two design phases. On the other hand, the two analysis activities are quite different and distinct from the design activities.

Finally, to finish the story of Figure 2-7, it should not be surprising that there is a fundamental similarity in the *products* of the two analysis phases and a similarity to the products of the two design phases. Of course, the two analysis products are quite different and distinct from the design products.

The following sections address analysis, design, their iterations, and their products separately.

Analysis Phases   The two analysis phases both deal with requirements. The systems analysis phase deals with the statement of the "essential" requirements of the customer, without regard to the technology used to implement the requirements.

The software analysis phase similarly deals with requirements, but now it deals with requirements in a piecewise fashion (using divide-and-conquer as a dominant strategy) to simplify the problem. Each separate analysis deals only with the specific essential requirements allocated to a specific piece of software, *plus* the requirements needed to satisfy the specific technology that has been chosen (during system design) to solve the customer's problem (the *derived* requirements).

For both of the analysis phases, it is frequently useful to make the assumption of perfect technology relative to the phase being analyzed, without considering the internal "technology" of the system. For example, system requirements are unconcerned with the speed of data communication channels internal to the system being developed (or whether there *are any* data communication channels); software requirements are similarly unconcerned with the speed of subprogram calls (or whether there *are any* subprogram calls). Therefore, they involve timing only in regard to the interval of time from an external stimulus to a response by the system or by the software for which the requirements are being specified.

Since the two phases are similar in nature and make similar assumptions about focus on more-or-less abstract requirements rather than internal technology, it is not surprising that the mechanisms for illustrating the requirements are similar. In fact, in SSEM, the graphics are identical. Both phases have a balanced emphasis on the functional processes that transform data and on the data itself in terms of flows, stores, origins, and destinations. The requirements of both phases are illustrated with data flow diagrams and associated techniques, as detailed in the separate chapters for each phase.

Design Phases The two design phases are quite different from the analysis phases: design deals with making decisions to select or devise components that can satisfy the requirements and the establishment of an overall architecture for the components. For system design, the components are computers, local area networks, data links, people, conveyor belts, analog-to-digital converters, and so on. For software design, the components are tasks, modules, data structures, and so on.

Distinct from the requirements analysis phases, the design phases do not deal with abstractions such as "processes" but with unique and technology-specific components. Being technology-specific, the design phases deal with factors such as efficiency, reliability, redundancy, weight, power, storage, and timing. The essence of the design phase is the selection of the distinct components, their architecture, and the allocation of requirements to the components.

Interactions There is an important interaction among the phases that can be illustrated with a response-time requirement example. Timing must be allocated among system components. During system design, an essential requirement of 15 milliseconds from stimulus to response may be allocated as 3 milliseconds to one computer, 2 milliseconds to a communication channel, 9 milliseconds to another computer, and 1 millisecond to some sort of sensor. The 9 milliseconds to the second computer may then become a derived requirement (during software requirements analysis) to a software configuration item. The 9 milliseconds is then further allocated during software design, perhaps as 1 millisecond for data acquisition, 2 milliseconds for interaction with the sensor, and so on. If existing, or affordable, technology does not exist to meet some of the requirements, the allocation may have to be changed, hence revisiting one or both design phases. If the total of the allocations cannot be satisfied, the requirements phases will be revisited, specifically involving the customer and the operational need—the essential requirement.

Products Since the system design phase differs significantly from the system requirements phase in terms of approach and desired result, it necessarily differs in its resulting product. The primary difference is in the graphic portrayal of components. Some of the differences are minor, even though important to assist the reader in comprehension. For example, requirements are shown in data flow diagrams as circles, while system components are shown (in SSEM) as rounded rectangles. (Similarly, schematic block diagrams are distinctly different from functional flow block diagrams.) The data flow diagrams are then *allocated to* the system components, with a logical nesting of circles in rectangles. More significantly, the graphics chosen for the system design must provide for the actual system interconnection, via data buses of various sorts, and for the technology-specific components that may not be *part of* the customer requirements, but are necessary for *the satisfaction of* the requirements. The same graphics show the system interfaces that *are part* of the customer requirement. Although we nominally have "essential" requirements, real customers in real systems development projects will often require specific hardware, especially at the interfaces.

Similarly, the software design graphics differ significantly from the software requirements graphics. As a small difference, but important for clarity and comprehension, the software graphics show tasks as parallelograms, even though they share some similarity with abstract processes. Similar to the system design/requirements relationship, data flow processes (circles) are allocated or are constituents of tasks (parallelograms). More significantly, other software design graphics provide for calling or invoking relationships and account for visibility among modules.

Transitions   The alternating analysis and design, with the corollary, alternating mental viewpoints and graphics, calls for a significant amount of attention to be paid to the transition from one phase to the next, as discussed in the sections earlier.

A final issue to be addressed is the general distinction between analysis and design. At one level the distinction is easy. If you are involved in the determination and representation of *what* is to be done, you are doing analysis. On the other hand, if you are involved in the determination and representation of *how* to accomplish the requirements, you are doing design. In fact, the situation is not so simple, because of the iteration between requirements and design and because it is almost always possible to view one person's design as another's requirements. As a simple example, it is usual to discuss the *specification* of a software module as a statement of what it *does*, whereas the implementation, the *how it does it,* is hidden from users of the module. Here is yet another what–how issue, but certainly within the context of the *how* of software design. Davis [DAV90, page 19ff] discusses the issue at length. We will almost always be satisfied with the simple distinction pointed out in the foregoing.

2.5 INTEGRATION OF IDEAS

We need to discuss two final topics: the integration of methods, concepts, ideas, and so on, and how such integration relates to the specifics of each project. SSEM integrates previous ideas; projects must integrate SSEM with project-specific issues.

SSEM Integration   Sir Isaac Newton is quoted as saying, "If I have seen further than others, it is because I stand on the shoulders of giants." The young field of computing doesn't seem to have this worked out yet; it has been pointed out that in the computing field innovators mostly stand on each other's feet! In the development of SSEM, we have tried to stand on shoulders. SSEM does not so much break new ground as it does integrate a large number of ideas that are in common practice. In fact, we have shied away from taking advantage of the new and potentially useful (but untried) ideas in favor of proven methods that have resulted in systems being placed in use by satisfied customers.

We have drawn from many sources, with extensive references in Chapters 4 through 8, in order both to acknowledge the ideas of others and to invite the interested reader to pursue the issues further. The following discussion mentions some of the authors of the works, with specific reference under the authors' names in the bibliography.

The requirements specification and system design graphics and philosophy are largely drawn from the work of Hatley & Pirbhai, with some integration of material from McMenamin & Palmer (especially the use of event analysis to help determine the first level of data flow decomposition), and Ward & Mellor. They, of course, have drawn on the work of others, with much of the general form of analysis based on the early work of DeMarco.

The software requirements-to-design transition has been strongly influenced by Nielsen & Shumate, with modularization concepts influenced primarily by the ideas of Parnas and task identification influenced by Gomma. Nielsen & Shumate also influenced the specific software design methods, as did the ideas of Yourdon & Constantine, Liskov & Guttag, and others. The notions of object-oriented design (at least the modularization aspects of that philosophy) have also been influential, with Booch being the primary spokesman for the methods. The early ideas of Dijkstra and Wirth have been of particular importance to the notion of having a balanced viewpoint of functional decomposition and data abstraction.

We have tried to integrate these ideas (in a not-too-large volume) into a consistent and understandable—and most of all, usable—methodology for software specification and design.

Project Integration   SSEM does not, and no one book can, address all the issues of system development. It will be necessary for projects (and of course organizations) to establish specific standards, checklists, review procedures, documentation formats, and so on. For example, although SSEM describes the products of analysis and design, they are not presented in an integrated format as a specific set of documents. They are left general in nature, with the assumption that different organizations and projects—and customers—will have different sorts of documentation requirements.

In addition, any individual project may have more or less emphasis on any specific aspects of SSEM or may need techniques to augment the general framework of SSEM. For example, although we place significant emphasis on data relationships (especially on relationships to processes) during the event–action analysis described in Chapter 4, we do not provide all the tools necessary for establishment of a large database-oriented system. Similarly, we do not deal with many important detailed techniques for real-time systems: mutual exclusion, synchronization, the determination and change of priorities, asynchronous task communication, and so on. All these sorts of methods and techniques can be integrated easily with SSEM to meet the needs of different sorts of systems software development projects.

2.6 KEYS TO UNDERSTANDING

- There is a long-standing and highly successful *systems* development process and set of methods; it is important that *software* specification and design stay within that mainstream.
- There are a number of excellent existing methods for the specification of software; it is useful to integrate a number of different ideas and to integrate the method with the process.
- Requirements for both systems and software are effectively stated functionally (in terms of what the system must accomplish), while software design is best expressed in terms of the major components (or modules) of code; this necessitates that particular concern and attention be given to the software requirements-to-design transition.
- When accomplishing requirements analysis, in addition to expressing *what sorts of activities occur* in a system (the process model), it is also vital to express *when they occur* (the control model). It is also important to pay attention to data relationship issues, particularly in regard to organization of the items in the process and control model.
- Software design based on information hiding and data abstraction—modular design—is becoming increasingly important in software development; these methods are new to many software development organizations.
- Software requirements analysis is similar to system requirements analysis, but narrows its focus to the piece-by-piece specification of requirements for each CSCI and its associated interfaces.
- The graphics and guidelines, and many of the steps, are identical in systems and software specification.
- Nominally, the software requirements specification makes no assumptions of the software design; the analogy with system requirements being "essential" or technology-independent is nearly exact.
- On the other hand, there is exactly the same sort of requirements–design iteration at the software level as occurs at the system level. Indeed, some software design actually takes place during requirements specification. However, it is important that the requirements specification only state *what* the software is to do, and not dictate or constrain *how* the software is to accomplish its function.

CHAPTER 3

The Systems Software Development Process

Objective: to define and provide an overview of the development process and methodology for systems software—the Systems Software Engineering Methodology (SSEM)

The purpose of this chapter is to provide an overview of a set of specific methods for accomplishing systems software engineering efforts as part of the systems development process. It describes the portions of the systems development process that are addressed and gives a brief description of the methods to be utilized. The final sections provide information that is relevant to the case study developed in the rest of the book.

3.1 OVERVIEW

We will deal with all aspects of system development shown in Figure 3-1, which repeats Figure 1-1. The overall approach that combines the *process* of system development with the *methodology* for accomplishing the development is called the *Systems Software Engineering Methodology* (SSEM). The primary interest of the methodology is software that is developed in accordance with and to satisfy the needs of overall systems development, as shown in Figure 3-1, as distinct from software that is created as a software-only development on existing or purchased hardware. The boxes representing the system requirements analysis and system design phases are half-highlighted (as is the cloud labeled "Systems Engineering") to illustrate that the methodology deals with the *software-related portions* of these phases. Indeed, the vital difference between systems software and software-only development is this concern with the systems engineering process. SSEM does not concern itself with any specific documentation standard, set of checklists, or review process (those being the realms of organization style, philosophy, and culture).

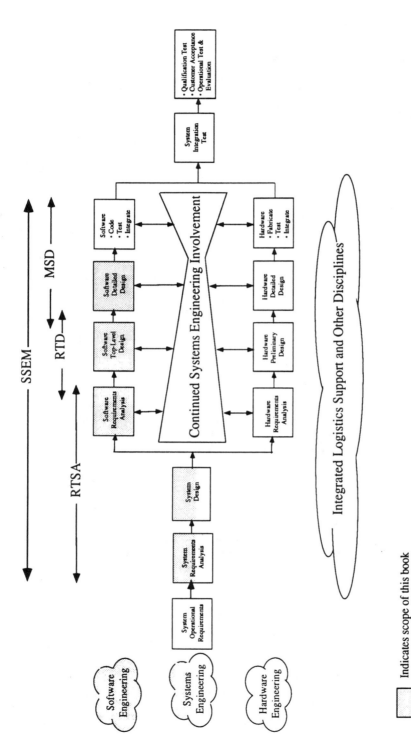

Figure 3-1 The Systems Development Process

Indicates scope of this book

SSEM: Systems Software Engineering Method
RTSA: Real-Time Structured Analysis
RTD: Real-Time Design Method
MSD: Modular Structured Design

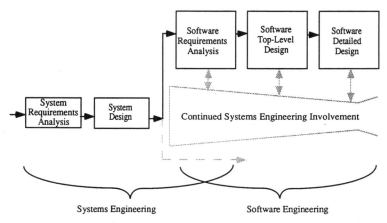

Figure 3-2 Systems Software Development Process

Figure 3-2, repeating Figure 1-2, summarizes the portions of the overall systems development process that are our concern and illustrates the overlap and transition between systems engineering and software engineering. The half-size boxes for the system requirements and design phases reemphasize the partial (that is, software-related) concern with systems engineering issues.

Some key aspects of the methodology are that:

- The system and software requirements analysis phases emphasize process and control modeling; they consider data relationships in regard to their influence on the determination of process and control transforms. The resulting specification is designed to take advantage of functionally oriented system requirements and system design models developed during earlier stages of concept exploration and demonstration/validation.

- The system design phase provides methods and graphic illustrations to distinguish it clearly from the preceding and following analysis phases.

- The two software design phases have as a fundamental principle the use of sophisticated software engineering approaches based on data abstraction and information hiding. To the degree appropriate, the methods take advantage of the modularization techniques and world-view of object-oriented design. These methods establish the basis for the primary partitioning, or decomposition, of the software.

- The two software design phases also make use of functional methods for a secondary software decomposition based on the step-by-step processing of the system.

- Therefore, the software design approach is characterized by a balance between functional decomposition and data abstraction. The graphical representation of the software design illustrates both viewpoints.

- The methodology has a special focus on the transition from phase to phase, particularly the transition in the overlapping area of systems engineering and software engineering. The transition is accomplished in two steps:

   1. Development of the software requirements, involving the final phases of allocation of system functions to software; completion of the representation of those requirements and interfaces
   2. Transition from software requirements analysis to top-level design, involving the transition from *what* is to be done in software to *how* it is to be accomplished

The remainder of this chapter addresses:

- Concept of a development cycle: a process model
- Overview of the development cycle: phase by phase
- Case study (problem statement)

3.2 CONCEPT OF A DEVELOPMENT CYCLE: A PROCESS MODEL

The primary purpose of this book is to define a *methodology*: a set of procedures, graphics, and guidelines that explains how to accomplish systems software engineering. It is important that the methodology be embedded within a *process*: the set of steps that must be accomplished to complete a task. The relationship of process and methodology is so important that one should reread the brief discussion in Section 2.1.

Although it is important to represent the process as an orderly or rational set of phases, the process is, in real projects, less orderly. Real systems have inconsistent and overlapping phases; they iterate phases and transitions; they use partial software developments or "builds"; they are dependent upon earlier products of development; they are affected by customer-directed changes. It is often useful to think of the "phases" instead as "sets of activities" that are conducted during the system development process. Nonetheless, it is important to discuss these activities in some orderly manner.

The remainder of this chapter and the rest of the book address the systems software engineering methodology in the context of the phases shown in Figure 3-2.

3.3 OVERVIEW OF THE DEVELOPMENT CYCLE: PHASE BY PHASE

The following sections address the activities of the development cycle, phase by phase:

- System requirements analysis
- System design
- Software requirements analysis
- Software top-level design
- Software detailed design

Each of the sections addresses the general characteristics of its phase and the methods used to accomplish the activities of the phase. The discussion of the first two (systems-oriented) phases focuses on the aspects of the development that are important for the later (software-oriented) phases.

3.3.1 System Requirements Analysis

System requirements analysis is the transformation of the customer's operational needs into a set of capabilities and performance requirements suitable for the (1) interactive and parallel *determination of a system design* and (2) *allocation of requirements to components* of the design.

This phase involves analysis of what is needed to accomplish the system operational requirements, a "needs statement" or "required operational capability." It involves a great deal of interaction with the people for whom the system is being built, whom we will call the "customer" or the "user." The input to this phase is the customer or user requirements, both written and oral, which are finally reduced to at least a general written form as the required operational capability.

It is useful to distinguish two different sorts of activities during this phase: *analysis* and *description*.

Analysis is the creative activity involved in understanding the problem, associated constraints, and methods of overcoming constraints and in determining how to organize the mass of information that is being gathered. This process goes on until the problem is well understood.

Description is the product of analysis that documents and communicates the results of analysis to others. "Description" sounds like merely the drudgework of documenting the results of analysis; however, although it *is* documentation, the writing down effort is iterative and interactive with the analysis effort. In fact, this is the time to organize and structure the results of the analysis, and that includes resolution of ambiguity, integration of conflicting views, and elimination of inconsistencies. *One of the most important aspects of writing something down is that it clarifies the thinking of the writer!* Further, the very form of documentation— text, ordered and consistent graphics, variety of pictures—can influence how one thinks about the problem and hence either help or hinder the analysis.

The SSEM approach to the development cycle uses the methods of traditional structured analysis, data flow diagrams and associated techniques—the process model—supplemented by increased emphasis on control, timing, and activation of the components of the process model. This addition to traditional methods is called the *control model* and adds control flows, state transition diagrams, and process activators to the model. The basic approach is that of Hatley & Pirbhai [HAT87]. Event-driven concepts are borrowed from McMenamin & Palmer [MCM84] and integrated with the basic process/control model. These methods are used to capture data-process relationships more fully, to address coupling and cohesion early in the analysis, and to provide a starting point for systematic decomposition of the requirements in a leveled manner. The combined methods are known as Real-Time

Structured Analysis (RTSA) which is, of course, a general-purpose and widely used phrase and acronym. What is different about the approach of SSEM/RTSA is the integration of several methods, the continued application of RTSA to system design, and the careful distinction of the various uses of RTSA across the phases of system development shown in Figure 3-1.

This phase cannot be considered a complete effort in of itself. It is necessary for the requirements analysis to be interactive with system design. (In the simplest sense, this is because the requirements must be consistent with the technology; more subtly, the technology and the requirements drive each other.) This was discussed in detail in Chapter 2.

Once the requirements are developed and are consistent with the technology to be employed, they are considered to be *essential,* in the sense that they must be satisfied in order to meet the operational needs, independent of any later technology advances or the specific technology used to implement the system. (Of course, such advances or technology introduction may later modify what the customer perceives as the requirements of the system. This is one of the factors that make systems development challenging and entertaining!)

The output is a set of overall detailed system requirements to be satisfied by the system to be developed. These requirements are linked to the customer's operational needs via specific traceability from the detailed requirements to the operational needs. These requirements are expressed in a functional manner, using Data Flow Diagrams (DFDs) and related tools of structured analysis. DFDs are hierarchical in nature, with the functions defined at the top level further decomposed using lower-level DFDs. This process proceeds until the functioning of the system is fully understood and described. This process of functional analysis is defined [DSM86, page 6-1] as:

> Functional analysis is a method for analyzing performance requirements and dividing them into discrete tasks or activities. It involves the identification and decomposition of the primary system functions into subfunctions at ever-increasing levels of detail. Functional analysis supports mission analysis in defining functional areas, sequences, and interfaces. Functional analysis is also used by engineering specialists and support organizations.
>
> A function is a characteristic action to be accomplished by one of the system elements of hardware, software, facilities, personnel, procedural data, or any combination thereof.

3.3.2 System Design

System design is the determination of the overall system architecture, consisting of a set of physical processing components—hardware, software, people, and the communication among them—that will satisfy the system's essential requirements.

This phase includes the *description* of all system components and how they work together and the *allocation* of each of the system requirements to components of the system design. For the purposes of SSEM, the components are those used for configuration control of hardware and software—the hardware configuration items (HWCI) and the computer software configuration items (CSCI). The input to this phase is the requirements developed during system requirements analysis.

The methods continue to borrow notation from Hatley & Pirbhai [HAT87], but are strongly influenced by traditional systems engineering approaches such as those expressed by Blanchard & Fabrycky [BLA90]. In fact, although the methods expressed for this phase are considered to be a continuation of RTSA, they could be completely replaced by other methods and notations with no disruption to the later software specification and design. What is important for SSEM is that *some* consistent and thorough approach be used for an explicit system design phase.

The primary work of this phase is often called *synthesis*. Synthesis is the determination of (usually alternative) solutions to the problem posed by the mission or operational need. Synthesis is design. Synthesis follows functional analysis, but it also interacts and affects functional analysis. Following synthesis is the evaluation of the alternatives, based on "trade" ("trade off" studies) which analyze and "trade off" the relative benefits and costs of the various alternatives.

An important aspect of this phase is that it begins the "handoff" of responsibility from the systems engineering function to the software engineering function. (Note that it is a *function* handoff. There may be no change in organization, or even in the engineers doing the work, but there is a change in *function* and *perspective*.) During the handoff, there is a continued interaction between statement of software requirements and system design/requirements.

The development of the software requirements may also partially occur during the system design phase. This allows a natural iteration of requirements/functional analysis with the ongoing system architecture design and provides for preparation of preliminary software requirements specification material.

The final output of this phase is the documented description of the system to be developed and its method of satisfying overall system requirements. The requirements are mapped or allocated to the system design; conversely, each component of the system design can be traced back to a set of specific requirements. The output of the phase includes preliminary software requirements for each software configuration item and related preliminary interface requirements.

The preliminary software-related output has two components: (1) for each software configuration item, a documented description—both processing- and data-structure-oriented—of the major logical components of software and their method of satisfying allocated system requirements; and (2) the interfaces between each of the software configuration items and the rest of the system or external world.

3.3.3 Software Requirements Analysis

Software requirements analysis is the detailed specification of the necessary functionality of each CSCI and the detailed specification of the interfaces among all CSCIs and HWCIs.

This phase consists of the detailed analysis and documentation of the system requirements that have been allocated to each of the software configuration items (CSCI) and of the interfaces external to each item. Each CSCI is a single, functionally cohesive portion of software that can be conveniently defined by a single specification. The interfaces are defined as part of the specification to show the linking among CSCIs and HWCIs. The analysis is repeated for each CSCI and for all interfaces. The input to the phase is the system design, particularly the identification and allocation of requirements to system components.

Except for the focus on a single CSCI, this phase has considerable similarity to the system requirements phase, particularly in its emphasis on what is to be accomplished. This is the continuation of RTSA to another phase; the similarity of the two requirements analysis phases is discussed at length in Chapter 2. As the system requirements phase is driven by a need to satisfy the customer's operational need, so the software requirements phase is driven by a need to satisfy the needs of the system design.

The process starts with the system requirements allocated during the previous phase and develops in great detail the functions that the software to be developed must accomplish, including specific algorithms and step-by-step processing. The details include technology-specific functions that go beyond the customer's essential requirements; these are the *derived* requirements needed to satisfy the system design.

The detailed analysis of requirements is accomplished through the use of data flow and control flow methods; the process and control models.

The product of this phase is a set of data and control flows, together with significant amounts of supplementary text and graphic material, that fully express the processing necessary to satisfy the allocated requirements. The requirements statements are traceable back to the components of the system design. They are therefore traceable either to derived requirements (necessary to satisfy the selected technology of the system design), or even further back, to the requirements of the system requirements analysis phase.

3.3.4 Top-Level Design

Top-level design is the determination and description of the overall software architecture, of the interfaces between the major modules within that architecture, and of the interfaces to components external to the CSCI.

This phase is sometimes known as *preliminary design*. Its primary purpose is to serve as a foundation for the later detailed design, but it is also a key step in ensuring a proper and maintainable software product that satisfies all requirements. This is the key phase for the requirements-to-design transition. The set of methods is called Real-Time Design (RTD), reflecting the usual real-time nature of large system developments. It incorporates non–real-time issues as a subset of real-time design. It also uses the basic principles of Modular Structured Design (MSD), discussed further in the next section on detailed design.

The basic approach of RTD is to define concurrent software elements, or tasks, from the products of RTSA, especially data flow diagrams. There are extensive guidelines for doing so, as well as extensive guidelines for grouping tasks into modules. The modules define the software architecture, based on modern software engineering principles. For non–real-time systems, the grouping of processes and data stores from data flow diagrams proceeds directly to software modules.

The starting point of RTD is the work of Nielsen & Shumate [NIE88], but it incorporates the work of many others, as discussed in Chapter 2, Section 2.5. MSD draws on the same background.

The input is the products of RTSA, providing details of interface to other components and the specific processing required to satisfy both essential and derived requirements. The output is a software design that contains a specification of software components subordinate to the configuration item, and graphics and text that describe the major modules and their interfaces.

The software is initially partitioned into *modules*. Modules are the building blocks for the software design; they provide sets of operations that either manipulate hidden data structures or provide the functionality needed to satisfy the requirements specified for the software. Major modules are the first-level decomposition of the software and typically encapsulate tasks and data structures used for task communication. Tasks are modules themselves, with the added feature that all tasks operate concurrently. Modules trace backward to satisfy each of the processes and control mechanisms of the software requirements.

Top-level design begins with the determination of the concurrency within the software (tasks) and the ways in which the tasks interact either directly or through the mechanism of a real-time executive. The tasks will depend on the capabilities of information-hiding and other helper modules, which are specified during top-level design. Helper modules are low-level components that provide operations and services that make the job of higher-level modules easier to understand. Much of the complexity of a system generally resides in such helper modules. Such modules contain tasks only if they are needed to control concurrent access to data structures. Helper modules are often reusable components. All the components are then packaged, or grouped, in ways that allow minimal interaction and data flow between them; this is accomplished by the use of the principles of data abstraction and information hiding.

This initial phase of top-level design is expressed as a set of concurrency-oriented graphics, which illustrate tasks and their interactions, and module-oriented graphics, which show the decisions that have been made to group the tasks and their means of communication.

The next step involves the decomposition of tasks into a set of callable subprograms. This incorporates the traditional structured design phase but continues to be influenced—"driven" is not too strong a term—by the notions of modularization and information hiding used to define the original set of modules. The product of this step consists of additional modules of the software architecture and an expression of how the modules work together to solve the given requirements. In addition to a graphical representation of the modules, the approach produces a structure chart, which shows the hierarchical nature of the software, the data flows and access to data structures, and some representation of iteration and selection of alternatives. The combination of modules and structure charts clarifies traceability to the requirements and eases the task of explaining the design to the customer for whom the system is being built.

3.3.5 Detailed Design

Detailed design is the determination of the low-level architecture of the system and the specification, in a pseudocode format, of algorithms in each callable software component.

Design continues with the determination of the characteristics of information-hiding and other helper modules and the development of their internal structure. This phase includes the decisions about specific data structures inside modules and all the mathematical and operational details of algorithms. This is a continuation of the methods of MSD discussed above.

The input is the task and module structure of the top-level design. The output is a software design that has as its focus the details internal to the modules and tasks; it incorporates all the information of the top-level design and adds the information about lower-level modules, data structures, and algorithms. The components of the detailed design are intrinsically traceable back to the top-level design, since they are simply the internal details of that design. In addition, each of the components of the detailed design is traceable back to the software requirements.

The detailed design is expressed by graphics that illustrate the software hierarchy (the calling structure) of the software and by graphics that illustrate the modularization of the components of the calling hierarchy. Both forms of graphics are vital in order to show the balance of functional decomposition and data abstraction that characterizes this phase of design. In addition to the details of the modules identified in the top-level design, there will be additional modularization at lower levels in the design in order to continue the philosophy of information hiding at all levels. There will be no additional expression of concurrency during detailed design. A program design language (PDL) will be used to express both the overall structure of the software (tasks and modules) and the internal algorithmic details of tasks and other components.

3.3.6 Summary

SSEM integrates methods of traditional structured analysis with increased emphasis on control modeling. It further integrates mutual data–process relationships, especially during the event analysis used to get the top-level decomposition of the hierarchical representation of requirements. It further integrates these logical analysis methods with a set of notations for the concrete representation of the system design, and shows how the phasing of system requirements analysis, system design, and software requirements analysis works in a systematic way to yield a software specification as a systems engineering activity.

The development of the software requirements is the beginning of the handoff from systems engineering to software engineering; that handoff is completed with the requirements-to-design transition of the top-level design phase. SSEM has a strong emphasis on this transition, with a combined process/method that uses guidelines for creating the top-level software design and continuing into detailed design.

3.4 CASE STUDY: FURNACE MONITORING SYSTEM (FMS)

The purpose of this section is to provide a sample problem, which will be solved in later chapters in order to demonstrate the systems software engineering methodology.

The same problem will be used as the example in all stages of the systems software engineering methodology. Each chapter will provide a solution that illustrates the methodology described in that chapter.

Problem Description   The Acme Steel Corporation (ASC) has a need to monitor the temperature and other status in 28 automatic blast furnaces scattered over 900 acres in its steel mill. The blast furnaces produce molten iron that is loaded into insulated railcars that carry it, still molten, to steel-making furnaces. The process is more or less continuous, with continual *charging* (or loading) with iron ore, limestone, and coke. The molten iron is drawn off periodically. Fuel is burned to provide heat to reduce the iron ore to molten iron (with various important chemical reactions taking place along the way), with temperature reaching 3500°F in the *bosh,* the area immediately above the hearth. There are other inputs (such as superheated oxygen) and outputs (such as slag and useful gases), but this problem will not be concerned with them.

The type and quality of molten iron produced depends upon the input mix to the furnace, on the temperature, and on proper functioning of the furnace. The Furnace Administrative Office (FAO) has knowledge of the input mix, but needs information from the furnace on temperature and functioning. At the worst level of functioning, the furnace simply stops and produces no output, at a significant cost to the company. (Various safety mechanisms ensure that there is no danger when the furnace halts operation.)

Currently, inspectors walk the floor of the mill to personally read the thermometers attached to the furnace, to check the amount of molten iron being produced, and to check whether there is any maintenance action required. The inspectors periodically report temperatures, maintenance status, and the output rate of molten iron. Each furnace has 15 locations at which the temperature must be checked. If the average temperature is too high, over 3500°F, or if any single temperature is over 3600°F, the inspector reduces the fuel flow, remaining with the furnace until the temperature is in specified bounds.

The inspectors report every few hours to the FAO on temperature, and as quickly as possible to the Maintenance Office (MO) when maintenance is required. However, sometimes it is as long as 30 minutes before they can reach a telephone and report maintenance status. In addition, it is typically several hours between each check; if a furnace halts right after being checked, several hours of iron production are lost.

The MO is on a somewhat remote edge of the mill complex, while the FAO is located downtown, about 12 miles from the steel mill. The overall situation is illustrated in Figure 3-3.

The information from the inspectors is manually input to the FAO central mainframe computer, which is housed in a temperature- and humidity-controlled com-

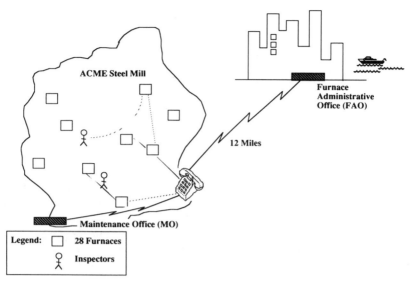

Figure 3-3   ACME Steel Corporation (ASC): Furnace Monitoring System (FMS)

plex. The key information for each furnace is:

- Temperature at each of 15 locations
- Rate of output (expressed as tons/minute)
- Maintenance status: one of
  - Normal
  - Degraded
  - Impaired
  - Critical
  - Safety Hazard

In addition to the monitoring and reporting activity above, there are special requirements to be met when the MO decides that a certain furnace is *troublesome* — needing a great deal of maintenance. In order to help determine the problem, the inspectors can be told to take lower-level reading of status, representing the basic electrical signals that make up the overall status; there are 10 different readings to be taken, each in the range 0 to 570 millivolts. These readings are called *detailed status*.

The schedule of the inspectors is not fixed. Depending on the product being produced, it may be necessary to check the temperature quite frequently, as often as every 10 minutes, or it may be satisfactory to check only every six hours. The schedule is established by the FAO. The environment is very harsh in the mill — heat, smoke, and so on — and it is difficult to retain qualified inspectors. The checking of each furnace is illustrated in Figure 3-4.

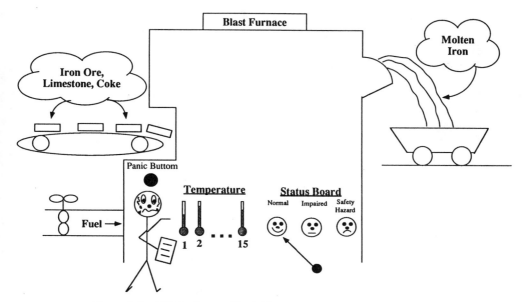

Figure 3-4   ASC Inspectors Check Temperature, Status, and Output Rate

The ASC intends to automate the process of furnace monitoring, including automatic sensing of the key information listed above, automatic reporting of status to the FAO and MO, control over the fuel flow to reduce temperature when necessary, and development of both management and maintenance reports based on the information.

The FAO desires to schedule the frequency of reading for each of the 15 locations for each of the 28 furnaces separately. The Maintenance Office is able to designate any number of furnaces as "troublesome," thereby causing the system to record the detailed status (electrical readings).

The furnace temperature is to be controlled in accordance with the following rules, which are to be applied each time any temperature is sensed. If the highest temperature is over 3600°F, the fuel flow is reduced by 20 percent. If no single temperature is over 3600°F, but the average temperature is over 3500°F, the fuel flow is reduced by 10 percent. In addition, until no temperature is above 3600°F *and* the average is below 3500°F, all temperatures are sensed once per minute. Therefore, the fuel flow is to be reduced once each minute until the temperature is in bounds.

There will be several different reports required by the FAO and the MO, to be defined later. The largest report will contain all the information for all furnaces. Such a report is to be generated within three minutes of the request, based on status and output information that is current as of the time of the request, and on the latest temperature readings scheduled prior to the request.

Both offices can also request an immediate update for an individual furnace on any item of information. Rate, status, or the temperature at a single location must be provided within 10 seconds, while temperature at all 15 locations must be provided within 30 seconds. The offices can also request total rate of output of any subset of furnaces, available within 90 seconds.

If maintenance status of any furnace falls to the "impaired" level, the system is to activate a flashing light in the MO within five seconds. Status is reported to the MO immediately and each five minutes until status returns to "normal."

If status falls to "critical," bells in each of the two offices are to be rung within one second. Status is to be reported to the MO immediately and at one minute intervals. In addition, detailed status (the 10 electrical readings) is to be collected for user-requested reports. Both one-minute status reporting and collection of detailed status continue until status has returned to "impaired" or "normal."

If status falls to "safety hazard," status is to be reported immediately to the MO; the conveyer belt and furnace are to be automatically shut down within three seconds; and the bells in both offices rung once per second until silenced by command from the MO.

A Note About Case Studies and Realism   It is important to strike a fine balance, in textbook or classroom case studies, between size/realism and practicality. We wanted a large and realistic case study—which is why only a single major problem is addressed throughout the book—but without the overwhelming complexity of real problems that take years to solve. We have taken the approach of presenting a very realistic problem, with the level of detail and specification essentially typical of what you might initially receive from a customer as part of the Mission Needs Statement (MNS) or a Required Operational Capability (ROC). (We usually call this an Operational Requirement or simply a Customer Need. It is the problem statement for which the engineering staff is to design and implement a solution.)

While realistic, the FMS is necessarily a simplification of an actual system, to be readily understandable and to fit into a classroom example and case study environment. An example of both the realism and the simplification is the situation relative to control of the furnace temperature.

The problem is realistic, in that there is *closed-loop control,* but the control is simplified to provide only for *reduction* in temperature. A real temperature controller would, first of all, also have a mechanism for increasing fuel flow; here we assume that fuel flow increases must be manual. In addition, the temperature controller would have a fine-grained sensing mechanism; would account for the amount by which the temperature is out of bounds; would consider the rate of change of temperature; would use techniques such as exponential smoothing; and would introduce delays to damp oscillation of temperature caused by frequent turn-on/turn-off. Nonetheless, this simple example is a good illustration of closed-loop control, common in the systems you will be building, and it is sufficient to illustrate the complex interactions of system and software specification and software design. The detail that is omitted has been as carefully considered as that which is included; the simplification is largely in the detailed algorithms, not in the overall specification and design.

Phased Solution   The final section in each of the chapters defining the system software methodology will contain an example solution to this problem, appropriate for the phase of the development cycle described by the chapter. That is, the examples will accomplish the corresponding phase of system development and, taken together, will illustrate a solution to the problem.

If you wish to test your knowledge of the methods presented, you may wish to solve the problem yourself before looking at the solution.

3.5   KEYS TO UNDERSTANDING

If you have not read Chapter 2, you should at least look at its Keys to Understanding; they are as true for this chapter as for Chapter 2.

PART 2

SOFTWARE SPECIFICATION

Part Two deals with the specification of software: what it is to accomplish. Since the focus of the book is on software developed within the context of a larger system, significant attention—the first two chapters—is paid to the specification of the requirements for the larger system and to the representation of the system design. Representation of the design includes hardware, software, people, and the allocation of requirements to these components of the larger system. It is vital for the software engineer to understand these issues, including details of the representation of *system* specification and design, in order to better understand the role of *software* specification and the transition to software design. The final chapter of Part Two deals specifically with the specification of the software-only portions of a system. The Furnace Monitoring System (FMS) posed as a problem or operational requirement in Part One is used as an example to show:

- System specification
- System design
- Software specification

CHAPTER 4

System Requirements Analysis

Objective: to provide a set of graphical notations, guidelines, and a step-by-step process for the analysis and presentation of system requirements

The purpose of this chapter is to describe the methods to be used during the system requirements analysis phase of the development cycle. Figure 4-1 illustrates the phases of the development cycle. This chapter covers the phase that is highlighted.

System requirements analysis is the transforming of the customer's operational needs into a set of capabilities and performance requirements suitable for the interactive and parallel:

- *determination* of a system design and
- *allocation* of requirements to components of the design.

This phase is the beginning of the development process. The inputs to it are the general operational needs of the customer. The output consists of the detailed requirements of the system being developed.

To accomplish the methodology definition, the following items are covered:

- Graphics
- Guidelines
- Methodology—step by step
- Example

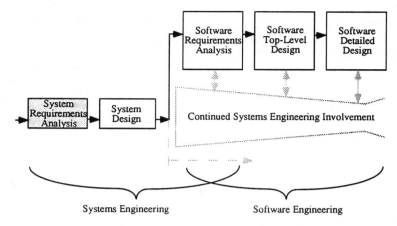

Figure 4-1   Phases of the Development Cycle

4.1   GRAPHICS

This section describes the graphics that are used for the methodology; they represent the *system requirements model*. The graphics presented in this section are not intended to tell the whole story of the methodology and are not necessarily tightly interrelated; they are only intended to introduce the *form* of the notation. The "FMS Example" in the final section of the chapter will use these graphics, the guidelines of the next section, and the step-by-step methodology to present an integrated picture. Recommended conventions are also listed. We will cover the following graphics and associated data, with relationships as illustrated in Figure 4-2.

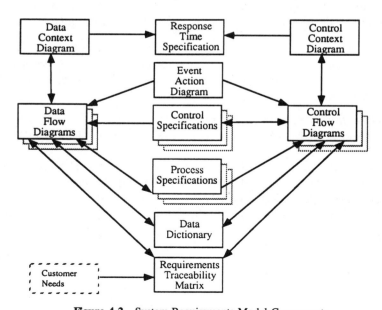

Figure 4-2   System Requirements Model Components

- Data context diagram (DCD)
- Data flow diagrams (DFD)
  - Diagram
  - Process specifications (PSpec)
- Data dictionary
- Control context diagram (CCD)
- Control flow diagrams (CFD)
  - Diagram
  - Control specifications (CSpec)
    - Decision tables
    - Process activation tables (PAT)
    - State transition diagrams/tables (STD/STT)
- Response time specification (RTS)
- Requirements traceability matrix (RTM)
- Event-action diagram (EAD)
- Action/store matrix

4.1.1 Data Context Diagrams (DCD)

The top-level diagram describing the functional behavior of the system, called the *data context diagram,* summarizes the requirements for the system under development to accept inputs from external entities and generate the associated outputs to the external entities. These requirements are purely functional and ignore any design or implementation. The entities with which the system is required to interface are also shown. Naming conventions for DCDs are discussed in the next section under DFDs.

Figure 4-3 is a generic example of a DCD. There is only one *process* (circle or bubble) on this diagram; it represents the system being developed. Any number of *data flows* (arrows) may be present, depicting the data interface with the environment. The entities outside the context of the system being developed, with which that system interfaces, are called *terminators* (shown as boxes); there may be any number of these.

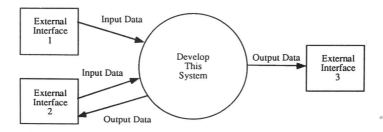

Figure 4-3 Generic Data Context Diagram (DCD)

4.1.2 Data Flow Diagrams (DFD)

The DFDs are the backbone of the graphical representation for system requirements analysis. They are constructed in a leveled manner, with each level providing more details of the requirements. The DFD consists of two parts: the diagram itself and—for the lowest-level processes—process specifications (PSpecs).

4.1.2.1 Diagram The top-level DFD is a breakdown of the functional requirements from the DCD. Figure 4-4 shows a DCD, and Figure 4-5 is the first-level breakdown from that diagram, numbered DFD 0. Exactly how to accomplish that top-level decomposition is a vital issue in problem analysis and requirements specification; it will be addressed in detail in Section 4.1.8.

Each level of DFDs shows more detail of the requirements and may include *processes* (circles), *data flows* (arrows), and *data stores* (parallel lines). Each new level (sometimes referred to as a *child*) is a breakdown of a process shown on the higher level (*parent*). These subprocesses and subflows do *not* make new statements about the system—only more detailed ones. Each process is numbered, and the child process inherits the parent's number and an additional number of its own. The title of the DFD showing the child processes is the name of the process (parent) that is being decomposed. Figures 4-5 and 4-6 illustrate this organization of DFDs into levels.

The following are some general naming conventions to use on the DFDs and DCDs. Since processes represent actions, their names should always start with a verb. Data flows and stores represent information; as such, their name should never contain a verb (it should be a noun phrase). Terminators (on data context diagrams) depict actual entities; as such, they should be named with noun phrases.

Any abbreviations should be chosen to be understandable without reference to a definition. Avoid abbreviations wherever possible (for example, use shorter words), but be consistent throughout the project when they are used.

Consistency throughout the project is of *vital* importance. Otherwise, readers and reviewers will be confused as to whether small name variations actually mean something different or are errors (inconsistencies).

Figure 4-5 gives the Level 0 DFD for "Monitor Furnaces." There are six processes shown, with the necessary data flow between them and to the "outside world" (the furnace or one of the offices). In order to understand the data flows to and from the outside world, you should always read a DFD in conjunction with its parent.

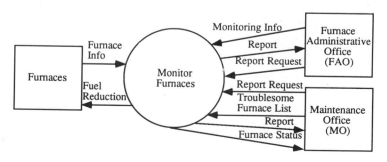

Figure 4-4 DCD for Furnace Monitoring System

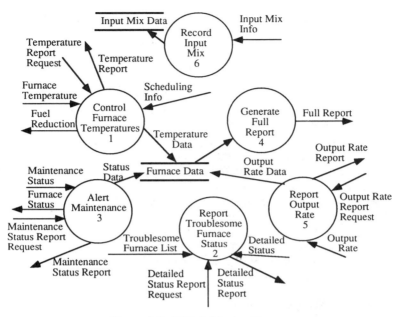

Figure 4-5 DFD 0: Monitor Furnaces

(Of course, you as the developer will always *create* a DFD based on the data flows and needed functionality of the parent.) Data stores are shown for data that needs to be accessed later than it is stored or more than once. "Furnace Data" is an example. Between the levels of DFDs, there needs to be consistency of data flow (called *balancing*). By this we mean that any data shown entering or leaving the parent process must be shown on the child DFD as flows to its outside world. The data flow names must be identical (for example, "Fuel Reduction" is present on both Figures 4-4 and 4-5), or the data must be decomposed into its component parts at

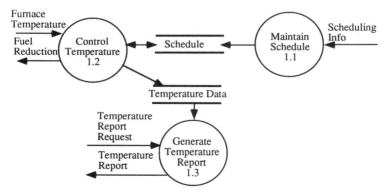

Figure 4-6 DFD 1: Control Furnace Temperatures

the lower level. For example, in Figure 4-4, "Monitoring Info" is received from the external Furnace Administration Office (FAO); in Figure 4-5, we see "Scheduling Info" entering Process 1 and "Input Mix Info" entering Process 6. These two flows make up "Monitoring Info" and would be defined as such in the data dictionary, to be discussed later. Data flows entering or leaving a data store need to be labeled only when a portion of the data in the store needs to be indicated (for example, "Temperature Data" going into "Furnace Data"). Again, the data dictionary gives the definitions of what makes up the data stores.

Figure 4-6 is the breakdown of Process 1, "Control Furnace Temperatures," on DFD 0 (see Figure 4-5). Notice that the numbering scheme is carried out (1.1, 1.2, 1.3). The data flows to the outside (external to "Control Furnace Temperatures") shown in this diagram must still be consistent with those leaving the parent process in the higher-level diagram, as discussed previously. Lower-level data flows or stores internal to this diagram may appear, showing more detail than was necessary or desired in the parent DFD. "Temperature Data" is an example of a lower-level data store; it is the only part of "Furnace Data" on DFD 0 that is accessed by Process 1, so it is consistent. No control flow is shown here; that is left for the CFD (discussed in Section 4.1.5).

4.1.2.2 Process Specifications (PSpec)   A PSpec shows how the output for the given process is generated from its inputs, nothing more and nothing less. The format of the PSpec can vary. Textual PSpecs describe a process that is procedural. Usually a "structured" English is used to make the text concise. When equations are used in PSpecs, one may also want to provide an informal descriptive comment that summarizes them.

Tables should be used in PSpecs whenever they are the most expressive way to convey the meaning of the requirements. However, be careful of using the process activation table (PAT) (described later) in a PSpec. It is usually used to show control in a CSpec. A good rule to follow is that if a figure, diagram, or table would have been included in a traditional narrative specification, it should be included in a PSpec. Another convention that is often useful is to show the actual names of data flows into or out of the process in all upper case in the PSpec and use lower case for the rest of the text.

PSpecs must be written for every functional primitive process (one that is not further decomposed) on a DFD. There are three ways to write the text in a PSpec, in increasing order of precision, as illustrated in Figure 4-7. Note that the name and number for the PSpec is inherited from the process that it describes.

4.1.3 Data Dictionary

The data dictionary consists of the definitions for all the information (data and control) that flows through the system. The following attributes should be present for each primitive flow or store:

- *Name* — actual name of the flow or store (such as MONITOR FREQUENCY)
- *Rate* at which a signal is to be updated (such as "once per second")

PSpec 2.1: **Manage Troublesome Furnace List**
The FMS shall maintain a list of furnaces that are considered troublesome. The furnaces currently in the list shall be monitored for their detailed electrical readings. The MO shall have the capability to update (add/delete) furnaces in the list.

(a)

PSpec 2.1: **Manage Troublesome Furnace List**
For each furnace in the change list
  Issue a command to start or stop monitoring detailed status as indicated by the change (add/delete).

(b)

PSpec 2.1: **Manage Troublesome Furnace List**
For each FURNACE NUMBER in TROUBLESOME FURNACE LIST
  if TROUBLESOME FURNACE INDICATOR = Add then
    Issue MONITOR CHANGE = On Troublesome List.
  otherwise * indicator is Delete *
    Issue MONITOR CHANGE = Off Troublesome List.

(c)

Figure 4-7 PSpec Styles: (*a*) Traditional English "Shall" Style; (*b*) Structured English; (*c*) Structured English with Actual Data Names

- *Range*—limits within which a *continuous* primitive signal exists (-1000 to $+60,000$ ft, $\pm300°$C, and so on)
- *Resolution* (*Precision*)—smallest magnitude increment the entry is required to represent (0.01 kg, 0.5 gal, for example), which also indicates the increments by which the value changes (for example, at a resolution of 0.5 gal we might have values such as 2.5 gal, but not 2.7 gallons—which is not a 0.5 increment from the starting point of 0.0)
- *Units*—physical units (pounds, feet, or gallons for example) as applicable (mandatory for continuous primitives)
- *Value Names*—names given for values of a given *discrete* primitive (for example, MAINTENANCE STATUS can be "Normal," "Degraded," "Impaired," "Critical," "Safety Hazard")

Accuracy and *repeatability* should be specified in PSpecs where needed. Accuracy is the characteristic of a numeric attribute that reflects how closely it represents an actual value. Measurement error causes many values to be not perfectly accurate. A closely related characteristic is repeatability: the degree to which repeated measurements of the same actual value result in the same measured value.

Accuracy is specified by placing bounds on a value, with associated confidence limits. For example, the altitude of an aircraft might be specified as being accurate within ± 100 feet, with 99 percent confidence. The bounds may be specific values as noted, or a percentage, as in ± 2 percent. Note that the accuracy description might be quite complex, perhaps being dependent upon the altitude itself and (perhaps for a radar system) the distance from the measuring device.

For grouped data, the name of the flow and the breakdown into its constituent parts should be given. Range, Rate, and Resolution are usually required for external flows but should rarely be used for internal ones—leave that for the designer.

SYMBOL	MEANING	DESCRIPTION
=	composed of	Indicates that the flow named on its left is composed of the flows named on its right.
+	together with	Collects members into a group, but does not imply order.
{ }	iterations of	Indicates that expression within these braces may occur any number of times. May be indexed: for example M { } N indicates any number of iterations from M to N.
[	]	select one of	Brackets contain two or more items separated by vertical bars. Any given instance of the flow will include exactly one of them
( )	optional	Expression enclosed may or may not appear in a given instance of the flow.
" "	literal	Symbols enclosed within quotes literally constitute the flow.
* *	comment	A statement that is not a formal part of definition but gives additional insight into its meaning.

Figure 4-8   Data Dictionary Symbols

The dictionary is to be constructed using the symbols shown in Figure 4-8. During system requirements analysis, the following information should be placed in the dictionary:

Internal Flows:

　　Data—Name and Units or Value Names

　　Control—Name and Value Names

External Flows:

　　Data—Name, Rate, and [Range, Resolution, and Units] or [Value Names]

　　Control—Name, Rate, and Value Names

The database may also include the identification of the originator and date entered; identification of person making change and change date; and a comment field, which provides additional insight into meaning while not being part of the formal definition. The fields used should be consistent for a given project.

Figure 4-9 shows portions of the data dictionary for the FMS. INDIVIDUAL ITEM REQUEST is an example of grouped data. It consists of an ITEM INDICATION, a FURNACE NUMBER, and, optionally, a THERMOMETER NUMBER (when ITEM INDICATION = Temperature). INPUT MIX INFO illustrates an item that contains repeated data. There may be from one to MAX FURNACES occurrences of the FURNACE NUMBER and INPUT MIX pair. Note that MAX FURNACES is a constant declared to make the system definition more flexible. Any item in the dictionary that pertains to each of the furnaces uses the constant rather than the actual number "28," allowing for the ability to change this in only one place. The primitive entry MONITOR FREQUENCY shows the Range, Units, Resolution, and Rate associated with it. The entry MAINTENANCE STATUS is an example of a primitive that is a selection of one value from a list of items; the quotes indicate that these are literal values of that status.

•••

FURNACE NUMBER = * Number assigned to furnace for automation/management purposes *
Range = 1 to Max Furnaces

INDIVIDUAL ITEM REQUEST = Item Indication + Furnace Number + (Thermometer Number)
* Thermometer Number is provided when Item Indication = Temperature *
Rate = event-driven

INPUT MIX = * Mixture of raw materials being placed in furnace *
(Not further defined for this example)

INPUT MIX INFO = 1{Furnace Number + Input Mix}Max Furnaces
Rate = event-driven

ITEM INDICATION = ["Temperature" | "Status" | "Output Rate"] * Indication of what type of
information is desired from the furnace *

MAINTENANCE STATUS = ["Normal" | "Degraded" | "Impaired" | "Critical" | "Safety Hazard"]
Rate = monitored "continuously"

MAX FURNACES = * Number of furnaces in plant that can be automatically monitored --
currently 28 *

•••

MONITOR FREQUENCY = * Frequency at which to monitor a thermometer*
Range = 0 to 144
Units = readings/day
Resolution = 10 minutes
Rate = change is event-driven

•••

Figure 4-9   Data Dictionary Excerpt

4.1.4   *Control Context Diagram (CCD)*

The top-level diagram showing the control of the system is called the control context
diagram (CCD). It establishes the control information interface between the system
and its environment. Naming conventions for the CCDs are consistent with those
discussed in the previous sections for DCDs and DFDs.

Figure 4-10 is a generic example of a control context diagram similar to the data
context diagram shown in Figure 4-3. All external interfaces (terminator boxes)
that were on the DCD are shown here, whether or not there is any control flow
associated. This aids in keeping the diagrams consistent as well as allowing completeness checking of control. Where no control is shown, one can check to be sure
that this also is correct. *Control flows* are shown as broken-line arrows with names.

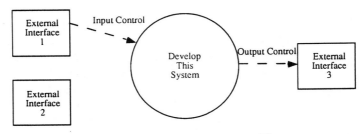

Figure 4-10   Generic Control Context Diagram

If the CCD and DCD are not too complex, the CCD may actually be superimposed on the DCD. That is the preferred method.

4.1.5 Control Flow Diagrams (CFDs)

Control flow diagrams (CFDs) are images of DFDs that show the flow of control, instead of data, through the system. They are produced after the DFDs and simply match them one for one, as necessary (if there is no control needed for a given DFD, no CFD is drawn). As with the recommended method for the CCD, the control information of the CFD may be added to the corresponding DFD. The CFD consists of two parts: the diagram itself and—optionally as needed for complexity—control specifications (CSpecs).

4.1.5.1 Diagram   For each level, CFDs show control of that section of the system. They include all the same processes (circles) that are on the corresponding DFD. As such, the processes still represent the processing of the *data* and *do not* represent processing of the *control flows*. The control flows simply enter the process—we say "are consumed by the process"—to be used later for control of lower-level processes. Therefore, a control flow entering a process never controls the entire process, but rather controls individual subordinate processes. Each CFD inherits the name and number of the associated DFD. Naming conventions for elements of CFDs follow those of the DFDs. There may be processes on the CFD without any control flows. These are kept on for consistency.

A *control bar* (single vertical line) shows control flow entering or exiting the associated CSpec, discussed in detail in Section 4.1.5.2, which provides the decision-making aspects of the CFD and indicates the activation and deactivation of processes. Multiple control bars may be used on a diagram, but all the bars on one diagram are associated with the same CSpec.

A CFD may also contain a *process event* (lightning bolt). This symbol represents the activation of one process on the diagram (at arrowhead) by another on the same diagram (at the other end of the bolt).

Notice the important difference between the process event and the control flow. The control flow *does not* activate the process it points to. Further, as we will see later, the process event is a one-time activation, while the control flow causes, via the CSpec, a process activation that is continuous, until explicitly deactivated. Why do we have both notations? The process event is simpler and clearer (because the control logic is expressed inside the PSpec and everything is shown on the same graphic), while the control flow, with associated methods described later, is more general and flexible in nature. (The process event is similar to the *event flows* of Ward & Mellor [WAR85, Vol. 1, page 47].) The process event may also be a signal to *deactivate* a process—to stop its continuous processing; there may be some terminating behavior, as specified in the process's own PSpec. The process event is optional. It could be stated within the CSpec instead; in fact, if there is anything complex about the control, a CSpec should be used. If the control is simple, then the use of the process event allows you to avoid creation of an additional CSpec and it should be used.

Sometimes a flow may be used as both data and control. In this case, one should show the flow in the way it is being used on the individual flow diagram. For a grouped flow, where part is data and part control, show it as data until it is broken down into the actual control component.

Figures 4-11 and 4-12 show the CFD for level 0 (see Figure 4-5 for DFD) and for the breakdown of Process 2 ("Report Troublesome Furnace Status"), respectively. Control flows (dashed arrow) entering a process do not activate or deactivate that process; they simply enter the process and go into a control bar at a lower-level CFD. Hence they indirectly control activity of the process. In Figure 4-11, "Furnace Trouble" is an example of such a control flow. This type of control flow controls something at a lower level. Figure 4-12 shows this same flow going into a control bar, indicating that the CSpec will tell us what the control really is. This will be discussed further under CSpecs in the next section. The CFD in Figure 4-12 is superimposed on the DFD.

Figure 4-13 shows the CFD for the breakdown of "Control Temperature" (Process 1.2), shown on the DFD in Figure 4-6. In it, we see an example of a process event ("Furnace Evaluation") shown on the CFD rather than using a CSpec. It activates Process 1.2.2, "Control Fuel Valve," on a *one-time* basis. The activated process takes the action specified in its PSpec, processing data available if any. Whether the process remains activated depends upon its own PSpec. The other processes (1.2.1 and 1.2.3) are said to be *data-activated*. They perform their function whenever the necessary input data is present. (Remember that the

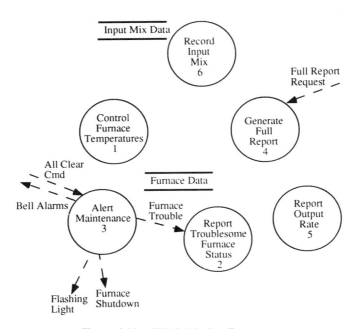

Figure 4-11   CFD 0: Monitor Furnaces

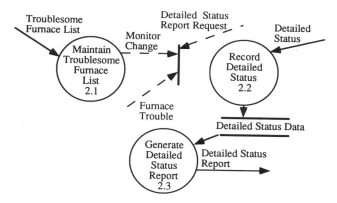

Figure 4-12 DFD/CFD 2: Report Troublesome Furnace Status

control flow "Temperature State Change," controls something at a lower level within Process 1.2.3.)

In Figure 4-12, "Monitor Change" and "Furnace Trouble" were shown entering a control bar rather than directly activating "Record Detailed Status." One reason for this is that one of the flows ("Furnace Trouble") came from outside the scope of the diagram. Another reason may be the complexity of the activate/deactivate criteria, which may need explanation within the CSpec. Actually, we can't determine that the control flow activates Process 2.2 from looking at DFD/CFD 2—but we will later see that this is what happens, when we look at the associated CSpec 2.

Control flows coming *out* of a bar are created within that CSpec and used to control processing outside the scope of the diagram. Figure 4-14 shows an example of this. "Furnace Trouble" is output from the CSpec here, to be used in Figure 4-12 as input to that CSpec to activate or deactivate "Record Detailed Status."

Control flows leaving a process, such as "Furnace Trouble" in Figure 4-11, show their generation in a lower-level process (see Figure 4-14) or, for lowest-level processes, in a PSpec. The PSpec in Figure 4-7c illustrates the issuing of the control flow "Monitor Change" (see also Figure 4-12).

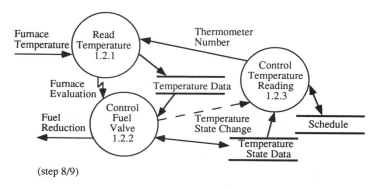

(step 8/9)

Figure 4-13 DFD/CFD 1.2: Control Temperature

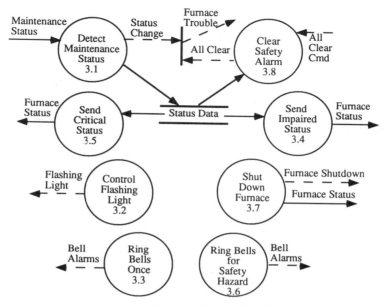

Figure 4-14 DFD/CFD 3: Alert Maintenance

Although we will not illustrate any additional notation, any specific project may have need of additional forms of control. For example, if a process does nothing but transform control signals as its processing, you might show it as a dashed circle. If you need to have storage for control flows, you can use a *control store,* shown in a manner analogous to the data store but with dashed lines.

4.1.5.2 *Control Specifications (CSpecs)*

The CSpecs represent the control behavior of the system. Their purpose is to show how their outputs are generated from their inputs. They are present only where process control is required on the associated DFD or where control signals are to be converted into new control signals. The inputs are control flows from the CFD and the outputs are process activators and control flows entering the CFDs. *Process activators* are simply system states, defined by the process activation tables, discussed below, that activate or deactivate processes on the associated CFD.

CSpecs are optional where no process activators are required. If a control bar is present on the CFD, there must be a CSpec associated with that CFD. Often a CSpec is made up of several pages consisting of tables and diagrams or text; the CSpec is the only component of the requirements model that is allowed to extend over several pages. The types of graphics included are:

- Decision tables
- Process activation tables
- State transition diagrams/tables

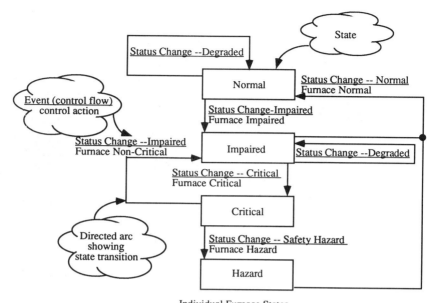

Individual Furnace States

Figure 4-15 CSpec 3: sheet 1 of 2 (State Transition Diagram)

Figures 4-15 and 4-16 illustrate portions of a multi-sheet CSpec corresponding to the CFD in Figure 4-14. Before the graphics shown are discussed, we need to introduce two categories of control structures:

- Combinational machines (no memory)
- Sequential machines (memory)

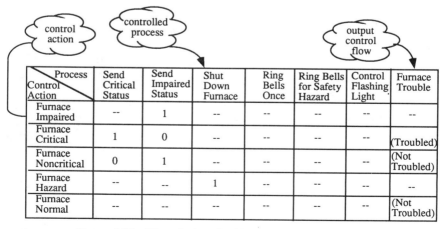

Figure 4-16 CSpec 3: sheet 2 of 2 (Process Activation Table)

Of the two, combinational machines are preferred because they are simpler: the output(s) are determined entirely by the current inputs.

Decision Table   A *decision table* (sometimes called a *truth table*) is a combinational machine. It can be drawn with a tabular arrangement of all combinations of input values, with required values of output for each combination. These combinations can be condensed if several produce the same output. Figure 4-17 gives an example. The input is a set of temperatures of the furnace, and the output is both a control action (amount of fuel reduction) and a possible state change for temperature ("Hot" or "Normal"). As usual, terms are defined in the data dictionary.

Process Activation Table (PAT)   A *process activation table* (PAT), a type of decision table in which some or all of the outputs happen to activate processes, represents a sequential machine. Therefore, it operates in cooperation with a mechanism for controlling state status and transition. Its input is a control action (which is based on the state of the system), and its output is a *process activator*, which serves to activate or deactivate a process. Figure 4-16 gives an example. For instance, when a furnace becomes impaired (input control action: "Furnace Impaired"), the process "Send Impaired Status" is activated (as denoted by the "1" in the intersecting box). The deactivation of a process is represented by a "0". Processes activated by a process activation table remain continuously active, until explicitly deactivated. Other boxes are left blank or have "—" inserted to indicate that that process is not affected by the control action. Where do the input control actions come from? They are derived from state information—the memory aspect of the machine. We need to look first at how state information is retained and changed; then we can revisit the PAT.

A sequential machine produces outputs that are determined both by its current and its past inputs. This implies that a memory must be kept. This memory can be represented in the form of states. To show these states graphically, two different diagrams, explained below, can be used. Figures 4-15 and 4-18 illustrate the equivalent state representations.

State Transition Diagram (STD)   In a *state transition diagram* (STD), the states of the system are shown in boxes. Arrows represent the direction of a

Inputs		Outputs	
Temperatures		Fuel Reduction	Temperature State
none above Hot Spot	avg > Hot Average	Low Fuel Reduction	Hot
	avg ≤ Hot Average	--	Normal
1 or more above Hot Spot	--	High Fuel Reduction	Hot

Figure 4-17   Decision Table Example

change from one state to another. For example, in Figure 4-15 one can change from "Critical" state to "Hazard", but not the other way. The data associated with each arrow indicates the event (control flow) that took place to cause the state change (text above line) and, optionally, the associated control action that is to occur (text below line). There may be multiple events or control actions associated with a state change. An event does not necessarily cause a change in state; this occurs when no control action is associated with it. The status change of "Degraded" is an example of such an event; no change in state takes place (arrow pointing into same box). Any control actions then map to a PAT, which shows what the action involves. When used together in this manner, the combination of diagrams is called a composite CSpec. An illustration of the composite CSpec occurs in the relationship between Figures 4-15 and 4-16. The event "Status Change—Critical" causes a state change from "Impaired" to "Critical". In addition, there is a control action of "Furnace Critical," which (in Figure 4-16) causes the process "Send Critical Status" to be activated, the process "Send Impaired Status" to be deactivated, and the control flow "Furnace Trouble" to be sent out, indicating that the furnace is "Troubled."

State Transition Table (STT)   The representation of the sequential machine in a *state transition table* (STT) follows a similar pattern to the STD. Here the intersection of the current state and each of the other columns indicate the associated event, control action, and next state (the state to make a transition to), respectively. Note that the STT can be used to accommodate more complex or larger cases without becoming as unmanageable as the STD (by confusion of lines crossing). See Figure 4-18 for an example.

PAT and STD Revisited   Let's review what is going on with the interaction between the STD and PAT. (We won't discuss the STT; it is just another form of STD.)

Current State	Event (status change)	Control Action	Next State
Normal	Impaired	Furnace Impaired	Impaired
	Degraded	--	Normal
Impaired	Normal	Furnace Normal	Normal
	Critical	Furnace Critical	Critical
	Degraded	--	Impaired
Critical	Hazard	Furnace Hazard	Hazard
	Non-Critical	Furnace Non-Critical	Impaired
Hazard	Normal	Furnace Normal	Normal

Figure 4-18   State Transition Table

First, a control flow enters a control bar with an associated CSpec, as shown in Figure 4-15 (for example, "Status Change—Impaired").

Second, the control flow is an event for the STD that causes a state transition. The state transition is shown as the directed arc between two states (the boxes), while the control flow/event is shown next to the directed arc, above the horizontal line (for example, the state transition from "Normal" to "Impaired").

Third (actually at the same time as the state change), there is an output control action, shown below the horizontal line next to the directed arc (for example, output of "Furnace Impaired").

Fourth, the *output* of the STD becomes the *input* of the PAT, shown in Figure 4-16 (for example, input of "Furnace Impaired").

Fifth, the output(s) of the PAT are *all the* non-blank (or "—") boxes in the row associated with the input control action. For the rows in which the corresponding column heading is a process from the DFD/CFD being controlled, the entry in the box is a "1" or "0" corresponding to process activation or deactivation, respectively. For the rows in which the corresponding column heading is a control flow, the box indicates that the control flow is an output from the control bar, with the value given. For example, the control action "Furnace Impaired" activates the process "Send Impaired Status." The control action "Furnace Critical" causes three things to happen: the process "Send Critical Status" is activated, the process "Send Impaired Status" is deactivated, and the control flow "Furnace Trouble" is emitted with the value of "Troubled."

The interaction between the PAT and STD associated with the use of control flows is somewhat complex, but it is an extremely powerful mechanism for precise control of complex interactions and timing issues. Careful review of the illustration (and the later full example) should make the interactions clear. It is partly because of these complexities that we also use the simpler *process event* mechanism described earlier.

4.1.6 Response Time Specification (RTS)

The response time specification (RTS) is used as a vehicle for thinking of the system as an event-driven model. It illustrates the external response times that need to be specified for the requirements model. The timing specification must balance with the requirements model; every external primitive signal from the DCD (and CCD) should appear at least once. No other signals should appear. Along with the requirements model and hardware characteristics (including hardware–software interfaces) determined during system design, this specification becomes one of the major inputs to the software designers.

Figure 4-19 is an example of an RTS. The input-to-output response time, usually the maximum response time, is shown from each event occurring as input to each resulting event occurring as output. Notice that it is OK to have an input event, such as "Scheduling Info", that does not have a specific external output signal associated with it. Instead, the output event is the effect that this has on the system as a whole (all later reports affected). The associated time for that effect to take place is given.

External Input Signal	Input Event	Frequency	External Output Signal	Output Event	Response Time
Scheduling Info	entered	event-driven	none	All later reports affected	new schedule in effect within 10 min
Input Mix Info	entered	event-driven	Report	displayed	as requested in reports
Troublesome Furnace List	entered	event-driven	Report	displayed/ recording start or stop	as requested in reports/ within 1 min
Furnace Temperature	received from furnace	according to schedule	Report	displayed	as requested in reports
		every min. (when hot)	Fuel Reduction (when hot)	fuel reduced	within 1 min
Output Rate	received from furnace	periodically	Report	displayed	as requested in reports
Detailed Status	received from furnace	"continuosly"	Report	displayed	as requested in reports

Figure 4-19   Response Time Specification

4.1.7   Requirements Traceability Matrix (RTM)

A requirements traceability matrix (RTM) must be provided to ensure completeness and consistency with the customer's needs. This can be done in the form of a simple (possibly large) table that lists the customer's needs along one axis and requirements model components on the other. On large systems, there may be too many requirements model components to fit on one page. In order to have some control over the structure of the matrix, leveled matrices can be drawn to correspond to the DFD/CFDs. An "X" in an intersection box indicates that the given customer need is satisfied (at least in part) by the requirements model component listed. Sometimes a requirement may be satisfied in more than one place.

Figure 4-20 shows an extract of an RTM. Customer need "7.1 Individual Item" is an example of a requirement that has been split across multiple components. "Control Furnace Temperatures" needs to get the temperature from the furnace when that is requested, while "Alert Maintenance" handles the maintenance status in a similar fashion. Notice that "Control Furnace Temperatures" has been allocated all of the requirements for "3. Control Furnace Temperature," so it does not need to show the allocation of the subsidiary requirements. It is assumed from the diagram that when a higher-level requirement has been allocated to a given component, then the lower-level ones have as well.

Note that automated tools can often be used to generate much of the traceability information; the analyst then needs only to perform the allocation.

Requirement Model Component / Customer Need	Control Furnace Temperatures 1	Report Troublesome Furnace Status 2	Alert Maintenance 3	Generate Full Report 4	Report Output Rate 5	Record Input Mix 6
1. Schedule temperature readings	X					
2. Designate Troublesome Furnaces-record detailed status		X				
3. Control Furnace Temperatures	X					
3.1 High temperature -- reduce 20%						
3.2 Avg temperature -- reduce 10%						
3.3 Monitor 1/minute						
4. Different Reports (TBD)						
5. Input Mix used for reports at FAO						X
6. Full Report requested				X		
7. Immediate Update						
7.1 Individual Item	X		X		X	

Figure 4-20   Requirements Traceability Matrix Extract

4.1.8   Event–Action Diagram (EAD)

The partitioning of the context diagram into the first-level decomposition of data flow diagrams, DFD 0, is by no means obvious, yet it is one of the most important decisions made by the system requirements analyst, because it provides the foundation for the specification and explanation of the system requirements. If the analysis proceeds strictly "top down," we wind up doing the most important decomposition when we know least about the problem! Traditional structured analysis handles this through iteration; when you later find out that the initial decomposition was faulty (that is, when you know more about the problem and can make better decisions) you revise that decomposition and all later partitioning. That's fine; it is always good to be flexible and willing to improve a representation of the requirements. But it would be even better if we had some way to improve our initial try at DFD 0.

This section introduces the graphics for a method to do exactly that. The general philosophy is to start with a decomposition that is rather in the "middle" of the set of leveled DFDs and then use principles of composition to aggregate upwards to DFD 0. The advantage of this method is that we can establish a set of guidelines for finding the "middle" decomposition, aggregate using well-established principles of coupling and cohesion, and wind up knowing much more about the problem when we develop the initial DFD 0. The approach is called *event partitioning*.

McMenamin & Palmer [MCM84] describe the use of event partitioning as a means to partition the system into its essential activities: those actions that must be performed by the system regardless of the implementation that will be employed. Thus, the purpose of the *event–action diagram* (EAD) is to provide a starting point (partitioning) for the development of data flow diagrams. It allows us to start with a pseudo-DFD based on external stimuli (events) and the responses to those events (actions). Actions have the same characteristics as processes, and will be aggregated (principle of composition) into higher-level processes for DFD 0. The event partitioning consists of the following components:

- Event list
- EAD
- Action/Store Matrix or List

Event List   In order to understand or draw the EAD, we first need to look at a definition of the system events. *Events* are the interactions between the system and its environment. They are changes in the system's environment that cause the system to respond in some manner. The set of activities that must be performed by the system whenever a certain event occurs. They are referred to as the *event response* or *action*. Events may be temporal or external. An *external* event usually produces an incoming data or control flow that crosses the boundary of the system. The *temporal* event (arrival of a particular time) does not result in a data flow crossing the system's boundary, mainly because the passage of time does not happen in any one specific place. A list can be made of all of the events for a system.

Figure 4-21 is a partial example of an event list. In it we see a statement of what the event—stimulus—is (such as Maintenance Status received from furnace) followed by the response that the system needs to make. It is this response that we need to capture in the EAD.

Event–Action Diagram   From the event list, we can now draw an EAD representing the responses to these events. See Figure 4-22 for an excerpt.

The EAD is a form of DFD/CFD with special constraints. Each circle on the EAD represents an *action;* it is numbered to correspond to the event list. The input and output associated with the action are shown with data and control flows. There is an additional limitation that communication between actions may only occur through data stores (in other words, no arrow directly from one action to another is allowed). The stores are lettered, so that if the same one occurs on more than one sheet, it receives the same letter. The control flows in the EAD are used to show the activation of temporal actions and to allow actions to communicate control to something outside the system. Periodic actions should be shown as separate (temporal) actions with a control flow indicating that it is "time to . . . ".

Action/Store Matrix or List   A number of data stores may appear on more than one sheet. This is particularly prevalent on large systems, and for that reason it is

1. FAO submits scheduling info (may be update): When FAO enters SCHEDULING INFO, update the internal SCHEDULE so that furnaces may be monitored accordingly.
   - •
   - •
   - •

4. Time to monitor a thermometer (temporal event): When it's TIME TO MONITOR a furnace thermometer, get the TEMPERATURE from the furnace and store that information. If this TEMPERATURE or the average temperature for the furnace is too hot, then send out FUEL REDUCTION and monitor every minute. If the TEMPERATURE is now returning to "normal" then return to regular scheduled monitoring.

5. Output rate received from furnace: When OUTPUT RATE is received from a furnace, store that information.

6. Detailed status received from furnace: When DETAILED STATUS is received from a furnace that is listed in TROUBLESOME FURNACE DATA, store that information.
   - •
   - •
   - •

10. Maintenance status received from furnace: When MAINTENANCE STATUS is received from a furnace store that information. In addition, check the value and send the appropriate information to the office(s). This information may include FURNACE STATUS, FLASHING LIGHT (on or off) and BELL ALARMS. Update TROUBLESOME FURNACE DATA as required (for furnace transitioning from/to CRITICAL)

11. Time to send impaired status (periodic): When it's TIME TO SEND STATUS, the current FURNACE STATUS is reported to the MO for any furnace that is still IMPAIRED or DEGRADED.
   - •
   - •
   - •

Figure 4-21 Event List Excerpt

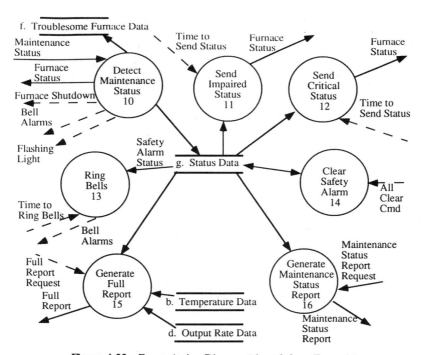

Figure 4-22 Event–Action Diagram (sheet 2 from Example)

useful to introduce the Action/Store Matrix. An example is shown in Figure 4-23a. The matrix shows which actions set (S) or use (U) the different stores. It helps in construction of the DFD 0 in terms of grouping together actions that operate on common data stores. For systems where this diagram would become too complex, a list can be constructed showing each store and the action(s) that access them (see Figure 4-23b).

Once we have established this initial system decomposition, we are ready to tackle the creation of DFD 0. The actions are aggregated together, using the coupling and cohesion principles related to composition (see Section 4.2.2), into the processes of DFD 0. The actions are not primitive processes, but are rather at a "middle" level of decomposition. Therefore, they may be split into pieces and allocated to several different higher-level processes on DFD 0. The other implication of their not being primitive processes is that when DFD 0 is further partitioned, there is no attempt made to partition into processes that are congruent with actions. Further, the continued subdivision of DFDs will go to a finer level of detail than shown by the actions themselves.

Remember that the purpose of the EAD is to provide a starting point for the decomposition, allowing us to have sound reasons for establishment of the processes of DFD 0. Where, then, do the EAD and event list fit in the documentation scheme? The answer is that they do not! The event list and EAD are typically not provided to a customer; they are saved, however, for future reference, especially for when a change in requirements occurs. Section 4.4 gives a complete example of this process.

Suppose you already have a good idea of what DFD 0 should be. Must you use event partitioning? Of course not. If the analysis and design team has a good sense for the top-level decomposition, perhaps from the "legacy" discussed in Chapter 2, there is no need to approach the problem at the event level. Event partitioning and the EAD are tools in the tool kit; you choose the ones you need for each specific job.

4.1.9   Graphics Summary

Now that we've seen all of the graphics individually, we will summarize the ways the major components interact with each other. Figure 4-24 is an illustration of the ways in which the DFD, CFD, and CSpec relate to each other to demonstrate the integrated requirements of the system. The CFD shows events (control flows), usually generated within a process, that enter a CSpec through the control bar. An event causes a state change within the CSpec, which results in one or both of the following actions: (1) process(es) being activated or deactivated on the associated DFD or (2) control signal(s) generated, as represented by control flow leaving the control bar on the CFD. Remember that this control signal is used to control something in another part of the system not shown on this particular CFD.

This association of diagrams could occur at any level of the decomposition, but the CFD/CSpec is most likely to be present near the top, since that is where most of the control takes place. At the bottom levels, PSpecs come into play to describe the control flows that a process may generate (such as C3 in Figure 4-24).

Data Store / Action	a.Schedule	b.Temperature Data	c.Input Mix Data	d.Output Rate Data	e.Detailed Status Data	f.Troublesome Furnace Data	g.Status Data
1. Maintain Schedule	S						
2. Record Input Mix			S				
3. Monitor Troublesome Furnace(s)						S	
4. Control Temperature	S,U	S					
5. Record Output Rate				S			
6. Record Detailed Status					S	U	
7. Generate Temperature Report		U					
8. Generate Output Rate Report				U			
9. Generate Detailed Status Report					U	U	
10. Detect Maintenance Status							S
11. Send Impaired Status							U
12. Send Critical Status							U
13. Ring Bells							U
14. Clear Safety Alarm							S,U
15. Generate Full Report		U		U			U
16. Generate Maintenance Status Report							U

(a)

Schedule
   Maintain Schedule
   Control Temperature
Temperature Data
   Control Temperature
   Generate Full Report
   Generate Temperature Report
Input Mix Data
   Record Input Mix
Output Rate Data
   Record Output Rate
   Generate Full Report
   Generate Output Rate Report
Detailed Status Data
   Record Detailed Status
   Generate Detailed Status Report
Troublesome Furnace Data
   Monitor Troublesome Furnace(s)
   RecordDetailed Status
Status Data
   Detect Maintenance Status
   Send Impaired Status
   Send Critical Status
   Ring Bells
   Clear Safety Alarm
   Generate Full Report
   Generate Maintenance Status Report

(b)

Figure 4-23 (a) Action/Store Matrix; (b) Action/Store List

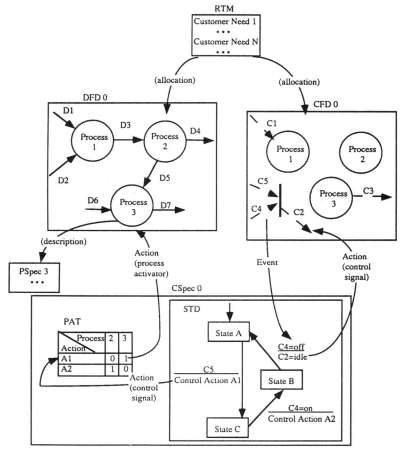

Figure 4-24   Relationship among Requirements Model Components

4.2   GUIDELINES

This section introduces several sets of guidelines for use in the methodology steps. The application of these rules will be indicated at the appropriate steps in the methodology. The guidelines include:

- Information to include in the system-level analysis
- Coupling and cohesion
- Events
  - ○ Identifying events
  - ○ Defining actions
  - ○ Grouping actions

- Data flow diagram hints
- Constructing a leveled set of processes
- Separating data and control
- Checklist for correctness and completion (balancing)

Most of these guidelines follow those given in Hatley & Pirbhai [HAT87].

4.2.1   Information to Include in the System-Level Analysis

What should be included in the requirements model during system requirements analysis?

1. Only those requirements that must be implemented regardless of the technology used! DO NOT include any design-specific "requirements" (but remember the interaction we stressed in Chapter 2, Figures 2-3 and 2-4; the requirements must be consistent with feasible designs).
2. Only the timing between events at the system inputs and outputs—the external timing—are of concern. Internal timing is entirely a design issue.

4.2.2   Coupling and Cohesion

There are two characteristics of the processes on a DFD that must be taken into account in order to analyze them effectively into levels. The first has to do with the complexity of the inter-process interactions; this is described in terms of *coupling*. The second has to do with the degree to which the lower-level processes each have a clearly stated focus—a single function to perform; this is described in terms of *cohesion*.

Partitioning a system involves not only decomposition into smaller components; certain phases make use of composition of smaller components into larger. Both composition and decomposition make use of the concepts of coupling and cohesion.

Coupling and cohesion are also important to the partitioning of software; this topic will be addressed again during the presentation of top-level design.

The following sections provide further discussion of coupling and cohesion and of how they relate to functional partitioning. They provide guidelines for both composition and decomposition. When we are aggregating actions into the upper-level processes of DFD 0, we are using composition. The rest of the DFD leveling activity consists of decomposition.

4.2.2.1   Coupling   The concept of coupling was introduced by Myers [MYE75] as a measure of the *independence* of processes. Coupling can also be thought of in terms of the *amount of knowledge* we need of one process in order to understand another. We will use the phrase *interconnected* to incorporate both the idea of independence and knowledge. The ideas we have introduced so far can be summarized as a definition:

Coupling is the characteristic of a number of processes that indicates the degree to which they are interconnected.

When the processes have little interconnection, they are said to be loosely (or weakly) coupled; otherwise they are said to be tightly coupled. In order to understand each process more easily, to understand the total of process interactions, and to reduce the effect of change in one process on another, it is desirable that processes be loosely coupled.

There are three ways in which processes can be coupled:

- Common access to a data store
- Control flow on a control flow diagram (CFD) or in a Control Specification (CSpec), by which one process generates an event that creates a process activator for the other process
- Data flow on the DFD

The most loosely coupled connection between two processes is common access to a data store. There is coupling via the data, but no activation. However, be cautious of this sort of coupling with many processes; when many processes access the same data store, they are *collectively* tightly coupled.

Control coupling is tighter than access to a data store, since the reader must understand both the controlling process and its associated CSpec in order to understand the activation of the process being considered. Remember that the control flow entering a process *does not* activate that process but rather activates some lower-level process by entering a control bar, and hence a CSpec. The process event, shown with the lightning bolt symbol, is somewhat simpler, in that it directly shows the process activation or deactivation, but still indicates tight coupling.

Data flow is the most tightly coupled interaction, but has the desirable characteristic that it shows both data and control flow in one diagram. If you need only one of data or control flow, use the other methods. If you need both sorts of control, which is a very common situation, show the relationship using data flow on a DFD. Avoid control flow unless you need activation without data flow, or if you need to illustrate repeated activation with information out of a data store.

Guidelines (Group processes to minimize interconnections.)

Composition: Group together in the same process those actions that have strong interconnections—particularly those that have significant access to common data stores.

Decomposition: Partition a process into lower-level processes in a way that tends to minimize the number of interconnections—particularly direct data flows.

4.2.2.2 Cohesion   Yourdon & Constantine [YOU79, page 106] introduce the phrase "cohesion" as a stand-in for what we might call "intramodular functional relatedness." But the clumsy long phrase is important to understand: cohesion deals with the degree to which the next-lower-level processes are related. The ideas we have introduced so far can be summarized as a definition:

Cohesion is the characteristic of a process that indicates the degree to which its components are working together to accomplish the same function.

By "components of the system" we mean lower-level processes of a DFD or the individual steps of processing in a PSpec. Another way of saying this is that the degree of "cohesion" in a process is an indicator of how well the individual components have a strong interrelationship.

Guidelines (Group together in same process only those actions that are closely related.)

Composition: Group together in the same process those actions that work together to accomplish a specific function.

Decomposition: Partition a process into lower-level processes in such a way that each of the lower-level processes has a single, clearly defined function.

4.2.2.3 Coupling and Cohesion Relationship Coupling and cohesion are two sides of the same coin. Almost always, a set of processes with strong cohesion will have loose or weak coupling to other sets or processes. Conversely, applying the guidelines for loose coupling will result in processes with strong cohesion.

This pairing of the two concepts comes about because when subcomponents are strongly functionally related, they are likely to have access to common data stores. Therefore, aggregating subcomponents into higher level processes based on strong functional cohesion has the net effect of keeping access to the data store within the higher-level process and simultaneously minimizing data flow between the higher-level processes: loose coupling. Conversely, again, performing the aggregation based on common access to data stores (explicitly looking for loose coupling) automatically results in higher-level processes that have strong functional cohesion.

Understanding this two-way relationship is important in understanding the similarity of functionally oriented analysis and data-oriented analysis. Functionally oriented analysis, which we emphasize in this book, looks at the functions or the things that have to be done in order to meet a customer's need or operational requirement. Data-oriented analysis, commonly called information modeling [FLA81, RUM91], has as its focus the data necessary to satisfy the requirements. Any specific system may need more of one flavor or more of the other, but actually both viewpoints are working toward the same end and are mutually compatible. In fact, as illustrated in the next section and in Section 4.4, we will often focus on grouping together actions that share common data stores—a data-oriented viewpoint with focus on loose coupling—in order to achieve strong functionality in DFD 0.

4.2.3 Events

The following has been adapted from McMenamin & Palmer [MCM84].

The main purpose of identifying the events of the system and their associated response is to gain an understanding of the system from a customer's point of view in order to construct an initial top-level DFD that is reasonably complete. This uses the coupling and cohesion rules for composition. Why do we need this starting point?

It is quite difficult, perhaps impossible, to partition the context diagram into good lower-level processes in a completely "top-down" fashion. That is, simply making guesses—even guesses based on functionality of system components—is likely to lead to a poor initial decomposition. This can be revised later, of course, but it is preferable to attempt to reach a good partitioning at our first attempt. That is what EADs help us to do, by capturing the system's response to all events that may occur.

The following paragraphs address the identification of events, the definition of the actions that need to take place in the system to satisfy the events, and how to group those actions in a reasonable way to proceed with system definition.

4.2.3.1   Identifying Events   *Events* are the interactions between the system and its environment. They are changes in the system's environment that cause the system to respond in some manner. The set of activities that must be performed by the system whenever a certain event occurs is called the *event response*. Partitioning the system into these event responses (we will refer to them as *actions*) has several benefits:

1. It helps in the quest for the system's true requirements, because it produces reasonably uniform results no matter who partitions the system.
2. It produces a model that is concise and is faithful to the system's essential requirements.
3. The results are precise enough for everyone on the engineering team to agree on, and because the partitions are at a middle level, the results do not overwhelm reviewers with too many details.
4. The partitioning also clearly shows that the system's responses to different events can be performed in any sequence. It reflects that systems typically don't interact with the entities in the environment in any set order. The actions can be thought of as occurring simultaneously or concurrently.

To recognize events, one must consider both the system and its environment, because events may be temporal or external. An external event usually produces an incoming data or control flow that crosses the boundary of the system. The temporal event (the arrival of a particular time) does not result in a data flow crossing the boundary of the system, because the passage of time happens everywhere and is independent of location. A list can be made of all of the events for a system.

4.2.3.2   Defining Actions   The following is a list of characteristics necessary for defining actions:

1. Each action must contain all of the activities that would be carried out in response to one and only one event.
2. An action is considered complete if, when all of the activities that make up that action have been performed, the system becomes idle until another event occurs. (Most systems do not *really* become idle, but this is a useful assumption to make.)
3. If there are too many actions to fit on a single page, then *try* to group them by functionality and by access to data stores on each page. This is not always

feasible, because several actions may access the same data store as well as many other data stores accessed by still other actions, and so on. Do as much of this grouping as you can, however, as it will help in the aggregation of actions into the top-level DFD. Note that this composition may take several levels (two or more) of effort for large systems with *many* (for example, more than 300) events.

4.2.3.3 *Grouping Actions* The primary rule for grouping the actions that respond to events is to minimize the complexity of the interfaces (the data flow). Another way to say this is that it is important that the processes be loosely coupled. The following list is in priority order:

1. *Common Data Access*: Since the only data coupling at this level is through data stores, minimizing coupling is accomplished by aggregating actions into processes based on common access to data stores.

2. *Common Functionality*: It will almost always turn out that by grouping the actions into the aggregate processes for the level 0 DFD, you will find a great deal of common functionality among the actions that you group together. A guideline that is nearly as important as grouping around data stores—in fact, essentially the same thing—is to group actions by common function. This circumstance of having common functionality leads to highly cohesive processes, with everything that the process does related to a common purpose.

3. *Common Terminator*: Actions can be grouped together by the terminating interface. This grouping tends to lead toward a more physical layout than the foregoing data grouping.

4. *Common Periodicity*: Events/actions that occur at the same time or with the same frequency can be combined.

5. *Experience*: Finally, the use of sound engineering judgment comes into play for areas that don't fit in the above categories or in which the engineer has worked on similar projects and knows what does (or doesn't) fit well together as one looks forward to design.

4.2.4 Data Flow Diagram Hints

The following ideas are adapted from Page-Jones [PAG88, page 162].

1. There are several strategies for partitioning a DFD. One can work from the outside in, from the middle out, from input to output, or from output to input. If you get stuck on one of these strategies, try another one. It may help you get through a tough spot.

2. Make sure that you know the composition of a new data flow or store before adding it to the DFD. It should be precisely named and recorded in the data dictionary.

3. Agree with colleagues (and clients) on a few levels of DFDs before plunging down deeper.

4. Normal data flows are of more importance than the exceptions, especially at the requirements level. Don't clutter the DFD with too many error flows.

5. Don't flowchart. There's no need for a loop back to get another data item. The data flow is like a conveyor belt of data—the next item will just come along when it's ready. Any control necessary should be dealt with on the CFD.

6. Ignore problems of initialization and termination; pretend that the system has been running forever and always will. The details will be taken care of during design.

7. Make sure all necessary input is given to a process to create its output.

4.2.5 Constructing a Leveled Set of Processes

The following guidelines are offered for constructing a set of processes.

1. Minimize both total number of flows on the diagram and the number of flows associated with a given process. This can be done by grouping flows together under a single name or by grouping processes together to push some flows down to a lower level. Here it is often good to apply the 7 ± 2 rule [MIL56]. This rule states that one can only comprehend a limited number of concepts at a time, approximately $7 + 2$, so that is the maximum amount of information to give on a page. Conversely, too few items (less than $7 - 2$) can lead to an excessive number of levels with very little progress made along the way. Thus, DFDs should contain approximately 7 ± 2 processes.

2. Try to distribute the flows evenly between the processes. A process with more flows than others in its diagram is a candidate for splitting into component processes. Possibly some of these components can then be grouped with other processes on the diagram.

3. A flow or a process for which you cannot think of an appropriate name is a candidate for repartitioning, because it probably consists of unrelated elements.

4. Concentrate, as far as possible, all the processing of one input or group of inputs in one region of the model, so as to avoid half-processed data.

The following additional partitioning heuristics are adapted from Ward & Mellor [WAR85, Vol. 2, Chapter 5]:

5. Partition to minimize interfaces. The best grouping of processes, flows, and stores is usually the one with the simplest, loosest connections. One importance of minimizing interfaces is that the understandability of a section of the model is proportional to its independence from other sections.

6. Identify hierarchies of control. Incorporation of the control hierarchy into the level analysis (the CFDs corresponding to DFDs) is useful because it allows grouping together processes that are activated and deactivated all at once. This permits the model's reader to understand the details of a group without having to refer continually to the activation/deactivation mechanism.

7. Use response-related groupings. Since the basic structure of the requirements model starts with stimuli and responses (input and output on the DCD), it is helpful to maintain this perspective when choosing upper-level groupings for processes.

8. Use terminator-related groupings. Terminators on the DCD provide an obvious source of information about the system environment. Sometimes it is helpful to group together processing whose inputs and outputs connect to a single terminator. In a system with a large number of terminators, it may be necessary to bundle together related terminators to achieve a reasonable number of top-level processes. They could then be separated at lower levels.

Finally, remember that the purpose of all the specification and level analysis is to provide a foundation for system design and that each of the requirements will be tested during customer acceptance.

9. Strive for lowest-level requirements (PSpecs and CSpecs) that are amenable to allocation to hardware/software/people components during system design. The PSpec (and CSpec) should mention every data flow (or control flow) in and out of the process (control bar).

10. Partition to a low enough level so that all the customer's needs are satisfied, but no lower. It is easy to fall into a trap of overspecification, which both limits options available during system and software design, and unnecessarily complicates the testing process.

4.2.6 Separating Data and Control

How does one distinguish between what is data and what is control?

1. Continuous signals and the processes that act on them are always categorized as data.

2. Discrete signals and the processes that act on them are usually categorized as control, but there may be exceptions.

3. Terms like "Activate," "Turn On," "Engage," and "Execute" are usually associated with control requirements.

4. Categorize according to the use to which the signal or process is put. Algebraic calculations and algorithms and the signals they use should be data. Decision-making processes and the signals they use (to determine operating mode of the system, or to decide which processes on the data side should be active) should be control.

5. Control structure is the area where it is most tempting to go beyond the true requirements and start getting into design. Beware of words such as "flag," or "bit".

DeMarco[DEM78, pages 68–69] provides the following guidelines for deciding on control or data. If you're ever in doubt about whether a flow is data or control in disguise, ask yourself:

1. What *information* flows across the line? If there is none, then it is likely control.
2. What does the destination process use the information for? If it is modified and put out as an outgoing data flow or part of one, then it is data. If it only serves to prompt the process to start doing its work or guide it in how to do its work, then it is control.

Finally, *only add control when absolutely necessary!*

4.2.7 Checklist for Correctness and Completeness (Balancing)

Much of this checking can be accomplished by automated tools.

1. A correct parent/child pair must have the same input and output data flows. A discrepancy implies that a flow has been shown that either does not come from anywhere, is not used anywhere, or has not been completed on the child diagram. This is equivalent to contradictory statements in different parts of a narrative document.
2. Verify by cross-checking that every data flow is defined in the dictionary and that definitions for groups and subgroups are consistent with each other.
3. To ensure completeness of a data/control store, all of the store's contents must leave it and be accounted for at some destination. The same rule applies for flows into the store, except for store contents that are read-only.

The data flow should be "balanced" in almost an esthetic sense: The picture should be "attractive"—not messy, not difficult to read or understand.

4.3 METHODOLOGY—STEP BY STEP

This section goes through the details of the methodology in a step-by-step style to give an understanding for the issues that come up. The guidelines introduced above are discussed at the appropriate step of the methodology.

The building of the requirements model is principally a process of interpreting the statements of needs from the various users and constructing the model from their statements. This process will test whether the statements are self-consistent and complete and should lead to further dialogue where they are not. The following lists the steps in the general order that they occur. In practice, some may be worked on in parallel and iteratively.

1. Draw preliminary data context diagram.
2. Establish data dictionary.
3. Determine events and actions.
4. Construct top-level data flow diagram.
5. Determine need for control at top level.
6. Document external timing.
7. Document allocation to top-level processes.
8. Draw next-level DFD.

9. Determine need for control at this level.
10. Update data dictionary.
11. Document traceability.
12. When am I done?

Step 1   Draw preliminary data context diagram. Identify external entities with which the system is required to communicate and the major information groups that must flow between the system and these external entities. Draw the DCD depicting this flow of information between the system and the environment in which it operates.

Step 2   Establish data dictionary. Establish the data dictionary to contain the definitions for all of the information that flows through the system as documented by the DCD.

Step 3   Determine events and actions. Using the guidelines given for identifying events, come up with an event list for the system. From this list, draw an EAD. Remember that there are no direct data flows between actions, because this would violate the requirement that the system becomes idle when the one action is complete. The main purpose of this drawing is to gain an understanding of the system from a customer's point of view in order to construct the top-level DFD that is reasonably complete. Construct the associated Action/Store Matrix or List.

It is intended that the event list, the associated event–action diagram(s), and the action/store matrix be internal documentation and, as such, not delivered to the customer but saved for future reference.

Step 4   Construct top-level data flow diagram. Construct a top-level DFD by representing the major functional grouping of actions determined above as processes and showing the major information group data flows between them and the external environment. If the EAD is simple enough, it could potentially become the top-level DFD itself, although direct flow between the processes would be allowed. Use the coupling and cohesion rules and action grouping guidelines here.

It is important to avoid putting the internal control flows in until the events list, EAD, and top-level DFD have been completed, so that one can be certain that they are really necessary.

Enter the flow information into the data dictionary.

Study the resulting diagram and ask:

1. Is the scope of the model right? Should any of the terminators on the DCD really be part of the system, or should any of the processes be terminators?
2. Do the processes relate well to the way that the customers view the system requirements? Would repartitioning make the requirements clearer?
3. Are the flows correct? Can the processes reasonably produce their stated outputs with the given inputs? Would the picture be clearer if the flow were regrouped?

Make any changes resulting from the answers to the preceding questions. Update the DCD as appropriate. Enter the flow information into the data dictionary.

Step 5   Determine need for control at top level. Examine the major requirements and decide if there are any modes or conditions of the system under which any of the top-level processes require activating or deactivating. If so, identify the signals representing those modes or conditions, assign them as control signals on the CFD or on the DFD, and then construct a CSpec that includes the appropriate diagrams, such as decision tables or STDs.

Also, examine the EAD created in Step 3 for necessary control. Before taking this step, be sure that the same effect would not be obtained though the inherent presence or absence of the appropriate data in these modes and conditions. Use the rules for separation of data and control to help make this decision.

If any of the necessary control is with an external interface, draw the appropriate CCD (or add to DCD). Update the data dictionary with the control information. A guideline here is that unless the diagram would be too complex, the control flows should be overlaid on the DFD rather than drawing separate diagrams. Remember, if you do use separate diagrams, show all the processes (and terminators) on both to allow for complete picture. If control is necessary, it is more likely to be at higher levels than at lower levels.

Step 6   Document external timing. Draw a response time specification to document the external timing of the system. Remember that only the external response times should be specified. Internal timing is left for design.

To do this, the following needs to be performed:

1. List all the primitive inputs to the system. These can be derived directly from the DCD and CCD.
2. Determine the input event(s) caused by these inputs and the output signal(s) and output event(s) associated with each input. This is essentially the filling-in of the table. The event list and EAD can be useful here for the mapping of input to output as well as the identification of the events.
3. Extract the timing requirements from the customer's needs and map to the inputs and outputs of the table.

Step 7   Document allocation to top-level processes. Draw a requirements traceability matrix depicting the allocation of the customer's needs to the top-level processes identified in DFD 0.

Step 8   Draw next-level DFD. Decompose each process into a child diagram, which gives more details about the accomplishment of the higher-level requirement. Remember to concentrate on *what* the system must do, not *how* it will do it. Apply the principles for constructing a leveled set of processes here at each iteration.

Step 9   Determine need for control at this level. Examine the requirements at this level, as in Step 5, to decide on the necessity for a CFD. Follow the same rules for separation of data and control. Note that most control will occur in the top levels of the system. Very low-level control can often be handled within a PSpec.
Only add control flows when absolutely necessary!

Step 10   Update data dictionary. Add any new information to the data dictionary, based on this level of diagrams, and update appropriate entries.

Step 11   Document traceability. Draw a requirements traceability matrix depicting the allocation of the customer's needs to the processes at this level. This matrix should have the same customer needs requirements listed along the side of the matrix as in the top-level traceability documented in Step 7 (or at least all of the requirements that had been allocated to the parent process).

Step 12   When am I done? For each process, iterate, performing Steps 8 through 11, until you can clearly express the function of that process in a few lines of text or equations or with a simple diagram (typically less than one page total). Then write a PSpec for that process. This becomes the "bottom" network of that DFD process. For very large systems, one should write a simple description of the DFDs at several intermediate levels. Although this may seem redundant to the diagrams, it can help clarify your thoughts as the analyst, and it provides the reader with some additional information as to where you are in the process. These intermediate descriptions may not be delivered to the customer, but they should be saved for future reference.

Since the top-level diagrams will determine how all the analysis from this point on is partitioned and, therefore, how the analysts will divide up the tasks, it is worth spending more time on it at this high level than at lower ones.

Each time that two or three levels have been done, review and revise them to improve their understandability and correctness. Check for balancing errors according to the guidelines and fix any that are found. Resolve requirements ambiguities and omissions as soon as possible. If they cannot be fixed at this time, be sure to note them for later resolution.

Remember that what you come up with here will form the basis for requirements traceability for the rest of the development cycle, so be as complete and unambiguous as possible without putting in technology constraints that should be decided upon during system design.

4.4   FMS SYSTEM REQUIREMENT ANALYSIS EXAMPLE

This section provides an example of the system requirements methodology, essentially solving the following problem. If you wish to test your knowledge of the methods presented, you may wish to solve the problem yourself, before looking at the solution.

Assignment: Perform a system requirements analysis for the automation of the Furnace Monitoring System (FMS) described in Chapter 3, including a complete system requirements model. Make whatever assumptions you feel are necessary, for example the temperature range of the furnaces, the bounds on output, and the various states of the furnace relative to maintenance status. Normally, this is the sort of information that would come about from your interview with the customer and more detailed analysis of the current process. For the purpose of this example, what is important is that you *identify your additional information needs* and then pick whatever values seem appropriate.

What follows is a completed system requirements model, including answers to the questions you asked yourself (or should have asked yourself).

Your requirements model is likely to vary somewhat from the textbook solution, but it is of central importance to the methodology that it should be *essentially* similar. Remember that the requirements model can also be called the *essential* model; both the book solution and yours should have captured this essential requirements.

4.4.1 Step 1: Draw Preliminary Data Context Diagram

Figure 4-25 is the preliminary DCD for the FMS. In coming up with this diagram, the following assumptions were made:

1. Input of INPUT MIX is needed to do calculations for FAO reports.
2. MAINTENANCE STATUS and OUTPUT RATE are monitored "continuously" in order to meet reporting requirements.
3. DETAILED STATUS is also monitored "continuously" for furnaces designated as troublesome. This is in addition to the MAINTENANCE STATUS above.
4. The flashing light is turned off when all furnaces are in NORMAL status.

Comments

- Notice that FURNACE STATUS automatically goes only to the MO. FAO needs to request the information by means of a report.
- Sometimes we're aware of control flow necessary while drawing the DCD. It's important to avoid putting it in until the events list and top-level DFD have been completed, so that we can be sure that it is really necessary. Examples in this case include the request for a report and control of alarms (bells and flashing light).

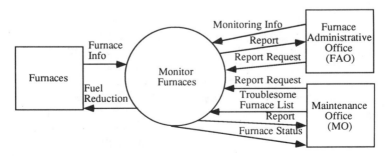

Figure 4-25 FMS Preliminary Data Context Diagram

4.4.2   Step 2: Establish Data Dictionary

The following is the initial establishment of the data dictionary for the FMS based on the DCD information.

DETAILED STATUS = Max Detailed Status Points {Electrical Reading}

DETAILED STATUS REPORT = * Report including Detailed Status currently available *
Rate = upon request

ELECTRICAL READING = * Single electrical status point *
Range = 0 to 570
Units = volt
Resolution = millivolt
Rate = monitored "continuously" when furnace is marked as troublesome

FUEL REDUCTION = [High Fuel Reduction | Low Fuel Reduction]
* Amount of fuel to reduce due to hot furnace *
Rate = event-driven; depends on temperature of furnace

FULL REPORT = * Report containing all info for all furnaces *
Rate = upon request

FURNACE INFO = [Furnace Temperature | Output Rate | Maintenance | Status | Detailed Status]

FURNACE NUMBER = * Number assigned to furnace for automation/management purposes *
Range = 1 to Max Furnaces

FURNACE STATUS = Furnace Number + Maintenance Status
Rate = Once every 5 minutes when furnace is impaired or
Once every minute when furnace is critical

FURNACE TEMPERATURE = * Actual temperature of furnace *
Units = °F
Range = 900 to 3700
Resolution = 1 degree
Rate = event-driven; according to schedule

HIGH FUEL REDUCTION = * Actual fuel reduction percentage = 20 percent *

INPUT MIX = * Mixture of raw materials being placed in furnace *
(Not further defined for this example)

INPUT MIX INFO = 1{Furnace Number + Input Mix} Max Furnaces
Rate = event-driven

LOW FUEL REDUCTION = * Actual fuel reduction percentage = 10 percent *

MAINTENANCE STATUS = ["Normal" | "Degraded" | "Impaired" | "Critical" | "Safety Hazard"]
Rate = monitored "continuously"

MAINTENANCE STATUS REPORT = * Report containing the Maintenance Status for a single furnace *
Rate = upon request

MAX DETAILED STATUS POINTS = * Number of electrical status points at a furnace—currently 10 *

MAX FURNACES = * Number of furnaces in plant that can be automatically monitored—currently 28 *

MAX THERMOMETERS = * Number of thermometers attached to a furnace—currently 15 *

MONITOR FREQUENCY = * Frequency at which to monitor a thermometer *
Range = 0 to 144
Units = readings/day
Resolution = 10 minutes
Rate = change is event-driven

MONITORING INFO = [Scheduling Info | Input Mix Info]

OUTPUT RATE = * Amount of molten iron being produced *
Units = tons/minute
Range = 0.0 to 50.0
Resolution = 0.05 tons
Rate = monitored "continuously"

OUTPUT RATE REPORT = * Report containing the Output Rate of a subset of furnaces *
Rate = upon request

REPORT = [Full Report | Maintenance Status Report | Temperature Report | Output Rate Report | Detailed Status Report | others??]
* "Others" may include a management report of type and quality of steel produced (depends on input mix, temperature, functioning of furnace) | maintenance report including problems over time per furnace *
(others *not* further defined for this example)

REPORT REQUEST = * Request for one of the available reports *
Rate = event-driven

SCHEDULING INFO = 1{Furnace Number + 1{Thermometer Number + Monitor Frequency}Max Thermometers}Max Furnaces
Rate = event-driven

TEMPERATURE REPORT = * Report of one or all temperatures for a single furnace *
Rate = upon request

THERMOMETER NUMBER = * Number assigned to thermometer for automation/management purposes *
Range = 1 to Max Thermometers

TROUBLESOME FURNACE LIST = 1{Furnace Number + Troublesome Status Indicator}Max Furnaces
Rate = event-driven

TROUBLESOME STATUS INDICATOR = ["Add" | "Delete"] * Indication to add or delete a furnace from the troublesome list *

Comments

- It is "legal" to have entries in the dictionary that don't appear on diagrams. They are typically details needed to explain or amplify the data items on the diagram. An example is constants used in definitions.

- Note: as new entries are added for the DFDs/CFDs in this example, they will be listed under the associated diagram. A "final" dictionary is at the end of the model.

4.4.3 Step 3: Determine Events and Actions

The following is the event list for the FMS. Figure 4-26a and 4-26b give the associated event–action diagram.

1. FAO submits scheduling info (may be an update): When FAO enters SCHEDULING INFO, update the internal SCHEDULE so that furnaces may be monitored accordingly.

2. FAO enters new input mix: When INPUT MIX INFO has been entered, store the INPUT MIX for the given furnace(s).

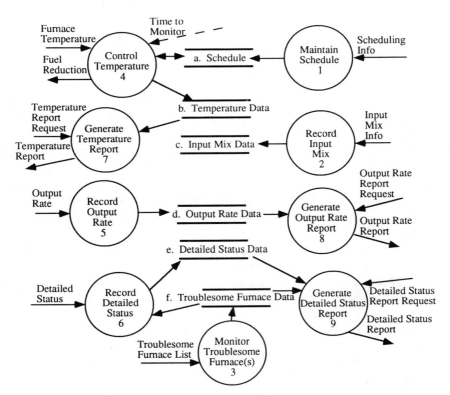

Figure 4-26a Event–Action Diagram—sheet 1 of 2

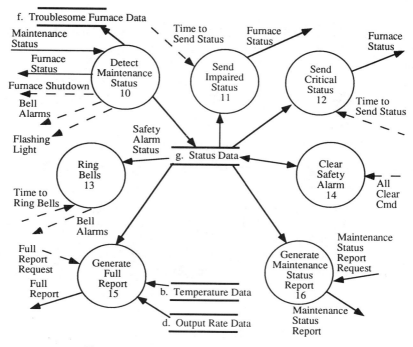

Figure 4-26b Event–Action Diagram—sheet 2 of 2

3. MO enters troublesome furnace list: When a TROUBLESOME FURNACE LIST has been entered, update the TROUBLESOME FURNACE DATA to indicate furnaces to monitor.

4. Time to monitor a thermometer (temporal event): When it's TIME TO MONITOR a furnace thermometer, get the TEMPERATURE from the furnace and store that information. If this TEMPERATURE or the average temperature for the furnace is too hot, then send out FUEL REDUCTION and monitor every minute. If the TEMPERATURE is now returning to "normal," then return to regular scheduled monitoring.

5. Output rate received from furnace: When OUTPUT RATE is received from a furnace, store that information.

6. Detailed status received from furnace: When DETAILED STATUS is received from a furnace that is listed in TROUBLESOME FURNACE DATA, store that information.

7. Temperature report request received form FAO of MO: When TEMPERATURE REPORT REQUEST is received, the report for the given thermometer(s) of a single furnace is generated and sent back.

8. Output rate report request received from FAO or MO: When OUTPUT RATE REPORT REQUEST is received, the report for the given furnace(s) is generated and sent back.

9. Detailed status report request received from MO: When DETAILED STATUS REPORT REQUEST is received, the report for all troublesome furnaces is generated and sent back.

10. Maintenance status received from furnace: When MAINTENANCE STATUS is received from a furnace, store that information. In addition, check the value and send the appropriate information to the office(s). This information may include FURNACE STATUS, FLASHING LIGHT (on or off), and BELL ALARMS. Update TROUBLESOME FURNACE DATA as required (for furnace transitioning from/to CRITICAL).

11. Time to send impaired status (periodic): When it's TIME TO SEND STATUS, the current FURNACE STATUS is reported to the MO for any furnace that is still IMPAIRED or DEGRADED.

12. Time to send critical status (periodic): When it's TIME TO SEND STATUS, the current FURNACE STATUS is reported to the MO for any furnace that is still CRITICAL or below.

13. Time to sound safety alarm (periodic): When it's TIME TO RING BELLS, the BELL ALARM is sent to each office if the SAFETY ALARM STATUS is still on.

14. All clear received: When the ALL CLEAR CMD is received, the FURNACE STATUS of each furnace is checked. The SAFETY ALARM STATUS is turned off.

15. Full report request: When FULL REPORT REQUEST is received from the FAO or MO, the FULL REPORT is generated and sent back.

16. Maintenance status report request: When MAINTENANCE STATUS REPORT REQUEST is received from the FAO or MO, the appropriate MAINTENANCE STATUS REPORT (for an individual furnace) is generated and sent back.

The following assumptions have been made.

1. Report requests (actions 7, 8, 9, 15, 16) retrieve the current data from the appropriate store(s) as it was placed there by another event (action 2, 4, 5, 6, or 10).

2. When a furnace is shut down for safety hazard, we will continue to monitor and receive data from it (if possible).

Comments

- Did you catch the Input Mix and Detailed Status Report Request as events? Note that Input Mix is only used for "other reports" at FAO and so is not looked at much further in this example—we will see the allocation in system design (Chapter 5) and then no more.

- It is useful to number the actions in diagram to match the event list. This allows for easy reference.

- Although we probably could have fitted all 16 actions on one page, we show here the example of how to split them onto more than one page. A large real-time system will have hundreds of events and actions.

- A number of data stores appear on more than one sheet. This is particularly prevalent on large systems, and for that reason it is useful to draw the action/store matrix shown in Figure 4-27. The matrix shows which actions set (S) or use (U) the different stores. It helps in construction of the top-level DFD in terms of grouping together actions that operate on common data stores. A list could have been drawn instead (see Figure 4-23b).

- Some of the events are "triggered" by control coming into the system (e.g., TIME TO MONITOR or REPORT REQUEST), or the response generates control to the environment (e.g., FURNACE SHUTDOWN). These are shown with control flows. They will be revisited when we determine the need for control at top level in Step 5.

Data Store / Action	a. Schedule	b. Temperature Data	c. Input Mix Data	d. Output Rate Data	e. Detailed Status Data	f. Troublesome Furnace Data	g. Status Data
1. Maintain Schedule	S						
2. Record Input Mix			S				
3. Monitor Troublesome Furnace(s)						S	
4. Control Temperature	S,U	S					
5. Record Output Rate				S			
6. Record Detailed Status					S	U	
7. Generate Temperature Report		U					
8. Generate Output Rate Report				U			
9. Generate Detailed Status Report					U	U	
10. Detect Maintenance Status							S
11. Send Impaired Status							U
12. Send Critical Status							U
13. Ring Bells							U
14. Clear Safety Alarm							S,U
15. Generate Full Report		U		U			U
16. Generate Maintenance Status Report							U

Figure 4-27   Action/Store Matrix

Dictionary Updates:

ALL CLEAR CMD = * Indicator to turn off safety alarm *

BELL ALARMS = FAO Bell + MO Bell

DETAILED STATUS DATA = Max Furnaces {Detailed Status}

DETAILED STATUS REPORT REQUEST = * Request for report of detailed status on all troublesome furnaces *
Rate = event-driven

FAO BELL = * Indication to ring bell in FAO *
Rate = once when first furnace becomes critical, and every second when a furnace is a safety hazard

FLASHING LIGHT = ["On" | "Off"] * Control the flashing light in the MO *

FULL REPORT REQUEST = * Request for a full report on all furnaces *
Rate = event-driven

FURNACE SHUTDOWN = * Indication to turn off furnace for safety purposes *

INPUT MIX DATA = Max Furnaces {Input Mix}

MAINTENANCE STATUS REPORT REQUEST = Furnace Number * Request for report of maintenance status for a given furnace *
Rate = event-driven

MO BELL = * Indication to ring bell in MO *
Rate = once when first furnace becomes critical, and every second when a furnace is a safety hazard

OUTPUT RATE DATA = Max Furnaces {Output Rate}

OUTPUT RATE REPORT REQUEST = 1 {Furnace Number} Max Furnaces * Request for report of output rate on subset of furnaces *
Rate = event-driven

REPORT REQUEST = [Full Report Request | Maintenance Status Report Request | Temperature Report Request | Output Rate Report Request | Detailed Status Report Request | others]
* Other reports are not defined at this point and will not be further defined for this example *
Rate = event-driven

SAFETY ALARM STATUS = ["On" | "Off"] * Indication to control periodic ringing of Bell Alarms *

SCHEDULE = Max Furnaces{Max Thermometers {Monitor Frequency}}

STATUS DATA = Max Furnaces{Maintenance Status}+ Safety Alarm Status

TEMPERATURE DATA = Max Furnaces {Max Thermometers {Furnace Temperature}}

TEMPERATURE REPORT REQUEST = Furnace Number + 1 {Thermometer Number}
Max Thermometers * Request for report of subset of temperatures for a given furnace *
Rate = event-driven

TIME TO MONITOR = * Activates reading of specific thermometer according to schedule *

TIME TO RING BELLS = * Activates ringing of bells—periodically *

TIME TO SEND STATUS = * Activates sending of status—periodically *

TROUBLESOME FURNACE DATA = 0 {Furnace Number} Max Furnaces

Some of the foregoing flows and stores may only show up in the event flow. In that case, they will not be in the final dictionary (see Section 4.4.9).

4.4.4 Step 4: Construct Top-Level DFD

There is no *one* correct way to group the actions to come up with the top-level DFD. The following are some ways in which it could be done, and some rationale for each. All of the rationales have to do with the coupling and cohesion criteria discussed in Section 4.2.2: minimizing data flow and grouping for high-functional commonality.

First Attempt

Record Monitoring Input: Group actions 1, 2, 3, because they all have to do with data inputs from one of the offices.

Monitor Furnace: Group actions 4, 5, 6, because they all deal directly with the furnace.

Alert Maintenance: Group actions 10, 11, 12, 13, 14, because they all pertain to the maintenance of the status and associated alarms. Except for reports, these are the only ones that access the data store STATUS.

Generate Report: Group actions 7, 8, 9, 15, 16, because they all generate reports.

A potential problem with this breakdown is that there is not much cohesion to the "Record Monitoring Input" group. Each action works entirely on different data; there is no communication between them.

Second Attempt

Monitor Furnace: Group actions 1, 3, 4, 5, 6, because they all have to do with monitoring the furnace.

Alert Maintenance: Group actions 10, 11, 12, 13, 14, as in the above grouping.

Generate Report: Group actions 2, 7, 8, 9, 15, 16, as in the preceding grouping, but with the addition of 2, since it is *only* needed for the generation of reports.

Since action 1 (Maintain Schedule) does not interface directly with the furnace, it could be a stand-alone function that simply maintains the schedule.

Third Attempt

Maintain Schedule: Set action 1 by itself, because it is a stand-alone function.

Monitor Furnace: Group actions 3, 4, 5, 6, all interfacing with the furnace.

Alert Maintenance: Group actions 10, 11, 12, 13, 14, as in the preceding grouping.

Generate Report: Group actions 2, 7, 8, 9, 15, 16 as in the preceding grouping.

Since "Maintain Schedule" and part of "Monitor Furnace" perform the processing of temperatures, it may be good to group them together. In that case, we would also group together the parts of "Monitor Furnace" that deal with the monitoring of detailed status, which would leave the output rate by itself. Functionally, these three areas should probably be separate, since at least two of them are rather complex and they don't interface with each other at all. "Generate Report" could also be split up along these same data lines.

Fourth Attempt

Control Furnace Temperatures: Group actions 1, 4, 7, since they are the only ones that have to deal with monitoring of temperatures. This also encapsulates the data store SCHEDULE. (TEMPERATURE DATA is only accessed outside of this process for FULL REPORT).

Report Troublesome Furnace Status: Group actions 3, 6, 9, since they are the only ones that have to do with monitoring of detailed status.

Alert Maintenance: Group actions 10, 11, 12, 13, 14, 16 as in the preceding grouping, with the addition of 16 to generate the associated report. (STATUS DATA is only accessed outside this process for FULL REPORT).

Report Output Rate: Group actions 5 and 8 as the only ones that monitor the output rate. (OUTPUT RATE DATA is only accessed outside this process for FULL REPORT).

Generate Full Report: Set action 15 by itself, because of its complexity and because it doesn't fit with the other data-oriented groupings.

Record Input Mix: Action 2 is used for "other reports" and will not be discussed further except to allocate in system design.

This final grouping is illustrated in Figures 4-28*a* and 4-28*b*. It is the one that will be used in the solution for this example. Note that some of the stores have been encapsulated within a top-level process such as SCHEDULE. Others are shown as a "grouped" data store accessed by processes at the top level. Figure 4-29 shows the resulting DFD 0.

Dictionary Updates:

FURNACE DATA = Temperature Data + Status Data + Output Rate Data

4.4.5 Step 5: Determine Need for Control at Top Level

From the EAD, the need for control with the environment is seen. The CCD is shown in Figure 4-30. We drew it as a separate diagram, because the complexity of all of the control and data flows on one drawing might have been hard to read or follow. Figure 4-31 shows the combined DCD/CCD. Notice that we grouped together the REPORT REQUESTs as a data flow, since they are really all requests for reports (some require special data associated with them at lower level). The control aspect will show up at the lower level(s). Figure 4-32 is the resulting DFD/CFD 0.

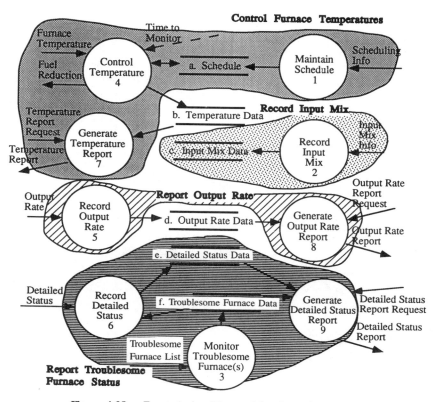

Figure 4-28a Event–Action Diagram Mapping—sheet 1 of 2

Comments

- Notice that the TIME TO MONITOR, TIME TO RING BELLS, and TIME TO SEND STATUS control flows from the event list do not show up at this level. They have been deferred to a lower level.

- No CSpec is necessary at this level. There are no overall system states, but we will see some at lower levels.

- An interesting flow here is BELL ALARMS. On the CCD we had to show the individual FAO BELL and MO BELL, because the terminators are on that diagram and one alarm goes to each office. Here, since they always go out at the same time, we've grouped them together to simplify the diagram. The meaning is not lost. This may only occur between the context diagram(DCD/CCD) and the top-level flow diagram (DFD/CFD).

- In this case the diagram is rather complex and may be easier to read on a separate diagram (the separate CFD is also shown in Figure 4-33). The decision is really often a matter of preference. Remember that you should show all of the processes even if no control is shown to them for consistency and completeness.

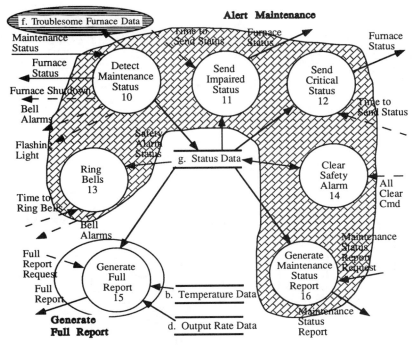

Figure 4-28b Event–Action Diagram Mapping—sheet 2 of 2

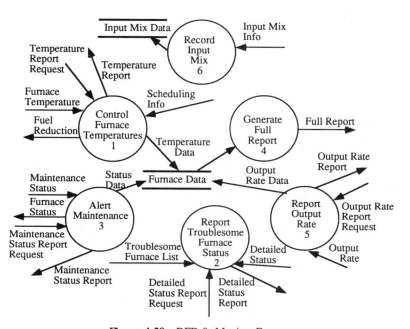

Figure 4-29 DFD 0: Monitor Furnaces

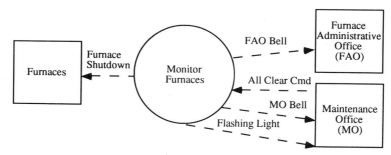

Figure 4-30 Control Context Diagram

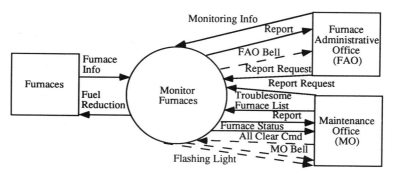

Figure 4-31 Combined DCD and CCD

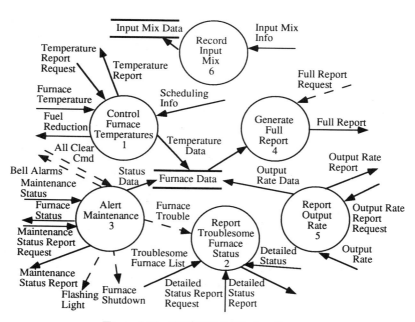

Figure 4-32 DFD/CFD 0: Monitor Furnaces

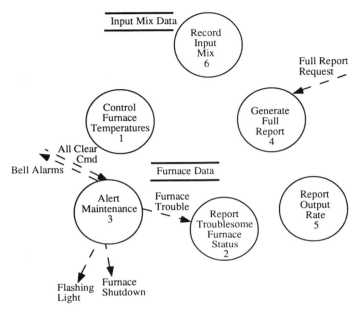

Figure 4-33   CFD 0: Monitor Furnaces

- Notice the control flow FURNACE TROUBLE. It *does not* control Process 2 (that would require a CSpec), but *does* control a lower-level process within "Report Troublesome Furnace Status." This flow is the result of the access to TROUBLESOME FURNACE DATA by "Detect Maintenance Status" (action 10 on the EAD).

Dictionary Updates:

FURNACE TROUBLE = ["Troubled" | "Not Troubled"] * Indication of furnace detected to be in trouble or no longer troubled *

4.4.6   Step 6: Document External Timing

The following is the list of timing requirements from the customer's needs that was used to determine the response times.

1. Fuel flow is to be reduced once each minute until the temperature is in bounds.
2. The largest report will contain all the information for all furnaces. Such a report is to be generated within 3 minutes of the request.
3. Both offices can also request an immediate update for an individual furnace on any item of information.
   - Rate, status, or temperature at a single location must be provided within 10 seconds.

○ Temperature of all 15 locations must be provided within 30 seconds.

○ Total rate of output of any subset of furnaces must be available within 90 seconds.

4. If maintenance status falls to Impaired:

○ The system is to activate a flashing light in the MO within 5 seconds.

○ Status is reported to the MO immediately and each 5 minutes until status returns to Normal.

5. If status falls to Critical:

○ Bells in each of the two offices are to be rung within 1 second.

○ Status is to be reported to the MO immediately and at 1-minute intervals.

6. If status falls to Safety Hazard:

○ Status is to be reported to the MO immediately.

○ The conveyer belt and furnace are to be automatically shut down within 3 seconds.

○ The bells in both offices are to be rung once per second until silenced by command from MO.

Figure 4-34 shows the response time specification for the FMS.

Comments

- All the inputs to the system are shown at the left under "External Input Signal."

- All the outputs from the system appear at least once under the column "External Output Signal." It is OK to list the primitive or grouped output here as appropriate. For example, we have listed BELL ALARM instead of the individual FAO BELL and MO BELL. On the other hand, we have listed the individual reports instead of the REPORT flow, because the timing for each is different.

- Sometimes the customer has not given a timing requirement for an input. An example of this is TROUBLESOME FURNACE LIST. The requirement to accept that entry is given, but no timing requirement on how soon the system should begin the detailed status monitoring is given. Here the response time given is based on the frequency at which the MAINTENANCE STATUS must be sent to the MO when the furnace falls to critical. The reason for this basis is that at that point the system is also to begin monitoring DETAILED STATUS.

- It is typical that the analyst will come up with additional timing requirements based on those given by the customer. For example, when all furnaces return to normal, the flashing light needs to be turned off within a reasonable amount of time. We decided here to give it the same length of time as to turn it on. Of course, all such decisions need to be discussed with the customer.

- Notice on SCHEDULING INFO that there is no external output signal. This is OK. Sometimes an event, like this one, causes changes in the output of other events instead (e.g., reports affected because of new monitoring schedule). The response time assigned here is based on the scheduling frequency given by the FAO—10 minutes is the minimum time interval for scheduling.

External Input Signal	Input Event	Frequency	External Output Signal	Output Event	Response Time
Scheduling Info	entered	event-driven	none	All later reports affected	new schedule in affect within 10 min
Input Mix Info	entered	event-driven	Report	displayed	as requested in reports
Troublesome Furnace List	entered	event-driven	Report	displayed/ recording start or stop	as requested in reports/ within 1 min
Furnace Temperature	received from furnace	according to schedule	Report	displayed	as requested in reports
		every min (when hot)	Fuel Reduction (when hot)	fuel reduced	within 1 min
Output Rate	received from furnace	periodically	Report	displayed	as requested in reports
Detailed Status	received from furnace	continuosly	Report	displayed	as requested in reports
Maintenance Status (received from furnace)	falls to Impaired	event-driven	Flashing Light/ Furnace Status	light on/ status displayed	within 5 sec/ within 5 sec and every 5 min
	returns to Normal	event-driven	Flashing Light	light off	within 5 sec
	falls to Critical	event-driven	Bell Alarm/ Furnace Status	ring bell/ status isplayed	within 1 sec/ within 1 sec and every 1 min
	falls to Safety Hazard	event-driven	Furnace Shutdown/ Bell Alarm	furnace off/ ring bell	within 3 sec/ once/second
Report Request	entered	event-driven	Full Report/ Temperature Report - single -- multiple/ Output Rate Report - single -- multiple/ Detailed Status Report/ Maintenance Status Report/ others (TBD)	displayed	within 3 min / within 10 sec within 30 sec / within 10 sec within 90 sec / within 3 min / within 10 sec / within 3 min
All Clear Cmd	entered	event-driven	Bell Alarm	bell turned off	within 5 sec

Figure 4-34   Response Time Specification

- You must be sure that this diagram is complete before continuing your analysis. Here the "other reports" are not fully defined (but we will not be using these in this example).

4.4.7 Step 7: Document Allocation to Top-Level Processes

The following is a list of the "customer's needs" extracted (e.g., parsed) from the description of the FMS in Chapter 3. We will use it as the basis for our traceability matrix.

1. The FAO desires to schedule the frequency of reading separately for each of the 15 locations for each of the 28 furnaces.
2. The Maintenance Office is able to designate any number of furnaces as "troublesome," thereby causing the system to record the detailed status (electrical readings: There are 10 different readings to be taken, each in the range 0 to 570 millivolts).
3. The furnace temperature is to be controlled in accordance with the following rules; the rules being applied each time any temperature is sensed:
   3.1 If the highest temperature is over 3600°F, the fuel flow is reduced by 20 percent.
   3.2 If no single temperature is over 3600°F, but the average temperature is over 3500°F, the fuel flow is reduced by 10 percent.
   3.3 In addition, until no temperature is above 3600°F *and* the average is below 3500°F, all temperatures are sensed once per minute. Therefore, the fuel flow is to be reduced once each minute until the temperature is in bounds.
4. There will be several different reports required by the FAO and the MO, to be defined later.
5. The Furnace Administrative Office (FAO) has knowledge of the input mix.
6. The largest report will contain all the information for all furnaces. Such a report is to be generated within 3 minutes of the request, based on status ("Normal," "Degraded," "Impaired," "Critical," or "Safety Hazard") and output information (expressed as tons/minute) that is current as of the time of the request and on the latest temperature readings scheduled prior to the request.
7. Both offices can also request an immediate update for an individual furnace on any item of information.
   7.1 Rate, maintenance status, or the temperature at a single location must be provided within 10 seconds.
   7.2 Temperature of all 15 locations must be provided within 30 seconds.
   7.3 The offices can also request total rate of output of any subset of furnaces, available within 90 seconds.
8. If maintenance status of any furnace falls to the Impaired level:
   8.1 The system is to activate a flashing light in the MO within 5 seconds.

8.2 Status is reported to the MO immediately and each 5 minutes until status returns to Normal.

9. If maintenance status falls to Critical:

9.1 Bells in each of the two offices are to be rung within 1 second.

9.2 Status is to be reported to the MO immediately and at 1-minute intervals.

9.3 In addition, detailed status (the 10 electrical readings) is to be collected for user-requested reports.

9.4 Both 1-minute status reporting and collection of detailed status continue until status has returned to Impaired or Normal.

10. If status falls to Safety Hazard:

10.1 Status is to be reported to the MO immediately.

10.2 The conveyer belt and furnace are to be automatically shut down within 3 seconds.

10.3 The bells in both offices are to be rung once per second.

10.4 The bells are to ring until silenced by command from the MO.

Figure 4-35 is the RTM for the FMS at this top level.

Comments

- The "Customer Needs" should be allocated at the highest level possible. For example, "3.0 Control Furnace Temperatures" has been allocated to Process 1: "Control Furnace Temperatures." This implies that the requirements under 3.0 (that is, 3.1, 3.2, 3.3) are also satisfied by the process.

- Sometimes a requirement is satisfied by several processes working together. An illustration of this is the handling of "7.0 Immediate Update." Processes 1, 3, 4, and 5 are all involved here. Process 1 is controlling temperatures, so it must get the temperature(s) for the furnace. Process 3 handles everything to do with maintenance status, which means that it must pass on the status for reports. Similarly, Process 5 brings in output rate. Process 4 then takes all the information needed to generate the actual report requested.

4.4.8 Steps 8 to 12: Lower-Level Decomposition

An aspect of the statement of requirements that is broadly applicable to the complete decomposition is that there are multiple furnaces. It is undesirable to replicate the processes, one for each furnace, but equally undesirable to pass furnace numbers constantly around the diagrams or to have the processes accessing a furnace data store. In fact, passing a furnace identification or having a data store (even a conceptual or essential one) may tend to constrain the design.

The solution is to assume that furnace information is broadly known and that at any time a process knows to which furnace its processing is applicable. We will frequently note that a process is done "for each furnace" without specifying how a specific furnace identification is provided.

Requirement Model Component / Customer Need	Control Furnace Temperatures 1	Report Troublesome Furnace Status 2	Alert Maintenance 3	Generate Full Report 4	Report Output Rate 5	Record Input Mix 6
1. Schedule temperature readings	X					
2. Designate Troublesome Furnaces-record detailed status		X				
3. Control Furnace Temperatures	X					
3.1 High temperature -- reduce 20%						
3.2 Avg temperature -- reduce 10%						
3.3 Monitor 1/minute						
4. Different Reports (TBD)						
5. Input Mix used for reports at FAO						X
6. Full Report requested				X		
7. Immediate Update						
7.1 Individual Item	X		X		X	
7.2 Temperatures of furnace	X					
7.3 Total rate of output					X	
8. Status - Impaired			X			
8.1 MO flashing light						
8.2 Report Status to MO						
9. Status - Critical			X			
9.1 Ring Bell (MO & FAO)						
9.2 Status to MO						
9.3 Record Detailed Status		X				
9.4 Every Minute						
10. Status - Safety Hazard			X			
10.1 Report Status						
10.2 Furnace Shutdown						
10.3 Ring Bells (MO & FAO)						
10.4 Silence bells on command						

Figure 4-35 Monitor Furnaces Requirements Traceability Matrix

Similarly, it is sometimes necessary to know the state of all furnaces in order to determine overall system state. We do not wish to constrain the design by assuming polling of all furnace processes to obtain the information, or by assuming some centralized data base or constantly updated table that contains complete furnace states. So we will use the same solution: Just as a process knows to which furnace it is applicable at any given time, a process dealing with system state will have available necessary status information from all furnaces.

This scheme allows for later designs that are centralized and sequential (with a single process iteratively cycling through furnaces), for a concurrent application with separate tasks for furnaces or for passing of furnace identification, for a multiprocessor application with a processor for each furnace, or for blended designs.

Note: It is often useful to write a description of what a process is in order to understand it. The next section describes the overall functions of the Control Furnace Temperatures process as an example of what you might want to write—and have others review —in order to clarify your thinking about the overall process.

4.4.8.1. *Process 1: Control Furnace Temperatures* This process controls the monitoring of furnace temperatures based on the input "Scheduling Info" as well as current temperature(s) of the furnace. If the furnace temperature is too hot, fuel supply is reduced. Temperature reports that are requested are generated based on current temperatures and sent out. Figure 4-36 shows the DFD/CFD breakdown for this process.

Comments

• This diagram is essentially the same as the portion of the EAD that was grouped together as Process 1. This is often the case, since the events are a "middle-level" representation of the system processing.

Dictionary Updates (step 10): None

Figure 4-37 shows only the requirements that were allocated to the parent process. Processes 1.1 and 1.3 are not further decomposed. Their PSpecs are shown in Figure 4-38.

Let's taken an informal look at what Control Temperature (Process 1.2) needs to accomplish. This process controls temperature by reducing the fuel flow when the furnace is too hot, in accordance with specified criteria for "hotness." In order to control temperature, the temperature must be sensed or read. Although a natural by-product of the need to control, the reading and reporting of temperature is also

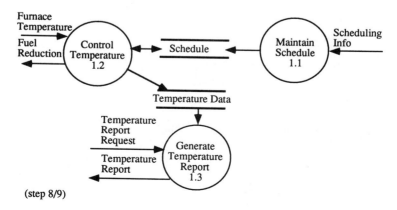

Figure 4-36   DFD/CFD 1: Control Furnace Temperatures

Requirement Model Component / Customer Need	Maintain Schedule 1.1	Control Temperature 1.2	Generate Temperature Report 1.3
1. Schedule temperature readings	X	X	
3.1 High temperature -- reduce 20%		X	
3.2 Avg temperature -- reduce 10%		X	
3.3 Monitor 1/minute		X	
7.1 Individual Item			X
7.2 Temperatures of furnace			X

(step 11)

Figure 4-37   Control Furnace Temperatures RTM

of importance in itself. The temperature is read on a furnace-by- furnace basis, and for each furnace, on a thermometer-by-thermometer basis. The discussion below focuses on an individual furnace, with its actions replicated for each of the MAX FURNACES in the system. The temperature is read in accordance with the following different prompts:

1. Periodically, based on a schedule of given rates.
2. Periodically, on HOT PERIODIC period, when the furnace is hot.

The normal situation is that the temperatures are read in accordance with the user-initiated SCHEDULE. Under certain circumstances, illustrated in the decision table in the PSpec 1.2.2 shown later, system-controlled periodic reading overrides

PSpec 1.1: Maintain Schedule
(NOTE: This processing occurs per furnace)

When SCHEDULING INFO is received then
Update the SCHEDULE.

PSpec 1.3: Generate Temperature Report
(NOTE: This processing occurs per furnace)

When TEMPERATURE REPORT REQUEST is received then
Generate TEMPERATURE REPORT
    for the thermometers requested.

(step 12)

Figure 4-38   PSpecs 1.1 and 1.3

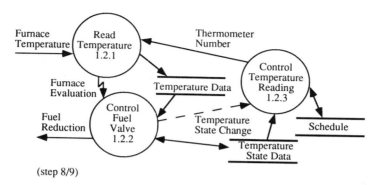

(step 8/9)

Figure 4-39   DFD/CFD 1.2: Control Temperature

the normal case. The temperatures are also read when a temperature request is received, regardless of whether the periodic reading is user- or system-specified. The process of reading the temperatures is simply sensing a temperature reading. The temperature readings are placed in storage for later use.

Given the reading and storage procedure above, the main job done by this process is to evaluate whether or not the furnace is too hot. This is done for each furnace, each time any thermometer is read for that furnace. For the conditions specified in the decision table in PSpec 1.2.2, the flow of fuel will be reduced. At the same time, the periodicity changes from user-controlled, by the schedule, to system-controlled, based on HOT PERIODIC.

Note: As usual, all these things are going on "at the same time." We don't know if they are *literally* going on at the same time (since we have not yet done the system design), but they are *logically* going on at the same time.

Figure 4-39 gives the breakdown for Control Temperature.

Comments

- Notice that Process 1.2.2, "Control Fuel Valve," is activated via the process activator from Process 1.2.1 (rather than a CSpec).
- The control flow TEMPERATURE STATE CHANGE enters Process 1.2.3 to control something at a lower level.

Dictionary Updates (step 10):

FURNACE EVALUATION = * process activator *

HOT AVERAGE = * Average temperature above which the furnace is considered too hot—currently = 3500°F *

HOT SPOT = * High single temperature above which the furnace is considered too hot—currently = 3600°F *

TEMPERATURE STATE = ["Normal" | "Hot"]

Requirement Model Component / Customer Need	Read Temperature 1.2.1	Control Fuel Valve 1.2.2	Control Temperature Reading 1.2.3
1. Schedule temperature readings	X		X
3.1 High temperature -- reduce 20%		X	
3.2 Avg temperature -- reduce 10%		X	
3.3 Monitor 1/minute		X	X

Figure 4-40 Control Temperature RTM

TEMPERATURE STATE CHANGE = * process activator *
TEMPERATURE STATE DATA = Max Furnaces {Temperature State}

Figure 4-40 shows only the requirements that were allocated to the parent process as step 11 of this decomposition. Processes 1.2.1 and 1.2.2 are not further decomposed. Their PSpecs are shown in Figure 4-41.

PSpec 1.2.1: Read Temperature
(NOTE: This processing occurs per furnace)

Read the FURNACE TEMPERATURE for the given THERMOMETER NUMBER.
Store FURNACE TEMPERATURE.
Issue FURNACE EVALUATION.

PSpec 1.2.2: Control Fuel Valve
(NOTE: This processing occurs per furnace)

Read TEMPERATURE DATA.

In accordance with Decision Table 1.2.2,
  If required, issue FUEL REDUCTION at appropriate level.

  Update TEMPERATURE STATE.

If there is a state change then
  Issue TEMPERATURE STATE CHANGE.

Inputs		Outputs	
Temperatures		Fuel Reduction	Temperature State
none above Hot Spot	avg > Hot Average	Low Fuel Reduction	Hot
	avg ≤ Hot Average	--	Normal
1 or more above Hot Spot	--	High Fuel Reduction	Hot

Decision Table 1.2.2

Figure 4-41 PSpecs 1.2.1 and 1.2.2

Now we need to address the more complex process 1.2.3. Let's do another informal analysis and description. This process has to do the following major things, at logically the same time. They are:

1. For each furnace with TEMPERATURE STATE of NORMAL
    Read the SCHEDULE then
        At the time indicated for each thermometer
            Issue THERMOMETER NUMBER.
2. When TEMPERATURE STATE changes then
    If the state is HOT then
        Send out THERMOMETER NUMBER for all thermometers, for a
        specific furnace, every HOT PERIODIC.
    otherwise *state is NORMAL*
        Stop sending out the THERMOMETER NUMBER.

In addition, the process must, at any time, be ready to update the state of a furnace when a TEMPERATURE STATE is received.

When parallel actions such as in these occur in a single process, it is often a clue that one more level of partitioning is required. For this simple example, the parallelism above might be OK, but it is likely better just to go ahead and show the parallelism graphically, with additional process partitioning. That is what we have decided to do in this case, with the resulting processes in the DFD shown in Figure 4-42.

Comments

- Part of the reason for further decomposition of Control Temperature Reading is to graphically show the logical concurrency mentioned in the overview above. The human mind can cope with a certain number of concurrent items in text but is better at visualizing concurrency by seeing parallel pictures.
- Here we see that the control flow TIME TO MONITOR, which was on the EAD, is not necessary because it can be handled within the PSpecs.
- The CSpec shows the activation and deactivation of Process 1.2.3.2 based on the TEMPERATURE STATE of the furnace when TEMPERATURE STATE CHANGE is received.
- Notice that the parent DFD for this one only had two processes on it, and this one also only has two. To follow the guidelines for leveled DFDs (7 ± 2 processes at a level), these two levels could be combined. We show them separate here to suggest something to look at and to illustrate multiple levels in the decomposition.

Dictionary Updates (step 10):

HOT PERIODIC = * Interval at which to monitor temperatures when a furnace is "hot"—currently = 1 minute *

process / control action	Initiate Periodic Temp. Reading
Temperature State = Hot	1
Temperature State = Normal	0

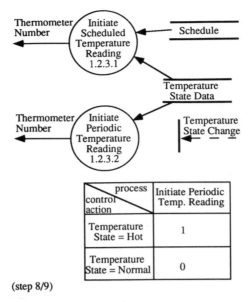

(step 8/9)

Figure 4-42 DFD/CFD 1.2.3: Control Temperature Reading (with CSpec)

Figure 4-43 gives the associated RTM. Figure 4-44 contains the PSpecs for Processes 1.2.3.1 through 1.2.3.2.

Comments

- Notice PSpec 1.2.3.2. Once activated (see CSpec), it will send out the THERMOMETER NUMBER(s) periodically until it is deactivated.

Requirement Model Component / Customer Need	Initiate Scheduled TempReading 1.2.3.1	Initiate Periodic TempReading 1.2.3.2
1. Schedule temperature readings	X	
3.3 Monitor 1/minute		X

(step 11)

Figure 4-43 Control Temperature Reading RTM

PSpec 1.2.3.1: Initiate Scheduled Temperature Reading
For each furnace with TEMPERATURE STATE of NORMAL
  Read the SCHEDULE then
    At the time indicated for each thermometer
  Output THERMOMETER NUMBER.

PSpec 1.2.3.2: Initiate Periodic Temperature Reading
(NOTE: This processing occurs per furnace)

Send out THERMOMETER NUMBER for all thermometers
  every HOT PERIODIC.

(step 12)

Figure 4-44   PSpecs 1.2.3.1 and 1.2.3.2

4.4.8.2 Process 2: Report Troublesome Furnace Status

Figure 4-45 shows the DFD/CFD for Process 2. Because the control bar is present showing control from outside the scope of this diagram, a CSpec (also shown here) is necessary.

Comments

- In this case, all that is needed is text explaining the situation. In fact, if we were to demonstrate the control of detailed status recording in a state transition

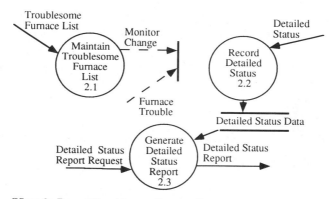

CSpec 2: Report Troublesome Furnace Status

Activate Record Detailed Status for a specific furnace if either or both
of the following conditions are true.
  a. MONITOR CHANGE = On Troublesome List
  b. FURNACE TROUBLE = Troubled

When monitoring is no longer necessary (neither condition is true),
  deactivate Record Detailed Status for that furnace.

(step 8/9)

Figure 4-45   DFD/CFD 2: Report Troublesome Furnace Status (with CSpec)

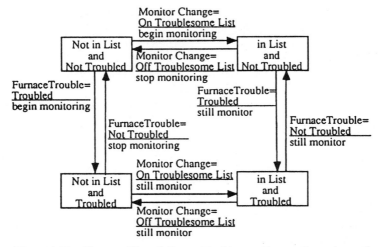

Figure 4-46   Alternate CSpec 2: Report Troublesome Furnace Status (example of overly complex STD)

diagram, it could look more complex and confusing (see Figure 4-46). Since there are four combinations of the two conditions (MONITOR CHANGE and FURNACE TROUBLE) there would need to be four "states" of the furnace. However, three of the states are really the same as far as processing is concerned, so it is easier to state the conditions in simple text. A PAT could also be used to express the control, as long as the interactions are not too complex.

• Notice FURNACE TROUBLE. That is the control flow that comes from another process (Process 3) on DFD/CFD 0, and is discussed in the comments from that step.

Dictionary Updates (step 10):

MONITOR CHANGE = ["On Troublesome List" | "Off Troublesome List"]

Figures 4-47 and 4-48 show the RTM and PSpecs, respectively.

Requirement Model Component — Customer Need	Maintain Troublesome Furnace List 2.1	Record Detailed Status 2.2	Generate Detailed Status Report 2.3
2. Designate Troublesome Furnaces-record detailed status	X		
9.3 Record Detailed Status		X	X

(step 11)

Figure 4-47   Report Troublesome Furnace Status RTM

PSpec 2.1: Maintain Troublesome Furnace List
For each FURNACE NUMBER In TROUBLESOME FURNACE LIST
  If TROUBLESOME FURNACE INDICATOR = Add then
    Issue MONITOR CHANGE = On Troublesome List.
  otherwise *indicator is Delete *
    Issue MONITOR CHANGE = Off Troublesome List.

PSpec 2.2: Record Detailed Status
Continuously monitor the furnace for DETAILED STATUS.
Store the DETAILED STATUS DATA received.

PSpec 2.3: Generate Detailed Status Report
Upon receipt of DETAILED STATUS REPORT REQUEST
Construct DETAILED STATUS REPORT from the current
DETAILED STATUS DATA.

(step 12)

Figure 4-48   PSpecs 2.1 through 2.3

Comments

- These PSpecs give simple text explanations of what is going on. The design will have to decide what "continuously" means in order to satisfy report timing requirements. The decision may need to be based on the hardware characteristics of the sensor chosen to allow for the monitoring.

4.4.8.3 Process 3: Alert Maintenance   Alert Maintenance is decomposed in the DFD shown in Figure 4-49. Note that this one is fairly complex, since it involves status of individual furnaces (so as, for example, to send furnace status) as well

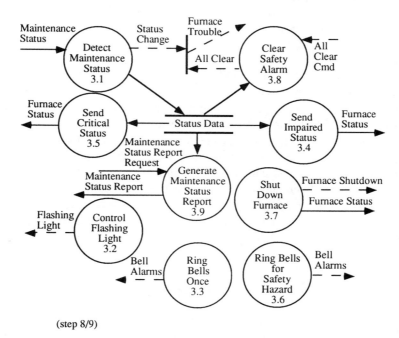

(step 8/9)

Figure 4-49   DFD/CFD 3: Alert Maintenance

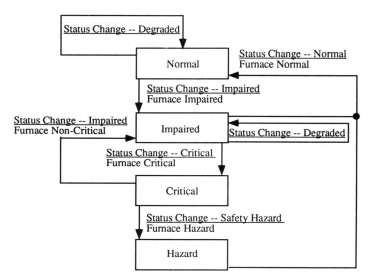

Figure 4-50a CSpec 3: Alert Maintenance—sheet 1 of 3 (furnace state diagram—per furnace)

as all the furnaces together (for example, all furnaces in NORMAL status implies that the flashing light is turned off). As one can see from the DFD/CFD, there is a lot of control going on here. A CSpec is definitely necessary and is shown in Figures 4-50a through 4-50c.

Comments

- Notice that the control flow STATUS CHANGE of Degraded does not cause a state change to take place (Figure 4-50a).
- It is OK to have a state change without an action taking place. The change to System NonCritical (Figure 4-50c) is an example.
- Notice that TIME TO SEND STATUS and TIME TO RING BELL did not show up in the CSpec, even though they were in the EAD. Here the periodic nature of the process(es) can be handled in the PSpecs as shown below, so no extra control has been added. This is based on the rule to avoid extra control.
- In the PAT the last column is the control to activate or deactivate a process on a separate diagram (actually Process 2.2—Record Detailed Status). Thus, we "issue" FURNACE TROUBLE.

Dictionary Updates:

ALL CLEAR = ["Normal" | "Impaired" | "Critical"] * Indication of worst furnace status *

CRITICAL PERIODIC = * Interval to send out furnace status when the furnace is critical—currently every 1 minute *

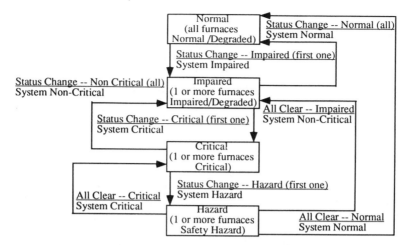

Figure 4-50*b* CSpec3: Alert Maintenance—sheet 2 of 3 (furnace system state diagram—all furnaces)

Process Control Action	Send Critical Status	Send Impaired Status	Shut Down Furnace	Ring Bells Once	Ring Bells for Safety Hazard	Control Flashing Light	Furnace Trouble
Furnace Impaired	--	1 (for furnace n)	--	--	--	--	--
Furnace Critical	1 (for furnace n)	0 (for furnace n)	--	--	--	--	(Troubled)
Furnace Non-Critical	0 (for furnace n)	1 (for furnace n)	--	--	--	--	(Not Troubled)
Furnace Hazard	--	--	1 (for furnace n)	--	--	--	--
Furnace Normal	--	--	--	--	--	--	(Not Troubled)
System Impaired	--	--	--	--	--	1 (on)	--
System Critical	--	--	--	1	--	--	--
System Non-Critical	--	--	--	--	--	--	--
System Hazard	--	--	--	--	1	--	--
System Normal	--	--	--	--	--	1 (off)	--
All Clear	--	--	--	--	0	--	--

Figure 4-50*c* CSpec3: Alert Maintenance—sheet 3 of 3 (process activation table)

HAZARD PERIODIC = * Interval to ring bells when the furnace is a safety hazard—currently every 1 second *

IMPAIRED PERIODIC = * Interval to send out furnace status when the furnace is impaired—currently every 5 minutes *

STATUS CHANGE = * Indication that furnace/system status has changed *

Figure 4-51 gives the RTM for Alert Maintenance. Notice that "9.3 Record Detailed Status" has been allocated to the CSpec. This is the part of the requirement that activates the process ("2.2 Record Detailed Status") when the furnace becomes Critical.

Figure 4-52 shows the associated PSpecs.

4.4.8.4 *Process 4: Generate Full Report*   "Generate Full Report" is not further decomposed or described for this example.

4.4.8.5 *Process 5: Report Output Rate*   Figure 4-53 shows the DFD for Report Output Rate. It is straightforward and simple processing. The RTM and PSpecs are given in Figure 4-54 and 4-55, respectively.

Requirement Model Component / Customer Need	Detect Maint. Status 3.1	Control Flashing Light 3.2	Ring Bells Once 3.3	Send Impaired Status 3.4	Send Critical Status 3.5	Ring Bells for Safety Hazard 3.6	Shut Down Furnace 3.7	Clear Safety Alarm 3.8	Generate Maint. Status Report 3.9	CSpec 3
7.1 Individual Item	X								X	
8. Status - Impaired	X									
8.1 MO flashing light		X								
8.2 Report Status to MO				X						
9. Status - Critical	X									
9.1 Ring Bell (MO & FAO)			X							
9.2 Status to MO					X					
9.3 Record Detailed Status										X
9.4 Every Minute					X					
10. Status - Safety Hazard	X									
10.1 Report Status					X					
10.2 Furnace Shutdown							X			
10.3 Ring Bells (MO & FAO)						X				
10.4 Silence bells on command								X		

(step 11)

Figure 4-51   Alert Maintenance RTM

PSpec 3.1: Detect Maintenance Status
(NOTE: This processing occurs per furnace)

Continually monitor the furnace for MAINTENANCE STATUS.
Check MAINTENANCE STATUS against current STATUS for change.
If change occurred
    Issue STATUS CHANGE according to state diagrams in CSpec.
    Record STATUS.

PSpec 3.2: Control Flashing Light
Based on the state of the system (as noted in CSpec), issue FLASHING LIGHT as
On or Off.

PSpec 3.3: Ring Bells Once
Issue FAO BELL.
Issue MO BELL.

PSpec 3.4: Send Impaired Status
Send out FURNACE STATUS for specific furnace every IMPAIRED PERIODIC.

PSpec 3.5: Send Critical Status
Send out FURNACE STATUS for specific furnace every CRITICAL PERIODIC.

PSpec 3.6: Ring Bells for Safety Hazard
Issue FAO BELL and MO BELL every HAZARD PERIODIC.

PSpec 3.7: Shut Down Furnace
(NOTE: This processing occurs per furnace)

Issue FURNACE SHUTDOWN.
Send out FURNACE STATUS of SAFETY HAZARD.

PSpec 3.8: Clear Safety Alarm
Check STATUS of all furnaces.
Issue ALL CLEAR based on lowest level of any STATUS.

PSpec 3.9: Generate Maintenance Status Report
When MAINTENANCE STATUS REPORT REQUEST is received then
Construct MAINTENANCE STATUS REPORT from STATUS DATA.

(step 12)

Figure 4-52   PSpecs 3.1 through 3.9

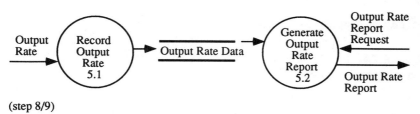

(step 8/9)

Figure 4-53   DFD 5: Report Output Rate

Requirement Model Component Customer Need	Record Output Rate 5.1	Generate Output Rate Report 5.2
7.1 Individual Item	X	X
7.3 Total rate of output		X

(step 11)

Figure 4-54 Report Output Rate RTM

PSpec 5.1: Record Output Rate
(NOTE: This processing occurs per furnace)

Continuously monitor the furnace for OUTPUT RATE.
Store OUTPUT RATE DATA received.

PSpec 5.2: Generate Output Rate Report

When OUTPUT RATE REPORT REQUEST is received then
Generate OUTPUT RATE REPORT from OUTPUT RATE DATA
for the subset of furnaces indicated in the request.

(step 12)

Figure 4-55 PSpecs 5.1 and 5.2

4.4.8.6 *Process 6: Record Input Mix* This process is part of "other reports" and is not expanded on further for this example.

4.4.9 Final Data Dictionary

ALL CLEAR = ["Normal" | "Impaired" | "Critical"] * Indication of worst furnace status *

ALL CLEAR CMD = * Indicator to turn off safety alarm *

BELL ALARMS = FAO Bell + MO Bell

CRITICAL PERIODIC = * Interval to send out furnace status when the furnace is critical—currently every 1 minute *

DETAILED STATUS = Max Detailed Status Points {Electrical Reading}

DETAILED STATUS DATA = Max Furnaces {Detailed Status}

DETAILED STATUS REPORT = * Report including Detailed Status currently available *
Rate = upon request

DETAILED STATUS REPORT REQUEST = * Request for report of detailed status on all troublesome furnaces *
Rate = event-driven

ELECTRICAL READING = * Single electrical status point *
Range = 0 to 570
Units = volt
Resolution = millivolt
Rate = monitored "continuously" when furnace is marked as troublesome

FAO BELL = * Indication to ring bell in FAO *
Rate = once when first furnace becomes critical and every second when a furnace is a safety hazard

FLASHING LIGHT = ["On" | "Off"] * Control the flashing light in the MO *

FUEL REDUCTION = [High Fuel Reduction | Low Fuel Reduction]
* Amount of fuel to reduce due to hot furnace * Rate = event-driven—depends on temperature of furnace

FULL REPORT = * Report containing all info for all furnaces *
Rate = upon request

FULL REPORT REQUEST = * Request for a full report on all furnaces *
Rate = event-driven

FURNACE DATA = Temperature Data + Status Data

FURNACE EVALUATION = * process activator *

FURNACE INFO = [Furnace Temperature | Output Rate | Maintenance Status | Detailed Status]

FURNACE NUMBER = * Number assigned to furnace for automation/management purposes *
Range = 1 to Max Furnaces

FURNACE SHUTDOWN = * Indication to turn off furnace for safety purposes *

FURNACE STATUS = Furnace Number + Maintenance Status
Rate = Once every 5 minutes when furnace is impaired or once every minute when furnace is critical

FURNACE TEMPERATURE = * Actual temperature of furnace *
Units = °F
Range = 900 to 3700
Resolution = 1 degree
Rate = event-driven—according to schedule

FURNACE TROUBLE = ["Troubled" | "Not Troubled"] * Indication of furnace detected to be in trouble or no longer troubled *

HAZARD PERIODIC = * Interval to ring bells when the furnace is a safety hazard—currently every 1 second *

HIGH FUEL REDUCTION = * Actual fuel reduction percentage = 20 percent *

HOT AVERAGE = * Average temperature above which the furnace is considered too hot—currently = 3500°F *

HOT PERIODIC = * Interval at which to monitor temperatures when a furnace is "hot"—currently = 1 minute *

HOT SPOT = * High single temperature above which the furnace is considered too hot—currently = 3600°F *

IMPAIRED PERIODIC = * Interval to send out furnace status when the furnace is impaired—currently every 5 minutes *

INPUT MIX = * Mixture of raw materials being placed in furnace *
(Not further defined for this example)

INPUT MIX DATA = Max Furnaces {Input Mix}

INPUT MIX INFO = 1{Furnace Number + Input Mix}Max Furnaces
Rate = event-driven

LOW FUEL REDUCTION = * Actual fuel reduction percentage = 10 percent *

MAINTENANCE STATUS = ["Normal" | "Degraded" | "Impaired" | "Critical" | "Safety Hazard"]
Rate = monitored "continuously"

MAINTENANCE STATUS REPORT = * Report containing the Maintenance Status for a single furnace *
Rate = upon request

MAINTENANCE STATUS REPORT REQUEST = Furnace Number * Request for report of maintenance status for a given furnace *
Rate = event-driven

MAX DETAILED STATUS POINTS = * Number of electrical status points at a furnace—currently 10 *

MAX FURNACES = * Number of furnaces in plant that can be automatically monitored—currently 28 *

MAX THERMOMETERS = * Number of thermometers attached to a furnace—currently 15 *

MO BELL = * Indication to ring bell in MO *
Rate = once when first furnace becomes critical/every second when a furnace is a safety hazard.

MONITOR CHANGE = ["On Troublesome List" | "Off Troublesome List"]

MONITOR FREQUENCY = * Frequency at which to monitor a thermometer *
Range = 0 to 144
Units = readings/day
Resolution = 10 minutes
Rate = change is event-driven

MONITORING INFO = [Scheduling Info | Input Mix Info]

OUTPUT RATE = * Amount of molten iron being produced *
Units = tons/minute
Range = 0.0 to 50.0
Resolution = 0.05 tons
Rate = monitored "continuously"

OUTPUT RATE DATA = Max Furnaces {Output Rate}

OUTPUT RATE REPORT = * Report containing the Output Rate of a subset of furnaces *
Rate = event-driven

OUTPUT RATE REPORT REQUEST = 1 {Furnace Number} Max Furnaces * Request for report of output rate on subset of furnaces *

REPORT = [Full Report | Maintenance Status Report | Temperature Report | Output Rate Report | Detailed Status Report | others??]
* Others may include a management report of type and quality of steel produced (depends on input mix, temperature, functioning of furnace) | maintenance report including problems over time per furnace *
("others" not further defined for this example)

REPORT REQUEST = [Full Report Request | Maintenance Status Report Request | Temperature Report Request | Output Rate Report Request | Detailed Status Report Request | others...]
* Other reports are not defined at this point and will not be further defined for this example *
Rate = event-driven

SAFETY ALARM STATUS = ["On" | "Off"] * Indication to control periodic ringing of Bell Alarms *

SCHEDULE = Max Furnaces {Max Thermometers {Monitor Frequency}}

SCHEDULING INFO = 1{Furnace Number + 1{Thermometer Number + Monitor Frequency}Max Thermometers}Max Furnaces
Rate = event-driven

STATUS CHANGE = * Indication that furnace/system status has changed *

STATUS DATA = Max Furnaces{Maintenance Status}+ Safety Alarm Status

TEMPERATURE DATA = Max Furnaces {Max Thermometers {Furnace Temperature}}

TEMPERATURE REPORT = * Report of one or all temperatures for a single furnace *
Rate = upon request

TEMPERATURE REPORT REQUEST = Furnace Number + 1 {Thermometer Number} Max Thermometers * Request for report of subset of temperatures for a given furnace *
Rate = event-driven

TEMPERATURE REQUEST = Furnace Number + Thermometer Number * Indication to check the temperature immediately *

TEMPERATURE STATE = ["Normal" | "Hot"]

TEMPERATURE STATE CHANGE = * process activator *

TEMPERATURE STATE DATA = Max Furnaces {Temperature State}

THERMOMETER NUMBER = * Number assigned to thermometer for automation/management purposes *
Range = 1 to Max Thermometers

TROUBLESOME FURNACE LIST = 1{Furnace Number + Troublesome Status Indicator}Max Furnaces
Rate = event-driven

TROUBLESOME STATUS INDICATOR = ["Add" | "Delete"] * Indication to add or delete a furnace from the troublesome list *

Note that the following from the response process flow diagram are not included in any of the DFDs/CFDs:

TIME TO MONITOR

TIME TO RING BELLS

TIME TO SEND STATUS

TROUBLESOME FURNACE DATA

4.5   KEYS TO UNDERSTANDING

- System requirements analysis is the transformation of the customer's operational needs into performance requirements. It results in a specification of what the system is to accomplish, stated in such a manner that it is possible to develop a system design.
- The requirements are tightly bound to the system design, in the sense that technological and cost feasibility must be taken into consideration during system requirements analysis; indeed, there is significant iteration between requirements and design. Nonetheless, a useful model or notion of development is to consider the final specification of requirements as an "essential" statement of what is needed to satisfy the customer operational needs.
- There are three aspects of system requirements specification:
  - Process Model: explicitly shown with context diagrams, data flow diagrams, and associated graphics/text.
  - Control Model: explicitly shown with control flows, CSpecs, state transition diagrams, and associated graphics/text.
  - Information Model: implicitly addressed by consideration of coupling and cohesion and embedded in the process and control models in the form of data stores, event–action diagram, and data dictionary.
- When developing a system specification, take into account the guidelines of this chapter. Some of the key concepts are:
  - Take advantage of the multiple levels of the data/control hierarchy to control complexity.

○ Partition for loose coupling and strong cohesion.

○ Prefer the process model to the control model when you can. Usually keep control at a high level. Combine DFDs and CFDs when you can.

○ Strive for lowest level requirements (PSpecs and CSpecs) that are easily testable and amenable to allocation to hardware, software, and people components during system design.

CHAPTER 5

System Design

Objective: to provide a set of graphical notations, guidelines, and a step-by-step process for the design of a system and the allocation of requirements to system components

The purpose of this chapter is to describe the methods to be used during the system design phase of the development cycle. This phase is highlighted in Figure 5-1, which illustrates the phases of the development cycle.

System design is the determination of the overall system architecture, which consists of a set of physical processing components—hardware, software, people, and the communication among them—that will satisfy the system's essential requirements.

The input to this phase is the detailed system requirements to be satisfied. The output is the specification of system components and allocation of system requirements to each component.

To accomplish the methodology definition, the following items are covered:

- Transition from system requirements analysis to system design
- Graphics
- Guidelines
- Methodology—step by step
- Example

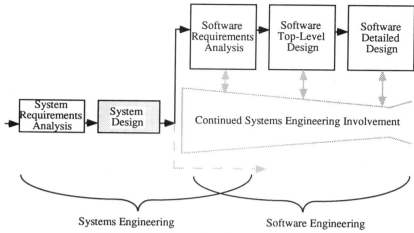

Figure 5-1   Phases of the Development Cycle

5.1   TRANSITION FROM SYSTEM REQUIREMENTS ANALYSIS TO SYSTEM DESIGN

This topic has already been addressed in Chapter 2 as an aspect of traditional system development, but it is worth revisiting at this point in order to shed more light on the topic, now that we have developed a set of system requirements. Although any discussion of moving from phase to phase of development is likely to sound as though one phase completes and then the other begins, remember that this is not the case, as elaborated in Chapter 2, especially Figures 2-3 and 2-4.

System design starts with the work products of the system requirements analysis: data and control flow diagrams, specifications, and so on. The *design* itself is the system architecture, which satisfies the requirements by having each of its components satisfy portions of the essential requirements. That is, portions of the requirements are allocated to components of the system design.

The system design phase includes the description of all system components and of how they work together as well as the allocation of each of the system requirements to components of the system design. The output is a documented description of the system to be developed and its method of satisfying overall system requirements. The question that naturally arises when looking at a completed, documented, system design is "How was this design derived?" This section illustrates the process of deriving a system design.

The determination of the design and the allocation of requirements is a very iterative process. It is also a very difficult process. It is not as though the system design arrives, full-blown so to speak, ready for the allocation of system requirements. Neither is it the case that the requirements are parceled out in some manner, and a system designed to accommodate the distribution of requirements. Rather, alternative designs are postulated that could, or are candidates to, satisfy the requirements. The determination of these designs is a fundamentally creative activity, a "cut and try" determination of what might work.

The methods for accomplishing this creative work are those of systems engineering, especially control theory. The methods of operations research are also of significant importance in order to determine best alternatives, often including true optimization. The specific techniques are numerous, can be considered "classical," and call upon a broad range of skills. In one of the best early texts on this topic, Shinners writes [SHI67, page vii]:

> The successful systems engineer must be a competent engineer, economist and manager. As an engineer, he must know theory, application, reliability, and testing techniques. In addition, he must be aware of state-of-the-art concepts and recognize their limitations. As an economist and manager, the systems engineer must know how to plan and control the fiscal and schedule aspects of the program. In addition, as a manager, he must be able to communicate with his superiors and subordinates in a manner which clearly and convincingly illustrates the problems and their solutions.

Shinners then goes on to note that the techniques include control theory, optimization, consideration of man–machine interface, and use of modern control test equipment. He also addresses queuing theory, communication and computer engineering, statistics, and other disciplines. These techniques are applied to factors such as performance, reliability, schedule, cost, maintainability, power consumption, weight, and life expectancy.

These factors are "traded off," one against the other, in terms of criteria important for the system being designed. Shinners uses, for example, a tradeoff of centralized vs. decentralized designs for a tactical command and control system. The kinds of tradeoffs that must be made are the lower cost vs. greater vulnerability of a centralized system for this application, speed of communication and decision making, and so on. Of course, in other application domains, vulnerability may not be such an important issue.

The point is that there is a broad range of issues to be addressed and a correspondingly broad range of engineering disciplines that are applicable to this process of designing the system to satisfy the essential requirements. When the systems engineering function successfully combines all these disciplines and activities, and simultaneously injects (when appropriate) consideration of hardware, software, and specialty engineering, the resulting approach is that of *concurrent engineering*. The methodology discussed in this chapter is not intended to teach all these techniques, but rather to provide the framework, and the graphic and textual notation, for *expressing the results* of the system design.

The design ensues from a series of technology decisions, which are documented with architecture diagrams that combine aspects of data and control flow. As an iterative component of making technology decisions, the functionality expressed by the data flow and control flow diagrams from system requirements analysis is allocated to the various components of the system. Although the methods for selection of specific technology components are not a part of the methodology, the consequences of the decisions are documented in internal performance requirements and timing diagrams.

The product of the system design is called an *architecture model*. The model expresses the components of the system, allocation of requirements, and topics such as maintenance, reliability, redundancy, and self-test. A key aspect of this phase, particularly important for purposes of this section and associated methodology, is that all the requirements are allocated to specific hardware and software configuration items, to manual operations, and to the interfaces among all system components.

In order to establish the context of the methods of graphic and textual notation recommended herein, it is also necessary to understand the steps in transition from system requirements analysis to system design and to show how the notation helps in making that transition. These steps are as "classic" as the methods themselves and are used on both systems engineering and systems analysis.

For example, the steps in making major decisions as expressed in [FIS71, page 8] are:

> FORMULATION (The Conceptual Phase)
> Clarifying the objectives, defining the issues of concern, limiting the problem, searching out good criteria for choice.
>
> SEARCH—Including the development of hypotheses (The Research Phase)
> Looking for data and relationships, as well as alternative programs of action that have some chance of solving the problem.
>
> EVALUATION (The Analytic Phase)
> Assessing the relative merit of alternatives in terms of value and cost, modeling the real world as affected by each alternative, and predicting the degree of satisfaction of objectives.
>
> INTERPRETATION (The Judgmental Phase)
> Using the predictions obtained from the models and whatever other information or insight is relevant to compare the alternatives further, derive conclusions about them, and indicate a course of action.
>
> VERIFICATION (The Testing Phase)
> Testing the conclusions wherever possible.

This approach is applicable to a broad range of problems. We will adapt the general approach, modifying the steps and techniques to suit the needs of real-time systems development. In order to understand fully the issue of *transition* from requirements to design, it is necessary to have an early partial understanding of the entire system design process. The traditional steps for the accomplishment of system engineering tradeoff studies for real-time systems are similar in nature, but more specifically focused on system design and hardware/software tradeoff issues. One way of looking at the steps is:

1. *Formulate alternative designs*. This step is fundamentally creative in nature and is actually the *transition* from one phase to the next. It involves the creation and exposition of system designs that can meet the essential requirements.

    This step involves the sort of technology decisions that were specifically and consciously avoided during the system requirements phase. The earlier phase was technology-independent: It made the assumption of perfect technology and focused on *what* the customer required, without regard to how the requirements were to be satisfied (that's the meaning of *essential*). The first step of the system design phase becomes technology-specific and focuses on *how* to satisfy the requirements.

2. *Analyze leading design candidates.* Some of the alternative designs will be quickly discarded; others will require more careful analysis. This step assesses the capability and quality of each design, using a set of design factors (specific to each application) and the methods of representing the system design.

3. *Perform tradeoff analyses.* Certain designs will be superior in some aspects, and other designs will be superior in other aspects. This step examines the tradeoff of the various factors based on relative capability and importance and identifies preferred alternatives for each aspect of the system.

4. *Choose system design.* The final step is to take all factors into account, including customer desires, political issues, and so on, to establish the complete system design.

Finally, remember again that these steps are not conducted in linear order. There is constant feedback to and modification of system requirements during the design process. There are prototypes, simulations, "chunks" of software development, and so on, that give us the insight we need to make requirements modification. But don't get lost in the chaos; it is our job to plan the development so as to place as much order on the chaos as we can—to make the process rational. One way we do so is to assume (even "pretend" is not too strong) that the requirements are essential, in the sense that they are the pure specification of customer needs that must be satisfied. Of course, we strip away the pretense whenever necessary, but between the necessary times we treat the requirements as essential. The viewpoint of the remainder of this chapter will be that the requirements are established, are essential, and will be allocated to the developing system design.

5.2 GRAPHICS

This section describes the graphics that are used for the methodology; they represent the *system architecture model.* The graphics presented in this section are not intended to tell the whole story of the methodology and are not necessarily tightly interrelated; they are only intended to introduce the *form* of the notation. The final section of the chapter,"FMS Example," will use these graphics, the guidelines of the next section, and the step-by-step methodology to present an integrated picture. Recommended conventions are also listed. We will cover the following graphics and associated data, with relationships as illustrated in Figure 5-2.

- Architecture context diagram (ACD)
- Architecture flow diagrams (AFD)
  - Diagram
  - Architecture module specifications (MSpec)
- Architecture interconnect diagrams (AID)
  - Diagram
  - Architecture interconnect specifications (AIS)

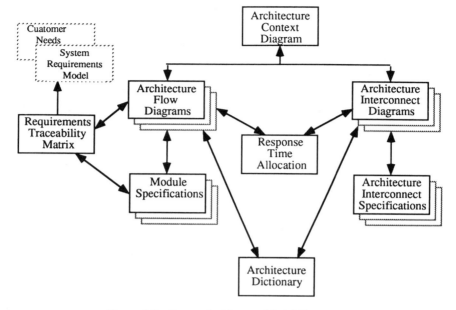

Figure 5-2 System Architecture Model Components

- Architecture dictionary
- Response time allocation (RTA)
- Requirements traceability matrix (RTM)

Although one could use the same types of graphics as were used during system requirements analysis, such as data flow diagrams (DFDs), there are benefits to using the distinct diagrams just listed. Since we are doing something different, namely, specifying physical components, it is useful to have different notation.

5.2.1 Architecture Framework

During system design, hardware-specific issues will require consideration of factors, including additional requirements that the components of the system must meet, that are not addressed during the system requirements analysis phase. The following are areas in which such considerations frequently arise:

- User interface processing
- Maintenance, self-test, and redundancy processing
- Input processing
- Output processing

These issues are addressed in [HAT87] in a relatively formal and rigid manner, called an *Architecture template,* which surrounds the control and process models.

We will adopt the concept, but in a less strict manner, allowing for other sorts of activities or factors. We will use the descriptive phrase "architecture template," however, and design or requirements representations for the factors just listed will be placed generally as shown in Figure 5-3.

The architecture template gives a general layout for all the architecture model diagrams (ACD, AFDs, AIDs) to follow. This template shows the addition of physical perspectives that had not existed in the system requirements model. An area of the diagram is assigned to each of the following:

User interface processing is the system-to-user interface, requiring some technology-based enhancements that were omitted in the requirements model. These enhancements are based on use of available technology and on various cost, operational environment, and other criteria. Design tradeoffs must be made to select the physical user–machine interface.

Maintenance, self-test, and redundancy processing requirements are also technology-dependent. We cannot identify these additional requirements for maintenance, self-test, and redundancy, such as fault tolerance, until we have selected an implementation technology that meets the system's reliability and performance criteria and we have analyzed its particular characteristics.

Input processing refers to the communications across the system's boundary that were not addressed in the requirements model and are not part of the user interface or a maintenance interface. Additional processing is added depending on technology decisions. The interface processing often includes definition of hardware devices and communication with them. The input processing accepts physical input from a source and converts it to a logical form usable by the system.

Output processing involves the same considerations as input processing. The output processing takes the system's logical output and converts it to a physical form acceptable to the output sink.

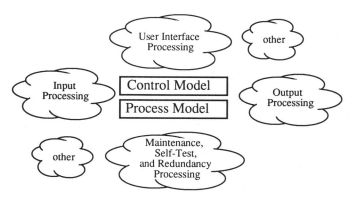

Figure 5-3   Architecture Framework

Control model and process model refer to control and functional processing, similar to that in the requirements model. The control and process portions of the architecture model are those requirements, from the requirements model, that have been allocated to the module on the ACD or AFD depicted by the template.

When the diagrams are drawn within the architecture model, terminators (on ACD) or architecture modules (on AFD or AID) can be placed within these areas to illustrate their place in the system's functionality graphically.

There are many benefits to using the template. An important aspect is that it can be used to organize and allocate tasks and responsibilities on a project. This allows for division of expertise in accordance with the template, not only during system design, but also during implementation, test, and maintenance of the system. It also draws the designer's attention to the different aspects of a system.

Remember that the physical perspectives used as specific illustrations in the architecture template of Figure 5-3 are illustrative and not necessarily exhaustive. These specific interfaces have been found to be useful in general, but each specific application may give rise to additional or different perspectives to consider.

5.2.2 Architecture Context Diagram (ACD)

The ACD is the top-level diagram for the architecture model. It contains the same information as the data context diagram (DCD) and control context diagram (CCD) from the requirements model, showing the system's place in its environment and, in addition, the actual physical interface to the environment. Another added value of this diagram comes from its layout. By following the architecture template, the reader can graphically see the types of interfacing that take place.

Figure 5-4 is a generic example of an ACD using the areas indicated in the template. Like the DCD, the diagram contains any number of terminators (boxes), one architecture module (rounded rectangle), and as many information flow vectors (arrows) as needed to show the data or control flow with the environment. Data flow is indicated with a solid line; control flow is shown with dashed lines.

Naming conventions follow those covered under AFDs.

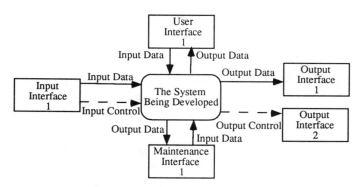

Figure 5-4 Generic Architecture Context Diagram

5.2.3 Architecture Flow Diagrams (AFDs)

An architecture flow diagram (AFD) is a network representation of the system's physical configuration. The AFD consists of two parts: the diagrams themselves and associated architecture module specifications (MSpecs).

5.2.3.1 Diagram   The AFD documents the information flow (arrows) between all architecture modules (rounded rectangles) in the system. The representation of these *physical* (implementation-dependent) entities as rectangles is useful in clearly distinguishing them from the *logical* (implementation-independent) entities represented as circles in the requirements model. The AFD also represents the allocation of processes and flows from the DFDs and CFDs of the requirements model into the architecture module. As such, the information that flows to and from the architecture module must be the same as the data and control flows to and from the allocated data and control processes.

In order to control the complexity inherent in very large systems, the AFDs can be hierarchically represented, with upper-level modules later decomposed into lower-level AFDs. The decomposition of the AFDs is *not* the same as the functional decomposition of the system during system requirements analysis. Each decomposition shows the next level of system architecture definition, which further defines the component *physical* entities. At upper levels, especially on very large systems, the partitioning shows architecture modules (segments or subsystems) without regard to whether they are hardware or software. Lower-level AFDs show the hardware and software modules and the manual operations derived from that upper-level system partitioning. The architecture template is applied successively to each module in the parent AFD to create the next level of AFDs and determine their component physical entities until the system is completely structured.

The number of modules at any given level depends on the actual physical entities that have to communicate at that same level of system definition. If two or more modules are exactly identical (perform exactly the same requirements), they may be shown as one module on the AFD. Their multiple occurrence is shown in the associated AID, to be discussed later. If they are not *totally* identical, they must be shown separately on the AFD as unique modules. Figures 5-5 and 5-6 give examples of AFDs and their hierarchical relationship.

These diagrams illustrate the use of the template layout. In Figure 5-5, the FAO (Furnace Administrative Office) computer and the MO (Maintenance Office) computer are in the user interface portion of the diagram, since they will be interfacing with the staff in those offices. Similarly, "System Status" and "Status Request" are flows to and from the maintenance section of the picture.

In Figure 5-6, the decomposition of the "Plant Subsystem" can be seen. Architecture modules 3.1 and 3.2 ("Plant Management Computer" and "Furnace Subsystem") are located in the control/process model portion, and one would therefore expect to see that many of the processes and control from the requirements model have been allocated to these modules. Other requirements would be allocated to the remaining architecture modules. The important thing is that all of the requirements will be allocated to some architecture module. Also at this level, several hardware

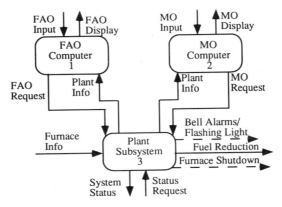

Figure 5-5   AFD 0: Furnace Monitoring System

devices, possibly hardware configuration items (HWCIs), have been identified. In this illustration, they are all output devices, located in the output processing section of the diagram. The control flows to them are shown (such as, "Flashing Light" to module 3.4, "Light Switch").

The following are some general naming conventions to use on the AFDs and ACDs. Since modules and terminators (on ACD) represent physical entities, their names should be noun phrases. The information flows (data or control) between these modules should also be a noun phrase, never containing a verb.

5.2.3.2   *Architecture Module Specifications (MSpec)*   An architecture module specification (MSpec) must be written for every architecture module in the model. The purpose of the MSpec is to describe the information and processing of the architecture module in narrative or graphical form. As with PSpecs in Chapter 4,

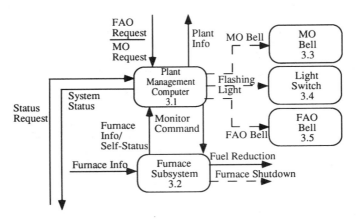

Figure 5-6   AFD 3: Plant Subsystem

MSpec 3.1: Plant Management Computer

(HWCI - Computer Model _____
  Memory _____
  • • •

CSCI - Software to perform processing allocated)

The Plant Management Computer (PMC) controls the interface to each furnace subsystem as well as to the offices and the Data Control Inspector. It provides the processing necessary to maintain system-level status, thus controlling the alarms sent to the offices (FAO BELL, MO BELL, FLASHING LIGHT, and periodic FURNACE STATUS).

All the control requirements except for the actual furnace shutdown from CSpec 3 in the requirements model have been allocated to this architecture module.

MSpec 3.2: Furnace Subsystem

The Furnace Subsystem handles the actual interface with the furnace. There will be one subsystem per furnace. The interfaces include receipt of MONITOR COMMANDs from the PMC, which are used to control the actual furnace monitoring. FURNACE INFO and SELF-STATUS are sent back to the PMC to provide the data necessary for its processing.

The control requirement for furnace shutdown from CSpec 3 in the requirements model is handled within this subsystem.

Figure 5-7   MSpec Examples

there are many different formats that the MSpec can take. It may include diagrams to describe the design. Details such as machine type, memory, disk, and system software (such as operating system, data base management system, or communications package) should also be listed here for the hardware identified. The use of the actual data names in uppercase in the description allows for easy reference to the AFD as well as the architecture dictionary.

The primary place to document requirements allocation is with the requirements traceability matrix. Sometimes portions of it, especially splitting of control requirements, are stated in the MSpecs. These requirements may be stated in textual format or by graphical representation.

Figure 5-7 gives an example of an MSpec for some of the architecture modules in the AFD of Figure 5-6 above. Notice that in this case, the control requirements from a portion of a Control Specification (CSpec) have been allocated. If this partial allocation cannot be described clearly in text, the diagram(s) from the CSpec must be redrawn to indicate the allocation to each associated architecture module. Also shown is a skeleton of the identification of the hardware and software components associated with the plant management computer. A common name for such software components, which we will adopt, is *computer software configuration item* (CSCI). The equivalent term for a hardware component is *hardware configuration item* (HWCI).

5.2.4 Architecture Interconnect Diagrams (AID)

An architecture interconnect diagram (AID) is a representation of the information flow channels by which the architecture modules communicate. It consists of the diagram itself and an architecture interconnect specification (AIS).

Actually, the whole mechanism of the AFD, AID, and AIS can be used for specification and flow of things other than information: power, time, heat, fuel, airplanes,

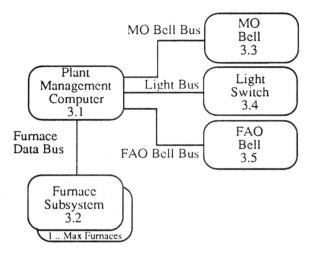

Figure 5-8 AID 3: Plant Subsystem

molten iron, bombs, and so on. Our primary concern is the aspect of system design that directly deals with software specification, and we correspondingly restrict our attention to issues of information flow.

5.2.4.1 Diagram The channels represent the physical means by which the information travels from one architecture module to another. This may be any material or energy medium, such as electrical buses, mechanical linkages, or an optical link. There is one AID corresponding to each AFD. In addition to the communication between the architecture modules, the duplication of modules and the channels that link them are also shown.

The AID inherits the names and numbers from the associated AFD, with additional notation for the duplicated modules. This is shown by using an additional rectangle behind the architecture module and noting the number of duplicate modules. In the example below, we see that the furnace subsystem occurs "Max Furnaces" times (numbered from 1 to "Max Furnaces").

Figure 5-8 shows the AID associated with the AFD in Figure 5-6. Each of the channels (such as "Furnace Data Bus") is labeled. The corresponding AIS, as described below, will provide the definitions of each channel.

5.2.4.2 Architecture Interconnect Specifications (AIS) The architecture interconnect specification (AIS) establishes the characteristics of the physical media connecting the architecture modules. The definitions of the characteristics may be given in either graphical or textual form. Since the information flow channels may be constructed of any medium, such as electrical, mechanical, or optical, the characteristics of each of the channels must be defined appropriately. The areas that one needs to be concerned with in the interface description include message formats, protocol associated with the bus, and the actual hardware addresses associated with

AIS: Temperature Bus

The Temperature Bus is used to gather temperature information from one of MAX THERMOMETERS (15) of a given furnace.

The bus operates as follows:
Place a THERMOMETER NUMBER in the thermometer buffer at address 16#00B4#.

A TEMPERATURE INTERRUPT will be sent from the hardware device to address 16#00B0# when the corresponding TEMPERATURE has been placed in the temperature buffer at 16#00B2#.

Figure 5-9 AIS Example

the interface. The detailed values of individual message fields are given in the architecture dictionary.

Figure 5-9 gives an example of an AIS. In it we see a detailed description of how the interface with the digital temperature sensor works. The specific hardware addresses are shown.

We also use the AIS to represent the software interfaces between CSCIs, such as detailed message definitions, more thoroughly. These are sometimes called "operational specifications", "message catalogs", or "interface requirements specifications". Figure 5-9 also shows such software-oriented detail.

5.2.5 Architecture Dictionary

The architecture dictionary is a listing of all data and control elements among architecture modules and external entities. There are two ways to establish the dictionary:

1. As a "first cut", the data dictionary from system requirements analysis can be used. This data would then be updated and added to as the system design progresses.

2. The dictionary can be created separately from the system requirements analysis dictionary.

The choice of which approach to use is a project decision.

At a minimum, the following information needs to be present. These are the same fields as in the system requirements dictionary discussed in Chapter 4.

- Name, range, rate, resolution, units, value names (for primitive flows)
- Breakdown of the flow into component parts (for grouped flows)

Additional attributes that are sometimes included are the origin module, the destination module, and the channel. This information is contained on the actual graphics (AFD, AID) and need not be repeated here. In fact, the situation often arises where a given data flow may occur between several different modules or on different channels. In that case it may be more confusing to list all the origin and destination modules and channels in the dictionary than simply to allow the reader to view it on the graphics.

···

FURNACE TEMPERATURE = * Actual temperature of furnace *
Units = °F
Range = 900 to 3700
Resolution = 1 degree
Rate = event-driven - according to schedule

···

MAX THERMOMETERS = *Number of thermometers attached to a furnace - currently 15*

MONITOR COMMAND = [Scheduling Info I Furnace Trouble I Temperature Request]

MONITOR FREQUENCY = * Frequency at which to monitor a thermometer*
Range = 0 to 144
Units = readings/day
Resolution = 10 minutes
Rate = change is event-driven

···

THERMOMETER NUMBER = * Number assigned to thermometer for automation /
management purposes *
Range = 1 to Max Thermometers

Figure 5-10   Architecture Dictionary Extracts

See Figure 5-10 for an example of architecture dictionary entries. Section 4.1.3 contains the detailed description of the dictionary notation.

5.2.6   Response Time Allocation (RTA)

The response time specification (RTS) from the requirements model must be allocated to the architecture modules, information flow vectors, and information flow channels in the same way as the other requirements model components are allocated. These timing specifications don't just get allocated; they play an important role in selecting the implementation technology. They are a determining factor in the tradeoff between different hardware technologies and in the tradeoff between hardware and software. Only after these tradeoffs have been made are the timing specifications allocated to the resulting architecture components. The timing requirements in the architecture model must take into consideration not only the external signals but also the specific timing constraints on the internal architecture modules.

The architecture model covers only the representation of the response time allocation, not the tradeoffs and trade studies involved in reaching the decisions. An example is given in Figure 5-11.

5.2.7   Requirements Traceability Matrix (RTM)

The requirements traceability matrix (RTM) during system design depicts the allocation of the system requirements to the system design chosen. The RTM graphic is discussed in detail in Section 4.1.7. For system design, the bottom-level system requirements model processes, and any CSpecs, are shown along one axis and architecture modules on the other. In addition, a design requirement (derived) needed within an architecture module to help satisfy the implementation of the essential requirement will also result in an X. A derived requirement can be defined as a requirement to be imposed on hardware or software because of a higher-level

INPUT EVENT	OUTPUT EVENT	ALLOCATION							TOTAL SYSTEM RESPONSE TIME
		Furnace Monitor Computer	Digital Temp. Sensor	Output Rate Sensor	Maint. Status Sensor	Elect. Status Sensor	Fuel Control	Furnace Control	
Temperature Received from Furnace	Fuel Reduction (when furnace hot)	30 seconds	3 seconds	--	--	--	20 seconds	--	within 1 minute
	sent to PMC	3 seconds	3 seconds	--	--	--	--	--	within 6 seconds
Output Rate Received from Furnace	sent to PMC	4 seconds	--	2 seconds	--	--	--	--	within 6 seconds
Maintenance Status Received from Furnace	sent to PMC	0.8 seconds	--	--	0.2 seconds	--	--	--	1 second
- falls to safety hazard	Furnace Shutdown	0.5 seconds	--	--	0.2 seconds	--	--	0.3 seconds	1 second
Scheduling Info Entered	All later reports affected	8 minutes	--	--	--	--	--	--	8 minutes
Troublesome Furnace List Entered	Recoding Started or Stopped	20 seconds	--	--	--	15 seconds	--	--	35 seconds
	sent to PMC	20 seconds	--	--	--	15 seconds	--	--	45 seconds
Individual Item Request Entered	Temperature sent to PMC	3 seconds	3 seconds	--	--	--	--	--	within 6 seconds

Figure 5-11   Response Time Allocation Extract

system technology decision. The duplication of software requirements in multiple components (if there are any) should be noted in MSpecs, so that it will only be designed and implemented once.

5.2.8 Graphics Summary

Now that we've seen all of the graphics individually, we will summarize how the major components are used with each other. At each level of decomposition of the system design, the AFD, AID, and RTM will be drawn and associated MSpecs and AISs written. Together these form the complete picture of that portion of the design, as illustrated in Figure 5-12. Each architecture module is fully described in its associated MSpec. Any duplication of architecture modules shows up in the AID, and the information flow channels are described in their AIS. Finally, requirements in the RTM show the mapping from the essential requirements of the requirements model (of system requirements analysis phase) to each component in the architecture model.

5.3 GUIDELINES

This section introduces several sets of guidelines for use in the methodology steps. The application of these rules will be indicated at the appropriate steps in the methodology. The guidelines include:

- Information to include in the system design
- Alternative design issues
- Design factors to consider

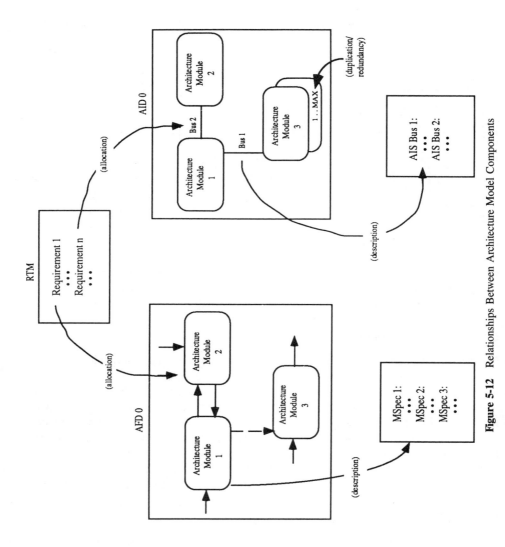

Figure 5-12 Relationships Between Architecture Model Components

- Allocation to architecture modules
- Partitioning between hardware and software
- Model consistency and balancing rules

Most of these guidelines follow those given in Hatley & Pirbhai [HAT87].

5.3.1 Information to Include in the System Design

What should be included in the architecture model during systems design?

1. Technical decisions based on the end-to-end flows that are critical to the system's safety and performance
2. Consideration of reusability of existing system components (tradeoffs will need to be made between the maintainability of these existing components and the more modern technology used in new ones)
3. Consideration of the real-world objects that these architecture modules will represent and the associated processing that they have to handle

DeMarco [DEM78] gives the following advice:

4. Defer physical considerations, such as formats, layouts, and internal system structure, for the software designers.
5. One may need to include:

   ○ Error messages
   ○ Startup and shutdown of system
   ○ User-sensitive formats (those that the user insists must be there before the software phase)
   ○ Conversions and algorithms
   ○ Performance

McMenamin & Palmer [MCM84] point out the differences between the deriving of the requirements model (the "essence") and the architecture model (the "incarnation") as follows:

System Requirements Model	System Architecture Model
1. Focus only on essential activities.	1. Focus on redefining the system's physical interface with the outside world.
2. Locate fragments of a single essential activity and unite them.	2. Allocate the pieces of the activites to processors.
3. Root out and eliminate infrastructure and administration.	3. Devise infrastructural and administrative activities that are right for the technology chosen.

5.3.2 Alternative Design Issues

There are many varying issues to be considered when formulating alternative system designs. Listed below are several of the issues to get you started. It is not the intention of this document to provide an exhaustive list.

- Centralized vs. distributed
- Star vs. multidrop vs. fully connected telecommunication systems
- A few powerful computers vs. many less capable processors
- Make vs. buy
- Specific model of processor (such as 68030 vs. 80386)
- Communication protocols, including error detection issues
- Hardware–software tradeoffs

5.3.3 Design Factors to Consider

There are many ways to configure a system to meet the given set of requirements. Some design factors that can play a critical role in the development of the system's architecture are:

1. *Reliability*: The system must be usable for prolonged periods of time without failure. Reliability is usually expressed in terms of mean time between failures (MTBF).

2. *Maintainability*: The system needs to be checked for correct operation in service and must collect data for error isolation. Maintainability is often expressed as mean time to repair (MTTR).

3. *Availability*: The design must result in a system that is up (available) for use more than a specified percentage of the time.

4. *Safety*: The design must be "fail-safe"—that is, when its performance degrades, it must do so gracefully so that safety is not jeopardized.

5. *Testability*: The system must be designed so that its requirements can be verified and validated.

6. *Cost*: The design must result in a system that can be built within a specified total dollar amount.

7. *Technology*: Decisions have to be researched to determine the technology that will best meet the system's cost constraints.

8. *Performance*: The system must meet some particular timing or behavioral constraints, such as overall response time to certain critical operations, or calculating flight paths to achieve a desired fuel economy.

9. *Growth and expansion capability*: The design must allow for future functional expansion.

10. *Schedule*: The design must result in a system that can be developed within a specified time.

5.3.4 Allocation to Architecture Modules

In allocating data and control processing from the system requirements model, ask the following questions:

1. Does any one module clearly dominate the control of the system's behavior?
2. Should any data processes be duplicated in more than one module to satisfy the control requirements as well as the technology decisions?
3. Should all modules contain the control necessary to be self-sufficient? That is, should each module contain the CFD control signals and those parts of the corresponding CSpecs such that it can make its own process activation and deactivation decisions?

If the answer to the third question is yes, then the simple allocation of the control and data processing applies. Affirmative answers to the first or second question can produce a different result. Consider each answer and the implications that it makes on the design of the system.

According to Ward & Mellor [WAR85, Vol. 3], the system design should:

1. Minimize distortion of the essential model given by the system requirements.
2. Be a satisfactory approximation to the ideal (perfect) technology implied in the system requirements model.
3. Allocate requirements to higher-level implementation units (architecture modules) before allocating to lower-level ones.
4. Classify the essential model by implementation technology used rather than by the system's subject matter. This may be based on either qualitative or quantitative grounds.

   ○ Qualitative classification implies that the decision is based on portions of the system that perform one type of processing versus another (for example, those portions that involve arithmetic calculations and those that do not).
   ○ Quantitative classification can be illustrated by the need to distribute a process control system among two microprocessors in order to avoid processor overload.

5. Search the essential model for common elements that will identify potential implementation resources; these elements may be subject matter-oriented.

5.3.5 Partitioning Between Hardware and Software

In the process of mapping individual system requirements to the architecture model, one must decide whether each module is going to be accomplished though hardware or software implementation.

Ward & Mellor [WAR85] provide the following discussion of allocation to hardware and software processing:

1. Data corresponding to the system requirements model process's *input flows* must be captured by the processor (hardware) and provided to the code that carries out the transformation of the data (software).

2. Data corresponding to the *output flows* must be obtained by the processor from the code that carried out the transformation and sent to the appropriate destination.
3. The *work* described by the process must be carried out by code within the processor.
4. Data corresponding to *connections between the process and a store* must be retrieved or placed in storage by the processor.

Once software has been identified, it must be allocated to individual CSCIs. A CSCI should have the following characteristics:

- All the activities of the CSCI should be related to a coherent function.
- It should usually exist entirely on one processor. There may be multiple occurrences, but each occurrence is only on a single processor.
- An exception to the above characteristic is a CSCI that handles such areas as a distributed data base or communication control for a network system.
- The average size should be around 50K source lines of code (SLOC). Any specific one may range from 10K SLOC to 120K SLOC, but one should become suspect of a CSCI that is predicted to be over 100K SLOC.
- A CSCI must be testable, both alone and in cooperation with other CSCIs.
- Contractual issues may be important.

5.3.6 Model Consistency and Balancing Rules

1. Every architecture module that appears on an AFD must also appear on the corresponding AID. In addition, the names and numbers must be the same on both graphics.
2. Every component of an information flow into an architecture module must be used within that module. It must be accounted for in the architecture dictionary.
3. Every PSpec and CSpec from the system requirements model must have a place in the architecture module. This is accomplished through the requirements traceability matrix.
4. Every data or control flow in the system requirements model must be assigned a place in the architecture model.

Note that an automated tool should be able to perform most of these checks.

5.4 METHODOLOGY—STEP BY STEP

This section goes through the details of the methodology in a step-by-step style to give an understanding for the issues that come up. The guidelines introduced above are discussed at the appropriate step of the methodology.

Figure 5-13 gives an overview of the basic steps performed during system design. The details are discussed below. The following lists the steps in the general order

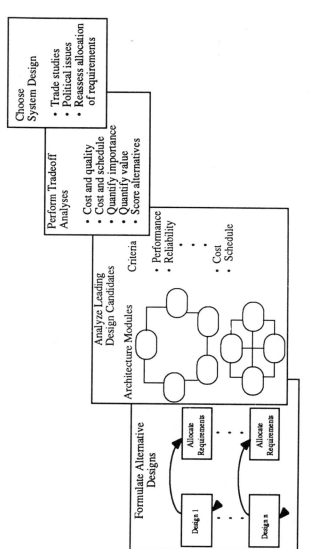

Figure 5-13 System Design Process

that they occur. In practice, some may be worked on in parallel and iteratively.

1. Formulate alternative designs.
2. Analyze leading candidate designs:
   2.1   Draw architecture context diagram.
   2.2   Establish architecture dictionary.
   2.3   Construct architecture flow diagram.
   2.4   Write MSpecs.
   2.5   Allocate response times.
   2.6   Document traceability.
   2.7   Iterate.
3. Perform tradeoff analysis.
4. Choose the system design:
   4.1   Create architecture interconnect diagram(s).
   4.2   Determine characteristics of each interface.
5. When am I done?

Step 1   Formulate alternative designs. This is the fundamentally creative step in system design, involving all the system engineer's knowledge, skill, and roles as engineer, manager, and economist. This process is often called *synthesis*. Consider the alternative-design issues, such as those listed in the guidelines, in order to develop a tentative design.

Many of the designs will be immediately, or at least quickly, recognized as being infeasible, uneconomical, or otherwise unsatisfactory. Those designs that pass the quick informal review are called "leading candidates" and are evaluated more formally during the next step of the process.

Step 2   Analyze leading candidate designs. The serious candidates—those not discarded quickly as infeasible or not economic—are to be documented using architecture flow diagrams and the other graphics and notational aids, as indicated in the substeps that follow. This provides the mechanism for communicating the designs to others and is the foundation for making system tradeoffs.

The degree to which each of the candidates is documented, compared to the deliverable documentation of the final design, is dependent upon the time, formality, and funding available for the system design process. The important issue is that the same graphics and other notation used for the documentation of the *final design* is also used during the process of *determining* the design.

There is a significant degree of iteration between development of the design itself and the allocation of requirements to the individual components of the design. That is, a tentative design is developed, an allocation is made, and the design is modified as necessary to accommodate the requirements better. This process repeats until the designer's engineering judgment is satisfied that an attractive alternative design has been developed. This iteration takes place for each of the alternative designs that are created. This is also the point at which there may be significant interaction and iteration with the system requirements.

Determine the characteristics of the design based on the specific design factors such as those given in the guidelines. The relative importance of the factors will vary from system to system (that is, they are application domain–dependent). The actual list of characteristics may be several pages long and ordered by relative importance for the specific system being designed. This may involve analytical models of the system, computer simulations, "what if" considerations, war games (both manual and computerized, sometimes involving actual forces in the field), and detailed cost analysis (taking into account, for example, inflation and time value of money).

The actual documentation of each serious design candidate is accomplished by the following substeps.

Step 2.1 Draw architecture context diagram. Use the system requirements model, and any trade studies that have already been performed, to create the ACD showing the actual physical terminators to the system. These terminators are real-world persons, places, or things. Start with flows from the DCD and CCD of the requirements model and, using the architecture model template as a guide, add any new information needed because of physical constraints.

Step 2.2 Establish architecture dictionary. This may simply involve a copy of the requirements model data dictionary, or it may mean starting from the ACD and creating a new dictionary with traceability back to the system requirements model data dictionary. This must be a project decision.

Step 2.3 Construct architecture flow diagram. Allocate the processes and flows of the system requirements model to the architecture modules determined in the formulation of the design alternative. Use the general design factor guidelines, as well as the detailed guidelines for allocation to architecture modules here to decide if the allocation is a good one. At lower levels in the system design, the guides for partitioning between hardware and software are also used. Update the architecture dictionary.

Step 2.4 Write MSpecs. Write a description of each architecture module identified in the AFD. Note any duplicate requirements or any special control. Remember to document the splitting of CSpec requirements for each affected module. Include new CSpec-type graphics as necessary.

Step 2.5 Allocate response times. Determine allocation of the response times from the RTS of the requirements model to the components identified in the AFD. Draw or update the architecture model RTA.

Make sure that the technology decisions made at this level will support those times indicated. This is another of the places where iteration between system requirement analysis and system design may occur. There may be no technology that satisfies some timing requirement, or the only available technology may be very expensive. The implication is that if none of the design candidates can meet the requirement, you must go back to Step 1 in order to determine new alternatives, or back to system requirements analysis (and possibly the customer) to arrive at a new and agreeable requirement that can be implemented.

Step 2.6   Document traceability. Draw a traceability matrix depicting the allocation of the requirements model processes and CSpecs to the architecture modules at this level.

Step 2.7   Iterate. For each architecture module, iterate, performing Steps 2.3 through 2.6, until all requirements have been allocated to the appropriate level of detail or it can be shown that this design alternative will not work. If you are doing system design to create segment- or subsystem-level specifications, the stopping point will be when everything has been allocated to the subsystem level. For the final system design, all requirements must be allocated to specific hardware or software portions (HWCIs and CSCIs) or manual operation.

Each time two or three levels have been done, review and revise them to improve their understandability and correctness; check for balancing errors according to the guidelines and fix any that are found. Resolve ambiguities and omissions as soon as possible. If they are not fixed at this time, be sure to note them for later resolution. This may be an indication that another alternative should be considered.

Document any major decisions made for future reference. Include why a seemingly reasonable alternative was discarded.

Step 3   Perform tradeoff analyses. Some design candidates will be superior in some characteristics, others superior in other characteristics. For example, the best-performing system may not have high reliability. Developing a low-cost-per-unit system might take so much engineering time that the production schedule cannot be met. Cost is almost always an important factor, with the usual tradeoff being between more capable, high-cost systems vs. less capable, lower-cost systems.

This is the step in which operations research and quantitative economics techniques become particularly important. It is often possible to quantify in cost terms the consequences of issues such as lower capability or lower reliability. This is the approach, for example, of *Cost Considerations in Systems Analysis* [FIS71]. In this case, the final decision is strictly on a cost or "pseudo-cost" basis.

More commonly, the various criteria (which may be thought of as a capability vector) are rank-ordered and often quantified in terms of relative *importance*. For example, weight may have a relative importance score of 0.04, while reliability may have a relative importance score of 0.13. Typically, importance scores sum up to 1.0.

It is also often possible to quantify the relative *value* of the different factors for each alternative. For example, a weight of 30 pounds may have a "value" of 100, while a weight of 40 pounds may have a value of only 20. Such figures are often referred to as "utility values."

If such quantification is possible, then techniques that combine the importance scores with the utility values can be applied in a quantitative assessment. Such techniques have been in use for a long time; specific methods are advocated in *Systems Analysis for Policy Planning* [QUA68] and *Quantitative Methods for Decision Making* [TRU77].

Step 4   Choose the system design. Remember that the entire process of design, analysis, tradeoffs, and so on is highly iterative. One of the important factors of iteration is the allocation of requirements in order to ensure the satisfaction of the essential needs of the customer. The choice of the alternative design is an outgrowth of the tradeoff analyses, although political factors may come into play during the final decision process. It is at this point that it is important to revisit the allocation of requirements and ensure that the complete system design will accomplish the job.

Once the analyses have been completed and the design chosen, the following substeps are performed to complete the definition of the system design.

Step 4.1   Create architecture interconnect diagram(s). Draw the AID for each AFD, depicting the actual physical interconnections between the modules. Any duplicate modules (either for redundancy or multiple occurrences) must be shown on this diagram.

Step 4.2   Determine characteristics of each interface. Write a description of the details of each bus shown in the AIDs. This description is an AIS. Update the architecture dictionary as needed for details such as message field ranges.

Step 5   When am I done? You are finished with system design when the architecture chosen meets the system requirements for functionality, timing, sizing, and cost as well as the project's budget and schedule. Remember that what you come up with here will become the basis for the hardware and software development, so be as complete and clear as possible.

5.5   FMS SYSTEM DESIGN EXAMPLE

This section provides an example of the system design methodology, essentially solving the following problem. If you wish to test your knowledge of the methods presented, you may wish to solve the problem yourself, before looking at the solution.

Assignment: Perform a system design, including a complete architecture model, for the automation of the process whose requirements model was developed in Chapter 4 for the Furnace Monitoring System (FMS). Make whatever assumptions you feel are necessary about the environment or the technology, for example the temperature on the factory floor, the availability of temperature-sensing devices, the speed and cost of telecommunication lines, and so on. Allocate requirements to CSCIs and HWCIs and establish the preliminary interfaces between all configuration items (CIs).

What follows is a completed system architecture model, including answers to the questions you asked yourself (or should have asked yourself).

5.5.1 Step 1: Formulate Alternative Designs

The following are some design alternatives considered for the FMS:

1. Have a large computer at the Maintenance Office (MO) with dial-in capability from the Furnace Administration Office (FAO). Connect the sensors for each furnace directly to the main computer in the MO.

2. Each office is to have a mainframe computer like the one currently at the FAO. Connect the sensors for each furnace directly to each of the offices over a network line.

3. Each office is to have a mainframe computer like the one currently at the FAO. Add a third large computer at the plant, connected to each furnace sensor. This last computer would then route the furnace information on to the offices.

4. Each office is to have a mainframe computer like the one currently at the FAO. Each furnace will have its own microprocessor to communicate with the sensors of the furnace. A plant computer will be used to manage the plant (for example, to perform the self-test based on status sent from each furnace computer, to determine overall system status, and to control the lights and associated bells at the offices) as well as to act as data concentrator to pass on normal operational information to the offices.

5. Each office is to have a mainframe computer like the one currently at the FAO. Add multiple data concentrators at the plant, each connected to several furnaces. At each furnace, install a microcomputer to connect to the sensors. These microcomputers will need to perform self-tests to ensure that their system is running properly. The furnace information will be passed on through the associated data concentrator to the offices.

Comments

- The first alternative, with all the processing going on in one centralized computer, will not be able to handle the interfacing to both offices as well as to all the furnace sensors. We will not consider it further.

- In the second alternative, some of the interfacing has been simplified, since each office will have its own computer. In fact, there will be a lot of duplicated software that can run at both offices. We will eliminate this alternative from further consideration, however, because of:

  Timing: How can the office computers collect information from all the sensors at once? Maybe we could try a larger, more powerful computer.

  Cost: The communication network from each of the sensors to each of the offices would be outrageous in price. In addition, the larger computer needed to support such a vast interface would be out of a reasonable budget price, especially since we had originally planned on using the current computer at the FAO at no cost to our project.

- We will use alternatives 3, 4, and 5 as our leading candidate designs and document them in Step 2.

5.5.2 Step 2: Analyze Leading Candidate Designs

The following are the candidates that will be discussed in the sections below.

Candidate 1: FAO and MO Computers with single Plant Computer (alternative 3)

Candidate 2: FAO and MO Computers with Plant Management Computer and microprocessors at each furnace (alternative 4)

Candidate 3: FAO and MO Computers with multiple Data Concentrators and microprocessor at each furnace (alternative 5)

5.5.2.1 Candidate 1

Step 2.1 Draw architecture context diagram. Figure 5-14 shows the ACD for Candidate 1.

Comments

- Should you show an overlay of the architecture template? This may be useful, especially when first drawing, to make sure you've thought about each area, but it is not necessary for final delivery. Notice that there is nothing within the "Maintenance . . . Processing" area. Sometimes an area will not have any module or terminator associated with it. That's OK; the important thing is that you have considered whether there should be something there or not.
- Although this is the only diagram that we will be showing it on in this case study, all the other diagrams *are* using the layout implied by the template, because it makes the diagram clearer and easy to follow. It *is* important to be able to demonstrate to an internal reviewer or the customer that the architecture is complete.
- One should be able to compare this diagram with the context diagram(s) of the requirements model (DCD/CCD) for consistency. Some grouping of data or added design constraints may be present on the ACD, but *all* the requirements from system requirements analysis must be there as well. Any differences because of design decisions should be documented and kept for future reference.
- An example of grouping of data from the DCD/CCD is the interface to the Furnace Administrator. FAO INPUT includes MONITORING INFO, REPORT REQUEST, and INDIVIDUAL ITEM REQUEST.
- Notice that the MO, from the DCD/CCD, has been divided into its physical components of the "Furnace Maintenance Staff" (user interface) and "MO Facility" (location of bell and light).

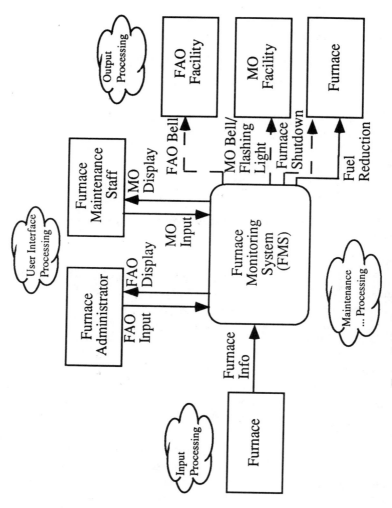

Figure 5-14 Candidate 1: Architecture Context Diagram

Step 2.2 Establish architecture dictionary. For Candidate 1, we will start with a new dictionary (separate from the requirements model):

ALL CLEAR CMD = * Indicator to turn off safety alarm *

DETAILED STATUS = Max Detailed Status Points {Electrical Reading}

DETAILED STATUS REPORT = * Report including Detailed Status currently available *
Rate = upon request

DETAILED STATUS REPORT REQUEST = * Request for Detailed Status Report *
Rate = event-driven

ELECTRICAL READING = * Single electrical status point *
Range = 0 to 570
Units = millivolt
Resolution = millivolt
Rate = monitored "continuously" when furnace is marked as troublesome

FAO BELL = * Indication to ring bell in FAO *
Rate = once when a furnace first becomes critical, and every second when a furnace is a safety hazard.

FAO DISPLAY = Report

FAO INPUT = [Monitoring Info | Report Request]

FLASHING LIGHT = ["On" | "Off"] * Control the flashing light in the MO *

FUEL REDUCTION = [High Fuel Reduction | Low Fuel Reduction]
* Amount of fuel to reduce due to hot furnace *
Rate = event-driven; depends on temperature of furnace

FULL REPORT = * Report containing all info for all furnaces *
Rate = upon request

FULL REPORT REQUEST = * Request for Full Report *
Rate = event-driven

FURNACE INFO = [Furnace Temperature | Output Rate | Maintenance Status | Detailed Status]

FURNACE NUMBER = * Number assigned to furnace for automation/management purposes *
Range = 1 to Max Furnaces

FURNACE SHUTDOWN = * Indication to turn off furnace for safety purposes *

FURNACE STATUS = Furnace Number + Maintenance Status
Rate = Once every 5 minutes when furnace is impaired, or once every minute when furnace is critical

FURNACE TEMPERATURE = * Actual temperature of furnace *
Units = °F
Range = 900 to 3700
Resolution = 1 degree
Rate = event-driven; according to schedule

HIGH FUEL REDUCTION = * Actual fuel reduction percentage = 20 percent *

INPUT MIX = * Mixture of raw materials being placed in furnace *
(Not further defined for this example)

INPUT MIX INFO = 1{Furnace Number + Input Mix}Max Furnaces
Rate = event-driven

LOW FUEL REDUCTION = * Actual fuel reduction percentage = 10 percent *

MAINTENANCE STATUS = ["Normal" | "Degraded" | "Impaired" | "Critical" |
"Safety Hazard"]
Rate = monitored "continuously"

MAINTENANCE STATUS REPORT = * Report containing the Maintenance Status
for a single furnace*
Rate = upon request

MAINTENANCE STATUS REPORT REQUEST = Furnace Number * Request for report of maintenance status for a given furnace *
Rate = event-driven

MAX DETAILED STATUS POINTS = * Number of electrical status points at a
furnace—currently 10 *

MAX FURNACES = * Number of furnaces in plant that can be automatically
monitored—currently 28 *

MAX THERMOMETERS = * Number of thermometers attached to a furnace—
currently 15 *

MO BELL = * Indication to ring bell in MO *
Rate = once when furnace first becomes critical, and every second when
a furnace is a safety hazard.

MO DISPLAY = [Report | Furnace Status]

MO INPUT = [All Clear Cmd | Report Request | Troublesome Furnace List]

MONITOR FREQUENCY = * Frequency at which to monitor a thermometer*
Range = 0 to 144
Units = readings/day
Resolution = 10 minutes
Rate = change is event-driven

MONITORING INFO = [Scheduling Info | Input Mix Info]

OUTPUT RATE = * Amount of molten iron being produced *
Units = tons/minute
Range = 0.0 to 50.0
Resolution = 0.05 tons
Rate = monitored "continuously"

OUTPUT RATE REPORT = * Report containing the Output Rate of a subset of
furnaces *
Rate = upon request

OUTPUT RATE REPORT REQUEST = 1 {Furnace Number} Max Furnaces * Request
for report of output rate on subset of furnaces *
Rate = event-driven

REPORT = [Full Report | Maintenance Status Report | Temperature Report | Output Rate Report | Detailed Status Report | Others??]
* "Others" may include a management report of type and quality of steel produced (depends on input mix, temperature, functioning of furnace) | maintenance report including problems over time per furnace *
(Others not further defined for this example.)

REPORT REQUEST = [Full Report Request | Maintenance Status Report Request |Temperature Report Request | Output Rate Report Request | Detailed Status Report Request | others...]
* Other reports are not defined at this point and will not be further defined for this example *
Rate = event-driven

SCHEDULING INFO = 1{Furnace Number + 1{Thermometer Number + Monitor Frequency}Max Thermometers}Max Furnaces
Rate = event-driven

TEMPERATURE REPORT = * Report of one or all temperatures for a single furnace *
Rate = upon request

TEMPERATURE REPORT REQUEST = Furnace Number + 1 {Thermometer Number} Max Thermometers
* Request for Temperature Report of the given furnace *
Rate = event-driven

THERMOMETER NUMBER = * Number assigned to thermometer for automation/management purposes *
Range = 1 to Max Thermometers

TROUBLESOME FURNACE LIST = 1{Furnace Number + Troublesome Status Indicator}Max Furnaces
Rate = event-driven

TROUBLESOME STATUS INDICATOR = ["Add" | "Delete"] * Indication to add or delete a furnace from the troublesome list *

Step 2.3   Construct architecture flow diagram. **Figure** 5-15 shows the top-level AFD for Candidate 1. It is being assumed that the INPUT MIX is used only for special report at FAO; that is, it does not need to be routed to the MO (either directly or through the Plant Computer).
Design Decisions:

1. The first decision is to retain the mainframe computer at the FAO and add a similar make and capacity machine at the MO.
2. Additional sensors such as "Electrical Status Sensor," and analog-to-digital converter interfaces, such as "Output Rate Sensor," will be installed at each furnace.
3. The Digital Temperature Sensor (DTS) that will be used has to be prompted with a thermometer number for it to return a temperature.

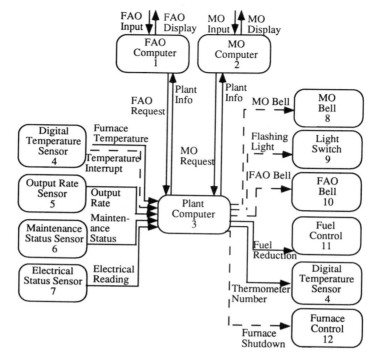

Figure 5-15 Candidate 1: AFD 0: Furnace Monitoring System

Comments

- Notice the addition of the TEMPERATURE INTERRUPT. This is for the actual interface with the DTS, which interrupts the Plant Computer when the FURNACE TEMPERATURE has been placed in the hardware buffer. Also added is the sending of a THERMOMETER NUMBER to the DTS to prompt it for the FURNACE TEMPERATURE.

- At this point in the analysis of this candidate design, we see that the Plant Computer must interface with the offices (2), the office devices (3), as well as the devices at each furnace (6 × 28). The total number of interfaces is 173. Either the computer (if indeed one exists that can handle this situation) must be very fast and have a great capacity for I/O interface processing, or we need to try another candidate. We will leave this candidate and look next at Candidate 2. Note that we are not showing a complete trade study here. This simple analysis is intended only to give the *flavor* of the kinds of things to consider as you analyze each design candidate.

5.5.2.2 Candidate 2

Step 2.1 Draw architecture context diagram. The architecture context diagram for Candidate 2 is given in Figure 5-16. The following design decisions were

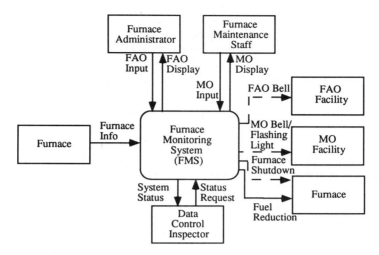

Figure 5-16 Candidate 2: Architecture Context Diagram

made:

1. The first decision is to retain the mainframe computer at the FAO, adding a similar make and capacity machine at the MO.

2. There will be a Plant Management Computer (PMC) to collect the information from the individual Furnace Monitor Computers (FMCs) to pass on to the offices.

3. Since we will be having a computer at each furnace, we have decided to provide for someone to monitor the system status of the automated furnace system for control and maintenance of the computer system that we are developing. This gives us the interface to a Data Control Inspector (a maintenance interface on the ACD).

Comments

- In comparing this diagram for consistency with the context diagrams (DCD/CCD) of the system requirements model, we see some grouping of data (for example, MO DISPLAY consists of REPORT and FURNACE STATUS) and the added design constraint of the Data Control Inspector, but all the requirements from system requirements analysis are there as well. The differences because of design decisions should be documented for future reference.

    The reasoning behind the flow grouping, besides making the diagram cleaner, is to make it appear more like the actual physical interface. For example, the interface with the FAO Administrator is a very user-intensive one. We've grouped the flows to simplify them as the input (FAO INPUT) and output (FAO DISPLAY) for this user interface.

- Make sure that the terminators are the final source or destination of the flow. For example, in our design we will be using a Digital Temperature Sensor

(DTS) to retrieve temperatures from the furnace. It requires that we send it a THERMOMETER NUMBER; then it interrupts when a FURNACE TEMPERATURE has been placed in a specific hardware buffer. Since this hardware device is part of the system being developed (even though it will be commercial and off-the-shelf (COTS)), the passing of the THERMOMETER NUMBER to the "furnace" and the receipt of the interrupt are not part of the ACD. They will be seen in the lower-level allocation to the hardware and software modules.

Step 2.2 Establish architecture dictionary. For Candidate 2, we will begin with the data dictionary from the requirements model (see Section 4.4.9) and add to it as necessary. The additions and changes will be noted as they come up in the steps. A final architecture dictionary for the candidate chosen will be presented at the end of this chapter.

Dictionary Updates (from ACD):

FAO DISPLAY = Report

FAO INPUT = [Monitoring Info | Report Request]
 * Note that FAO cannot request detailed status report *

MO DISPLAY = [Report | Furnace Status]

MO INPUT = [All Clear Cmd | Report Request | Troublesome Furnace List]

STATUS REQUEST = 1{Furnace Number}Max Furnaces
 * Request for status of Furnace Monitoring System *

SYSTEM STATUS = * Overall status of the Furnace Monitoring System and individual furnace status *
 * System Status is not further defined for the purposes of this case study *

Comments
 • Note that FAO DISPLAY is a redefinition or alias for REPORT, to give it the individual user interface perspective and to be consistent with MO DISPLAY, which can also be a REPORT.

Step 2.3   Construct (top-level) architecture flow diagram. Figure 5-17 shows the top-level AFD for the FMS. The following assumptions were made:

1. INPUT MIX is used only for special report at FAO; it does not need to be routed to the MO, either directly or through the Plant Subsystem.
2. The MAINTENANCE STATUS is always displayed at the MO. Thus, whenever an update is sent to the MO (for example, every 5 minutes when impaired), it will be displayed.
3. When an individual temperature report is requested, the furnace should be queried for the temperature at that time rather than using the last scheduled information.

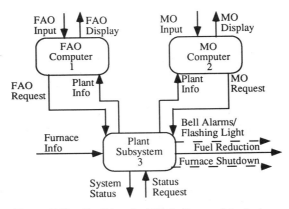

Figure 5-17   Candidate 2: AFD 0: Furnace Monitoring
System

Comments

- Remember, these modules represent the physical breakdown of the system, assigning the requirements to individual subsystems, to individual processor(s), and to hardware and software. By identifying each of these components, we can defer some of the details to a lower level as needed. For example, the plant subsystem is fairly complex, but its interface to the FAO computer and the MO computer can be illustrated here and understood without those details.
- Note the definition of new data flows between the architecture modules. Often, as is the case here, these are a (re)grouping of the requirements data flows to fit the design.

Dictionary Updates:

FAO REQUEST = [Scheduling Info | Temperature Request]

MO REQUEST = [Troublesome Furnace List | Temperature Request]

PLANT INFO = 1 {Furnace Info + Furnace Number} Max Furnaces

TEMPERATURE REQUEST = Furnace Number + Thermometer Number
   * Indication to check the temperature immediately *

Step 2.4   Write MSpecs. The MSpecs associated with the architecture modules in the top-level architecture diagram are shown in Figure 5-18.

Comments

- Notice that we wrote a short MSpec for the plant subsystem, even though it will be broken down to lower levels. This is to get an understanding of the subsystem as a whole and to provide the information for possible use in a segment specification.

MSpec 1: FAO Computer
   (HWCI - Computer Model _____
        Memory _____
   . . .

CSCI - Software to perform the processing allocated)

The FAO Computer handles the interface to the Furnace Administrator. This includes the acceptance and validation of input from the FAO, the routing of the FAO REQUEST to the Plant Subsystem for furnace monitoring, the acceptance of PLANT INFO from the Plant, and the generation of reports for display based on that information.

MSpec 2: MO Computer
   (HWCI - Computer Model _____
        Memory _____
   . . .

CSCI - Software to perform the processing allocated)

The MO Computer provides the user interface to the Furnace Maintenance Staff. This includes the acceptance and validation of input from the MO, the routing of the MO REQUEST to the Plant Subsystem for furnace monitoring, the acceptance of PLANT INFO from the Plant, and the generation of reports for display based on that information.

MSpec 3: Plant Subsystem
The Plant Subsystem handles all communication with the furnaces and interprets the FAO REQUEST and MO REQUEST for monitoring. In addition, it provides the information about each furnace to the offices as PLANT INFO for use in generation of reports.

Figure 5-18   Candidate 2: MSpec 1 through MSpec 3

- Details of the computers have been left blank in this example, but they need to be filled in for an actual system design to be complete.

Step 2.5   Allocate response times. The allocation of response times from the system requirements to the system architecture (design) is illustrated in Figure 5-19.

Comments
- For items used in various reports, the actual timing is given under the report for the office timing requirements. There is some time allocated to the plant subsystem to be able to pass the data to the office(s).
- Remember to check for consistency between timing requirements. For example, although there is no strict timing stated for "Temperature Received from Furnace" to be displayed in a report, there is a definite 10-second deadline under "Individual Item Report Request." To be consistent, the Plant Subsystem should always be allowed the same amount of time to send the temperature to the offices.

Step 2.6   Document traceability. Figure 5-20 and Figure 5-21 show the traceability of the system design back to the system requirements.

The actual database for keeping all of the furnace data records needs to be kept somewhere. For now, we are assuming that it is in the office(s), so some of it is just passed through the Plant Subsystem. This issue is left for the reader to decide and carry out.

INPUT EVENT	OUTPUT EVENT	ALLOCATION			TOTAL SYSTEM RESPONSE TIME
		FAO Computer	MO Computer	Plant Subsystem	
Temperature received from furnace	Fuel Reduction (when furnace Hot)	-	-	within 1 minute	within 1 minute
	Report Displayed	see individual reports below	see individual reports below	8 seconds	as requested in reports
Output Rate received from furnace	Report Displayed	see individual reports below	see individual reports below	8 seconds	as requested in reports
Detailed Status received from furnace	Report Displayed	see individual reports below	see individual reports below	8 seconds	as requested in reports
Maintenance Status received from furnace	Flashing Light ON	-	-	within 5 seconds	within 5 seconds
- falls to impaired	Furnace Status displayed	-	1 second	4 seconds	within 5 seconds /every 5 minutes
- returns to normal	Flashing Light OFF	-	-	within 5 seconds	within 5 seconds
	Bell Alarm Rung	-	-	within 1 second	within 1 second
- falls to critical	Furnace Status displayed	-	0.5 second	2.5 seconds	within 3 seconds /every 1 minute
- falls to safety hazard	Furnace Shutdown	-	-	within 3 seconds	within 3 seconds
	Bell Alarm Rung	-	-	within 1 second	once per second
Scheduling Info entered	All later reports affected	1 minute	-	9 minutes	new schedule in affect within 10 minutes
Input Mix Info entered	Report Displayed	see individual reports below	-	-	as requested in reports
Troublesome Furnace List entered	Recording Started or Stopped	-	5 seconds	55 seconds	within 1 minute
	Report Displayed	-	see individual reports below	1 minute	as requested in reports
Report Request entered - Full	Full Report displayed	within 3 minutes	within 3 minutes	-	within 3 minutes
- Temperature (single) (multiple)	Temperature Report displayed	within 2 seconds within 30 seconds	within 2 seconds within 30 seconds	within 8 seconds -	within 10 seconds within 30 seconds
- Output Rate (single) (multiple)	Output Rate Report displayed	within 10 seconds within 80 seconds	within 10 seconds within 80 seconds	-	within 10 seconds within 90 seconds
- Detailed Status	Detailed Status Report displayed	--	within 2 minutes	-	within 3 minutes
- Maintenance Status	Maintenance Status Report displayed	within 10 seconds	within 10 seconds	-	within 10 seconds
- others...	other... Report displayed	within 3 minutes	within 3 minutes	-	within 3 minutes

Figure 5-19 Candidate 2: Furnace Monitoring System Response Time Allocation

Requirements Model Component \ Architecture Model Component	FAO Computer 1	MO Computer 2	Plant Subsystem 3
1.1 Maintain Schedule	X		X
1.2.1 Read Temperature			X
1.2.2 Control Fuel Valve			X
1.2.3 Control Temperature Reading			X
1.3 Generate Temperature Report	X	X	X
2.1 Maintain Troublesome Furnace List		X	X
2.2 Record Deatiled Status			X
2.3 Generate Deatiled Status Report		X	
CSpec 2		X	X
3.1 Determine Maintenance Status			X
3.2 Control Flashing List			X
3.3 Ring Bells Once			X
3.4 Send Impaired Status		X	X
3.5 Send Critical Status		X	X
3.6 Ring Bell-Safety Hazard			X
3.7 Shutdown Furnace			X
3.8 Clear Safety Alarm		X	X
3.9 Generate Maintenance Status Report	X	X	

Figure 5-20 Candidate 2: Furnace Monitoring System Requirements Traceability Matrix — sheet 1 of 2

Comments

- Note the splitting onto multiple sheets (pages). This allows readability of the text. Real systems do have more than one page of requirements.
- By constructing this matrix at this level, we can see the complete allocation of the system requirements model. The lower-level architecture (the decomposition of the Plant Subsystem) will show the further allocation of requirements within that area.

Requirements Model Component \ Architecture Model Component	FAO Computer 1	MO Computer 2	Plant Subsystem 3
CSpec 3			X
4 Generate Full Report	X	X	
5.1 Record Output Rate			X
5.2 Generate Output Rate Report	X	X	
6 Record Input Mix	X		

Figure 5-21 Candidate 2: Furnace Monitoring System Requirements Traceability Matrix — sheet 2 of 2

- Note that some requirements need to be allocated to more than one module (for example, "Clear Safety Alarm"). This is because of the additional interfaces between the modules. When a requirement overlaps, check to be sure that you are allocating it correctly and completely. Divide up the requirement to fit into each module.
- Duplicate requirements may occur, as with (1.3) "Generate Temperature Report." Indeed the generation of any report common to both offices is a duplication. The software developed should be reused for the second office.
- Notice that derived requirements will often occur because of the added interface between architecture modules, such as computers. For example, to generate a report, the information must be passed from the Plant Subsystem and saved at the offices (we've assumed that the database is in the offices). This data must then be displayed.

Step 2.7   Lower-level decomposition (repeat Steps 2.3 through 2.7). The following shows the further decomposition of the system.

Architecture Module 3: Plant Subsystem   Figure 5-22 shows the construction of the AFD for the Plant Subsystem. The following design decisions were made:

1. Because of the expense of communication links from each of the furnaces to the FAO Computer and the MO Computer, a computer will be added to serve as a *data concentrator;* it will link individual furnace microprocessors with the office computers. In addition this computer can serve as the link between the FAO and the MO for any requirements that are likely to occur in the future. A further, and very important, use of this computer will be to serve as the maintenance center for the automated FMS and interface to the Data Control Inspector. Therefore, this computer will be called the Plant Management Computer (PMC). Note that this is not the maintenance

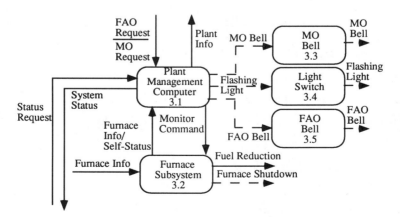

Figure 5-22   Candidate 2: AFD 3: Plant Subsystem

center for the production of iron and control of the blast furnaces, but the maintenance center for the control and maintenance of the computer systems.

2. Various alternatives were considered for the communication between the multiple furnace subsystems and the PMC, with the decision being a multi-drop line, in order to minimize costs of communication within the plant itself. There is some concern about response time in the system, but initial analyses indicate that buffering at each furnace, combined with high data rates once the furnace is polled, will satisfy the stated needs.

Comments

- Note that the Plant Subsystem is still very complex. With further trade studies, especially into the cost for communication lines between each furnace and the offices, it has been determined that it is best to add a data concentrator on the site, which will interface to the offices and poll each furnace computer for data (as discussed in the assumptions above). These design decisions and the trade studies supporting them should be saved for future reference.

- What if a module doesn't fit entirely into one of the template components? Then it may not be fully decomposed; at least, that is something to look at. An example is the furnace subsystem, which is still handling all inputs and outputs directly. If these were simple data interfaces, that might be accomplished in one module. Here we have a complex controlling of the furnace to carry out, so we need to break it down further.

- Since 3.3 through 3.5 are actual hardware devices, the control leaving them is the ringing of the bell or the light flashing. The bell itself is part of the FMS.

- Notice that the PMC can handle the processing necessary for determining if a furnace is troublesome (that is, on TROUBLESOME FURNACE LIST received from the MO, or furnace falling to CRITICAL status). Thus, only an indication to start or stop monitoring of detailed status need be sent down to the individual furnace as FURNACE TROUBLE. This allows the Furnace Subsystem to operate without any extra knowledge of how the status influences further monitoring.

Dictionary Updates:

SELF-STATUS = * Status of individual computer *

MONITOR COMMAND = [Scheduling Info | Furnace Trouble | Temperature Request]

Figure 5-23 gives the MSpecs associated with this level.

Comments

- Here we see the first hint of duplicate/identical modules: "There will be one subsystem per furnace." The associated AID would show the duplicate modules.

MSpec 3.1: Plant Management Computer
(HWCI - Computer Model _____
        Memory _____
. . .

CSCI - Software to perform the processing allocated)

The Plant Management Computer (PMC) controls the interface to each furnace subsystem as well as to the offices and the Data Control Inspector. It provides the processing necessary to maintain system-level status, thus controlling the alarms sent to the offices (FAO BELL, MO BELL, FLASHING LIGHT, and periodic FURNACE STATUS).

All the control requirements except for the actual furnace shutdown from CSpec 3 in the requirements model have been allocated to this architecture module.

MSpec 3.2: Furnace Subsystem
The Furnace Subsystem handles the actual interface with the furnace. There will be one subsystem per furnace. The interfaces include receipt of MONITOR COMMANDs from the PMC, which are used to control the actual furnace monitoring. FURNACE INFO and SELF-STATUS are sent back to the PMC to provide the data necessary for its processing.

The control requirement for furnace shutdown from CSpec 3 in the requirements model is handled within this subsystem.

MSpec 3.3: MO Bell
The MO Bell is the HWCI that will actually ring a bell in the MO.

MSpec 3.4: Light Switch
The Light Switch is the HWCI that will actually turn the flashing light on/off in the MO.

MSpec 3.5: FAO Bell
The FAO Bell is the HWCI that will actually ring a bell in the FAO.

Figure 5-23   Candidate 2: MSpec 3.1 through MSpec 3.5

- Notice the reference to the partial CSpec that has been allocated to the PMC. If the splitting of the CSpec can be clearly stated in text as above, there is no need to redraw the entire diagram in two (or more) parts. On the other hand, if there is a significant breaking up of the CSpec, then the new control would be drawn in each of the affected MSpecs. We'll see the allocation of the rest of this CSpec later in the breakdown of the Furnace Subsystem.

The allocation of response times to the plant subsystem is illustrated in Figure 5-24.

Comments

- This level shows only those timing requirements that have been allocated to this subsystem.
- Notice that some output events have been changed from "Report displayed" to "sent to FAO/MO," since that is the real event from this subsystem's point of view.
- An interesting allocation that at first glance doesn't add up is the allocation of time to ring the bell alarm. If we simply add across the line, we get

0.8 (PMC) + 0.2 (MO Bell) + 0.2 (FAO Bell) = 1.2 seconds.

However, once the signal gets to the offices, the two bells can execute in

INPUT EVENT	OUTPUT EVENT	ALLOCATION					TOTAL SYSTEM RESPONSE TIME
		Plant Mgt Computer	Furnace Subsystem	MO Bell	Light Switch	FAO Bell	
Temperature received from furnace	Fuel Reduction (when furnace Hot) sent to FAO/MO	--	within 1 minute	--	--	--	within 1 minute
Output Rate received from furnace	sent to FAO/MO	2 seconds	6 seconds	--	--	--	8 seconds
Detailed Status received from furnace	sent to FAO/MO	2 seconds	6 seconds	--	--	--	8 seconds
Maintenance Status received from furnace	Flashing Light ON	within 3 seconds	1 second	--	within 1 second	--	within 5 seconds
- falls to impaired	Furnace Status sent to MO	within 2 seconds	1 second	--	--	--	4 seconds
- returns to normal	Flashing Light OFF	within 3 seconds	1 second	--	within 1 second	--	within 5 seconds
	Bell Alarm Rung	within 0.8 seconds	--	within 0.2 seconds	--	within 0.2 seconds	within 1 second
- falls to critical	Furnace Status sent to MO	within 1.5 seconds	1 second	--	--	--	2.5 seconds
- falls to safety hazard	Furnace Shutdown	--	3 seconds	--	--	--	within 3 seconds
	Bell Alarm Rung	within 0.8 seconds	--	within 0.2 seconds	--	within 0.2 seconds	within 1 second
Scheduling Info entered	All later reports affected	1 minute	8 minutes	--	--	--	9 minutes
Troublesome Furnace List entered	Recording Started or Stopped	20 seconds	35 seconds	--	--	--	55 seconds
	sent to MO	15 seconds	45 seconds	--	--	--	1 minute
Temperature Report Request entered (single)	temperature sent to FAO/MO	within 2 seconds	within 6 seconds	--	--	--	8 seconds

Figure 5-24 Candidate 2: Plant Subsystem Response Time Allocation

Requirements Model Component / Architecture Model Component	Plant Mgmt. Computer 3.1	Furnace Sub-system 3.2	MO Bell 3.3	Light Switch 3.4	FAO Bell 3.5
1.1 Maintain Schedule	X	X			
1.2.1 Read Temperature	X	X			
1.2.2 Control Fuel Valve		X			
1.2.3 Control Temperature Reading		X			
1.3 Generate Temperature Report	X	X			
2.1 Maintain Troublesome Furnace List	X				
2.2 Record Detailed Status	X	X			
CSpec 2	X				
3.1 Determine Maintenance Status	X	X			
3.2 Control Flashing Light	X			X	
3.3 Ring Bells Once	X		X		X
3.4 Send Impaired Status	X				
3.5 Send Critical Status	X				
3.6 Ring Bell - Safety Hazard	X		X		X
3.7 Shutdown Furnace		X			
3.8 Clear Safety Alarm	X				
CSpec 3 - Furnace Shutdown		X			
Other	X				
5.1 Record Output Rate	X	X			

Figure 5-25 Candidate 2: Plant Subsystem Requirements Traceability Matrix

parallel, so that what we really have is

0.8 (PMC) + 0.2 (MO Bell) = 1.0 seconds and
0.8 (PMC) + 0.2 (FAO Bell) = 1.0 seconds.

Figure 5-25 shows the traceability of requirements at this level.

Comments

- This RTM (and the ones that follow) shows only those requirements that have been allocated to the parent architecture module.
- This design has completely allocated CSpec 2 to the PMC, rather than let the Furnace Subsystem keep part of the determination of a troublesome furnace. This allows the Furnace Subsystem to require only an interface to start or stop the monitoring of detailed status, without knowing why. This decision also affects the splitting of CSpec 3: Now that the Furnace Subsystem has no knowledge of how a furnace becomes troublesome, it will not check the maintenance status to determine when the furnace falls to CRITICAL or returns to NORMAL. It can just keep monitoring as usual until it receives notice of FURNACE TROUBLE.
- Note the splitting of CSpec 3. Only the Furnace Shutdown has been allocated to the Furnace Subsystem. This is because it needs to have complete control

of the furnace but does not need to know anything about how often to send statuses to the MO. At first, we had thought of putting all the furnace state control in the Furnace Subsystem, with the system state control in the PMC. However, that would have meant that the Furnace Subsystem needed to know about five-minute and 1-minute status reporting, which really has nothing to do with the actual monitoring of the furnace.

- The PMC is allocated the portion of "Read Temperature," "Record Detailed Status," "Determine Maintenance Status," and "Record Output Rate" necessary to send the data to the office(s).

Architecture Module 3.2: Furnace Subsystem   Figure 5-26 shows the decomposition of the Furnace Subsystem into its architectural components. The following design decisions were made:

1. The Furnace Monitor Computer (FMC), the microprocessor used to gather the data and control each furnace, will be installed at the same time as additional sensors and analog-to-digital converter interfaces to existing sensors.

2. The Digital Temperature Sensor (DTS) that will be used must be prompted with a thermometer number for it to return a temperature.

Comments
- The TEMPERATURE INTERRUPT has been added. This is for the actual interface with the DTS, which interrupts the Furnace Monitor Computer when the FURNACE TEMPERATURE has been placed in the hardware buffer. Also added is the sending of a THERMOMETER NUMBER to the DTS to prompt it for the FURNACE TEMPERATURE. Since this protocol takes place within

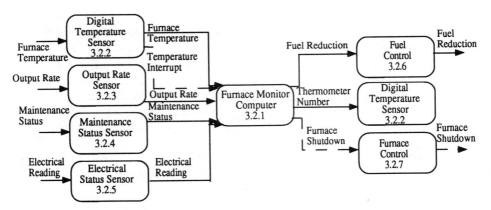

Figure 5-26   Candidate 2: AFD 3.2: Furnace Subsystem

the system, there is no THERMOMETER NUMBER shown as an output from the DTS to the furnace.

Dictionary Updates:

TEMPERATURE INTERRUPT = * Hardware interrupt indicating that a temperature has been placed in the associated hardware buffer *

The associated MSpecs for the Furnace Subsystem components are given in Figure 5-27.

Comments

- Here we see the rest of the allocation of CSpec 3 from the requirements model. Again, simple text is enough.
- The actual hardware devices are identified as such. The details of the characteristics of each device should be given.

Figure 5-28 shows the allocation of response times to the furnace subsystem. The final traceability to the actual software and hardware identified is given in Figure 5-29.

MSpec 3.2.1: Furnace Monitor Computer
(HWCI - Computer Model _____
   Memory _____
 ...

CSCI - Software to perform the processing allocated)

The Furnace Monitor Computer handles the interface to an individual furnace in order to monitor the FURNACE TEMPERATURE, DETAILED STATUS, MAINTENANCE STATUS, and OUTPUT RATE of that furnace. This is done through the individual hardware devices for the control. The SCHEDULING INFO received from the PMC is used to determine the time to acquire the temperature from each thermometer. FURNACE TROUBLE is used to determine if the detailed status needs to be collected. The statuses and output rate are monitored "continuously" in order to meet timing requirements for their output.

The requirement from CSpec 3 in the requirements model to shutdown the furnace when it transitions to SAFETY HAZARD status has been allocated to this architecture module.

MSpec 3.2.2: Digital Temperature Sensor
The HWCI that provides FURNACE TEMPERATURE for a requested THERMOMETER NUMBER for the furnace.

MSpec 3.2.3: Output Rate Sensor
The HWCI that will provide OUTPUT RATE for the furnace.

MSpec 3.2.4: Maintenance Status Sensor
The HWCI that will provide the MAINTENANCE STATUS of the furnace.

MSpec 3.2.5: Electrical Status Sensor
The HWCI that will provide the DETAILED STATUS of the furnace.

MSpec 3.2.6: Fuel Control
The HWCI that will control the FUEL REDUCTION to the furnace.

MSpec 3.2.7: Furnace Control
The HWCI that will shut down the furnace as needed.

Figure 5-27 Candidate 2: MSpec 3.2.1 through MSpec 3.2.7

INPUT EVENT	OUTPUT EVENT	ALLOCATION							TOTAL SYSTEM RESPONSE TIME
		Furnace Monitor Computer	Digital Temp. Sensor	Output Rate Sensor	Maint. Status Sensor	Elect. Status Sensor	Fuel Control	Furnace Control	
Temperature received from furnace	Fuel Reduction (when furnace Hot) sent to PMC	30 seconds	3 seconds	-	-	:	20 seconds	:	within 1 minute
	sent to PMC	3 seconds	3 seconds	-	-	:	:	:	within 6 seconds
Output Rate received from furnace	sent to PMC	4 seconds	:	2 seconds	-	:	:	:	within 6 seconds
Detailed Status received from furnace	sent to PMC	4 seconds	:	-	-	2 seconds	:	:	within 6 seconds
Maintenance Status received from furnace	sent to PMC	0.8 seconds	:	-	0.2 seconds	:	:	:	1 second
- falls to safety hazard	Furnace Shutdown	1.3 seconds	:	-	0.2 seconds	:	:	0.5 seconds	within 3 seconds
Scheduling Info entered	All later reports affected	8 minutes	:	-	-	:	:	:	8 minutes
Troublesome Furnace List entered	Recording Started or Stopped	20 seconds	:	-	-	15 seconds	:	:	35 seconds
	sent to PMC	20 seconds	:	-	-	15 seconds	:	:	45 seconds
Temperature Report Request entered (single)	temperature sent to PMC	3 seconds	3 seconds	-	-	:	:	:	within 6 seconds

Figure 5-28 Candidate 2: Furnace Subsystem Response Time Allocation

Requirements Model Component \ Architecture Model Component	Furnace Monitor Computer 3.2.1	Digital Temp. Sensor 3.2.2	Output Rate Sensor 3.2.3	Maint. Status Sensor 3.2.4	Electrical Status Sensor 3.2.5	Fuel Control 3.2.6	Furnace Control 3.2.7
1.1 Maintain Schedule	X						
1.2.1 Read Temperature	X	X					
1.2.2 Control Fuel Valve	X					X	
1.2.3 Control Temperature Reading	X						
2.1 Record Detailed Status	X				X		
3.1 Determine Maintenance Status	X			X			
3.7 Shutdown Furnace	X						X
CSpec 3 - Furnace Shutdown	X						
5.1 Record Output Rate	X		X				

Figure 5-29   Candidate 2: Furnace Subsystem Requirements Traceability Matrix

Comments

- Again, notice that this RTA covers only those timing requirements allocated to the Furnace Subsystem.
- The output event for "reports" has been changed to reflect this architecture module: "sent to PMC."
- Notice that the timing requirements for MAINTENANCE STATUS we have been combined together in this RTA rather that stated separately, as in the RTA for Plant Subsystem, since all of them are treated the same within the Furnace Subsystem: the status is sent to the PMC.

5.5.2.3 Candidate 3

Step 2.1   Draw architecture context diagram.   The ACD for Candidate 3 is given in Figure 5-30. The following design decisions were made:

1. The first decision is to retain the mainframe computer at the FAO, adding a similar make and capacity machine at the MO.
2. There will be multiple Data Concentrator Computers (DCCs) to collect the information from the individual Furnace Monitoring Computers (FMCs) and to pass that data on to the offices.
3. Since we will be having a computer at each furnace, we have decided to provide for someone to monitor the status of the automated furnace system for control and maintenance of the computer system that we are developing. This gives us the interface to a Data Control Inspector (a maintenance interface on the ACD). The self-test aspect that this implies must be done at each of the FMCs.

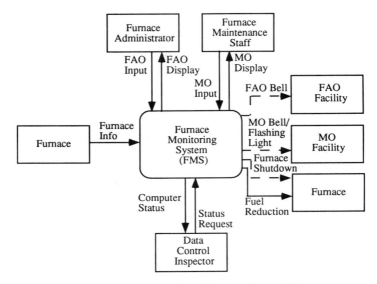

Figure 5-30   Candidate 3: Architecture Context Diagram

Comments

- In comparing this diagram with the context diagrams of the requirements model for consistency, we see some grouping of data and the added design constraint of the Data Control Inspector, but all the requirements from system require-ments analysis are there as well. The differences due to design decisions should be documented for future reference.

Step 2.2 Establish Architecture Dictionary. For Candidate 3, we will begin with the data dictionary from the requirements model (see Section 4.4.9) and add to it as necessary. The additions or changes will be noted as they come up in the steps. A final architecture dictionary for the candidate chosen will be presented at the end of this chapter.

Dictionary Updates (from ACD):

COMPUTER STATUS = * Overall status of the Furnace Monitor Computer *

   * Computer Status is not further defined for the purposes of this example *

FAO DISPLAY = Report

FAO INPUT = [Monitoring Info | Report Request]

   * Note that the FAO cannot request detailed status report *

MO DISPLAY = [Report | Furnace Status]

MO INPUT = [All Clear Cmd | Report Request | Troublesome Furnace List]

STATUS REQUEST = * Request for status of Furnace Monitor Computer *

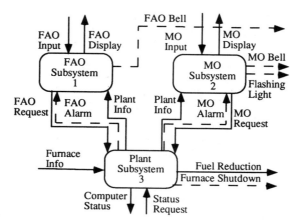

Figure 5-31 Candidate 3: AFD 0: Furnace Monitoring System

Step 2.3 Construct (top-level) architecture flow diagram. The top-level AFD is shown in Figure 5-31. An assumption was made that INPUT MIX is used only for special report at FAO; therefore, it does not need to be routed to the MO, either directly or through the Plant Subsystem.

Comments

- Remember, these modules represent the physical breakdown of the system, assigning the requirements to individual subsystems, to individual processor(s), and to hardware and software. By identifying each of the components, we can defer some of the details to a lower level as needed. For example, the Plant Subsystem is fairly complex, but its interface to the FAO subsystem and the MO subsystem can be illustrated here and understood without those details.

- Note the definition of new data flows between the architecture modules. Often, as is the case here, these are a (re)grouping of the requirements data flows to fit the design.

Dictionary Updates:

FAO ALARM = FAO Bell

FAO REQUEST = [Scheduling Info | Temperature Request]

MO ALARM = [MO Bell | Flashing Light]

MO REQUEST = [Troublesome Furnace List | Temperature Request]

PLANT INFO = 1 {Furnace Info + Furnace Number} Max Furnaces

TEMPERATURE REQUEST = Furnace Number + Thermometer Number
* Indication to check the temperature immediately *

Step 2.4   Write MSpecs. The MSpecs for this top level are shown in Figure 5-32.

Comments

- Notice that we wrote a short MSpec for each of the subsystems, even though they will be broken down to lower level(s). This is to get an understanding of the subsystem as a whole and to provide the information for possible use in a segment specification.

Step 2.5   Allocate response times. The allocation of the system response times to the top-level architecture are given in Figure 5-33.

Comments

- For items used in various reports, the actual timing is given under the report for the office timing requirements. There is some time allocated to the Plant Subsystem to allow it to pass the data to the offices.
- Remember to check for consistency between timing requirements. For example, although there is no strict timing given for "Temperature received from furnace" to be displayed in a report, there is a definite 10-second deadline under "Individual Item Report Request". To be consistent, the Plant Subsystem should always be allowed the same amount of time to send the temperature to the offices.

Step 2.6   Document traceability. Figure 5-34 shows the traceability of the system design back to the system requirements that they satisfy.

MSpec 1: FAO Subsystem
   The FAO Subsystem handles the interface to the Furnace Administrator. This includes the acceptance and validation of input from the FAO, the routing of the FAO REQUEST to the Plant Subsystem for furnace monitoring, the acceptance of PLANT INFO from the Plant, and the generation of reports for display based on that information. The FAO ALARM is used to ring the FAO Bell.

MSpec 2: MO Subsystem
   The MO Subsystem provides the user interface to the Furnace Maintenance Staff. This includes the acceptance and validation of input from the MO, the routing of the MO REQUEST to the Plant Subsystem for furnace monitoring, the acceptance of PLANT INFO from the Plant, and the generation of reports for display based on that information. The MO ALARM is used to ring the MO Bell or to flash the warning light.

MSpec 3: Plant Subsystem
   The Plant Subsystem handles all communication with the furnaces and interprets the FAO REQUEST and MO REQUEST for monitoring. In addition, it provides the information about each furnace to the offices as PLANT INFO for use in generation of reports and alarms for warning the personnel there.

Figure 5-32   Candidate 3: MSpec 1 through MSpec 3

| INPUT EVENT | OUTPUT EVENT | ALLOCATION | | | TOTAL SYSTEM RESPONSE TIME |
		FAO Subsystem	MO Subsystem	Plant Subsystem	
Temperature received from furnace	Fuel Reduction (when furnace Hot)	-	-	within 1 minute	within 1 minute
	Report Displayed	see individual reports below	see individual reports below	8 seconds	as requested in reports
Output Rate received from furnace	Report Displayed	see individual reports below	see individual reports below	8 seconds	as requested in reports
Detailed Status received from furnace	Report Displayed	see individual reports below	see individual reports below	8 seconds	as requested in reports
Maintenance Status received from furnace	Flashing Light ON	-	-	within 5 seconds	within 5 seconds
- falls to impaired	Furnace Status displayed	-	1 second	4 seconds	within 5 seconds /every 5 minutes
- returns to normal	Flashing Light OFF	-	-	within 5 seconds	within 5 seconds
	Bell Alarm Rung	-	-	within 1 second	within 1 second
- falls to critical	Furnace Status displayed	-	0.5 second	2.5 seconds	within 3 seconds /every 1 minute
- falls to safety hazard	Furnace Shutdown	-	-	within 3 seconds	within 3 seconds
	Bell Alarm Rung	-	-	within 1 second	once per second
Scheduling Info entered	All later reports affected	1 minute	-	9 minutes	new schedule in affect within 10 minutes
Input Mix Info entered	Report Displayed	see individual reports below	-	-	as requested in reports
Troublesome Furnace List entered	Recording Started or Stopped	-	5 seconds	55 seconds	within 1 minute
	Report Displayed	-	see individual reports below	1 minute	as requested in reports
Report Request entered - Full	Full Report displayed	within 3 minutes	within 3 minutes	-	within 3 minutes
- Temperature (single) (multiple)	Temperature Report displayed	within 2 seconds within 30 seconds	within 2 seconds within 30 seconds	within 8 seconds -	within 10 seconds within 30 seconds
- Output Rate (single) (multiple)	Output Rate Report displayed	within 10 seconds within 80 seconds	within 10 seconds within 80 seconds	-	within 10 seconds within 90 seconds
- Detailed Status	Detailed Status Report displayed	-	within 2 minutes	-	within 3 minutes
- Maintenance Status	Maintenance Status Report displayed	within 10 seconds	within 10 seconds	-	within 10 seconds
- others...	other... Report displayed	within 3 minutes	within 3 minutes	-	within 3 minutes

Figure 5-33 Candidate 3: Furnace Monitoring System Response Time Allocation

Requirements Model Component \ Architecture Model Component	FAO Subsystem 1	MO Subsystem 2	Plant Subsystem 3
1.1 Maintain Schedule	X		X
1.2.1 Read Temperature			X
1.2.2 Control Fuel Valve			X
1.2.3 Control Temperature Reading			X
1.3 Generate Temperature Report	X	X	X
2.1 Maintain Troublesome Furnace List		X	X
2.2 Record Detailed Status			X
2.3 Generate Detailed Status Report		X	
CSpec 2		X	X
3.1 Determine Maintenance Status			X
3.2 Control Flashing Light		X	X
3.3 Ring Bells Once	X	X	X
3.4 Send Impaired Status		X	X
3.5 Send Critical Status		X	X
3.6 Ring Bell-Safety Hazard	X	X	X
3.7 Shutdown Furnace			X
3.8 Clear Safety Alarm		X	X
3.9 Generate Maintenance Status Report	X	X	
CSpec 3			X
4 Generate Full Report	X	X	
5.1 Record Output Rate			X
5.2 Generate Output Rate Report	X	X	
6 Record Input Mix	X		

Figure 5-34 Candidate 3: Furnace Monitoring System Requirements Traceability Matrix

The following assumption was made in allocating the requirements: The actual database for keeping all of the furnace data records needs to be kept somewhere. For now we are assuming that it is in the office(s), so some of it is just passed through the Plant Subsystem. This issue is left for the reader to decide and carry out.

Comments

The same comments as given for Candidate 2 (top-level) apply here.

Step 2.7   Lower-level decomposition (repeat Steps 2.3 through 2.7). The following is the further decomposition for candidate 3.

Architecture Module 1: FAO Subsystem   Figure 5-35 is the AFD for the FAO Subsystem. The associated MSpecs are shown in Figure 5-36.

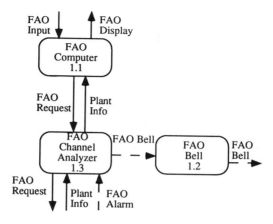

Figure 5-35   Candidate 3: AFD 1: FAO Subsystem

Comments

- Here we see that there will be duplicate software functionality for the FAO and MO. During software development, this should be taken into consideration so that it will only be developed once. Software reuse on the same project is a vital issue that many projects do not sufficiently address. It is frequently the case on large systems that the same or similar software functionality is needed in multiple places. The sort of orderly and well-documented development in the SSEM approach helps clarify instances of such duplication, but it is still a project responsibility to encourage, in all the engineering staff, the habit of looking for software reuse.

The allocation of response times is illustrated in Figure 5-37.

MSpec 1.1: FAO Computer
(HWCI - Computer Model _____
Memory _____

• • •

CSCI - Software to perform the processing allocated)

The FAO Computer handles the interface to the Furnace Administrator. This includes the acceptance and validation of input from the FAO, the routing of the FAO REQUEST to the channel for furnace monitoring, and the acceptance of PLANT INFO for generation of reports for display.

(Note that the MO has many similar software requirements)

MSpec 1.2: FAO Bell
The FAO Bell is the HWCI that will actually ring a bell in the FAO.

MSpec 1.3: FAO Channel Analyzer
The FAO Channel Analyzer (HWCI) performs the functionality necessary to route plant information to the FAO Computer or the FAO Bell for processing. It also takes the FAO REQUEST and routes it to the Plant Subsystem.

Figure 5-36   Candidate 3: MSpec 1.1 through MSpec 1.3

INPUT EVENT	OUTPUT EVENT	ALLOCATION FAO Computer	FAO Bell	FAO Channel Analyzer	TOTAL SYSTEM RESPONSE TIME
Temperature received from Plant	Report Displayed	see individual reports below	:	0.05 seconds	as requested in reports
Output Rate received from Plant	Report Displayed	see individual reports below	:	0.05 seconds	as requested in reports
Maintenance Status received from Plant	Furnace Status displayed	see individual reports below	:	0.05 seconds	as requested in reports
FAO Alarm Received from Plant	Bell Alarm Rung	:	within 0.45 second	0.05 seconds	within 0.5 second
Scheduling Info entered	Sent to Plant	55 seconds	:	5 seconds	1 minute
Input Mix Info entered	Report Displayed	see individual reports below	:	:	as requested in reports
Report Request entered - Full	Full Report displayed	within 3 minutes	:	:	within 3 minutes
- Temperature (single) (multiple)	Temperature Report displayed	within 1.5 seconds within 30 seconds	:	0.5 seconds	within 2 seconds within 30 seconds
- Output Rate (single) (multiple)	Output Rate Report displayed	within 10 seconds within 80 seconds	:	:	within 10 seconds within 90 seconds
- Maintenance Status	Maintenance Status Report displayed	within 10 seconds	:	:	within 10 seconds
- others...	other... Report displayed	within 3 minutes	:	:	within 3 minutes

Figure 5-37 Candidate 3: FAO Subsystem Response Time Allocation

Requirements Model Component \ Architecture Model Component	FAO Computer 1.1	FAO Bell 1.2	FAO Channel Analyzer 1.3
1.1 Maintain Schedule	X		X
1.3 Generate Temperature Report	X		X
3.3 Ring Bells Once		X	X
3.6 Ring Bell-Safety Hazard		X	X
3.9 Generate Maintenance Status Report	X		X
4 Generate Full Report	X		X
5.2 Generate Output Rate Report	X		X
6 Record Input Mix	X		

Figure 5-38 Candidate 3: FAO Subsystem Requirements Traceability Matrix

Comments

- This level shows only those timing requirements that have been allocated to this subsystem.
- Notice that some input events have been changed from " . . . received from furnace" to " . . . received from plant," since that is the real event from this subsystem's point of view.

Figure 5-38 shows the requirements traceability for the FAO Subsystem.

Architecture Module 2: MO Subsystem The MO Subsystem is similar to the FAO Subsystem. The architecture and its description are shown in Figure 5-39 and Figure 5-40, respectively. Figure 5-41 gives the response time allocation, and Figure 5-42 illustrates the requirements traceability.

Architecture Module 3: Plant Subsystem Figure 5-43 illustrates the decomposition of the Plant Subsystem into its components. The following design decisions were made:

1. Trade studies were performed to determine the ratio of Data Concentrator Computers (DCCs) to Furnace Monitor Computers (FMCs). It was concluded that there would be 4 DCCs, with 7 FMCs assigned to each.
2. The microprocessor (FMC) used to gather the data and to control each furnace will be installed at the same time as additional sensors and analog-to-digital converter interfaces to existing sensors.
3. The Digital Temperature Sensor (DTS) that will be used must be prompted with a thermometer number for it to return a temperature.

Comments

- The duplication of DCCs and FMCs would show up in the AID. We will also see it mentioned in the MSpecs.

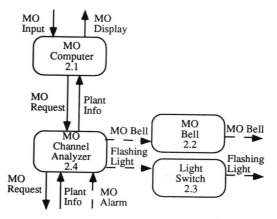

Figure 5-39 Candidate 3: AFD 2: MO Subsystem

- Note the addition of the TEMPERATURE INTERRUPT. This is for the actual interface with the DTS, which interrupts the Furnace Monitor Computer when the FURNACE TEMPERATURE has been placed in the hardware buffer. Also added is the sending of a THERMOMETER NUMBER to the DTS to prompt it for the FURNACE TEMPERATURE.

Dictionary Updates:

MONITOR COMMAND = (FAO Request — MO Request)

OFFICE CONTROL + (Bell Alarm — Flashing Light)

TEMPERATURE INTERRUPT = * Hardware interrupt indicating that a temperature has been placed in the associated hardware buffer *

MSpec 2.1: MO Computer
 (HWCI - Computer Model _____
 Memory _____
 • • •

 CSCI - Software to perform the processing allocated)

 The MO Computer handles the interface to the Furnace Maintenance Staff. This includes the acceptance and validation of input from the MO, the routing of the MO REQUEST to the channel for furnace monitoring, and the acceptance of PLANT INFO for generation of reports for display.

 The portion of CSpec 2 to activate Generate Detailed Design Status Report is allocated to this module.

 (Note that the FAO has many similar software requirements)

MSpec 2.2: MO Bell
 The MO Bell is the HWCI that will actually ring a bell in the MO.

MSpec 2.2: Light Switch
 The Light Switch is the HWCI that will actually turn the flashing light on or off.

MSpec 2.4: MO Channel Analyzer
 The MO Channel Analyzer (HWCI) performs the functionality necessary to route plant information to the MO subsystem components for processing. It also takes the MO REQUEST and routes it to the Plant Subsystem.

Figure 5-40 Candidate 3: MSpec 2.1 through MSpec 2.4

INPUT EVENT	OUTPUT EVENT	ALLOCATION			MO Channel Analyzer	TOTAL SYSTEM RESPONSE TIME
		MO Computer	MO Bell	Light Switch		
Temperature received from Plant	Report Displayed	see individual reports below	-	-	0.05 seconds	see individual reports below
Output Rate received from Plant	Report Displayed	see individual reports below	--	--	0.05 seconds	see individual reports below
Detailed Status received from Plant	Report Displayed	see individual reports below	-	-	0.05 seconds	see individual reports below
Maintenance Status received from furnace - falls to impaired	Flashing Light ON	-	-	within 2 seconds	0.05 seconds	within 2 seconds
	Furnace Status displayed	0.55 seconds	-	--	0.05 seconds	1 second
- returns to normal	Flashing Light OFF	-	-	within 2 seconds	0.05 seconds	within 2 seconds
- falls to critical	Bell Alarm Rung	-	within 0.45 second	-	0.05 seconds	within 0.5 second
	Furnace Status displayed	0.55 second	-	--	0.05 seconds	0.5 second
- falls to safety hazard	Bell Alarm Rung	-	within 0.45 second	--	0.05 seconds	within 0.5 second
Troublesome Furnace List entered	Recording Started or Stopped	4 seconds	--	--	1 seconds	5 seconds
	Report Displayed	see individual reports below	--	--	--	see individual reports below
Report Request entered - Full	Full Report displayed	within 3 minutes	--	--	--	within 3 minutes
- Temperature (single) (multiple)	Temperature Report displayed	within 1.5 sec / within 30 sec	--	--	0.5 seconds / --	within 2 seconds / within 30 seconds
- Output Rate (single) (multiple)	Output Rate Report displayed	within 10 sec / within 80 sec	--	--	--	within 10 seconds / within 80 seconds
- Detailed Status	Detailed Status Report displayed	within 2 minutes	--	--	--	within 2 minutes
- Maintenance Status	Maintenance Status Report displayed	within 10 sec	--	--	--	within 10 seconds
- others...	other... Report displayed	within 3 minutes	--	--	--	within 3 minutes

Figure 5-41   Candidate 3: MO Subsystem Response Time Allocation

Requirements Model Component \ Architecture Model Component	2.1 MO Computer	2.2 MO Bell	2.3 Light Switch	2.4 MO Channel Analyzer
1.3 Generate Temperature Report	X			X
2.1 Maintain Troublesome Furnace List	X			X
2.3 Generate Detailed Status Report	X			X
CSPEC 2 (generation of report)	X			
3.2 Control Flashing Light			X	X
3.3 Ring Bells Once		X		X
3.4 Send Impaired Status	X			X
3.5 Send Critical Status	X			X
3.6 Ring Bell-Safety Hazard		X		X
3.8 Clear Safety Alarm	X			X
3.9 Generate Maintenance Status Report	X			X
4 Generate Full Report	X			
5.2 Generate Output Rate Report	X			X

Figure 5-42   Candidate 3: MO Subsystem Requirements Traceability Matrix

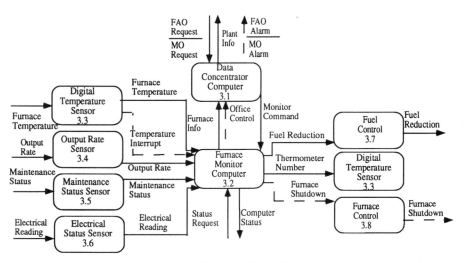

Figure 5-43   Candidate 3: AFD 3: Plant Subsystem

MSpec 3.1: Data Concentrator Computer
(HWCI - Computer Model _____
    Memory _____
    •••
CSCI - Software to perform the processing allocated)

The Data Concentrator Computer (DCC) controls the interface between several
individual Furnace Monitoring Computers and the FAO and MO. It provides the
processing necessary to send and receive data.

There will be one DCC per seven FMC.

MSpec 3.2: Furnace Monitor Computer
(HWCI - Computer Model _____
    Memory _____
    •••
CSCI - Software to perform the processing allocated)

The Furnace Monitor Computer handles the interface to an individual furnace in order to
monitor the FURNACE TEMPERATURE, DETAILED STATUS, MAINTENANCE
STATUS, and OUTPUT RATE of that furnace. This is done through the individual
hardware devices for the control. The SCHEDULING INFO received from the DCC is
used to determine the time to acquire the temperature from each thermometer.
TROUBLESOME FURNACE LIST is used to determine if the detailed status needs to
be collected for this furnace. The statuses and output rate are monitored "continuously"
in order to meet timing requirements for their output.

MSpec 33: Digital Temperature Sensor
The HWCI that provides FURNACE TEMPERATURE for a requested
THERMOMETER NUMBER for the furnace.

MSpec 34: Output Rate Sensor
The HWCI that will provide OUTPUT RATE for the furnace.

MSpec 3.5: Maintenance Status Sensor
The HWCI that will provide the MAINTENANCE STATUS of the furnace.

MSpec 36: Electrical Status Sensor
The HWCI that will provide the DETAILED STATUS of the furnace.

MSpec 3.7: Fuel Control
The HWCI that will control the FUEL REDUCTION to the furnace.

MSpec 3.8: Furnace Control
The HWCI that will shut down the furnace as needed.

Figure 5-44   Candidate 3: MSpec 3.1 through MSpec 3.8

The associated MSpecs are shown in Figure 5-44. Here we see the first hint
of duplicated identical modules: "There will be one DCC per seven FMCs." The
associated AID would show the duplicate modules.

Figure 5-45 gives the allocation of the response times to the components of the
Plant Subsystem.

Comments

- This level shows only those timing requirements that have been allocated to
  this subsystem.

- Notice that some of the output events have been changed from "Report displayed" to "sent to FAO/MO," since this is the real event from this subsystem's
  point of view.

The Plant Subsystem requirements traceability is given in Figure 5-46.

INPUT EVENT	OUTPUT EVENT	ALLOCATION								TOTAL SYSTEM RESPONSE TIME
		Data Concentrator Computer	Furnace Monitor Computer	Digital Temp. Sensor	Output Rate Sensor	Maint. Status Sensor	Elect. Status Sensor	Fuel Control	Furnace Control	
Temperature received from furnace	Fuel Reduction (when furnace Hot) sent to FAO/MO	-	30 seconds	3 seconds				20 seconds	-	within 1 minute
Output Rate received from furnace	sent to FAO/MO	2 seconds	3 seconds		2 seconds				-	8 seconds
Detailed Status received from furnace	sent to FAO/MO	2 seconds	4 seconds				2 seconds		-	8 seconds
Maintenance Status received from furnace	Flashing Light Sent to MO (ON)	within 1 second	within 2 seconds						-	within 3 seconds
- falls to impaired	Furnace Status sent to MO	within 1 second	within 1.8 seconds			0.2 seconds			-	4 seconds
- returns to normal	Flashing Light Sent to MO (OFF)	within 3 seconds	within 2 seconds						-	within 3 seconds
	Bell Alarm Sent to FAO/MO	within 0.2 seconds	within 0.6 seconds						-	within 1 second
- falls to critical	Furnace Status sent to MO	within 1 seconds	within 1.8 seconds			0.2 seconds			-	2.5 seconds
- falls to safety hazard	Furnace Shutdown	-	within 1.3 second			0.2 seconds			0.5 seconds	within 3 seconds
	Bell Alarm Sent to FAO/MO	within 0.2 seconds	within 0.6 seconds						-	within 1 second
Scheduling Info entered	All later reports affected	1 minute	8 minutes						-	9 minutes
Troublesome Furnace List entered	Recording Started or Stopped sent to MO	1 second	35 seconds				15 seconds		-	55 seconds
Temperature Report Request entered (single)	temperature sent to FAO/MO	10 seconds	50 seconds				15 seconds		-	1 minute
	temperature sent to FAO/MO	within 2 seconds	within 6 seconds						-	8 seconds

Figure 5-45 Candidate 3: Plant Subsystem Response Time Allocation

5.5.3   Step 3: Perform Tradeoff Analyses

In order to decide between the candidate designs, more trade studies may need to be performed that trade off the values of each candidate. Although trade studies themselves are beyond the scope of this methodology, the following are some of the things we looked at to decide between Candidate 2 and Candidate 3.

1. Candidate 3 would probably be cheaper to build than Candidate 2, since the Data Concentrator Computers (DCCs) are much less complex than the Plant Management Computer (PMC).

2. However, the individual Furnace Monitor Computers (FMCs) in Candidate 3 must perform more complex processing than the computers in Candidate 2. For instance, each FMC must maintain its own status instead of sending the computer (self) status to the PMC and allowing for the self-test and maintenance in one central location. This implies that the staff will have to go to each furnace (to determine its computers status), which is what the customer was striving to get away from.

3. The complexity of the system status (based on MAINTENANCE STATUS) and determination of FURNACE TROUBLE are dealt with in one location (the PMC) in Candidate 2. In Candidate 3, each FMC must check the status and know to send the bell and light alarms to the offices; the FMC also needs to look at the TROUBLESOME FURNACE LIST to determine if it is on the list.

4. Because of the added complex processing that the FMCs would need to perform for the Candidate 3 design, as well as the self-test at the furnaces, Candidate 2 will probably be more cost-effective in the long run.

Comments

- At this point, you may also decide to go with a new alternative that combines the best of two or more candidates. For example, the Plant Subsystem of Candidate 2 could be modified to send alarm signals to the offices (as in Candidate 3) instead of communicating with the bells and light more directly. Then the FAO and MO Subsystems of Candidate 3 could be used. If a decision is made to combine alternatives into a new design, then the previous steps to analyze that design must be performed and these decisions documented for future reference. This example is food for thought, but we will be using Candidate 2 as it stands for the rest of the solution.

5.5.4   Step 4: Choose the System Design

We have chosen Candidate 2 and will complete the design for this solution. Figure 5-47 illustrates the design chosen. The description below addresses the design in an informal manner prior to continuing the steps of the methodology.

- The first decision is to retain the mainframe computer at the FAO, adding a similar make and capacity machine at the MO. The computers will be called the FAOC and MOC, respectively.

- In order to gather the data at each furnace, a microprocessor controller will be installed at the same time as additional sensors and analog-to-digital converter

Requirements Model Component \ Architecture Model Component	Data Concentrator Computer 3.1	Furnace Monitor Computer 3.2	Digital Temp. Sensor 3.3	Output Rate Sensor 3.4	Maint. Status Sensor 3.5	Electrical Status Sensor 3.6	Fuel Control 3.7	Furnace Control 3.8
1.1 Maintain Schedule	X	X						
1.2.1 Read Temperature		X	X					
1.2.2 Control Fuel Valve		X					X	
1.2.3 Control Temperature Reading		X						
1.3 Generate Temperature Report	X	X						
2.1 Maintain Troublesome Furnace List	X	X						
2.2 Record Detailed Status	X	X				X		
CSpec 2		X						
3.1 Determine Maintenance Status	X	X			X			
3.2 Control Flashing Light	X	X						
3.3 Ring Bells Once	X	X						
3.4 Send Impaired Status	X	X						
3.5 Send Critical Status	X	X						
3.6 Ring Bell-Safety Hazard	X	X						
3.7 Shutdown Furnace		X						X
3.8 Clear Safety Alarm	X	X						
CSpec 3		X						
5.1 Record Output Rate	X	X		X				

Figure 5-46   Candidate 3: Plant Subsystem Requirements Traceability Matrix

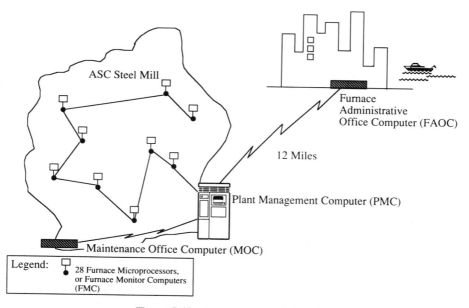

Figure 5-47   Chosen System Architecture

(ADC) interfaces to existing sensors. This will be called the Furnace Monitor Computer (FMC).

- Because of the expense of communication links from each of the 28 FMCs to the FAOC and MOC, a computer will be added at the plant to serve as a data concentrator; it will link the 28 microprocessors with the FAOC and MOC.
- In addition, this computer will serve as the link between the FAOC and MOC, to satisfy likely future requirements for communication between those offices.
- A further, and very important, use of the computer at the plant will be to serve as the maintenance center for the automated FMS. This computer will be called the Plant Management Computer (PMC). (Note: this is not the maintenance center for the *production of iron* and control of the blast furnaces, but the maintenance center for the *control and maintenance of the computer systems*.)
- Various alternatives were considered for the communication between the 28 FMC microprocessors and the PMC; the decision was to use a multidrop line in order to minimize cost of communication within the plant itself. There is some concern about response time in the system, but initial analyses indicate that buffering at each furnace combined with high data rates once the furnace is polled will satisfy the stated needs.

Step 4.1   Create (top-level) architecture interconnect diagram. Figure 5-48 illustrates the top-level interfaces.

Comments

- This diagram illustrates the identification of the interface between architecture modules in the associated AFD. Notice that the interfaces to the "outside world" are not shown. This sometimes takes place because those interfaces need to be defined or documented in a place that is often beyond the scope of this system. Another possibility is that the actual interface will be defined within the breakdown of the individual architecture module that implements it. The latter is the case here, especially within the Plant Subsystem.

Step 4.2   Determine characteristics of each interface. The AIS associated with the top-level AID is given in Figure 5-49.

Comments

- The description of each bus is to be detailed in the associated AIS(s). We are only showing the skeleton here. Others within this example will be described in more detail.

Architecture Module 3: Plant Subsystem   Figure 5-50 shows the AID for the Plant Subsystem. The associated AIS skeletons are given in Figure 5-51.

Comments

- Here is where the duplication actually shows up. For example, there are Max Furnaces Furnace Subsystems, numbered from 1 to "MAX FURNACES" (28). The breakdown of the Furnace Subsystem does not need to show the duplication of the individual pieces, since the whole diagram is duplicated.

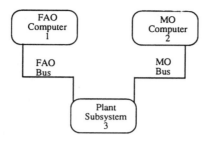

Figure 5-48 AID 0: Furnace Monitoring System

Architecture Module 3.2: Furnace Subsystem Figure 5-52 shows the architecture interfaces for the Furnace Subsystem. As mentioned earlier, the duplication need not show up here, since the entire Furnace Subsystem is duplicated per furnace. If all the modules for the entire system were drawn on one diagram (see Figure 5-53), then the duplication would have to be shown for each. This is about as large and complex a system for which it is useful to draw this overall diagram. It demonstrates the duplication of all architecture modules (hardware or software) in one place. For larger, more complex systems, this may not be feasible; it could then be done on a subsystem level.

The associated interface specifications for the Furnace Subsystem are illustrated in Figure 5-54.

Comments

- Notice details of the temperature bus, showing the actual hardware characteristics that the software will need to know in order to interface with the DTS.

Configuration Item List The following is the list of CSCIs and HWCIs identified for the Furnace Monitoring System.

CSCIs:

1. FAO Computer application software
2. MO Computer application software
3. Plant Management Computer (PMC) application software
4. Furnace Monitor Computer (FMC) application software

HWCIs:

1. FAO Computer hardware
2. MO Computer hardware (duplicate of #1)

AIS: FAO Bus
The information on this bus will be ...
The characteristics of this bus will be ...

AIS: MO Bus
The information on this bus will be ...
The characteristics of this bus will be ...

Figure 5-49 AIS associated with AID 0

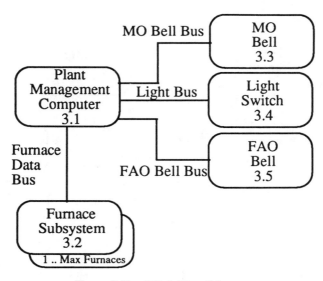

Figure 5-50 AID 3: Plant Subsystem

AIS: **MO BELL BUS**
•••

AIS: **Light Bus**
•••

AIS: **FAO Bell Bus**
•••

AIS: **Furnace Data Bus**
The Furnace Data Bus provides the interface between the PMC and the Furnace Subsystem, specifically with the Furnace Monitor Computer (FMC).
•••

Figure 5-51 AIS associated with AID 3

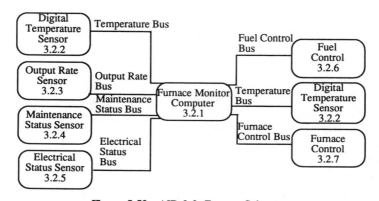

Figure 5-52 AID 3.2: Furnace Subsystem

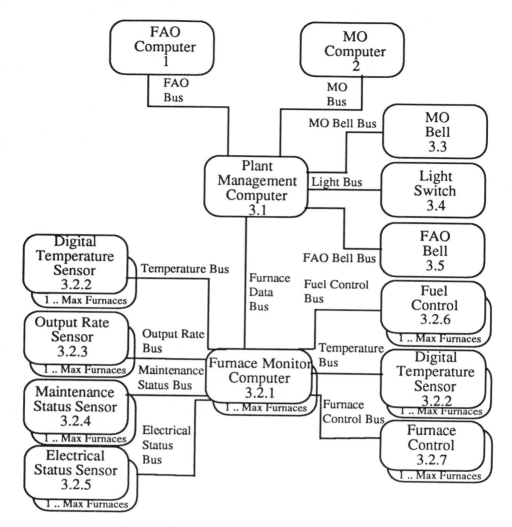

Figure 5-53 "Overall" Architecture Interconnect Diagram

3. PMC hardware
4. FMC hardware (one for each furnace)
5. MO bell
6. Light switch
7. FAO bell
8. Digital temperature sensor (one for each furnace)
9. Output rate sensor (one for each furnace)
10. Maintenance status sensor (one for each furnace)
11. Electrical status sensor (one for each furnace)

AIS: Temperature Bus
The Temperature Bus is used to gather temperature information from one of MAX THERMOMETERS (15) of a given furnace.

The bus operates are as follows:
Place a THERMOMETER NUMBER in the thermometer buffer at address 16#00B4#.

A TEMPERATURE INTERRUPT will be sent from the hardware device to address 16#00B0# when the corresponding TEMPERATURE has been placed in the temperature buffer at 16#00B2#.

AIS: Output Rate Bus
•••

AIS: Maintenance Status Bus
•••

AIS: Electrical Status Bus
•••

AIS: Fuel Control Bus
•••

AIS: Furnace Control Bus
•••

Figure 5-54   AIS associated with AID 3.2

12. Fuel control (one for each furnace)
13. Furnace control (one for each furnace)

5.5.5   Final Architecture Dictionary

ALL CLEAR CMD = * Indicator to turn off safety alarm *

BELL ALARMS = FAO Bell + MO Bell

DETAILED STATUS = Max Detailed Status Points {Electrical Reading}

DETAILED STATUS REPORT = * Report including Detailed Status currently available *
Rate = upon request

DETAILED STATUS REPORT REQUEST = * Request for report of detailed status on all troublesome furnaces *

ELECTRICAL READING = * Single electrical status point *
Range = 0 to 570
Units = millivolt
Resolution = millivolt
Rate = monitored "continuously" when furnace is marked as troublesome

FAO BELL = * Indication to ring bell in FAO *
Rate = once when first furnace becomes critical, and every second when a furnace is a safety hazard

FAO DISPLAY = Report

FAO INPUT = [Monitoring Info | Report Request]
* Note that FAO cannot request detailed status report *

FAO REQUEST = [Scheduling Info | Temperature Request]

FLASHING LIGHT = ["On" | "Off"] * Control the flashing light in the MO *

FUEL REDUCTION = [High Fuel Reduction | Low Fuel Reduction]
* Amount of fuel to reduce due to hot furnace *
Rate = event-driven; depends on temperature of furnace

FULL REPORT = * Report containing all info for all furnaces *
Rate = upon request

FULL REPORT REQUEST = * Request for a full report on all furnaces *

FURNACE INFO = [Furnace Temperature | Output Rate | Maintenance Status | Detailed Status]

FURNACE NUMBER = * Number assigned to furnace for automation/management purposes *
Range = 1 to Max Furnaces

FURNACE SHUTDOWN = * Indication to turn off furnace for safety purposes *

FURNACE STATUS = Furnace Number + Maintenance Status Rate = once every 5 minutes when furnace is impaired, or once every minute when furnace is critical

FURNACE TEMPERATURE = * Actual temperature of furnace *
Units = °F
Range = 900 to 3700
Resolution = 1 degree
Rate = event-driven; according to schedule

FURNACE TROUBLE = ["Troubled" | "Not Troubled"] * Indication of furnace detected to be in trouble or no longer troubled *

HIGH FUEL REDUCTION = * Actual fuel reduction percentage = 20 percent *

INPUT MIX = * Mixture of raw materials being placed in furnace *
(Not further defined for this example)

INPUT MIX INFO = 1{Furnace Number +Input Mix}Max Furnaces
Rate = event-driven

LOW FUEL REDUCTION = * Actual fuel reduction percentage = 10 percent *

MAINTENANCE STATUS = ["Normal" | "Degraded" | "Impaired" | "Critical" | "Safety Hazard"]
Rate = monitored "continuously"

MAINTENANCE STATUS REPORT = * Report containing the Maintenance Status for a single furnace *
Rate = upon request

MAINTENANCE STATUS REPORT REQUEST = Furnace Number * Request for report of maintenance status for a given furnace *
Rate = event-driven

MAX DETAILED STATUS POINTS = * Number of electrical status points at a furnace—currently 10 *

MAX FURNACES = * Number of furnaces in plant that can be automatically monitored—currently 28 *

MAX THERMOMETERS = * Number of thermometers attached to a furnace—currently 15 *

MO BELL = * Indication to ring bell in MO *
Rate = once when first furnace becomes critical, and every second when a furnace is a safety hazard.
MO DISPLAY = [Report | Furnace Status]
MO INPUT = [All Clear Cmd | Report Request | Troublesome Furnace List]
MO REQUEST = [Troublesome Furnace List | Temperature Request]
MONITOR CHANGE = ["On Troublesome List" | "Off Troublesome List"]
MONITOR COMMAND = [Scheduling Info | Furnace Trouble | Temperature Request]
MONITOR FREQUENCY = * Frequency at which to monitor a thermometer *
Range = 0 to 144
Units = readings/day
Resolution = 10 minutes
Rate = change is event-driven
MONITORING INFO = [Scheduling Info | Input Mix Info]
OUTPUT RATE = * Amount of molten iron being produced *
Units = tons/minute
Range = 0.0 to 50.0
Resolution = 0.05 tons
Rate = monitored "continuously"
OUTPUT RATE REPORT = * Report containing the Output Rate of a subset of furnaces *
Rate = upon request
OUTPUT RATE REPORT REQUEST = 1 {Furnace Number} Max Furnaces * Request for report of output rate on subset of furnaces *
Rate = event-driven
PLANT INFO = 1 {Furnace Info + Furnace Number} Max Furnaces
REPORT = [Full Report | Maintenance Status Report | Temperature Report | Output Rate Report | Detailed Status Report | Others??]
* "Others" may include a management report of type and quality of steel produced (depends on input mix, temperature, functioning of furnace) | maintenance report including problems over time per furnace *
(Others not further defined for this example)
REPORT REQUEST = [Full Report Request | Maintenance Status Report Request | Temperature Report Request | Output Rate Report Request | Detailed Status Report Request | Others...]
* Other reports are not defined at this point and will not be further defined for this example *
Rate = event-driven
SCHEDULING INFO = 1{Furnace Number + 1{Thermometer Number + Monitor Frequency}Max Thermometers}Max Furnaces
Rate = event-driven
SELF-STATUS = * Status of individual computer *

STATUS REQUEST = 1{Furnace Number}Max Furnaces
* Request for status of Furnace Monitoring System *

SYSTEM STATUS = * Overall status of the Furnace Monitoring System - and individual furnace status *
* System Status is not further defined for this example *

TEMPERATURE INTERRUPT = * Hardware interrupt indicating that a temperature has been placed in the associated hardware buffer *

TEMPERATURE REPORT = * Report of one or all temperatures for a single furnace *
Rate = upon request

TEMPERATURE REPORT REQUEST = Furnace Number + 1 {Thermometer Number} Max Thermometers * Request for report of subset of temperatures for a given furnace *
Rate = event-driven

TEMPERATURE REQUEST = Furnace Number + Thermometer Number
* Indication to check the temperature immediately *

THERMOMETER NUMBER = * Number assigned to thermometer for automation/management purposes *
Range = 1 to Max Thermometers

TROUBLESOME FURNACE LIST = 1{Furnace Number + Troublesome Status Indicator}Max Furnaces
Rate = event-driven

TROUBLESOME FURNACE INDICATOR = ["Add" | "Delete"] * Indication to add or delete a furnace from the troublesome furnace list *

Comments

- Notice that the architecture dictionary does *not* contain the flows from the system requirements model that are internal to a given architecture module. Examples of this include the data stores, such as FURNACE DATA, and process activators, such as EVALUATE FURNACE.

5.6 KEYS TO UNDERSTANDING

- System design has to do with the establishment of the physical components of the system. It is conducted iteratively with system requirements analysis.
- It is a fundamentally creative process, with primary steps of Formulation, Analysis, Tradeoff, and Selection/Validation.
- The graphics, guidelines, and steps of SSEM will help you understand and conduct system design, especially as it is relevant to the specification of software requirements.
- For the software engineer, the key outputs of system design are the:
  ◦ Identification of CSCIs
  ◦ Allocation of essential requirements to the CSCIs
  ◦ Identification of derived requirements
  ◦ Specification of interfaces to the CSCIs, both hardware and software

CHAPTER 6

Software Requirements Analysis

Objective: to show how to derive the more detailed requirements necessary to conduct a successful software development; the requirements are similar to the essential model for the system requirements analysis, adapted to software needs

The purpose of this chapter is to describe the methods to be used during the software requirements analysis phase of the development cycle. This phase is highlighted in Figure 6-1, which illustrates the phases of the development cycle.

Software requirements analysis is the detailed specification of the necessary functionality of each CSCI, and the interfaces among all CSCIs and HWCIs.

This phase is a vital transition point, with an overlap of systems engineering and software engineering viewpoints. The input to this phase is the system design expressed for each individual CSCI, along with the system requirements allocated to each CSCI. The output is the detailed set of software requirements for each .CSCI.

To accomplish the methodology definition, the following items are covered:

- Transition from system design to software requirements analysis
- Graphics
- Guidelines
- Methodology — step by step
- Example

The discussion of graphics and guidelines in this chapter is quite short; it only addresses the few things that are different from system requirements analysis. *All the lessons, graphics, guidelines, and so on from system requirements analysis are applicable to the specific issues of software requirements analysis.*

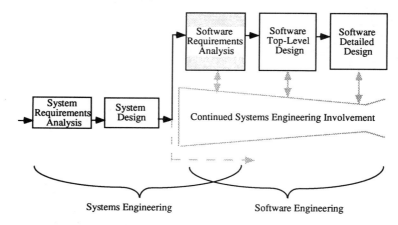

Figure 6-1 Phases of the Development Cycle

6.1 TRANSITION FROM SYSTEM DESIGN TO SOFTWARE REQUIREMENTS ANALYSIS

The system design process produced an allocation of requirements to CSCIs and HWCIs and a specification of the interfaces between these configuration items (CIs).

The transition to this phase involves a change of focus from the overall system to the individual CSCIs and their interfaces among each other and the other parts of the system. The creation of additional requirements to satisfy the system design (the *derived* requirements) illustrates how the system design drives the software requirements.

The transition from systems design to software requirements analysis is primarily functional. This means that a change in perspective is required by the engineers performing the task. Because systems engineering is a function performed on a project, the transition is not organizational in nature and should not be viewed that way. Rather, the engineers performing software engineering and the engineers performing system engineering now need to view those CSCIs they specified during the system design process as separate entities to be defined and created. The "handoff" is fundamentally a continuation of interactions between the statement of software requirements and system design, to a lower level of refinement.

Systems engineering is responsible for the completeness of the data and transmission of a complete understanding of the requirements, while software engineering is responsible for ensuring that the software can meet the performance requirements in the specified environment. Hence, the handoff is the checking, verification, understanding, and acceptance of the system design (as complete and capable of being implemented) by the software engineering function. There is likely to be continued iteration as the software requirements are analyzed and as preliminary specification materials are prepared and reviewed. This iteration occurs because as the requirements are refined into greater levels of detail, items previously unknown will become more apparent. It is important to understand that each successive iteration may cause additional system design activities to ensure a complete view of the overall system. It is, in fact, this iteration that refines the system design, and resulting software requirements, into an acceptable solution to system requirements.

In addition to the iteration *backward,* with the system design, there is iteration *forward,* with the software design. This requirements–design iteration is just like the requirements–design iteration at the system level discussed in detail in Chapter 2. This is accomplished in any of a number of ways. For example, there may already be preliminary designs existing from an earlier Demonstration and Validation phase. Alternatively, there may be explicit efforts for "trial" designs as risk reduction efforts, much in the same way as alternate system designs were developed and "traded off" with regard to the requirements. Such trial designs are likely to be evaluated with analytical tools, simulations, prototypes, and so on. These activities are all legitimately part of the software requirements specification phase.

Emphasis on trial designs, prototypes, and risk reduction activity—combined with the sort of iteration shown in Figures 2-3 and 2-4 and the legacy and repeated development shown in Figures 2-1 and 2-2—leads to a development approach called "spiral." The original form of the spiral model was shown as Figure 2-6. SSEM is entirely consistent with—even encourages—such spiral management approaches.

With the understanding of both backward and forward iteration, and of chaos, legacy, and spirals, we can now return to our attempt to provide our nominal or *rational* model of development. The remainder of this chapter progresses through the process, assuming a fixed allocation of requirements to a CSCI, and resulting in a single statement of software requirements for the CSCI.

6.2 GRAPHICS

This section describes the graphics that are used for the methodology; they represent the *software requirements model.* The graphics presented in this section are not intended to tell the whole story of the methodology and are not necessarily tightly interrelated; they are only intended to introduce the *form* of the notation. The final section of the chapter, "FMS Example," will use these graphics, the guidelines of the next section, and the step-by-step methodology to present an integrated picture. Recommended conventions are also listed. The graphics used for software requirements analysis and associated data are listed as follows, with relationships as illustrated in Figure 6-2.

- Enhanced flow diagram (EFD)
- Data context diagram (DCD)
- Data flow diagrams (DFD)
    - Diagram
    - Process specifications (PSpec)
- Data dictionary
- Control context diagram (CCD)
- Control flow diagrams (CFD)
    - Diagram
    - Control specifications (CSpec)
        - Decision Tables

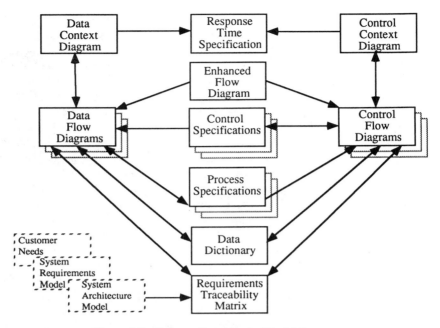

Figure 6-2 Software Requirements Model Components

- Process activation tables (PAT)
- State transition diagrams/tables (STD/STT)
- Response time specification (RTS)
- Requirements traceability matrix (RTM)

Most of the graphics are the same as those used for systems requirements analysis (see Section 4.1). Therefore, we will cover in detail only the new graphics (namely the EFD) or different contexts of graphics (RTM) already discussed.

6.2.1 Enhanced Flow Diagram (EFD)

The purpose of the enhanced flow diagram (EFD) is to provide a starting point for the development of data flow diagrams (DFDs). It allows us to start with a DFD that captures all of the system requirements (from system requirements analysis) that have been allocated to this CSCI during system design and then add any derived requirements based on the system architecture of system design. These processes will be aggregated into higher-level processes for DFD 0.

Figure 6-3 gives an example of an EFD. In it we see that all the procedures from the system requirements model (such as "Maintain Schedule" (1.1)) are shown with the process number from the system model kept. Derived requirements (such as "Received Command from PMC") are included to show the interfaces added to satisfy the system design; these are labeled as being "derived." The processes are then assigned a number for the purposes of this diagram, so that they can be easily referred to when grouping them for DFD 0.

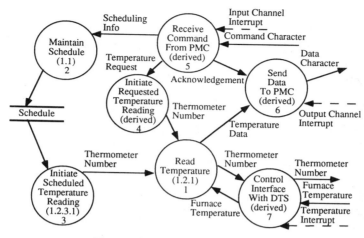

Figure 6-3 Enhanced Flow Diagram

It is useful to show the derived processes separate to keep the essential requirements as pure as possible, to organize the routing of information to or from another CI, and to provide traceability as discussed in earlier chapters.

Once we've established this initial CSCI decomposition, we are then ready to tackle the creation of DFD 0. The processes are aggregated together, using the coupling and cohesion principles related to composition, into the processes of DFD 0.

Remember that the purpose of the EFD is to provide a starting point for the decomposition, allowing us to have sound reasons for the establishment of the processes of DFD 0. Where, then, does the EFD fit in the documentation scheme? The answer is that it does not! The EFD is never provided to a customer; it is saved, however, as an integral part of project information for future reference.

6.2.2 Requirements Traceability Matrix (RTM)

The RTM during software requirements analysis depicts the allocation of the system requirements (from system requirements model and system architecture model) to the components of the software requirements model. The RTM graphic is discussed in detail in Section 4.1.7.

6.3 GUIDELINES

This section introduces several sets of guidelines for use in the methodology steps. The application of these rules will be indicated at the appropriate steps in the methodology. The guidelines include:

- Information to include in the software requirements analysis*
- Coupling and cohesion
- Physical perspectives*
- Grouping of EFD processes*
- Data flow diagram hints
- Constructing a leveled set of processes

- Separating data and control
- Checklists for completion and consistency (balancing)

Most of these guidelines follow those given in Hatley & Pirbhai [HAT87]. Only those guidelines which have not already been discussed in Section 4.2 will be covered here (as indicated by an asterisk, *).

6.3.1 Information to Include in the Software Level Analysis

What should be included in the requirements model during software requirements analysis?

1. Include only those requirements that must be implemented regardless of the technology used! Do *not* include any software design-specific "requirements."
2. Only the timing between events at the CSCI inputs and outputs—the external timing—is of concern. Internal timing is entirely a design issue. An exception to this is for distributed CSCIs, such as Network Controllers or distributed data base managers. For these CSCIs, it may be necessary to specify the timing involved with the network.

6.3.2 Physical Perspectives

The following is a list of some physical perspectives that it is useful to consider during the analysis of the software.

1. *User interface processing* refers here to enhancements to the system-to-user interface that are not described in the system requirements model. These enhancements are based on use of available technology and on various cost, operational environment, and other criteria. Design tradeoffs were made during system design to select the physical user–machine interface and need to be reflected as derived requirements in the software specification.
2. *Maintenance, self-test, and redundancy processing* refers to various types of additional, design-specific requirements for maintenance, self-test, and redundancy (fault tolerance), which arose in system design when an implementation technology that met the system's reliability and performance criteria was selected and its particular characteristics were analyzed.
3. *Input processing* refers to additional processing, dependent on technology decisions of system design, to handle the communications across the CSCI's boundary that were not addressed in the system requirements model and are not part of the user interface or a maintenance interface. The interface processing often includes communication with HWCIs. The input processing accepts physical input from a source and converts it to a logical form usable by the CSCI.
4. *Output processing* considerations are the same as those for input processing. The output processing takes the CSCI's logical output and converts it to a physical form acceptable to the output sink.

Not ever CSCI will need additional processing in every one of these areas. For example, there are CSCIs that do not interface with other CSCIs but only with users. These CSCIs need no processing un the input areas, but they do need processing in the user interface area. An important aspect of looking at these areas is that it can be used to organize and allocate tasks and responsibilities on a project. This allows for division of expertise in accordance with these areas throughout software development. They also draw the software analyst's attention to the different aspects of the CSCI.

The four perspectives are those used as specific illustrations in the *architecture template* of Figure 5-3. As stated in the discussion at the end of Section 5.2.1, they are not necessarily exhaustive. These specific interfaces have been found to be useful in general, but each specific application may give rise to additional or different perspectives to consider.

6.3.3 Grouping EFD Processes

The guidelines for grouping of processes on the EFD are similar to those for grouping actions during system requirements analysis. The primary rule is to minimize the complexity of the interfaces (the data flow). In other words, it is important that the processes be loosely coupled. The following list is in priority order (see Section 4.2.3.3 for details).

1. Common Data Access
2. Common Functionality
3. Common Terminator
4. Common Periodicity
5. Experience

6.4 METHODOLOGY—STEP BY STEP

This section goes through the details of the methodology in a step-by-step style to give an understanding for the issues that come up. The guidelines introduced above are discussed at the appropriate step of the methodology.

The building of the software requirements model is a process of interpreting the requirements from the previous phase that have been allocated to this CSCI in the preliminary software requirements specification. This process will test whether the statements are self-consistent and complete, and it should lead to further dialogue where they are not. The following lists the steps in the general order that they occur. In practice, some may be worked on in parallel and iteratively.

1. Draw preliminary data and control context diagrams.
2. Establish data dictionary.
3. Construct enhanced flow diagram.
4. Construct top-level DFD.
5. Determine need for control at top level.
6. Document external timing.
7. Document allocation to top-level processes.
8. Draw next-level DFD.
9. Determine need for control at this level.
10. Update data dictionary.
11. Document traceability.
12. When am I done?

Step 1   Draw preliminary data and control context diagrams.   Identify external entities with which the CSCI is required to communicate and the major information groups that must flow between the CSCI and these entities. The entities may be external to the system as a whole or be other portions of the system being developed (HWCIs or CSCIs) identified within the system design. Draw the DCD depicting the flow of information between the CSCI and the environment in which it operates. If there is any control indicated by the preliminary requirements, then draw the appropriate CCD (or add to the DCD).

If there are so many interfaces that it becomes difficult to show the context diagram on a single sheet, consideration should be given to returning to the systems engineering methods (system design process) for potential decomposition into two or more CSCIs (see Chapter 5).

Step 2   Establish data dictionary.   Establish the data dictionary to contain the definitions for all of the information that flows through the CSCI as documented by the DCD and CCD. This dictionary will be a new one, separate from the one used during system requirements analysis and system design. Much of the contents can be extracted from the earlier dictionary, but this one will contain only information necessary for this CSCI to operate. The amount of detail for each entry at this point depends on how well the interface to the external entity is defined. The full definition will be necessary before software requirements analysis is complete.

Step 3   Construct enhanced flow diagram.   Draw a preliminary EFD that includes all of the essential requirements (processes and control) that have been allocated to this CSCI in the requirements traceability matrix (RTM) of the system architecture model. Retain the process numbers from the RTM, annotating as necessary to indicate partial assignment of a process.

Enhance this diagram to include any physical characteristics and derived requirements as indicated by the system architecture model (RTM, MSpec, AFD, AID, and AIS). This may include deriving processes (bubbles) to add to the EFD for these requirements. Use the guidelines for physical perspectives in order to ensure coverage of all of the derived requirements.

It is intended that the EFD be internal documentation, not delivered to the customer but saved for future reference.

Step 4   Construct top-level data flow diagram.   Construct a top-level DFD by representing the major functional grouping of processes in the EFD and showing the major information group data flows between them and the external environment. Coupling and cohesion principles apply here, as well as the aggregation rules for grouping of the EFD processes. If the EFD is simple enough, it could potentially become the top-level DFD itself. The rationale for the grouping should be captured for future reference (such as when customer requirements change).

Study the resulting diagram and ask:

- Do the processes relate well to the way that the customers view the system requirements? Would repartitioning make the requirements clearer?

- Are the flows correct? Can the processes reasonably produce their stated outputs with the given inputs? Would the picture be clearer if the flows were regrouped?
- Are the physical interfaces to other CSCIs or HWCIs represented clearly? Refer to the physical perspectives guidelines.

Make any changes resulting from the answers to the above questions. Update the DCD and data dictionary as appropriate.

Often on systems where the engineers have worked on similar projects before, there is an "intuition" or engineering judgment that can be used in conjunction with these techniques to verify and validate the functions presented.

If there are a large number of system design–related interfaces and associated events for the CSCI (in other words, many derived requirements that result in events), you may wish to do a complete event analysis, as described in Chapter 4. Then the aggregation of bubbles into DFD 0 proceeds as before. The advantage of the EFD approach is that it is easier to accomplish and clearly separates the requirements of the system design from the essential customer requirements.

Step 5   Determine need for control at top level.   Examine the EFD and the allocated CSpecs from the RTM of the system architecture model to decide if there are any modes or conditions of the CSCI under which any of the top-level processes require activating or deactivating (or a portion of one needs to be controlled by another top-level process). If so, identify the signals representing those modes or conditions, assign them as control signals on the CFD or on the DFD, and then construct a CSpec that includes the appropriate diagrams (such as decision tables or STDs). Before taking this step, be sure that the same effect would not be obtained through the inherent presence or absence of the appropriate data in these modes and conditions. Remember that we prefer data flows when possible, using control flows only when necessary. Use the rules for separation of data and control to help make this decision.

A guideline here is that unless the diagram would be too complex, the control flows should be overlaid on the DFD rather than drawn on a separate diagram. If you do use separate diagrams, remember to show all the processes on both to allow for a complete picture.

Update the data dictionary with the control information.

Step 6   Document external timing.   Draw a response time specification (RTS) to document the external timing of the CSCI. This will include a subset from the response time allocation (RTA) of system design. It will also contain the allocated, or derived, response times. The table contains all the required responses of this CSCI (often called a *timing budget*) necessary to allow the CSCI to satisfy overall essential response times. Remember that only the external response times should be specified. Internal timing (within the CSCI) is left for design. An exception to this is for distributed CSCIs, such as Network Controllers or distributed data base managers. For these CSCIs, it may be necessary to specify the timing involved with the network. Additional response times may be added as needed for derived requirements in areas such as handling of interrupts and other I/O protocol.

Step 7   Document allocation to top-level processes.   Draw an RTM depicting the allocation of the system requirements model processes and CSpecs to the top-level processes identified. Include traceability to any derived requirements from the system architecture model as well.

Step 8   Draw next-level DFD.   Decompose each process into a child diagram that gives more details about the accomplishment of the higher-level requirement. Remember to concentrate on *what* the software must do, not *how* it will do it. Apply the principles for analyzing a set of processes by level here at each iteration.

Step 9   Determine need for control at this level.   Examine the requirements at this level, as in Step 5, to decide on the necessity for a CFD. Follow the same rules for separation of data and control. Note that most control will occur in the top levels of the CSCI. Very low-level control can often be handled within a PSpec.

Step 10   Update data dictionary.   Based on this level of diagrams, add any new information to the data dictionary and update appropriate entries.

Step 11   Document traceability.   Draw an RTM depicting the allocation of the system requirements model and system architecture to the processes at this level, as in Step 7. All requirements must eventually be satisfied by a PSpec.

Step 12   When am I done?   Iterate for each process, performing the steps until you can clearly express the function of the process in text or equations or with a simple diagram. For these bottom-level (primitive) processes, a PSpec must be written, describing what the process does. The PSpecs become the "bottom" network of the DFD process. An important guideline is that each of the requirements stated in the PSpec will result in a customer-witnessed test at the CSCI level. Although it is important to specify thoroughly what the CSCI is to accomplish, take care not to overspecify the system or to constrain the software design.

For very large CSCIs, write a simple description of the DFDs at several intermediate levels. Although this may seem redundant to the diagrams, it helps clarify your thoughts as the analyst, and it provides the reader with some additional information as to where you are in the process. They become useful when generating the actual documentation associated with this phase.

Since the top-level diagrams are the ones that will determine how all the analysis from this point on is partitioned and, therefore, how the analysts will divide up the tasks, it is worth spending more time on it at this high level than at lower ones.

Each time that two or three levels have been done, review and revise them to improve their understandability and correctness; check for balancing errors according to the guidelines and fix any that are found; resolve requirements ambiguities and omissions as soon as possible.

Software requirements analysis is considered complete when the following questions can be answered in the affirmative.

1. Are the requirements complete?
2. Are the requirements free from extraneous information or design?

3. Is the software requirements model consistent within itself and balanced?
4. Is the model consistent with the rest of the system?
5. Do all software requirements trace back to system (or derived) requirement(s)?
6. Have all system requirements for this CSCI been allocated to software requirement(s)?

Remember that what you come up with here must continue the requirements traceability to the system requirements and that it forms the basis for requirements traceability for the rest of the software development cycle. Be as complete and unambiguous as possible.

6.5   FMS SOFTWARE REQUIREMENTS ANALYSIS EXAMPLE

This section provides an example of the software requirements analysis methodology, essentially solving the following problem. If you wish to test your knowledge of the methods presented, you may wish to solve the problem yourself before looking at the solution.

Assignment: Perform a software requirements analysis for the automation of the CSCI for the Furnace Monitor Computer (FMC). Provide the analysis for the full automation of the process described in the systems requirements model, with the system design of the system architecture model. (You may wish to use the interface description between the FMC and the Plant Management Computer (PMC) that follows this assignment.) Make whatever assumptions you feel are necessary, for example the temperature range of the furnaces, the bounds on output, and the various states of the furnace relative to maintenance status. Normally, this is the sort of information that would come about from your interview with the customer and more detailed analysis of the current process. For the purpose of this example, what is important is that you *identify your additional information needs* and then pick whatever values seem appropriate.

The interface used for this solution between the PMC and the FMC, known as the Furnace Data Bus, is as follows. We are not going to be showing the interface to send the Self Status information from the FMC to the PMC. Except for hardware-specific issues such as interrupts, this information is also typical of CSCI-to-CSCI interface information in a single processor.

This bus is made up of two channels: one for input to the FMC and one for output from the FMC. *Furnace Monitor Packets* are sent to the FMC and *Furnace Temperature Packets* are received from the FMC by the PMC. Acknowledgments are sent or received for each of the data packets listed above. The packets are received and transmitted one ASCII character at a time; their formats follow. Details of each individual packet field are described in the dictionary entry for that field.

Furnace Monitor Packet Format   (STX)(M)(other data based on M)(ETX)

The "other data" is one of the following formats, based on the value of M (0, 1, or 2):

   0. Scheduling Info data   (NN)(FFF)
   1. Immediate Temperature Request data   (NN)
   2. Troublesome Furnace Indication data   none

Furnace Data Packet Format   (STX)(D)(other data based on D)(ETX)

The "other data" is one of the following formats, based on the value of D (0, 1, 2, 2, or 3):

   0. Temperature Data data   (NN)(TTTT)
   1. Maintenance Status data   (S)
   2. Detailed Status data   (10 * EEE)
   3. Ouput Rate data   (OOOO)

Acknowledgment Format   (STX)(A)(ETX)

where

M = MONITOR COMMAND TYPE (1 character)
    0 = Scheduling Info
    1 = Immediate Temperature Request
    2 = Troublesome Furnace Indication

D = FURNACE DATA TYPE (1 character)
    0 = Temperature Data
    1 = Maintenance Status
    2 = Detailed Status
    3 = Output Rate

NN = THERMOMETER NUMBER (2 characters)

FFF = MONITOR FREQUENCY (3 characters)

$TTTT$ = FURNACE TEMPERATURE (4 characters)

S = MAINTENANCE STATUS (1 character)
    N = Normal
    D = Degraded
    I = Impaired
    C = Critical
    H = Safety Hazard

EEE = Electrical Status (3 characters per point, 30 characters total)

$OOOO$ = Output Rate (4 characters; it is assumed that the decimal point is between the second and third character)

A = single ACK or NAK character

ACK = positive acknowledgment character

NAK = negative acknowledgment character

STX = start of text character

ETX = end of text character

The same message protocol is used by each end of this interface as follows:

Receive processing: Receive a packet and check for validity. If valid, send positive acknowledgment (ACK). If invalid, send negative acknowledgment (NAK). The criteria for validity are that the packet must have an STX and an ETX. The fields of the packet must contain numbers in the correct range.

Transmit processing: Transmit the packet and wait for one of the following events:

1. Receive positive acknowledgment (ACK). Send next packet.
2. Receive negative acknowledgment (NAK). Retransmit same packet.
3. Time-out (two-second delay). Retransmit same packet.

If the same packet is transmitted three times without a positive acknowledgment, it is to be discarded and the next available packet transmitted.

The following hardware addresses are associated with each channel:

Input channel:

Interrupt address: 16#00A4# (generated when character is in buffer)

Buffer address: 16#00A6#

Output channel:

Interrupt address: 16#00A0# (generated when character has been taken)

Buffer address: 16#00A2#

Note: Although the communication protocol is highly simplified—even overly simplified—it is satisfactory for our purposes of showing the interfaces and their effect on the software design.

What follows is a completed software requirements model for the FMC, including answers to the questions you asked yourself (or should have asked yourself).

6.5.1 Step 1: Draw Preliminary Data and Control Context Diagrams

Figure 6-4 shows the preliminary DCD/CCD for the FMC CSCI.

Comments

According to the description of the interface to the Plant Management Computer (PMC), there is an input channel and an output channel of communication. Because of this, the interface(s) shown in the software requirements analysis will be to those channels rather than to the PMC directly.

• We might have shown the interface to the PMC as a direct one rather than through the PMC Input and Output Channels (see Figure 6-5). That may be the way in which a customer would view the system, but now we need to consider the view of the developer as well. This alternate diagram does not allow for the identification of the real protocol of the interface, in which one character, rather than an abstract packet, is sent or received at a time, with an associated interrupt. This is a good example of a case where the technology constraints—the derived requirements obtained from system design—are part of the "outside world." For the internal analysis of the CSCI, we will still

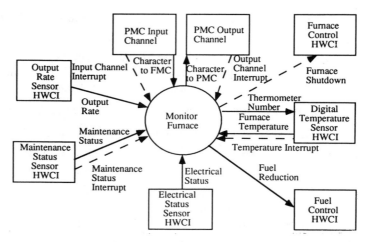

Figure 6-4 Data/Control Context Diagram for Furnace Monitor Computer CSCI

assume a "perfect" technology in order to develop the essential requirements for the software.

- Notice that the HWCIs identified in the system design (Output Rate Sensor, Maintenance Status Sensor, Electrical Status Sensor, Furnace Control, Digital Temperature Sensor (DTS), and Fuel Control) are shown here as terminators for this CSCI. Also shown are the PMC Input Channel and PMC Output Channel, as discussed in the item above. This diagram becomes important to illustrate all interfaces outside the CSCI being developed.

- Here we showed the data and control on one diagram. If they had been drawn separately, we would still have shown all terminators on the CCD, even where there was no control, for consistency.

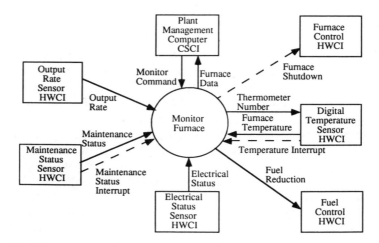

Figure 6-5 Alternate Data/Control Context Diagram (not used for example)

6.5.2   Step 2: Establish Data Dictionary

We need to establish the new data dictionary for this CSCI. The amount of detail for each entry is dependent on the level of definition of the interfaces to the externals within the system-level requirements and design. A great deal of the information in the data dictionary for this CSCI is captured from the earlier system data dictionary and architecture dictionary.

   Data Dictionary:

ACK = * ASCII ACK character, designating positive acknowledgment *

ACKNOWLEDGMENT = STX + [ACK | NAK] + ETX
   * Acknowledgment ASCII string sent to and received from PMC *
   Rate = event-driven

CHARACTER TO FMC = 1 character of [Acknowledgment | Furnace Monitor Packet]
   Rate = event-driven

CHARACTER TO PMC = 1 character of [Acknowledgment | Furnace Data Packet]
   Rate = event-driven

DETAILED STATUS = Max Detailed Status Points {Electrical Status}

ELECTRICAL STATUS = * Single electrical status point *
   Range = 0 to 570
   Units = millivolt
   Resolution = millivolt
   Rate = monitored "continuously" when furnace is marked as troublesome

ETX = * ASCII End of Text character *

FUEL REDUCTION = [High Fuel Reduction | Low Fuel Reduction]
   * Amount of fuel to reduce due to hot furnace *
   Rate = event-driven; depends on temperature of furnace

FURNACE DATA = [Temperature Data | Maintenance Status | Detailed Status | Output Rate]
   Rate = event-driven

FURNACE DATA PACKET = STX + Furnace Data Type + ASCII of Furnace Data + ETX
   Rate = event-driven

FURNACE DATA TYPE = * Type of Furnace Data contained in packet *
   Range 0 to 3 (ASCII character)
      where 0 = Temperature Data
            1 = Maintenance Status
            2 = Detailed Status
            3 = Output Rate

FURNACE MONITOR PACKET = STX + Monitor Command Type + ASCII of Monitor Command + ETX
   Rate = event-driven

FURNACE SHUTDOWN = * Indication to turn off furnace for safety purposes *

FURNACE TEMPERATURE = * Actual temperature of furnace *
Units = °F
Range = 900 to 3700
Resolution = 1 degree
Rate = event-driven; according to schedule

HIGH FUEL REDUCTION = * Actual fuel reduction percentage = 20 percent *

INPUT CHANNEL INTERRUPT = * Hardware interrupt indicating that a Character To FMC has been placed in the associated hardware buffer *
Rate = event-driven

LOW FUEL REDUCTION = * Actual fuel reduction percentage = 10 percent *

MAINTENANCE STATUS = ["Normal" | "Degraded" | "Impaired" | "Critical" | "Safety Hazard"]
Rate = monitored "continuously"

MAINTENANCE STATUS INTERRUPT = * Hardware interrupt indicating that the Maintenance Status has been placed in the associated hardware buffer *
Rate = event-driven; change in status

MAX DETAILED STATUS POINTS = * Number of electrical status points at a furnace—currently 10 *

MAX THERMOMETERS = * Number of thermometers attached to the furnace—currently 15 *

MONITOR COMMAND = [Scheduling Info | Temperature Request | Troublesome Furnace Indicator]
Rate = event-driven

MONITOR COMMAND TYPE = * Type of Monitor Command contained in packet *
Range = 0 to 2 (ASCII character)
    where 0 = Scheduling Info
          1 = Temperature Request
          2 = Troublesome Furnace Indicator

MONITOR FREQUENCY = * Frequency at which to monitor a thermometer *
Range = 0 to 144 (where 0 = stop monitoring)
Units = readings/day
Resolution = 10 minutes
Rate = change is event-driven

NAK = * ASCII NAK character − designating negative acknowledgment *

OUTPUT CHANNEL INTERRUPT = * Hardware inerrupt indicating that a Character To PMC has been taken from the associated hardware buffer *
Rate = event-driven

OUTPUT RATE = * Amount of molten iron being produced *
Units = tons/minute
Range = 0.0 to 50.0

Resolution = 0.05 tons
Rate = monitored "continuously"

SCHEDULING INFO = Thermometer Number + Monitor Frequency
Rate = event-driven

STX = * ASCII Start of Text character *

TEMPERATURE DATA = Thermometer Number + Furnace Temperature

TEMPERATURE INTERRUPT = * Hardware interrupt indicating that a temperature has been placed in the associated hardware buffer *
Rate = event-driven

TEMPERATURE REQUEST = Thermometer Number
* Indication to check the temperature of this thermometer immediately *
Rate = event-driven

THERMOMETER NUMBER = * Number assigned to thermometer for automation/management purposes *
Range = 1 to Max Thermometers

TROUBLESOME FURNACE INDICATOR = ["Start Monitoring" | "Stop Monitoring"]
* Indication to start or stop monitoring of detailed status *

6.5.3 Step 3: Construct Enhanced Flow Diagram

Figure 6-6 shows the enhanced flow diagram for the FMC CSCI.

Comments

- The processes from the system requirements model have their process number retained in parentheses. The *derived* processes from system design are marked "derived."

- Notice derived processes to handle the new physical interfaces with the PMC Channels and the DTS. The derived flows (from the architecture model) include the TEMPERATURE INTERRUPT from the DTS, the THERMOMETER NUMBER to the DTS, the INPUT_CHANNEL_INTERRUPT, COMMAND CHARACTER and OUTPUT_CHANNEL_INTERRUPT from the PMC, and the DATA CHARACTER to the PMC. The derived process "Initiate Requested Temperature Reading" has been added to portray the functionality required on receipt of a TEMPERATURE REQUEST.

  The reasons for adding the new processes for the physical control include the following:

1. The essential requirements should be kept as free as possible from worries about the actual technology used. For example, "Control Interface With DTS" shields "Read Temperature" from the physical processing involved to place the THERMOMETER NUMBER in a hardware buffer, process the TEMPERATURE INTERRUPT coming in, and copy the FURNACE TEMPERATURE from another hardware buffer.

2. The interface with the PMC is a derived interface, since it is internal to the system as a whole. We want to separate the derived requirements from the essential requirements.

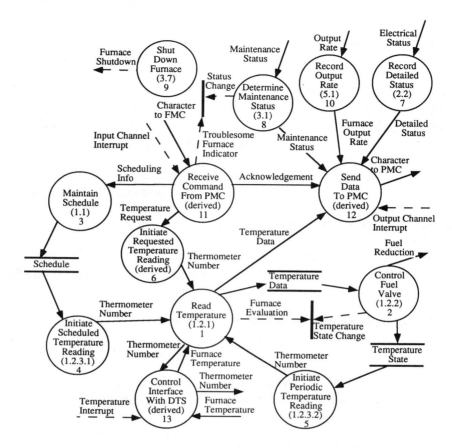

Figure 6-6 Enhanced Flow Diagram

3. Organize the routing of information to or from another CSCI. "Receive Command From PMC" handles the validation of the command data coming in and routes it appropriately. It also handles the protocol and interrupts that go along with that interface. These interrupts were derived from the AIS for the FURNACE DATA BUS.

- You may also wish to reconstruct a CSpec that contains only the control for the CSCI being developed. We will not show it here.

6.5.4 Step 4: Construct Top-Level Data Flow Diagram

The processes on the EFD are grouped to form the top-level DFD as shown in Figure 6-7.

Comments

- By grouping together Processes 1, 2, 5, 6, and 13, we have encapsulated all of the processing that deals with furnace temperatures. This includes the control

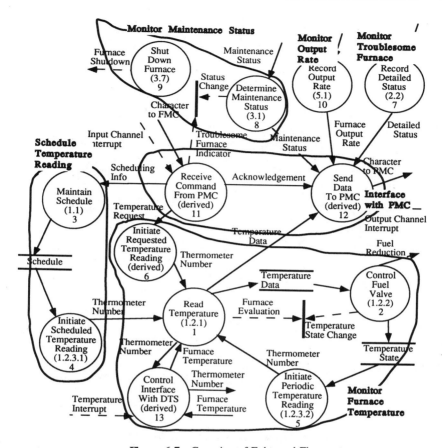

Figure 6-7 Grouping of Enhanced Flow

of the Fuel Valve and the DTS. This functionality's complexity (that it must be able to respond to either a scheduled reading or an immediate request) is hidden within it for decomposition later.

- Grouping of Processes 3 and 4 encapsulates the data store SCHEDULE.
- The interface to the PMC has been grouped together. The complexity of constructing packets for output to the PMC is hidden within the process.
- Processes 8 and 9 are grouped together, because they both operate based on maintenance status.
- Process 7 (Record Detailed Status) and Process 10 (Record Output Rate) are left by themselves, because their functionality is independent and distinct from the other processing.

Figure 6-8 shows the top-level DFD for the FMC CSCI.

Comments

- We are showing only the data flow here. Any control necessary will be added in the next step.

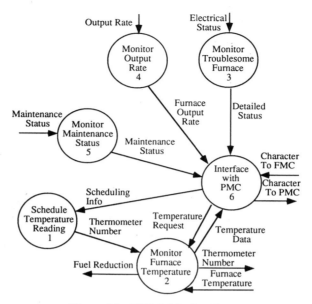

Figure 6-8   DFD 0: Monitor Furnace

- Note that we see the beginning of the numbering scheme for the software requirements model. These become the basis for the future traceability of software design.

6.5.5   Step 5: Determine Need for Control at Top Level

The control flow for the top level is shown in Figure 6-9. The associated CSpec is given in Figure 6-10.

Comments

- The control flow to get the interrupts (INPUT CHANNEL INTERRUPT, OUTPUT CHANNEL INTERRUPT, MAINTENANCE STATUS INTERRUPT, and TEMPERATURE INTERRUPT) and to shut down the furnace (FURNACE SHUTDOWN) have been added from the context diagram.
- The control to "switch" between reading temperatures according to SCHEDULE and reading them periodically (because of a hot furnace) is shown by the control flow from Process 2 to Process 1. It controls the activation and deactivation of a process at a lower level.

Dictionary updates:

TEMPERATURE MONITOR INDICATOR = ["Normal" | "Hot"]
* process activator/deactivator *

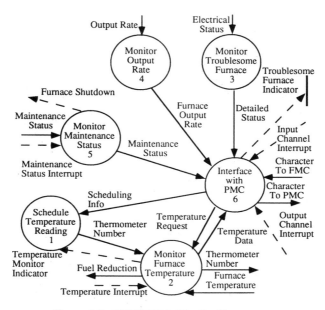

Figure 6-9   DFD/CFD 0: Monitor Furnace

6.5.6   Step 6: Document External Timing

The allocated response times are shown in Figure 6-11.

Comments

- Notice that it is OK for an event (such as SCHEDULING INFO) to have no external output signal. The implication is that the event causes changes in the output of other events. In this case, reports affected (that is, TEMPERATURE DATA) will be according to the new schedule within the allocated time. The response time assigned here is based on the scheduling frequency given for temperature gathering: 10 minutes is the minimum time interval for scheduling (part of that time is used within other CSCIs).

process control	Monitor Troublesome Furnace (3)
Troublesome Furnace Indicator	
- Start Monitoring	1
- Stop Monitoring	0

Figure 6-10   CSpec 0: Monitor Furnace

External Input Signal	Input Event	Frequency	External Output Signal	Output Signal	Response Time
Scheduling Info	received from PMC	event driven	none	All later reports affected	within 8 min.
Troublesome Furnace Indicator	received from PMC	event driven	none	recording started/ stopped	within 20 sec.
		every 30 sec.	Detailed Status Packet	sent to PMC	within 20 sec.
Furnace Temperature	received from furnace	according to schedule	Temperature Data Packet	sent to PMC	within 3 sec.
		every min. (when hot)	Fuel Reduction (when hot)	fuel reduced	within 30 sec.
Output Rate	received from furnace	every 5 sec.	Output Rate Packet	sent to PMC	within 4 sec.
Maintenance Status	received from furnace	whenever value changes	Maintenance Status Packet	sent to PMC	within 0.8 sec.
	(falls to Safety Hazard)	rare	Furnace Shutdown	furnace off	within 1.3 sec.
Temperature Request	received from PMC	event driven	Temperature Data Packet	sent to PMC	within 3 sec.
Acknowledge-ment	received from PMC	event driven	Furnace Data Packet	sent to PMC (when available)	within 3 sec.
Temperature Interrupt	received from furnace	event driven	none	take data from buffer	within 0.05 sec.
Input Channel Interrupt	received from PMC	event driven	none	take character from buffer	within 0.05 sec.
Output Channel Interrupt	received from PMC	event driven	none	place next character into buffer	within 0.05 sec.
Maintenance Status Interrupt	received from furnace	event driven	none	take character from buffer	within 0.05 sec.

Figure 6-11 Response Time Specification

- An event may also cause multiple outputs based on the value or state. For example, receipt of FURNACE TEMPERATURE produces TEMPERATURE DATA PACKET and, if hot, FUEL REDUCTION.
- Timing from system design was for TEMPERATURE DATA, SCHEDULING INFO, and TEMPERATURE REQUEST. Although we actually get one character at a time (including ACKNOWLEDGMENTs), the response time needs to be for the entire packet. One character of the packet wouldn't do either side of the interface any good.
- The additional timing requirements necessary for each of the interrupts and the acknowledgment protocol have been added here as well.

System Requirement \ Software Requirement	Schedule Temperature Reading 1	Monitor Furnace Temperature 2	Monitor Troublesome Furnace 3	Monitor Output Rate 4	Monitor Maintenance Status 5	Interface with PMC 6
1.1 Maintain Schedule	X					
1.2.1 Read Temperature		X				
1.2.2 Control Fuel Valve		X				
1.2.3.1 Initiate Scheduled Temperature Reading	X					
1.2.3.2 Initiate Periodic Temperature Reading		X				
2.2 Record Detailed Status			X			
3.1 Determine Maintenance Status					X	
3.7 Shutdown Furnace					X	
CSpec 3 - Furnace Shutdown					X	
5.1 Record Output Rate				X		
derived requirements						
Initiate Requested Temperature Reading		X				
Send Data to PMC						X
Receive Command from PMC						X
Control Interface with DTS		X				

Figure 6-12   Monitor Furnace Requirements Traceability Matrix

6.5.7   Step 7: Document Allocation to Top-Level Processes

The requirements traceability for the top level is shown in Figure 6-12.

Comments

- This matrix shows only the system-level requirements that have been (at least partially) allocated to this CSCI.
- Notice the allocated requirements from the system requirements model and the derived requirements from the system design.

6.5.8   Steps 8–12: Lower-Level Decomposition

6.5.8.1   Process 1: Schedule Temperature Reading   The decomposition for "Schedule Temperature Reading" is given in Figure 6-13. It is essentially the same as the processes grouped together on the EFD for this functionality. The associated CSpec is also shown.

Dictionary Updates (step 10): None.

Figure 6-14 shows only those requirements that were allocated to the parent process. This DFD is not further decomposed. The PSpecs are given in Figure 6-15.

6.5.8.2   Process 2: Monitor Furnace Temperature   The decomposition for "Monitor Furnace Temperature" is given in Figure 6-16. It shows the activation of Process 2.3 whenever a new temperature is received.

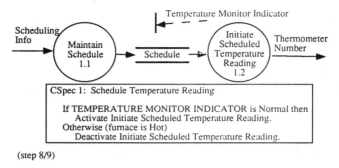

(step 8/9)

Figure 6-13   DFD/CFD 1: Schedule Temperature Reading (with CSpec)

Comments

- Notice the control from "Evaluate Temperatures" (Process 2.3), which activates and deactivates "Initiate Periodic Temperature Reading," as well as going off page to control something else (see Figure 6-13).

Dictionary Updates (step 10):

TEMPERATURE EVALUATION = * process activator *

TEMPERATURES = Max Thermometers {Furnace Temperature}

Figure 6-17 shows the requirements traceability for only the requirements allocated to this DFD. The PSpecs are given in Figure 6-18.

Comments

- Notice the long explanation of the first step in PSpec 2.2. Part of this is to ensure that all of the inputs and outputs of the process are mentioned in the PSpec.
- We have added some constants (originally in the system-level data dictionary) that need to be entered into the data dictionary, as follows.

System Requirement \ Software Requirement	Maintain Schedule 1.1	Initiate Scheduled Reading 1.2
1.1 Maintain Schedule	X	
1.2.3.1 Initiate Scheduled Temperature Reading		X

(step 11)

Figure 6-14   Schedule Temperature Reading Requirements Traceability Matrix

PSpec 1.1: Maintain Schedule

Update MONITOR FREQUENCY within SCHEDULE for the given THERMOMETER NUMBER.

PSpec 1.2: Initiate Scheduled Reading

Determine time to monitor each thermometer according to MONITOR FREQUENCY. Output THERMOMETER NUMBER at appropriate time.

(step 12)

Figure 6-15 PSpecs 1.1 and 1.2

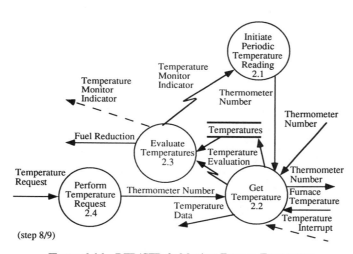

(step 8/9)

Figure 6-16 DFD/CFD 2: Monitor Furnace Temperature

System Requirement / Software Requirement	Initiate Periodic Temperature Reading 2.1	Get Temperature 2.2	Evaluate Temperature 2.3	Perform Temperature Request 2.4
1.2.1 Read Temperature		X		
1.2.2 Control Fuel Valve			X	
1.2.3.2 Initiate Periodic Temperature Reading	X			
derived requirements				
Initiate Requested Temperature Reading				X
Control Interface with DTS		X		

(step 11)

Figure 6-17 Monitor Furnace Temperature Requirements Traceability Matrix

PSpec 2.1: Initiate Periodic Temperature Reading

Output THERMOMETER NUMBER for all thermometers
every HOT PERIODIC.

PSpec 2.2: Get Temperature

Get the FURNACE TEMPERATURE for the given THERMOMETER NUMBER
according to the protocol for the DTS. (i.e., output the THERMOMETER NUMBER
and accept the TEMPERATURE INTERRUPT)

Store FURNACE TEMPERATURE in TEMPERATURES.

Issue TEMPERATURE EVALUATION.

Output TEMPERATURE DATA.

PSpec 2.3: Evaluate Temperatures

Read TEMPERATURES

In accordance with Decision Table 2.3,
   If required, issue FUEL REDUCTION at appropriate level

Issue Temperature Monitor Indicator.

Inputs		Outputs	
Furnace Temperature(s)		Fuel Reduction	Temperature Monitor Indicator
none above Hot Spot	avg > Hot Average	Low Fuel Reduction	Hot
	avg ≤ Hot Average	--	Normal
1 or more above Hot Spot	--	High Fuel Reduction	Hot

Decision Table 2.3

PSpec 2.4: Perform Temperature Request

Output THERMOMETER NUMBER to be read based on the input
TEMPERATURE REQUEST.

(step 12)

Figure 6-18   PSpecs 2.1 through 2.4

Dictionary Updates:

HOT AVERAGE = * Average temperature above which the furnace is considered too hot—currently = 3500°F *

HOT PERIODIC = * Interval at which to monitor temperatures when a furnace is "hot"—currently = 1 minute *

HOT SPOT = * High single temperature above which the furnace is considered too hot—currently = 3600°F *

6.5.8.3 *Process 3: Monitor Troublesome Furnace*   "Monitor Troublesome Furnace" is not further decomposed. The PSpec is shown in Figure 6-19.

Comments

- Here we see that the process performs its periodic function as long as it is activated (refer back to CSpec 0 in Figure 6-10).

PSpec 3: **Monitor Troublesome Furnace**

Every DETAILED STATUS PERIODIC
Get ELECTRICAL STATUS from each status point
Use this to construct DETAILED STATUS.

(step 12)

Figure 6-19   PSpec 3

- The constant for the periodic needs to be entered into the data dictionary:

DETAILED STATUS PERIODIC = * Interval at which to monitor the electrical status when the furnace is "troublesome"—currently 30 seconds *

6.5.8.4   *Process 4: Monitor Output Rate*   No further breakdown is necessary for this straightforward function. The PSpec is shown in Figure 6-20.

Comments

- Update data dictionary with constant:

OUTPUT RATE PERIODIC = * Interval at which to monitor output rate—currently 5 seconds *

6.5.8.5   *Process 5: Monitor Maintenance Status*   No further breakdown is necessary for this straightforward function. The PSpec is shown in Figure 6-21.

6.5.8.6   *Process 6: Interface with PMC*   Figure 6-22 shows the breakdown of "Interface with PMC."
Dictionary Updates (step 10): None.
The associated RTM is given in Figure 6-23.

Process 6.1: Receive Command from PMC   Figure 6-24 shows the breakdown of "Receive Command from PMC."

Comments

- This breakdown shows us the physical characteristics of the interface and the different types of packets that may be input.

Dictionary Updates (step 10): None.

PSpec 4: **Monitor Output Rate**

Every OUTPUT RATE PERIODIC
Get OUTPUT RATE from the furnace.
Generate OUTPUT RATE.

(step 12)

Figure 6-20   PSpec 4

PSpec 5: Monitor Maintenance Status

Upon receipt of MAINTENANCE STATUS from the furnace, perform the following:
If MAINTENANCE STATUS is "Safety Hazard" then
  Issue FURNACE SHUTDOWN.

Output MAINTENANCE STATUS.

(step 12)

Figure 6-21   Pspec 5

Since only one requirement has been allocated to this process, no RTM is given. Each of the subprocesses must satisfy a portion of that requirement. The PSpec for 6.1.1 is shown in Figure 6-25. Process 6.1.2 is further decomposed, as follows.

Process 6.1.2: Analyze Packet   The decomposition of "Analyze Packet" is given in Figure 6-26.

Comments

- Although this may seem rather low-level, we are showing it to demonstrate the common functionality that occurs in several of the processes (6.1.2.2, 6.1.2.3, 6.1.2.4). This is something to look for across the system—not just within a single DFD.

Dictionary Updates (step 10):

VALIDITY INDICATION = ["Valid", "Invalid"]

Since only one "derived" requirement has been allocated to this DFD, an RTM is not provided. The associated PSpecs are shown in Figure 6-27.

Comments

- Here we see an example of reference back to another process that performs the same basic functionality.

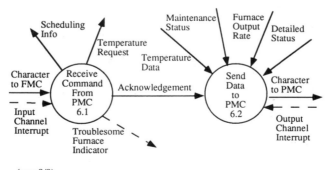

(step 8/9)

Figure 6-22   DFD/CFD 6: Interface with PMC

System Requirement \ Software Requirement	Receive Command from PMC 6.1	Send Data to PMC 6.2
derived requirements		
Send Data to PMC		X
Receive Command from PMC	X	

(step 11)

Figure 6-23   Interface with PMC Requirements Traceability Matrix

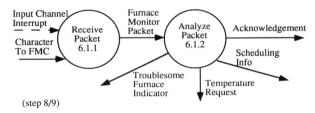

(step 8/9)

Figure 6-24   DFD/CFD 6.1: Receive Command from PMC

PSpec 6.1.1: Receive Packet

In a loop
  Accept INPUT CHANNEL INTERRUPT

  If CHARACTER TO FMC is STX then
    Build PACKET out of characters received with each interrupt until
      ETX is received.
    Output PACKET
  Otherwise
    Discard character -- noise on line
  end if
end loop

(step 12)

Figure 6-25   PSpec 6.1.1

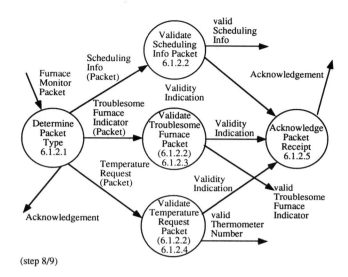

(step 8/9)

Figure 6-26 DFD 6.1.2: Analyze Packet

PSpec 6.1.2.1: Determine Packet Type

Determine the type of FURNACE MONITOR PACKET received.
Route by individual packet type (SCHEDULING INFO,
    TROUBLESOME FURNACE INDICATOR. TEMPERATURE REQUEST,
    ACKNOWLEDGEMENT).

PSpec 6.1.2.2: Validate Scheduling Info Packet

Check the value of the fields within the SCHEDULING INFO (PACKET).

If all fields are valid then
    Output valid SCHEDULING INFO.
    Set VALIDITY INDICATION to "Valid".
Otherwise
    Set VALIDITY INDICATION to "Invalid".

Output VALIDITY INDICATION.

PSpec 6.1.2.3: Validate Troublesome Furnace Indicator Packet

Equivalent to process 6.1.2.2; Validate Scheduling Info Packet, with:

TROUBLESOME FURNACE INDICATOR PACKET =>
    SCHEDULING INFO PACKET
TROUBLESOME FURNACE INDICATOR => valid SCHEDULING INFO

PSpec 6.1.2.4: Validate Temperature Request Packet

Equivalent to process 6.1.2.2; Validate Scheduling Info Packet, with:

TEMPERATURE REQUEST PACKET => SCHEDULING INFO PACKET
THERMOMETER NUMBER => valid SCHEDULING INFO

PSpec 6.1.2.5: Acknowledge Packet Receipt

Output ACKNOWLEDGEMENT based on VALIDITY INDICATION.

(step 12)

Figure 6-27 PSpecs 6.1.2.1 through 6.1.2.5

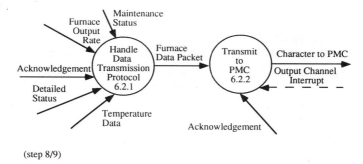

(step 8/9)

Figure 6-28   DFD/CFD 6.2: Send Data to PMC

Process 6.2: Send Data To PMC   Figure 6-28 shows the breakdown of "Send Data to PMC."

Comments

* We have broken this process down so as to be able to describe the protocol and the transmission functionality clearly.

Dictionary Updates (step 10): None.

Since only one requirement has been allocated to this process, no RTM is given. The associated PSpecs are shown in Figure 6-29.

Comments

* The protocol is rather complex, but it can be expressed in the PSpec without further breakdown for the timeout.

PSpec 6.2.1: Handle Data Transmission Protocol

Construct FURNACE DATA PACKET from data received
    (TEMPERATURE DATA, DETAILED STATUS, FURNACE OUTPUT
    RATE, MAINTENANCE STATUS).
Initially send FURNACE DATA PACKET to Transmit to PMC (6.2.2).

Wait for one of the following to occur:
If ACKNOWLEDGEMENT received is positive then
    Construct and send next FURNACE DATA PACKET to Transmit to PMC.

If ACKNOWLEDGEMENT received is negative then
    Send same FURNACE DATA PACKET for transmission (up to MAX
    TRANSMISSION ATTEMPTS).

If PROTOCOL TIMEOUT occurs then
    Send same FURNACE DATA PACKET for transmission (up to MAX
    TRANSMISSION ATTEMPTS).

PSpec 6.2.2: Transmit To PMC

For each character in packet received (FURNACE DATA PACKET
    or ACKNOWLEDGEMENT)

Set CHARACTER TO PMC to the individual character
Wait for OUTPUT CHANNEL INTERRUPT

(step 12)

Figure 6-29   PSpecs 6.2.1 and 6.2.2

Dictionary updates (step 10):

MAX TRANSMISSION ATTEMPTS = * Maximum number of times to attempt transmission of a packet before going on to the next one—currently 3 times *

PROTOCOL TIMEOUT = * Time to wait without receipt of acknowledgment before reattempting transmission—currently 2 seconds *

6.5.9 Final Data Dictionary

ACK = * ASCII ACK character—designating positive acknowledgment *

ACKNOWLEDGMENT = STX + [ACK | NAK] + ETX
* Acknowledgment ASCII string sent to and received from PMC *
Rate = event-driven

CHARACTER TO FMC = 1 character of [Acknowledgment | Furnace Packet]
Rate = event-driven

CHARACTER TO PMC = 1 character of [Acknowledgment | Furnace Data Packet]
Rate = event-driven

DETAILED STATUS = Max Detailed Status Points {Electrical Status}

DETAILED STATUS PERIODIC = * Interval at which to monitor electrical status when the furnace is "troublesome"—currently 30 seconds *

ELECTRICAL STATUS = * Single electrical status point *
Range = 0 to 570
Units = millivolt
Resolution = millivolt
Rate = Monitored "continuously" when furnace is marked as troublesome

ETX = * ASCII End of Text character *

FUEL REDUCTION = [High Fuel Reduction | Low Fuel Reduction]
* Amount of fuel to reduce due to hot furnace *
Rate = event-driven; depends on temperature of furnace

FURNACE DATA = [Temperature Data | Maintenance Status | Detailed Status | Output Rate]
Rate = event-driven

FURNACE DATA PACKET = STX + Furnace Data Type + ASCII of Furnace Data + ETX
Rate = event-driven

FURNACE DATA TYPE = * Type of Furnace Data contained in packet *
Range 0 to 3 (ASCII character)
        where 0 = Temperature Data
            1 = Maintenance Status
            2 = Detailed Status
            3 = Output Rate

FURNACE MONITOR PACKET = STX + Monitor Command Type + ASCII of Monitor Command + ETX
Rate = event-driven

FURNACE SHUTDOWN = * Indication to turn off furnace for safety purposes *

FURNACE TEMPERATURE = * Actual temperature of furnace *
Units = °F
Range = 900 to 3700
Resolution = 1 degree
Rate = event-driven; according to schedule

HIGH FUEL REDUCTION = * Actual fuel reduction percentage = 20 percent *

HOT AVERAGE = * Average temperature above which the furnace is considered too hot—currently 3500°F *

HOT PERIODIC = * Interval at which to monitor temperatures when a furnace is "hot"—currently = 1 minute *

HOT SPOT = * High single temperature above which the furnace is considered too hot—currently = 3600°F *

INPUT CHANNEL INTERRUPT = * Hardware interrupt indicating that a Character to FMC has been placed in the associated hardware buffer *
Rate = event-driven

LOW FUEL REDUCTION = * Actual fuel reduction percentage = 10 percent *

MAINTENANCE STATUS = ["Normal" | "Degraded" | "Impaired" | "Critical" | "Safety Hazard"]
Rate = Monitored "continuously"

MAINTENANCE STATUS INTERRUPT = * Hardware interrupt indicating that the Maintenance Status has been placed in the associated hardware buffer *
Rate = event-driven; change in status

MAX DETAILED STATUS POINTS = * Number of electrical status points at a furnace—currently 10 *

MAX THERMOMETERS = * Number of thermometers attached to the furnace—currently 15 *

MAX TRANSMISSION ATTEMPTS = * Maximum number of times to attempt transmission of a packet before going on to the next one—currently 3 times *

MONITOR COMMAND = [Scheduling Info | Temperature Request | Troublesome Furnace Indicator]
Rate = event-driven

MONITOR COMMAND TYPE = * Type of Monitor Command contained in packet *
Range = 0 to 2 (ASCII character)
    where 0 = Scheduling Info
          1 = Immediate Temperature Request
          2 = Troublesome Furnace Indication

MONITOR FREQUENCY = * Frequency at which to monitor a thermometer*
Range = 0 to 144 (where 0 = stop monitoring)
Units = readings/day
Resolution = 10 minutes
Rate = change is event-driven

NAK = * ASCII NAK character—designating negative acknowledgment *

OUTPUT CHANNEL INTERRUPT = * Hardware interrupt indicating that a Character to PMC has been taken from the associated hardware buffer *
Rate = event-driven

OUTPUT RATE = * Amount of molten iron being produced *
Units = tons/minute
Range = 0.0 to 50.0
Resolution = 0.05 tons
Rate = Monitored "continuously"

OUTPUT RATE PERIODIC = * Interval at which to Monitor Output Rate of a furnace—currently = 5 seconds *

PROTOCOL TIMEOUT = * Time to wait without receipt of acknowledgment before reattempting transmission—currently 2 seconds *

SCHEDULE = Max Thermometers {Monitor Frequency} + Hot Furnace Indication

SCHEDULING INFO = Thermometer Number + Monitor Frequency
Rate = event-driven

STX = * ASCII Start of Text character *

TEMPERATURE DATA = Thermometer Number + Furnace Temperature

TEMPERATURE EVALUATION = * process activator *

TEMPERATURE INTERRUPT = * Hardware interrupt indicating that a temperature has been placed in the associated hardware buffer *
Rate = event-driven

TEMPERATURE MONITOR INDICATOR = ["Hot" | "Normal"]

TEMPERATURE REQUEST = Thermometer Number
* Indication to check the temperature of this thermometer immediately *
Rate = event-driven

TEMPERATURES = Max Thermometers {Furnace Temperature}

THERMOMETER NUMBER = * Number assigned to thermometer for automation/management purposes *
Range = 1 to Max Thermometers

TROUBLESOME FURNACE DATA = ["Troublesome" | "Not Troublesome"]

TROUBLESOME FURNACE INDICATOR = ["Start Monitoring" | "Stop Monitoring"]
* Indication to start or stop monitoring of detailed status *

VALIDITY INDICATION = ["Valid" | "Invalid"]

6.6 KEYS TO UNDERSTANDING

- Software requirements analysis is similar to system requirements analysis but narrows its focus to the piece-by-piece specification of requirements for each CSCI and its associated interfaces.

- The graphics and guidelines, and many of the steps, are identical in systems and software specification.

- Nominally, the software requirements specification makes no assumptions of the software design; the analogy with system requirements being "essential" or technology-independent is nearly exact.

- There are, however, exactly the same sort of requirements–design iteration at the software level as occurs at the system level. Some software design actually takes place during requirements specification.

- However, it is important that the requirements specification *in no way constrain or dictate* the software design.

- SSEM specification and design methods are consistent with "spiral" process management approaches.

PART 3

SOFTWARE DESIGN

Part Three addresses the transition from software requirements to software design. The general strategy is to use the specification of requirements from the final chapter of Part Two to determine the concurrent elements of a system and, hence, its major modules. (For sequential systems, the allocation to modules proceeds directly without regard to concurrency.) This strategy makes traceability from the software back to the requirements easy, almost trivial. Additional significant issues of top-level design are addressed, with a consistent bias toward a balanced blend of functional decomposition and increased modularization.

The Furnace Monitoring System (FMS), which is posed as a problem or operational requirements in Part One and used in Part Two, culminating in the software specification of one of the computer software configuration items (CSCIs), continues to be used to illustrate

- *Software Top-Level Design*
- *Software Detailed Design*

CHAPTER 7

Top-Level Design

Objective: to provide a set of graphical notations, guidelines, and a step-by-step process for the top-level design of a single computer software configuration item (CSCI) and its interfaces

The purpose of this chapter is to describe the methods to be used during the top-level design phase of the development cycle. It includes the part of the Systems Software Engineering Methodology (SSEM) called *real-time design* (RTD) and the first portions of *modular structured design* (MSD). Figure 7-1 illustrates the phases of the development cycle. This chapter covers the phase that is highlighted.

Top-level design is the determination and description of the overall software architecture, the interfaces between the major modules within that architecture, and the interfaces to components external to the CSCI.

This phase is a critical transition point. Not only does it involve the change from what is to be done in software to how to accomplish the job, but it also completes the transition of viewpoints from systems engineering to software development, a traditionally difficult step. The input to this phase is the software requirements for a CSCI, expressed as a set of data flow and control flow diagrams (DFDs and CFDs) and associated products and specifications.

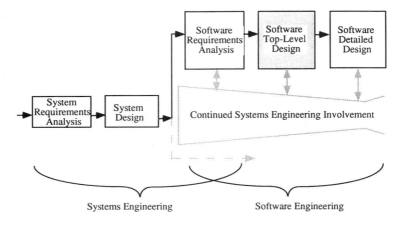

Figure 7-1 Phases of the Development Cycle

To accomplish the methodology definition, the following items are covered.

- Transition from software requirements analysis to top-level design
- Graphics
- Guidelines
- Methodology—step by step
- Example

Appendix A, "Software Design Concepts," addresses a number of discrete issues vital to this phase. You might wish to scan it at this time and then read it thoroughly after the RTD graphics and guidelines are introduced.

7.1 TRANSITION FROM SOFTWARE REQUIREMENTS ANALYSIS TO TOP-LEVEL DESIGN

An important consequence of the close tie between the software requirements model and the ultimate software design is that the transition from the model to the design becomes a major issue. The characteristics of this transition are similar to those of the system requirements-to-design transition, particularly the fact that the software design is a fundamentally creative activity.

Usually, the various software design alternatives are not analyzed and traded off in quite as formal a manner as for the earlier transition, but the creative process is quite similar. In addition, there are the following four differences between requirements representation and software architecture, which are described in Chapter 2, Section 2.3:

- Processes vs. tasks
- Functional vs. modular

- Flat vs. hierarchical
- Logical vs. physical

Appendix A-4, "Modular Real-Time Design," addresses the transition issues further, including rationale for the RTSA–RTD style of requirements-to-design approach.

7.2 GRAPHICS

This section describes the graphics that represent the top- level *software architecture* in the methodology. The graphics presented in this section are not intended to tell the whole story of the methodology and are not necessarily tightly interrelated; they are only intended to introduce the *form* of the notation. The final section of the chapter, "FMS Example," will use these graphics, the guidelines of the next section, and the step-by-step methodology to present an integrated picture. Recommended conventions are also listed. We will cover the following graphics and associated data, with relationships as illustrated in Figure 7-2.

- Flattened flow diagram (FFD)
- Task communication graph (TCG)
- Software architecture diagram (SAD)
- Structure charts
- Requirements traceability matrix (RTM)
- Program design language (PDL) (optional)

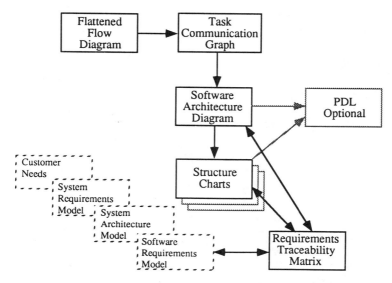

Figure 7-2   Top-level Design Structure Components

7.2.1 Flattened Flow Diagram (FFD)

The purpose of the FFD is to provide a starting point for the development of the software architecture. It allows us to start with a DFD and CFD that capture all the software requirements from software requirements analysis, and then to aggregate these processes into higher-level processes based on concurrency (two or more tasks operating simultaneously) within the CSCI.

The FFD is composed of the bottom-level (primitive) processes from software requirements analysis. For large systems, you will need a *big* piece of paper. By this, we mean that you need to do whatever it takes to have the entire architecture visible at the same time, even if you have to use an entire wall. You are encouraged to cut and paste or pin pages to a wall or whatever to get the processes all connected on one "page," so that the entire CSCI can be studied and contemplated at once. Without this, one cannot easily be certain that all the processes are grouped into the appropriate tasks. Since this diagram is not delivered to the customer, it doesn't have to be perfect; hand-drawn, pasted together or pinned to the wall, is acceptable. All the pieces of it should be saved for future reference. Remember that the entire system will never be illustrated with the FFD; it has already been partitioned into CSCIs. If the CSCI is so large (over 200 processes) that the FFD is intractable, it is a strong indicator of a need for revisiting the CSCI partitioning. A final simplifying factor is that the FFD often need not literally go to the lowest level. Some of the lowest-level processes are likely to deal with small issues of step-by-step processing and have nothing to do with concurrency; such processes will always follow their higher-level (parent) process. The net effect of these issues is that the FFD will typically contain fewer than 100 processes—a readily handled level of abstraction.

Figure 7-3 gives an example of an FFD. We see the processes (circles) from software requirements analysis (and their associated DFD process numbers) with the flow of data (solid arrows) and control (dashed arrows) between them and with the environment. Data stores (parallel lines) are shown for data that needs to be accessed at some time later than it is stored or that is accessed more than once. Data flows entering or leaving a data store need to be labeled only when a portion of the data in the store needs to be indicated. A control bar (single vertical line) shows control flow entering or exiting an associated control specification (CSpec). The CSpecs should be kept alongside the FFD for reference.

What if, despite your best efforts, there are too many processes? For large systems that have not been partitioned into CSCIs, or for large CSCIs that cannot be further partitioned, you can proceed in a strictly top-down manner. At each level of decomposition of DFDs, you can identify processes that you judge to be strictly sequential. Such processes either become tasks themselves or become candidates for combining with other such processes, using the same guidelines given later for FFDs. This approach is particularly sensitive to processes having been partitioned effectively around common data stores (high coupling and low cohesion), since the structure of the requirements specification tends to

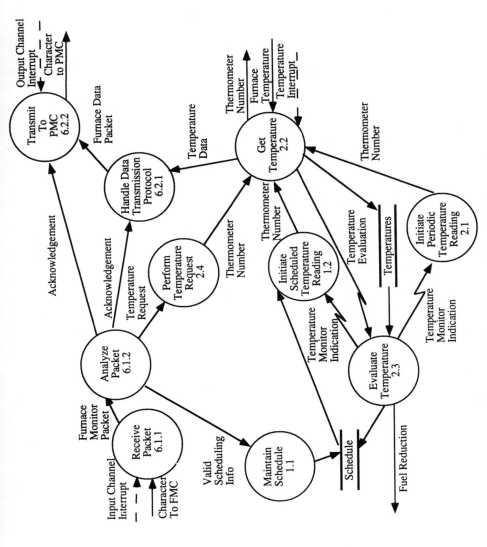

Figure 7-3 Flattened Flow Diagram

determine this step in the software design. This is potentially harmful, since the requirements analysis has a different focus: the statement of *what* is to be accomplished, as opposed to a description of *how* to create software to meet the requirement.

7.2.2 Task Communication Graph (TCG)

The FFD just described is used, along with a set of task identification rules, to determine the concurrency of the CSCI. Concurrency does not usually "fall out" as a by-product of designing a system—it must be seriously thought out and planned for. The determination of concurrency at the beginning of the design process allows for, among other things, structured breakdown of the CSCI that takes into consideration the timing involved for complex processing in relationship to other processing that could be occurring simultaneously (concurrently).

The task communication graph (TCG) provides a language-independent graphical representation of the concurrent tasks and the interfaces between them. Parallelograms are used to designate each of the tasks that operate concurrently. Data flows (solid arrows) and control flows (dashed arrows) are shown between the tasks. If the data is to be buffered (for example, queued) between tasks, "(buffered)" is added to the flow name. Shared data between two or more tasks is shown with the data store symbol (parallel lines). The arrowheads indicate the data flow into or out of the data area. To indicate that a single interface between two tasks has data or control flowing in both directions, such as input and output parameters, a double-headed arrow is used. Place the flow on the line by the task that will receive it. Figure 7-4 gives a generic example of this.

For large systems, you might think that you would need more than one (large) page to draw the TCG. The fact is that needing more than a page can serve as a warning that the CSCI allocation may need revisiting. Large CSCIs, unless they control many devices, don't have that many more concurrent elements than smaller (medium-size) ones; it is only that each piece (task) is itself larger.

The TCG is also used in the performance of some initial timing analysis, in which the *thread* or path of each input event to its output response activity is traced through the tasks (and task interactions) identified on the chart.

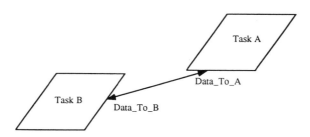

Figure 7-4 Task Interface with IN and OUT Parameters

Naming conventions for TCGs are as follows. Tasks are active (performing the work of the CSCI), but they can be thought of as things or entities (or objects) that take action, so they should be named with noun phrases (for example, "PMC_Data_Receiver"). The data and control flows indicate information and as such should be named with noun phrases (they should not contain a verb phrase). The operations or services not shown in this diagram that are provided by a task will be named with a verb phrase, indicative of the processing they perform; these will be seen in the SAD and PDL described in following sections. Since these names will potentially be used in the actual software (code), underscores are placed between the words in these names.

Figure 7-5 gives an example of the TCG. We see seven tasks with data flows between them and to and from with the external entities (hardware, software, or operator interfaces). "Temperature_Data" is an example of a flow that needs to be buffered. "Temperatures" is shared data.

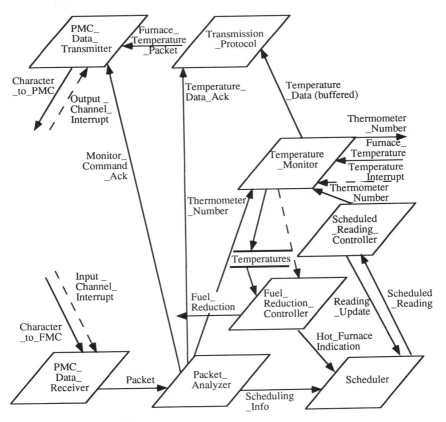

Figure 7-5 Task Communication Graph

7.2.3 Software Architecture Diagram (SAD)

The purpose of the software architecture diagram (SAD) is to describe the overall software architecture without internal details. It includes the intermodule dependencies. It is used to aid in requirements traceability: software requirements can be allocated to and traced from the individual modules shown on this diagram (the software architecture).

A "first cut" at the SAD will illustrate the design decisions made regarding the software architecture in terms of the encapsulation of tasks into *application modules*. An application module performs the main processing of the program; it contains the subprograms and tasks to accomplish the work. *Helper modules* are then added to assist in the decomposition of the software into testable and easily maintained components.

Each module (application and helper) is shown as a rectangle. The dependency of one module on another is illustrated using an arrow; the arrowhead points to the module being used. A module (called the *server*) is used by another module (called the *client*) when the client calls a visible subprogram of the server or uses constant definitions of the server. Rarely, the server will have data made visible that the client accesses directly; this becomes *global,* or a *common pool* of data. For languages that allow type definitions, a server may also provide type definitions. We say that the server *exports* subprograms, type definitions, and so on, and the client *imports* them.

The smaller boxes protruding from the side of the module rectangle represent the services (visible subprograms) that are available for use by other modules. The name of each subprogram is given. When a module provides more services than can fit clearly on a single diagram, the diagram can be extended over multiple pages. For modules that do not provide any services (they only use other modules), no service boxes are shown.

The naming conventions are as follows. Each module is given a name that is a noun phrase indicative of the abstraction provided. Services are named with verb phrases indicative of the processing they perform.

Figure 7-6 gives an example of a SAD. We see the application modules that were identified and the helper modules determined as needed by the application modules. "Temperature_Manager" is an example of a helper module. It is used by "DTS_Handler" and "Fuel_Reduction_Handler". These application modules depend on "Temperature_Manager" to perform some service(s) for them. Specifically, it encapsulates the data store "Temperatures," which is shown in Figure 7-5. This encapsulation ensures that the data will be accessed in a consistent manner. "Temperature_Data_Buffer" is a helper module that encapsulates the buffering of "Temperature_Data". "PMC_Input_Analyzer" is an example of a module that does not provide services to others.

The way we understand the functioning and design of large systems is a mix of overall viewpoint and component-by-component analysis. This implies that we must have one simple picture that shows the overall architecture of the system (see Figure 7-6). Real systems, however, are often too large and complex to be viewed in an all-at-once manner. The solution to this problem is layers of abstraction.

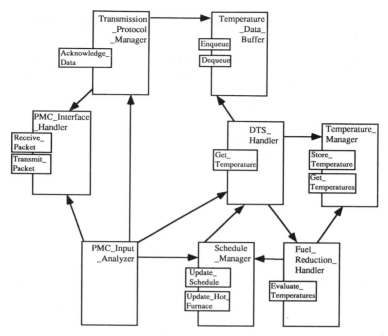

Figure 7-6   Software Architecture Diagram

We have already seen how the requirements-to-design transition process results in a relatively simple top-level view of the system, based on tasks that accomplish the function or the application of the CSCI being designed. These tasks were then grouped into modules forming the "first-cut" or top-level SAD (see Figure 7-7*a*). This view of the software is the top-level, or most abstract, view; it ignores both the internal details of the module and the details concerning "helpers" of the top-level modules.

The next level of abstraction of design, still hiding detail internal to the modules, consists of the helper modules for the top-level modules. This is shown in Figure 7-7*b*. The next level is the helpers of the helpers, and so on for lower levels.

Now, this is exactly the view of the system that, for many levels, becomes too complex to manage. It is an important view of the system, however, and can be represented by looking only at two or three levels at a time.

An alternate way of understanding the system is to look at all levels of support for a single (and eventually, for each) top-level module. This viewpoint is shown in Figure 7-8. This viewpoint is useful for understanding the full support and development needed for a single abstraction. It may also be useful to include top-level modules that depend on this module.

Both of these representations can be useful not only for understanding the system, but for defining and specifying partial software developments, or "builds," of the system. However, neither viewpoint gives all the information about the system,

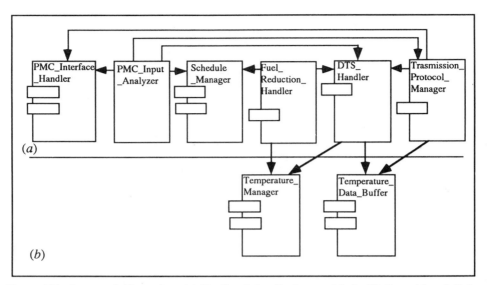

Figure 7-7 Layers of Abstraction: (*a*) Top-Level (application modules); (*b*) Second-Level (helper modules)

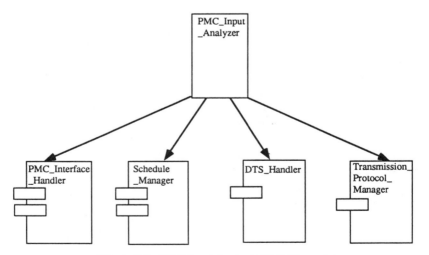

Figure 7-8 PMC_Input_Analyzer SAD Viewpoint

especially how top-level modules might be coupled or tied together by lower-level relationships. There is no substitute for a representation of all the modules in one logical and physical viewpoint. This might be accommodated by a computer-aided browsing tool or simply by large sheets of paper combined with careful analysis. Remember that the software components we are dealing with are only large, not gargantuan. (The assumption is that during system design the software is broken into reasonably sized CSCIs.) Even a very large CSCI is likely to contain fewer than 100 or so modules. If the software has not been so composed, then an early part of the software design process must be to identify subsystems or CSCIs (or whatever one wishes to call them) that are reasonably sized and have very low interconnection (coupling) between them.

7.2.4 Structure Chart

The structure chart describes the data and control flow of a set of subprograms that are executed sequentially, and it shows the calling hierarchical organization of these subprograms. Thus, it illustrates the architecture within each of the tasks identified for the CSCI. The structure chart is the primary graphic notation of structured design [YOU79]. In SSEM/RTD, we use structure charts for the design of each task.

Figure 7-9 shows a structure chart. Each rectangle represents a subprogram. Predefined subprograms are those defined elsewhere in the system (another module) or reused from other programs. They are indicated with the double bar on each side of the rectangle. A rectangle with "hat" does not represent a separate subprogram in itself but is used to show processing that is accomplished within the subprogram above it. Such a subprogram is referred to as a *lexical* and is often used to make the algorithm clearer. The large arrows indicate the direction of the call, whereas the small arrows show data (open circle) and control (black circle) flow. Control flows are used to make decisions in the higher-level subprogram making the call. A diamond is used to indicate decision. When more than one subprogram call is connected to the diamond, at most only one of them will be called. The oval with an arrowhead under a subprogram is used to denote looping on the subprogram calls within that oval. Data stores are represented by rectangles whose sides have been replaced with an arc. When the breakdown of a structure chart does not fit on a single page, off-page connectors, in the form of a page number within the box(es) still to be expanded, are used to indicate the page on which the chart is continued. In SSEM/RTD, the use of helper information-hiding modules leads to compact designs in which off-page connectors are almost never required.

Naming conventions for structure chart components are as follows. A subprogram should be named with a verb phrase representative of the processing performed by it as well as its subordinates. A predefined subprogram name should be prefixed with its associated module name and a "." (for example, "DTS_Handler.Get_Temperature"). The data and control flows continue to be named with noun phrases, since they are information. Data stores are entities and, as such, should be given a name with a noun phrase. Many of the flows and stores will in-

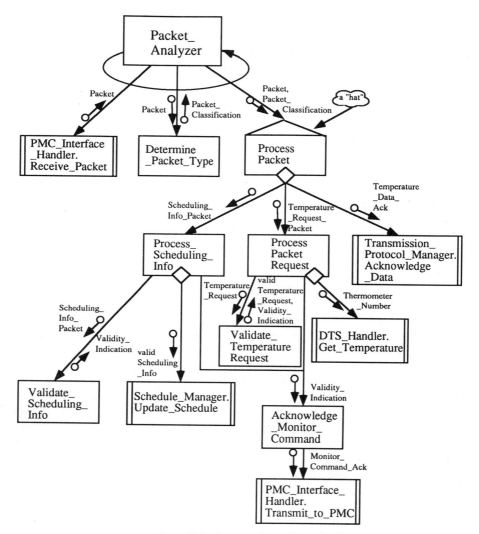

Figure 7-9 Structure Chart Example

herit their names from the DFDs of software requirements analysis. The processes of the DFD are not exactly the same as the subprograms of the structure chart— although some of them are—but since the DFD contains good user-recognizable descriptions of what the system is to do, it is good practice to strive to use similar names for the software components. Again, underscores are used to separate the words.

In Figure 7-9, "Packet_Analyzer" executes calls to the four subprograms beneath it within a loop. "Route_Valid_Command" is called only if the "Validity_Indication" (a control flow) is true; it is passed the "Valid_Monitor_Command" (data flow).

"PMC_Interface_Handler.Receive_Command" is an example of a predefined subprogram. Its definition (that is, its breakdown) would be found on another structure chart elsewhere in the CSCI. "Perform Immediate Temperature Request" is a lexical: Its code is in line with that of "Route_Valid_Command.

Figure 7-10 gives an excerpt from another structure chart to illustrate the data store symbol. "Schedule" is a store accessed by several subprograms. Notice that the large lines connecting the store to the subprograms do not have arrowheads. This is because the subprograms do not *call* the data store but access it directly. The small arrows and flow names indicate the components of the data store that are accessed. Since the procedures access data directly, and since we virtually never use global data, it is necessarily the case that they are all procedures inside a module, with the module containing the data structure. In Figure 7-10 these procedures are contained in the module "Schedule_Manager."

7.2.5 Requirements Traceability Matrix (RTM)

The requirements traceability matrix (RTM), during top-level design, depicts the allocation of the software requirements to the modules identified. The traceability is used to support test development. The RTM graphic is discussed in detail in Section 4.1.7. For top-level design, the software requirements are listed along one axis and the modules are listed along the other.

This allocation can be accomplished in a relatively straightforward manner, based on the FFD and grouping into tasks and modules. It is a major feature of SSEM that traceability becomes easy, because the requirements specified by the process specifications (PSpecs) of the DFDs are directly allocated to software components.

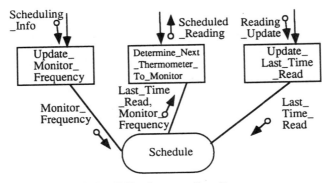

Figure 7-10 Structure Chart Excerpt

7.2.6 Program Design Language (PDL)

Program design language (PDL) is used to describe each component of the software design that will result in actual code such as subprograms or (in Ada) packages. Using structured English design descriptions, the PDL enables developers to understand a software designer's intent. When using a language such as Ada for implementation, it is also wise to use it as the PDL as early as top-level design.

PDL establishes the module structure that defines the information hiding or data abstraction aspects of the design. Most languages will not allow this module structure to be visible in the code; it is only a logical structure. It is vital, however, that this architecture be established, reviewed, and agreed upon during the design phase and clearly documented for the benefit of maintenance. When Ada is used as the PDL, the module structure is captured by the use of Ada packages. We also use the Ada task to represent concurrency aspects of the design, both for review and for maintenance.

PDL also represents the low-level details within modules. This has traditionally been the main role of PDL, essentially stating *how* to implement the functionality. Since it gives much more detail about the subprogram than simply looking at the interface (such as on a structure chart), there is less margin for error when it is actually translated into code. Indeed, PDL resembles a programming language, in that explicit operations can be specified such as "Convert Lat/Long to X/Y Coordinates" or "Print Error Message." It differs from the programming language in that these operations may be specified at any level. One needs to be careful, however, not to become too verbose. That would make the PDL unwieldy and of less use to the coder or during test and maintenance phases. Thus, we want to be sure to make the PDL succinct and to the point. The program logic in the PDL should be kept as simple as possible to reduce probability of errors and minimize the maintenance effort.

Figure 7-11 shows an example of some PDL. Examples of structured English PDL and Ada PDL are shown side by side to illustrate both ways of using PDL.

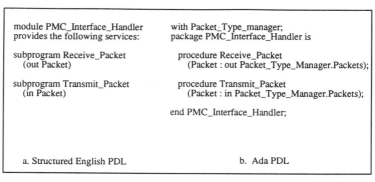

```
module PMC_Interface_Handler          with Packet_Type_manager;
provides the following services:      package PMC_Interface_Handler is

subprogram Receive_Packet                 procedure Receive_Packet
  (out Packet)                                (Packet : out Packet_Type_Manager.Packets);

subprogram Transmit_Packet                procedure Transmit_Packet
  (in Packet)                                 (Packet : in Packet_Type_Manager.Packets);

                                          end PMC_Interface_Handler;



a. Structured English PDL               b. Ada PDL
```

Figure 7-11   PDL Example for Top-Level Design: (*a*) Structured English PDL; (*b*) Ada PDL

7.2.6.1 Compilable PDL   The most effective way to use a strongly typed language that provides interface specifications, such as Ada, as a PDL is actually to compile the code written into the program library. This requires that a good deal of data definition, both types and data structures, be accomplished during design; this is a generally a good idea in any event. This allows the designer to generate sufficiently detailed program representations to allow compilation, and it allows the compiler to check the consistency of interfaces. Don't worry that you are writing "code" at this time while you are designing. In fact, this coding style of PDL is a distinct advantage, because the PDL need not be transformed into code during a separate phase; the coding phase simply *adds to* what has been done during detailed design. (On the other hand, you do have to be careful to avoid completing the coding during the design phase. The issue in regard to Ada is addressed in [NIE88].)

7.2.6.2 PDL at Top-Level Design   Everything we have just noted above in regard to interfaces is doubly true for top-level design. With languages such as Ada, the use of PDL should start during top-level design, with considerable detail in the package and task specifications, and significant type and data structure definitions in the package bodies.

7.2.7 Graphics Summary

Now that we've seen all of the graphics individually, we will summarize with how the major components interact with each other. Figure 7-12 is an illustration of the ways in which the FFD, TCG, structure chart, SAD, RTM, and (optionally) PDL relate to each other to demonstrate the integrated design of the CSCI. Software requirements are analyzed using the FFD to determine concurrency, and processes are allocated to the tasks of the CSCI to form the TCG. The tasks in the TCG are then grouped into application modules to form the basis of the SAD. Complex tasks are further decomposed with structure charts. The application modules and any identified support modules from the task decomposition (structure charts) are assigned a place on the SAD. The RTM shows the mapping from the software requirements to each module in the software architecture (the SAD). When PDL is used, it describes the modules identified and allows for checking of their interfaces.

7.3 GUIDELINES

This section introduces several sets of guidelines for use in the methodology steps. The application of these rules will be indicated at the appropriate steps in the methodology. The guidelines include:

- Task identification
- Task interfaces
- Module identification
- Transform analysis

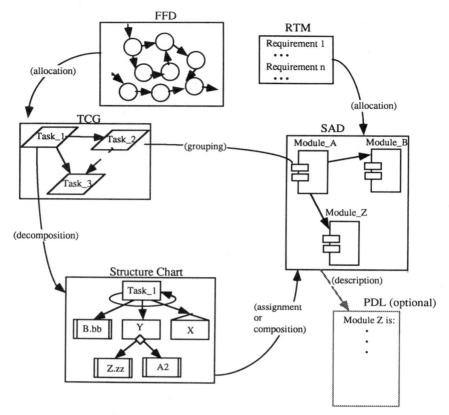

Figure 7-12   Relationship Between Top-Level Design Structure Components

- Transaction analysis
- Coupling and cohesion quality
- Factoring
- Modular structured design (MSD)

7.3.1 Task Identification

An important aspect of the methodology is that it emphasizes early identification of the concurrency within of the software. These concurrent elements are called *tasks*. This section provides guidelines for determination of the tasks based on the data flow diagrams. It uses as a primary method the approach by Gomaa [GOM84], adapted by Nielsen & Shumate [NIE88], called "Design Approach for Real-Time Systems" (DARTS). It also addresses Gomaa's recent Ada DARTS [GOM89] for the improved task identification guidelines. Although not a primary part of the methodology, a useful adjunct approach deals with concurrency identification based on concurrency in the real world, sometimes referred to as "Entity-Life Modeling" [SAN89a and SAN89b].

Early task identification is absent in object-oriented design (OOD)-style approaches to design [B0086]. The emphasis on early identification of concurrency gives SSEM a distinctly different approach from OOD. However, the *representation* of the design may be identical in OOD and this methodology, even though the *process* and steps in preparation of the design are different.

The sections below discuss:

- General Issues of task identification
- Specific guidelines

Task Identification: General Issues There are several approaches to determination of concurrency during top-level design of a real-time system. They are:

- Analogy to previous systems
- Modeling the external world
- Deferring the decision
- Aggregating processes from a data flow diagram (DFD)

Determination of concurrent tasks by analogy to previous systems is highly effective when the designers are familiar with a previous well-designed system to use as a model. This is not, however, the general case. Therefore, a method is required to determine concurrency in the general situation.

Modeling the external world is partially a subset of the use of DFDs, since some of the processes on the DFDs are exactly concerned with interacting with the real world. This is made obvious by the context diagram's illustration of all interfaces with the terminators of the external world. Nonetheless, there are some general techniques that have been advocated that can be useful adjuncts to the use of DFDs. They will be discussed under the topic of event modeling.

Deferring the decision is essentially the approach of object-oriented design, in which the top-level design has as its primary focus the tangible entities of the external world, which may or may not require the software to express concurrency. Specific concurrency issues then become a topic for detailed design. Consideration of objects is a useful adjunct to the methodology for the identification of modules, which will be discussed in Section 7.3.3, but less so for concurrency.

The approach taken to the determination of concurrency is based on grouping or aggregating the processes of a data flow diagram into elements of concurrency in the software—in other words, into tasks. The approach is strongly influenced by work of Gomaa [GOM84 and GOM89] and of Nielsen & Shumate [NIE88]. It builds on the results of the software requirements analysis phase, especially the DFDs, to perform the aggregation. An important element of the approach (shared with entity-life modeling) is that concurrency must be addressed "up front" as part, of top-level design.

Specific Guidelines The general approach is to begin with a complete flattened flow diagram (FFD). This may be upwards of 100 or more processes, but should not be much more, for the usual CSCI. In order to avoid off-page connectors, this analysis should use large sheets of paper containing all of the processes of the CSCI from software requirements analysis. The reason that the FFD is used is that the task boundaries will not necessarily match the boundaries of upper-level or intermediate processes. In determination of tasks in systems with multiple CSCIs, it is vital that each CSCI designer check interfaces (both explicit and implicit) with logically adjacent CSCIs. This is particularly important to control the number of tasks specified, their direct interactions, and access to and protection for common data stores.

The following list gives guidance for areas to look at in identifying concurrency. The list is *not* in any priority order, although it is usually easiest to first identify tasks that interact with external devices.

External Devices: The general guideline is that each external device, especially those that interact with the system via interrupts, should be assigned its own task. This is by no means a hard and fast rule, since timing issues may allow a single task to deal with several devices. In addition, those devices that are polled by the software may well all be served by a single task. A task established by this guideline should be kept as "simple" as possible: It should know only what it absolutely needs to in order to perform the interface with the device, and should not be tied to the application of the data. Besides being a clearer and more maintainable design, this also makes the software more reusable.

Periodic Events: All the actions that occur at the same periodic time interval should be grouped into a single task.

Aperiodic Events: There may be events that occur in the system aperiodically and require response—for example, some combination of circumstances or a stimulus from the outside world. Tasks that execute state transition diagrams may fall into this category, with the event being the cause of the state transition. Except for trivial responses, a task handling an external device will not respond to asynchronous events. Such device handlers should only deal with the hardware-dependent issues of handling the device.

Time-critical or hard-deadline processing: Those functions that must respond quickly or be completed before some deadline are generally separated into different tasks. This criterion overlaps with others; for example, a periodic task may be time-critical and hence have a high priority. There may be two functions with the same period but placed into different tasks as a consequence of this criterion.

Computational intensiveness: Tasks that require a great deal of processing, especially those which are iterative in nature and asymptotically approach some correct value with greater and greater precision, can be isolated as low-priority or "background" tasks.

Functional cohesion: Processes may be allocated to tasks because they perform a closely related function, and the modularization by tasks clarifies the design. This criterion leads to an extra task when the functionality of the task could be "lumped in" with that of some other task on other grounds, but lumping would lead to a loss of clarity in the design. This criterion can also lead to a design that is easier to modify and maintain. Efficiency concerns must be dealt with: There is a tradeoff between the extra clarity in the design and the extra overhead of the additional task.

Mutual exclusion: Depending upon the real-time executive used, additional tasks may have to be added to ensure that concurrent processes sharing data access the data in sequential order.

Process activation tables (PATs): The PATs from the software requirements model can make explicit concurrency defined in the requirements. These processes can be considered for grouping with other processes but, in most cases, not with each other.

Event modeling: This is a "checkback" on the other guidelines. The basic rule is that each "thread of real-world events is mapped onto a task" [SAN89a and SAN89b]. Looking at real-world events in this way may help clarify the design and help make task analysis decisions.

Often the grouping of activities is based on time of execution in a particular implementation (without regard to data flow or to order of execution). This is referred to as *temporal cohesion*. Specific guideline areas given above that may imply temporal cohesion are periodic and aperiodic events.

7.3.2 Task Interfaces

The particular interface between tasks that we choose depends on the degree of coupling desired between each pair of tasks, as follows:

- A loose coupling is depicted by stating "(buffered)" after the flow name. It signifies that a queue or buffer of some type is required for handling the data passed from one task to another.
- A slightly tighter coupling is a signal sent from one task to another. This is represented as a control flow.
- A tight coupling is shown as data flow (parameters) from one task to another.
- The tightest coupling between a pair of tasks occurs when there is data going in both directions between them. This signifies that one task is passing a parameter to another, and that the former is waiting for a reply from the latter.
- Be careful about coupling through shared data (stores) between two tasks, because you must be sure that mutual exclusion is provided for the data being stored. Often a data store must be a task by itself, providing services to access the data and guaranteeing mutual exclusion.

Additional guidelines and graphics for task interface identification for use with Ada are discussed in detail in [SHU88] and [NIE88] respectively.

7.3.3 Top-Level Module Identification

A *module* is a collection of software components (tasks, subprograms, and so forth) that interact closely together to perform functions necessary to satisfy the requirements. The primary form of module is that based on principles of data abstraction and information hiding.

The key aspect of establishing an effective top-level software architecture is the definition of a set of strong data abstractions [LIS86] or information-hiding modules [PAR72b]. These modules must be capable of being used based only on their specification, not their implementation [PAR72a]. In order to ensure that the software design satisfies the requirements, and to simplify traceability, a primary basis for the identification of information-hiding modules is that they be derived from "real-world" elements of the problem to be solved.

Examples of such elements are ships, radars, sonars, furnaces, aircraft, jammers, windmills, displays, and so on. The net effect of such an approach to top-level design is that the software architecture is a reflection of the customer's viewpoint of the system. This both helps the designer create a cohesive and coherent design ("clean" and "elegant" are useful adjectives) and helps satisfy the customer's need to visualize how the requirements will be satisfied.

Identification of information-hiding modules can result from any consideration of the problem space, but it comes most effectively and methodically from the products of the software requirements analysis phase: the DFD, CFD, and associated documentation. The tasks identified on the task communication graph (TCG) and the interfaces between them also become a source for module identification.

There are several general guidelines for identifying modules:

- External interfaces
- Task functionality
- Data stores in the DFD
- System states from associated CSpec(s)
- Data abstraction
- Information hiding

Each aspect of module identification is concerned with the module boundaries and the interfaces between the modules. Therefore, the identification of the module itself is only part of the job. The other important part of the decisions about module boundaries is the choice of what operations the module should export and what operations it should import from other modules. Such decisions should be made while selecting modules. In fact, the selection of boundaries and the selection of operations is an interactive and iterative process. Once a module is identified, it is useful to determine all likely operations required for the module. This is useful in helping think through the entire problem and helps the continual development of structure charts. Frequently, one of the functions necessary to satisfy some requirement will already be available as an exported operation of a module that was defined in this style. Additional guidelines, and a rationale for the SSEM type of module, are provided in Appendix A, "Software Design Concepts."

The decisions about module boundaries are documented in a graphic manner. It is not important to use graphics to show the operations; they need be only documented in a list. (For a simple module, the graphics might be useful, but a complex module may have dozens or more of exported operations, rendering graphic illustration worse than useless.) The formal expression of module interfaces is made during detailed design using program design language (PDL). Each of the following sections gives some guidance about modules and the operations that may be exported or imported.

External Interfaces There are actually three aspects of this guideline that are essentially equivalent:

- "Real-world" elements, or Entities in the problem space (objects)
- Hardware devices
- Terminators in the context diagram

The first aspect—elements, objects, or "tangible things" such as radars, ships, operators, consoles, thermometers, fuel gauges or controls—is the criterion invoked by object-oriented design. In terms of the software development, such elements are almost always important because of interaction through some hardware device and, hence, a terminator on a context diagram. Nonetheless, a useful checkback on the design is to look at the object or tangible elements in the problem space to see if the design might be simplified or clarified by modeling such objects.

The second aspect is straightforward information hiding: The module would hide the device characteristics and export operations on the device.

The third aspect is the most simple and easy to use when developing a design from context flow and data flow diagrams. The terminators usually represent hardware devices, which in turn represent real-world objects. The advantage of using the terminators is that they are already identified. The operations exported and imported by the module are largely defined by the process (or processes) interacting with the terminator and by the data flows connected to the terminator. In addition, the interactions and data flows of the TCG give additional imported and exported operations.

A general guideline is that each terminator will be encapsulated in a module. This is usually easy to apply, and it also serves to encapsulate the task that is (almost always) associated with the terminator. It is not an absolute rule, however, as it may be clearer to have one module deal with two terminators that have similar functioning. There will never be two modules dealing with a single terminator. This is actually yet another application of the usual information hiding principles; the secret of the module is the detailed characteristics of the terminator.

Task Functionality There are likely to be additional tasks in the system that are not associated with terminators. It will frequently be the case that each of these tasks is encapsulated in its own module. However, two or more tasks with similar functionality and working together to provide operations for other modules may be in the same module. (Such tasks should be looked at closely to see if they might be better combined into a single task.)

The description of the problem, given in PSpecs and CSpecs, may identify elements or objects, such as "radar analyzer," "speed comparator," "transmission protocol handler," or "radar jammer," that give hints as to good groupings of tasks for this purpose. Note that sometimes "objects" and "functions" are not clearly delineated. The objects above might just as well be expressed with functional language, such as "analyze radar signals," "compare desired and actual speed," "handle transmission protocol," or "jam enemy radar."

Data Stores in the DFD   As a general rule, each of the data stores in the DFD should be encapsulated in a module. (The only exception is a simple data store used only by a single task.) If the store is used for only a single task, the data store module is logically part of the task. If the store is used for two or more tasks, it may be actually or logically embedded in one of the tasks, or it may be embedded in another task created specifically and solely to control access to the data. The exact mechanism is dependent upon a specific real-time executive and tasking model.

This guideline is also closely related to the notion of identifying elements in the problem space. A data store may be closely associated with a tangible element in the world or at least a "logical element" that is part of the problem statement—a desired speed, temperature limits for some process, minimum altitude for certain maneuvers, and so on.

System States from CSpec(s)   The knowledge of system states and the management of the events causing change from one state to another form a good candidate for the creation of a module. Hiding this information, so that no other module would need to know the details of how these system states are managed, allows the system to be more maintainable and easier to modify when criteria for state transitions change.

Data Abstraction   During the development of the structure charts of the top-level design, or when one observes the interfaces between tasks (or concurrent modules), it may become apparent that a number of subprograms are operating on the same data structure; for example, inserting, deleting, and performing other operations on a queue. An important way to improve the understandability of software is to separate the complexity of application-type algorithms from the complexity of manipulation of data structures. The way to do this is to use data abstractly (for example, to think in terms of queuing or dequeuing elements to or from a list rather than in terms of the specific details of arrays, pointers, and so on). Encapsulating the specific data structure inside a module, with access to the data structure done by operations exported by the module, is an application of *data abstraction*. Application of principles of data abstraction give rise to the need for a module to encapsulate the data structure of the queue. Such modules are called helper modules, but they are identified as part of the top-level design and documented at this time.

The ideas of data abstraction, and the following notion of information hiding, are addressed further in Appendix A-2, "Information Hiding and Data Abstraction."

Information Hiding Parnas offers another view of the same ideas in his article "Enhancing Reusability With Information Hiding" [PAR89], where he points out that the overall goal of decomposition into modules is the reduction of software development and maintenance cost by allowing modules to be designed, implemented, and revised independently; these properties are synonymous with reusability. Specific goals of the module decomposition are:

1. Each module's structure should be simple enough that it can be understood fully.

2. It should be possible to change the implementation of one module without knowledge of the implementation of other modules and without affecting the behavior of other modules.

3. The ease of making a change in the design should bear a reasonable relationship to the likelihood of the change being needed. It should be possible to make likely changes without changing any module interfaces; less likely changes may involve interface changes, but only for modules that are small and not widely used. Only very unlikely changes should require changes in the interfaces of widely used modules. There should be few widely used interfaces.

4. It should be possible to make a major software change as a set of independent changes to individual modules; that is, except for interface changes, programmers changing the individual modules should not need to communicate. If the interfaces of the modules are not revised, it should be possible to run and test any combination of old and new module versions.

In keeping with these goals, the software design may be composed of many small modules, organized in a hierarchy. This makes the following additional goals achievable:

5. A software engineer should be able to understand the responsibility of a module without understanding the module's internal design.

6. A reader with a well-defined concern should easily be able to identify the relevant modules without studying irrelevant modules. This requires that the reader be able to distinguish relevant modules from irrelevant modules without looking at their internal structure.

The following types of modules form the top-level decomposition of a system:

1. The *hardware-hiding module* includes the tasks and subprograms that need to be changed if any part of the hardware is replaced by a new unit having a different hardware–software interface but with the same general capabilities. It hides the hardware–software interfaces described in the requirements. It

may also hide the data structures and algorithms that are used to implement the virtual hardware.

2. The *behavior-hiding module* includes the tasks or subprograms that need to be changed if there are changes to the requirements that describe the required behavior. This behavior of the system is the primary secret of this module. This module determines the values to be sent to the virtual output devices provided by the hardware-hiding module.

3. The *software decision module* hides software design decisions that are based upon mathematical theorems, physical facts, and programming considerations such as algorithmic efficiency and accuracy. Its secrets are not described in the requirements themselves but are instead a result of the software design. Changes in this module are more likely to be motivated by a desire to improve performance than by externally imposed changes.

Figure 7-13 is adapted from a similar figure in the article [PAR89] and illustrates examples of modules that were identified for the A-7E flight software using the principles of information hiding and these module goals.

7.3.4 Transform Analysis

The following has been adapted from *The Practical Guide to Structured Systems Design* [PAG88, Chapter 10]. We will only repeat the general steps here.

Transform analysis, or *transform-centered design,* as it is also known, is a strategy for converting into a structure chart each piece of the FFD that we isolated into tasks. It also yields balanced systems, which are easier to develop and to maintain than physically input- or output-driven systems.

The general idea is that a data flow diagram for a single task or a sequential system will usually have one primary point, consisting of several data transforms, at which the data flows change nature from "input" to "output." The data transforms accomplishing that transition are called the *central transforms*, which become the top-level steps to solve the problem. All data flows input to the transition point are called *efferent* data flows, and those leaving the transition point are said to be *afferent* data flows.

Of the several data transforms at the transition point, one of them will typically tend to be more-or-less directive in terms of order of processing. We will call this transform the "boss." If there is no obvious directive transform, we insert a transform (perhaps adding data flows as necessary) with the primary function of controlling the order of processing of the other central transforms. The inserted transform is then the "boss" of the transition point. Of course, we no longer have a proper DFD, and are just doing this to transition to the structure chart.

The "boss" becomes the top-level subprogram in the structure chart, while the other transforms become the next lower layer. (Remember that we are now talking about a calling or invoking relationship, independent of the direction of data

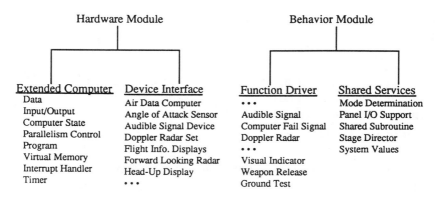

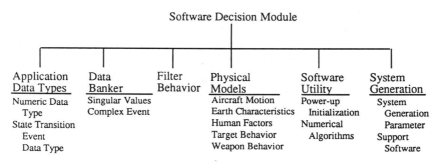

Figure 7-13   Module Examples From A-7E Flight Software

flows.) The transforms that are providing the efferent data, and disposing of the afferent data, become successively lower levels (expanding to the left and right, respectively) of the structure chart.

You can visualize the process by imagining that the DFD is a network of ping-pong balls connected by string. To create the first-cut structure chart, you just pick up the "boss" ping-pong ball and hold it high in the air, arranging the other balls in an orderly manner. This is a pretty rough cut, of course, and a lot of judgment goes into "orderly manner," but it gets the idea across. Then the first-cut structure chart is refined by coupling, cohesion, and factoring.

The transforms directly accessing the data stores are not initially treated any differently than other transforms. However, they really have a special role to play as subprograms, since they must have visibility to the actual formats of the data stores that become physical data base items. Eventually, the data stores in the data flow diagram become objects encapsulated in modules, with the data transforms immediately accessing the data store becoming the operations on the object.

When you carry out transform analysis, remember that it is a strategy. It starts with a seemingly mechanical process, but you cannot unthinkingly follow its steps as you could those of an algorithm. From time to time, to stay on the right track, you must bring to mind your knowledge of what the system is supposed to accomplish. When you derive your first structure chart, you must use structured design criteria of coupling, cohesion, and factoring to improve it.

Transform analysis is composed of the following steps:

1. Draw a DFD/CFD.
2. Find the central process(es) of the DFD/CFD.
3. Convert the DFD/CFD into a first-cut structure chart.
4. Refine this structure chart by means of structured design criteria.
5. Verify that the final structure chart meets the software requirements.

7.3.5 Transaction Analysis

Transaction analysis is used when a DFD (or a portion of it) has a configuration such that data or control information passes to a process that initiates one of several alternative processes or sequences of processes based on the incoming data. The first process on the DFD is called the *transaction center,* and it performs the following:

1. Receives incoming data (called *transactions*) in raw form
2. Analyzes each transaction to determine its type
3. Selects a *process path* based on the transaction type

The transaction center becomes the top-level control subprogram for the structure chart with the input, analysis, and routing (steps 1, 2, and 3) as lower-level subprograms on the structure chart.

As you can see, this design strategy for transaction-centered DFDs differs somewhat from the transform analysis above. An important property of the DFDs, however, is that transform- and transaction-centered structures may be combined to form building blocks for the overall software architecture. For example, a transform-centered structure may occur on a process path of a transaction process, or a transaction process may comprise the afferent branch of a transform-centered structure.

7.3.6 Coupling and Cohesion Quality

Coupling is the degree to which two subprograms are interconnected and, conversely, the degree to which they are independent. Loose coupling (little interconnection) is best for a good design. Coupling can be kept to a minimum by eliminating unnecessary relationships between subprograms, reducing the number of necessary relationships, and easing the tightness of necessary relationships. The types of coupling from best to worst (loose to tight) are:

Data coupling by passing elementary parameters

Stamp coupling by composite parameters, where not all elements of a parameter are needed

Control coupling by parameters used explicitly to control the behavior of the recipient subprogram

Global or common coupling via a globally accessible data area

Content or pathological coupling by direct connection between the internals of the subprograms

The most flexible and maintainable designs are typically those with the simplest interfaces between modules. The coupling between them is of the loosest possible (data coupling through control coupling).

Cohesion is the measure of an individual subprogram that indicates the degree to which its components are working together to accomplish the same function. High cohesion (single, clearly understood individual function) is desirable for a good design. In sequence from best to worst (high to low), the levels of cohesion are:

Functional cohesion: Elements contribute to a single, problem-related activity.

Sequential cohesion: Activities within the module are connected in that the output from one serves as the input to another.

Communicational cohesion: Activities share the same input or output, but order is not important.

Temporal cohesion: Activities can be carried out at the same time.

Logical cohesion: Activities appear to belong to the same general category.

Coincidental cohesion: Activities have no relationship to one another.

The maintainability of subprograms with functional, sequential, and communicational cohesion tends to be significantly higher than that of subprograms of the lower levels of cohesion.

Proper balancing of functional decomposition and information hiding should lead to a design exhibiting high cohesion and low coupling. However, there may be conflict between this and the mapping of the requirements model to the design model. The quality of the software design (for example, good modularity) is to be favored over traceability, because requirements traceability will be achieved through the linking within the requirements store and generation of an RTM.

7.3.7 Factoring

Factoring is the removal of a function contained as code in one subprogram to a new subprogram of its own. This needs to be done to decompose the software into a good design. Page-Jones [PAG88] gives the following reasons for factoring to be done:

- To reduce subprogram size
- To clarify the system, and so get the modular advantage of classic top-down design—thus making the system easier to understand and making modification to the system more localized and straightforward

- To minimize duplication of code by avoiding having the same function carried out by more than one subprogram
- To separate work (calculating and editing) from management (calling and deciding)
- To provide more generally useful subprograms
- To simplify implementation

7.3.8 Modular Structured Design

Sections 7.3.3 to 7.3.7 address various issues of modularity and information hiding and of decomposition and structured design. The modularity material addresses the importance of structuring the software design around encapsulated data; the other sections largely deal with expression of algorithms, the step-by-step processing of the system. What is really important in software design is that we address *both* data encapsulation and step-by-step processing. Since "modular design" addresses encapsulation and "structured design" has become widely known as the expression of the functional behavior or step-by-step processing of the system, we call the approach that includes both philosophies "Modular Structured Design" or MSD.

The MSD style of design, as well as an overview of some of its constituent parts, is expressed in Appendix A, "Software Design Concepts." Although the material in the appendix presents MSD as a step-by-step process, it is not so much the steps that are important as is the general approach—the philosophy of concern with both data encapsulation and functional decomposition.

You should read all of Appendix A at this time, as an integral part of this chapter leading to the remaining guidelines and steps, and also to set the foundation for Chapter 8, "Detailed Design."

7.4 METHODOLOGY—STEP BY STEP

This section goes through the details of the methodology in a step-by-step style to give an understanding for the issues that come up. The guidelines introduced above are discussed at the appropriate step of the methodology.

The following lists the steps in the general order that they occur. In practice, some may be worked on in parallel and iteratively.

1. Identify tasks (concurrent components).
2. Define task interfaces.
3. Perform timing thread analysis.
4. Develop preliminary software architecture.
   4.1 Identify application modules.
   4.2 Make preliminary identification of helper modules.
   4.3 Illustrate module relationships.
   4.4 Document module interfaces in PDL (optional).

5. Decompose tasks.
6. Finalize top-level software architecture.
7. Document traceability.
8. When am I done?

Step 1   Identify tasks (concurrent components).   To identify the concurrent elements within the CSCI, the following steps need to be performed:

1. Construct an FFD containing all the bottom-level processes from software requirements analysis on one chart (or wall). It is important to be able to see all the processing in one place in order to fully identify the concurrent components.
2. Identify the concurrency within the CSCI by marking it on the FFD. Use the guidelines for task identification. Make sure you give each concurrent component (task) a name indicative of the processing being performed.
3. Save the FFD for future reference along with a description of the reasons behind the grouping.

Step 2   Define task interfaces.   Draw a task communication graph (TCG) depicting each of the tasks identified above to illustrate the interfaces that must occur between them. Follow the guidelines for task interfaces.

In addition, for an Ada implementation, caller/called decisions between the tasks must be made. Refer to [NIE88] for details of guidelines and graphics for Ada tasking.

Step 3   Perform timing thread analysis.   The purpose of a timing thread analysis is to identify threads, allocate response times to tasks, and provide the basis for management of software time budgets. A *thread* is all the processing (literally all the instructions) necessary to respond to an event. All aspects of the processing of the task must be considered when coming up with the allocated times for these threads. Some of the issues are processor speed, algorithms, numerical analysis, number of subprogram calls, and the compiler, implementation language, and run-time executive that will be used for the individual project. Specific timing issues include time for interrupt handling, task synchronization, and so on. Timing thread analysis requires the following procedures:

1. Analyze each of the external timing events (external input signals) from the software requirements analysis phase to determine its criticality. The inputs, outputs, and required response times are provided in the response time specification (RTS). A noncritical time line is one which will clearly be satisfied if the critical response times are met, and there is no need to expend the effort to manage these noncritical time requirements.
2. For each critical event, identify the thread or path by drawing the line through the tasks involved on the TCG.

3. Partition the total response time and allocate it to the tasks (and associated task interactions). It is necessary to analyze the task or interaction execution time—using simulation, instruction step timing, or other means—in order to demonstrate that this concurrent design will satisfy the timing requirements. Remember that the most difficult aspects of the timing analysis are not the single threads (although the analysis must begin there), but the interaction of multiple concurrent threads of control interacting in complex ways. Problems uncovered at this point may cause a revisit to Steps 1 and 2 of top-level design. Indeed, if the timing discrepancy cannot be resolved there, then software requirements analysis (or system design or system requirements analysis) may also need to be reexamined.

4. Retain the timing analysis for future reference. Critical timing threads are likely to be presented to the customer during reviews and in appropriate documentation. The timing analysis will critically depend upon the language and real-time executive being used. The allocated times become the timing budget for the task, which will then be managed throughout the software development.

This step only outlines the general concept of timing analysis. Detailed analysis methods are beyond the scope of this text and are, in any event, largely dependent on specific language and real-time executive choices and on problem-specific issues. In fact, analysis and determination of timing is not a completely mastered discipline; it deserves a look all by itself.

A particularly important component of timing analysis is the frequency and type of input data and signals, called the *system load*. In systems of significant complexity, with combinations of periodic and aperiodic behavior, the most practical approach is simulation. For somewhat less complex, but still practicable, systems, there is an emerging theory of how analytically to address timing issues and ensure completion of deadlines (the most important of these is "Rate Monotonic Scheduling" [SHA90].) Although the analysis is highly likely to change during detailed design, it is important to perform this preliminary analysis during top-level design.

Even though it is not a formal step in the methodology, this is also the right time to perform *sizing* analysis. (In many companies, "sizing and timing analysis" is virtually one word.) We have little additional to say about sizing, although the early emphasis on tasks (and hence early determination of task control blocks for the real-time executive) will make the sizing issues clearer at an early stage in design.

Step 4 Develop preliminary software architecture. Develop a preliminary cut at the top-level software architecture, based on the concurrency identified for the CSCI, using the following substeps.

Step 4.1 Identify application modules. Mark the grouping of the tasks for development on the TCG. These become the application modules. Use the module identification guidelines to determine the grouping. Save the reasons for your grouping for future reference. Decide on the services that will need to be provided by each module.

Step 4.2 Make preliminary identification of helper modules. Examine the application modules and their interfaces with each other to make a preliminary determination of helper modules that will be needed. Use the guidelines for module identification. Data abstraction and information hiding are very important concepts here. In addition, identify the likely operations (subprograms) that each application and helper module will need to provide.

Step 4.3 Illustrate module relationships. Draw a preliminary SAD depicting the interrelationships between the application and helper modules.

Step 4.4 Document the module interfaces in PDL (optional). If you are using a language such as Ada, write PDL to document the actual interfaces between the modules. This allows for early checking of the consistency of the interface data definition.

Step 5 Decompose tasks. Using transform analysis, transaction analysis, and the structured design criteria of coupling, cohesion and factoring (described in Section 7.3), and using the modular structured design philosophy, create a structure chart that defines the first-level breakdown of each complex task (each task to which several software requirement processes have been allocated). For simple tasks, which contain only one process on the FFD, no decomposition is necessary during top-level design. It is enough that you have identified the task.

To do the decomposition, follow the transform or transaction analysis steps, using as the starting DFD/CFD the portion of the FFD that was allocated to the task being decomposed.

It is during this step that the need for additional helper modules appears. They could already exist in the preliminary SAD. Use information hiding and data abstraction principles to determine the helper modules. Although the methodology for performing transform analysis is language-independent, the actual design can be very much dependent on the model of concurrency or real-time executive used.

Step 6 Finalize top-level software architecture. Reexamine the application modules, their interfaces with each other, and their structure charts to identify any additional support needed. The module identification guidelines apply. Update the SAD to document the interrelationships between the application and helper modules. Update the list of operations provided by each module (or PDL).

Step 7 Document traceability. Generate an RTM to depict the allocation of the software requirements to each of the modules identified in the SAD. The FFD with the concurrency identified is a good place to start searching for the allocation. The allocation to each task can easily be seen on the FFD and applied to the application modules identified on the SAD. Determine the additional allocation of requirements to the helper modules as identified on the structure charts and on the SAD.

Step 8   When am I done? Top-level design is considered complete when the following questions can be answered in the affirmative:

1. Has all concurrency been identified?
2. Have the task interfaces been defined?
3. Has a structure chart been used to show top-level decomposition of each complex task?
4. Have helper modules been identified and their services determined?
5. Has the top-level software architecture been determined (using SAD)?
6. Does each module trace back to CSCI requirement(s)?
7. Have all CSCI requirements been allocated to module(s)?

The output of top-level design is the first-cut decomposition of the software architecture. Once the top-level design is complete, the most important graphic for illustrating the overall software architecture is the SAD. The SAD is also the key to traceability: Requirements are allocated to and traced from the modules on the SAD. In terms of explaining the design to others, in both engineering and customer reviews, it is best to *begin* with the SAD. (There is a distinct difference in how we develop the design and how we explain it—the development of the design *ended* with the SAD.) The structure chart and the TCG remain important in explaining the step-by-step processing—the *functionality*—in the context of the software architecture, based on principles of information hiding and data abstraction.

Remember, also, both in refining the SAD and in explaining the design to others, that the most important of the information-hiding modules on the SAD are software representations and abstractions of tangible components of the problem to be solved. This helps both in formulating good data abstractions and in ensuring that requirements have been met. These factors, in turn, lead to designs that are easy to implement, test, and modify and that are ultimately easy for the customer to maintain.

7.5   FMS TOP-LEVEL DESIGN EXAMPLE

This section provides an example of the top-level design methodology, essentially solving the following problem. If you wish to test your knowledge of the methods presented, you may wish to solve the problem yourself before looking at the solution.

Assignment: Develop a top-level design, including all graphics, for the software requirements specified in Chapter 6. This should include all identification of concurrency and all identification and documentation of top-level modules.

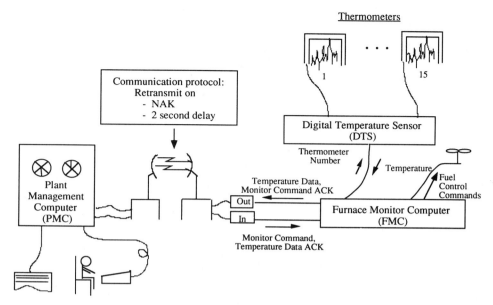

Figure 7-14   FMC Prototype

A prototype version of the software, implementing only part of the requirements shown in Chapter 6 and simplifying the communications interface, will be sufficient to illustrate all the points we need to make about software design. Implementation of a prototype is common practice, is often a good development approach, and will simplify and shorten the exposition and illustration of software design principles.

Figure 7-14 illustrates the prototype components of the FMC. The prototype covers only the temperature-sensing and related portions of the FMC. The scheduling information is received from the PMC, temperatures are monitored accordingly and reported back, and the fuel supply is controlled when the furnace gets too hot. Figure 7-15 and 7-16 give the context diagram and first-level breakdown (from software requirements) for the portion implemented. Also reference Section 6.5.8.1 for the requirement breakdown of this functionality. Detailed descriptions of the interfaces to the PMC and the DTS are given in Section 6.5 and Figure 5-54, respectively.

What follows is a completed top-level design, including answers to the questions you asked yourself (or should have asked yourself).

7.5.1 Step 1: Identify Tasks (Concurrent Components)

Figure 7-17 shows the flattened flow diagram for the temperature sensing portion of the FMC CSCI.

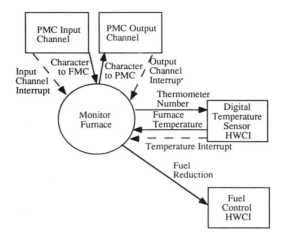

Figure 7-15   Data/Control Context Diagram for Furnace
Monitor Computer Prototype CSCI

Comments

• The FFD is composed of all the bottom-level processes from software requirements analysis. For large systems, you will need a bigger piece of paper or
indeed an entire wall. You are encouraged to cut and paste or whatever to get
them all connected on one "page," is so that the entire CSCI can be studied
and contemplated at once. Since this diagram is not delivered to the customer,
it doesn't have to be beautifully drawn. Hand drawings are acceptable. Re-

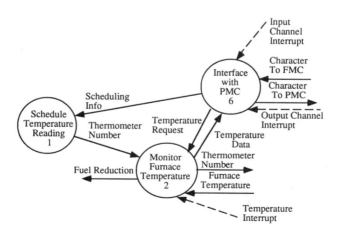

Figure 7-16   FMC Prototype DFD/CFD 0

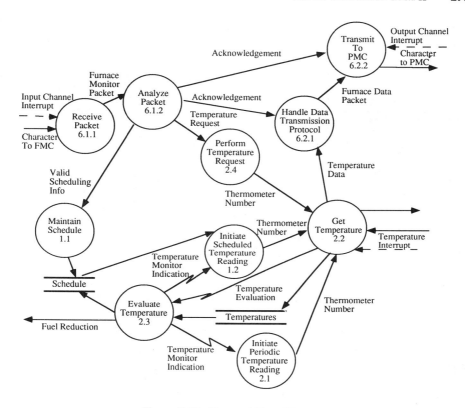

Figure 7-17 Flattened Flow Diagram

member to save it (or the pieces) for future reference. If any modification to the system comes up later, this diagram will prove invaluable in determining the best way to incorporate those changes.

- Since the breakdown of Process 6.1.2 contains only sequential processing for an individual packet (see Figure 5-26), we have used the higher-level process for the FFD.

The next (sub)step is to identify the concurrency on the FFD that was just drawn. The task identification is shown in Figure 7-18.

Comments

- Here we drew over the FFD to group the processes into concurrent tasks. Names are added to identify each task.
- When doing this with a "wall-sized" FFD, you will probably want to have colored pens and list the processes that are being grouped together along with the task name.

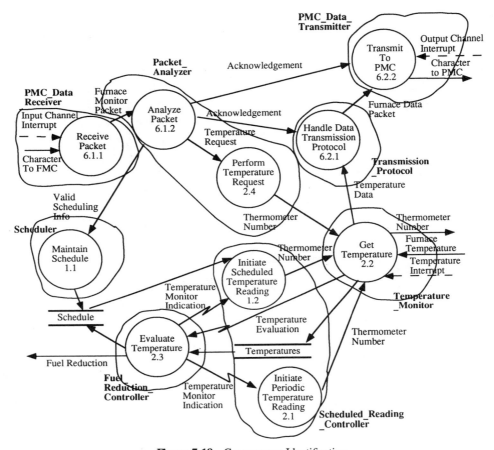

Figure 7-18   Concurrency Identification

- The rationale for these groupings is as follows:

    PMC_Data_Receiver is a device driver, and one of the rules is to keep device drivers as simple as possible so that they can handle the interrupts for the interface. This task must be ready to accept the INPUT CHANNEL INTERRUPT at any time. It cannot wait for the validation and routing to take place.

    Packet_Analyzer performs the determination of the type of input received from the PMC. ACKNOWLEDGEMENTs received are passed on for the protocol handling. Monitor commands are validated, acknowledged, and routed. Since this task does both validation and routing, it is temporally cohesive. These steps always occur together in time.

Scheduler encapsulates everything about the data store SCHEDULE. It is functionally cohesive. It will have to provide a service to the Scheduled_Reading_Controller task to update LAST TIME READ (a design decision about the SCHEDULE data store), since visibility directly to the data store is gone. The control of temperature reading (TEMPERATURE MONITOR INDICATION) will be handled here, so this is the only task with knowledge of scheduling.

Scheduled_Reading_Controller is simply a time-out task that will wait for the TIME TO READ and then send the THERMOMETER NUMBER for retrieving the temperature. We cannot combine it with the Scheduler task, because that task needs to be able to update the SCHEDULE at any time and thus cannot be waiting for a time-out.

Temperature_Monitor is a simple device driver.

Transmission_Protocol needs to function separately from PMC_Data_Transmitter because of the protocol involved. It needs to be able to time out or receive an ACK or new TEMPERATURE DATA when available.

PMC_Data_Transmitter, a device driver, cannot be combined with Transmission_Protocol, because it needs to be able to send a COMMAND ACK at any time as well as the TEMPERATURE DATA.

Fuel_Reduction_Controller is triggered separately, since we don't want to hold up "Get_Temperature," to evaluate the temperatures and reduce fuel flow as necessary.

Document your reasons, as shown here, and save them along with the diagram for future reference.

- Notice the shared data store (TEMPERATURES). The access to this data structure must include a mechanism for mutual exclusion, so that the two tasks are not reading or writing at the same time. The method for providing this varies depending on the implementation language. For example, in the Ada tasking model, a "monitor" package (containing a task) would be added to protect the data. In most languages, which use a real-time executive, the access by either task could be done within a critical section (for example, using semaphores). This difference in methods of data access is an example of why the actual top-level design, including the timing analysis, must be programming language–and run-time system–dependent.

7.5.2 Step 2: Define Task Interfaces

Figure 7-19 is the task communication graph, illustrating the tasks that have just been identified and the interfaces between them.

Comments

- Here we see the addition of data buffering of the Temperature_Data to be output to the PMC. This data needs to be buffered so that Temperature_Monitor is not held up if Transmission_Protocol is not finished with sending out the previous set of Temperature_Data. This buffer will be an overwriting one; that is, when the maximum number of elements are in it, the oldest one will be written over with new data coming in. This design is OK, because of our knowledge of the scheduling requirements and their timing.

- The incoming Packet information does not need to be buffered, because the protocol is such that new information will not be sent until this packet is acknowledged.

- The other interfaces should be straightforward and quick enough not to need buffering. If preliminary tests of the software indicate that this is not the case, then this diagram will need to be revisited at that time.

- The interface between the Scheduler and the Scheduled_Reading_Controller tasks is actually two separate interfaces (*not* the "tightest coupling" discussed in the task interface guidelines). This is illustrated by the two distinct flow lines between the task instead of a double-headed arrow:

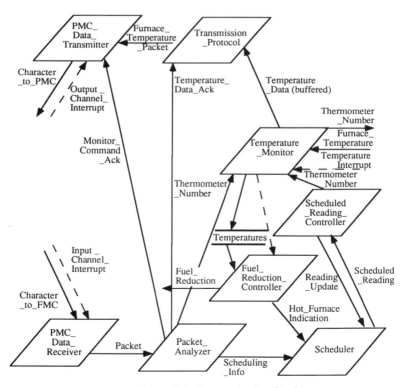

Figure 7-19   Task Communication Graph

1. The first interface is to pass Scheduled_Reading to Scheduled_Reading_Controller. The Scheduler can then go back to its other work.

2. The second interface is the Reading_Update coming back. Notice that this is a new parameter that we will have to define – it consists of Last_Time_Read and the Thermometer_Number. We needed to add this, because Scheduled_Reading_Controller no longer has direct visibility to the Schedule data store.

7.5.3 Step 3: Perform Timing Thread Analysis

The following is the list of external timing events from the RTS in the software requirements analysis phase that have to be considered for tracing through our initial task identification. The time-critical ones have been drawn on Figure 7-20. We then estimate the time for each portion of the thread and perform the allocation to each task.

SCHEDULING INFO received from PMC results in the following responses taking place:

1. COMMAND ACK sent (3 seconds): The thread is (solid line on Figure 7-20):

    ○ PMC_Data_Receiver receives the interrupt(s) and characters (Character_to_FMC) to make up a Packet, which is passed on to Packet_Analyzer. *Allocated Time*: 1.0 seconds.

    ○ Packet_Analyzer performs the validation on the individual fields of the Monitor_Command and passes the appropriate Monitor_Command_Ack on to PMC_Data_Transmitter. *Allocated Time*: 0.5 seconds.

    ○ PMC_Data_Transmitter places the characters of the Monitor_Command_Ack in the hardware buffer and gets the interrupt that each character has been taken. *Allocated Time*: 0.1 seconds.

2. Updated SCHEDULE used (8 minutes): This thread is not time-critical; there is plenty of time. We will not show this one on the graph.

TEMPERATURE REQUEST received from PMC results in the associated TEMPERATURE DATA being sent to the PMC within 3 seconds. The thread is (dashed line on Figure 7-20):

*   PMC_Data_Receiver receives the interrupt(s) and characters (Character_to_FMC) to make up a Packet, which is passed on to Packet_Analyzer. *Allocated Time*: 1.0 seconds.

*   Packet_Analyzer validates the command received and passes the Thermometer_Number on to Temperature_Monitor. *Allocated Time*: 0.25 seconds.

*   Temperature_Monitor places the Thermometer_Number into the hardware buffer. It then waits to receive interrupt from the digital temperature sen-

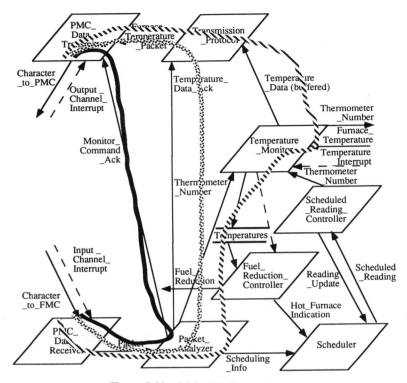

Figure 7-20 TCG with Timing Threads

sor (DTS) and retrieves the Furnace_Temperature from the hardware buffer. It buffers the Temperature_Data for transmission. *Allocated Time*: 0.5 seconds.

- Transmission_Protocol takes the Temperature_Data from the buffer, formats it into the ASCII characters that need to be sent to the PMC, and passes that Furnace_Temperature_Packet to PMC_Data_Transmitter. *Allocated Time*: 0.25 seconds.

- PMC_Data_Transmitter places the characters one at a time into the hardware buffer and waits for the interrupt after each character indicating that that character has been taken. *Allocated Time*: 1.0 seconds.

FURNACE TEMPERATURE, received from the DTS, results in TEMPERA-TURE DATA being sent to the PMC within 3 seconds. This thread is really a subset of the one just discussed, and if that one can be accomplished within the time allotted, so can this one. We will not show this one on the graph.

ACKNOWLEDGEMENT received from the PMC results in the next TEMPER-ATURE DATA being sent to the PMC within 3 seconds. The thread is (dotted line on Figure 7-20):

- PMC_Data_Receiver receives the interrupt and the characters that form the (acknowledgement) Packet. It passes this on to Analyze_Packet. *Allocated Time*: 0.1 seconds.
- Analyze_Packet determines that the Packet is indeed a Temperature_Data_Ack. It passes this on to Transmission_Protocol. *Allocated Time*: 0.1 seconds.
- Transmission_Protocol checks the value and either retrieves the next Temperature_Data from the buffer, when the acknowledgement is positive, and formats it into the ASCII characters that need to be sent to the PMC, or else uses the one last transmitted. That Furnace_Temperature_Packet is passed to PMC_Data_Transmitter. *Allocated Time*: 0.5 seconds.
- PMC_Data_Transmitter places the characters one at a time into the hardware buffer and waits for the interrupt after each character indicating that that character has been taken. *Allocated Time*: 1.0 seconds.

FUEL REDUCTION needs to occur within 30 seconds of receipt of a "hot temperature". This is not a critical time.

The interrupt/hardware buffer timing constraints are:

- TEMPERATURE INTERRUPT, received from DTS, implies that the character must be taken from the hardware buffer within 0.05 seconds.
- INPUT CHANNEL INTERRUPT, received from the PMC, implies that the character must be taken from the hardware buffer within 0.05 seconds.
- OUTPUT CHANNEL INTERRUPT, received from the PMC, implies that the next character (or a pulse) should be placed in the hardware buffer within 0.05 seconds.

These threads appear to be generous, are part of some of the threads previously discussed, and are localized within a single task.

Comments

- Notice that we simply drew the threads onto the TCG. If there are too many threads to show clearly on one copy of the TCG, use several copies.
- All aspects of the processing of the task must be considered when coming up with allocated times for these threads. Some of the issues are processor speed, algorithms, numerical analysis, number of subprogram calls, and the compiler, implementation language, and run-time executive that will be used for the individual project. Specific timing issues include time for interrupt handling, task synchronization, and so on.
- The allocated times become the timing budget for the task, which will then be managed throughout the software development.

Let's consider the timing thread, for handling TEMPERATURE REQUEST. In order to meet the three-second timing on this event, we would need to be sure that the interface between the furnace computer and the PMC is running smoothly (no line errors requiring frequent retransmissions). If not, the Transmission_Protocol may be busy retransmitting an old temperature (with a two-second delay between attempts) when the temperature request comes in. If this new temperature has to wait until the protocol completes up to two retransmissions on the old message, there is no way the timing requirement can be met. There are a couple of possible solutions to this, both of which would probably involve the customer.

1. Apply the timing requirement to the preparation of the response with a certain data error rate. Then say that the timing (3 seconds) must be met 95% of the time. The requested temperature would be the next one sent (in other words, move ahead of any other messages already waiting to go out).

2. Change the protocol so that this requested temperature can go out without regard to retransmission of the older data. A problem with this solution is how to keep in sync with the data acknowledgements coming in on each message. We may have to add a sequence number to the Temperature_Data and the Temperature_Data_Ack and allow time for the interrupts associated with these characters going out and coming in. If there is some reusable software that already handles the original protocol, we would not be able to use that either. This solution also affects more than one CSCI: the one being developed here and the one handling the other end of the interface at the PMC. We are going to assume here that the customer agrees to go along with the proposed solution (number 1).

Remember that the discussion here is only the beginning of the full timing analysis. This was discussed under Step 3 of Section 7.4. A particularly difficult aspect of the timing analysis is that it is impossible to assess fully the effect of design decisions on an individual thread-by- thread basis; this is because the concurrent execution of tasks leads to the timing threads actually being interleaved, rather than executing to completion. For complex systems, it is likely necessary to either simulate or prototype the design—including a simulation or prototype of the tasking model or real-time executive—in order to assess the effect of the interleaving of threads of control on each of the individual timing constraints.

7.5.4 Step 4: Develop Preliminary Software Architecture

Step 4.1   Identify application modules.   The application modules are identified in Figure 7-21. This diagram shows how we are going to group the software into application modules. The grouping is drawn over the TCG. Names have been assigned to each module.

The reasons for the grouping are as follows:

PMC_Interface_Handler: PMC_Data_Receiver and PMC_Data_Transmitter are the device drivers that handle the interface to the PMC. If the input protocol is such that the Packets need buffering, we would include that buffer in this module. This

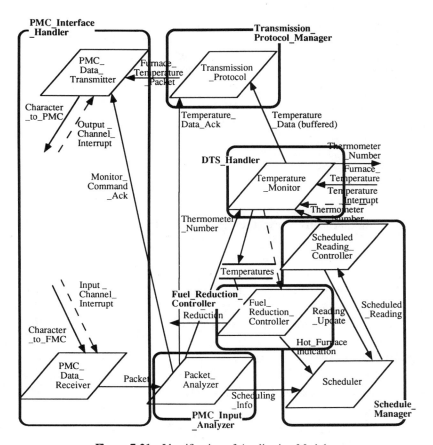

Figure 7-21 Identification of Application Modules

allows for the flexibility a concurrent component needs to handle the buffering depending on timing analysis. The interface to this module from Packet_Analyzer would still look the same.

PMC_Input_Analyzer: Packet_Analyzer has been left by itself to perform the analyzing of packets and associated routing of the command as it has time. In this way, it will not hold up any of the other tasks. The name of this module implies that any input from the PMC that requires actual input data processing, such as validation, would be included here.

Schedule_Manager: Scheduler and Scheduled_Reading_Controller together encapsulate all of the processing necessary for the Schedule. Scheduler is the actual data manager for Schedule, and Scheduled_Reading_Controller is a task that helps carry our the schedule.

DTS_Handler: Temperature_Monitor is a device driver and should be left by itself for reusability purposes. Note that the use of an abbreviation or acronym in the name of a module should be carefully looked at. If the name is not well known to the people that will need to see this, it should be spelled out. We are assuming that DTS is a common acronym (for this example).

Transmission_Protocol_Handler: Transmission_Protocol is by itself. This module handles all of the transmission protocol.

Fuel_Reduction_Handler: Fuel_Reduction_Controller is by itself to handle the calculation and interface involved with reduction of fuel input.

The following is the list of "services" provided by each application module.

1. PMC_Interface_Handler
   - This module can receive the hardware interrupts associated with the interface (Input_Channel_Interrupt and Output_Channel_Interrupt).
   - Receive_Packet allows the Packet to be passed on to the PMC_Input_Analyzer module.
   - Transmit_Packet allows input of Monitor_Command_Ack or Furnace_Temperature_Packet to be sent to the PMC.
2. PMC_Input_Analyzer: This module provides no services but uses the services of others to accomplish its work.
3. Schedule_Manager
   - Update_Schedule allows the new Scheduling_Info to be input.
   - Update_Hot_Furnace allows furnace to be marked as hot or normal.
4. DTS_Handler
   - Get_Temperature allows a Thermometer_Number to be input, indicating that that temperature will be taken.
5. Transmission_Protocol_Manager
   - Acknowledge_Data allows the Temperature_Data_Ack received from the PMC to be used to determine the Furnace_Temperature_Packet to send.
6. Fuel_Reduction_Handler
   - Evaluate_Temperature allows the initiation of the temperature evaluation and possible fuel reduction.

Step 4.2   Make preliminary identification of helper modules.   The Helper Modules identified from the application modules and the services they will provide are:

1. Temperature_Manager, to control the interface to the Temperatures data store.
   - Store_Temperature allows the input of Temperature retrieved from a thermometer to be stored.
   - Get_Temperatures allows the retrieval of the Temperatures that have been stored.

2. Temperature_Data_Buffer, as a lower-level helper module to perform the actual buffering of the outgoing Temperature_Data.

   ○ Enqueue allows storage of a Temperature_Data into the buffer.

   ○ Dequeue allows retrieval of a Temperature_Data from the buffer.

Note that either of these could potentially be a concurrent component itself, depending on the implementation language.

Step 4.3 Illustrate module relationships.   Figure 7-22 illustrates the application modules and the helper modules that have been identified. Their interfaces (dependencies) are also shown. This representation is often difficult to accomplish in a concise manner. For complex systems, one may wish to organize the modules in "levels," as illustrated in Step 4 of Section 7.4, or show the design on a module-by-module basis, showing each module only with those it directly provides services to or depends upon.

Step 4.4 Document the module interfaces in PDL (optional).   Since this example is using Ada as PDL, we will give the PDL for the modules (Ada packages) that provide interface information (either as services or type definitions):

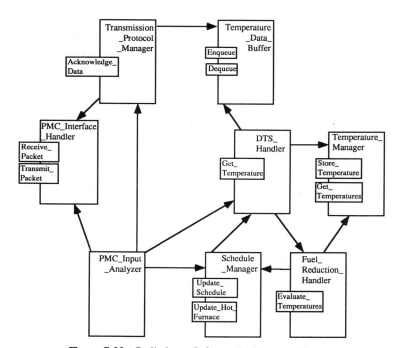

Figure 7-22 Preliminary Software Architecture Diagram

Application modules:

- DTS_Handler
- Schedule_Manager
- PMC_Interface_Handler
- Transmission_Protocol_Manager
- Fuel_Reduction_Handler
- Packet_Analyzer (not shown because no services provided)

Helper modules:

- Temperature_Manager
- Temperature_Data_Buffer
- Monitor_Command_Type_Manager (Ada type definitions and management)
- Packet_Type_Manager (Ada type definitions and management)

DTS_Handler package specification PDL

```
package DTS_Handler is
  Max_Thermometers : constant := 15;

  type Thermometer_Numbers is range 1 .. Max_Thermometers;

  procedure Get_Temperature (Thermometer_Number : in
      DTS_Handler.Thermometer_Numbers);
end DTS_Handler;
```

Comments

- Each project will have its own standards for PDL, including "prologue" information about the module, subprogram, or other component. The purpose of this book is not to establish those standards but rather to give the example of the actual PDL: the part that is (or will become) executable code.
- This use of PDL formalizes the information stated in Steps 4.1 through 4.3. The modules are represented by package specifications containing subprogram specifications representing the services. The type definitions help make the program specific to the FMS problem.

Schedule_Manager package specification PDL

```
with DTS_Handler;
package Schedule_Manager is
  Min_Frequency : constant := 0;
  Max_Frequency : constant := 144;
  type Monitor_Frequencies is range Min_Frequency .. Max_Frequency;

  type Scheduling_Info_Type is
    record
      Thermometer_Number : DTS_Handler.Thermometer_Numbers;
      Monitor_Frequency  : Monitor_Frequencies;
    end record;

  type Hot_Furnace_Indicators is (Hot, Normal);
```

```
procedure Update_Schedule (Scheduling_Info : in
    Scheduling_Info_Type);

procedure Update_Hot_Furnace (Indicator : in
    Hot_Furnace_Indicators);
end Schedule_Manager;
```

PMC_Interface_Handler package specification PDL

```
with Packet_Type_Manager;
package PMC_Interface_Handler is
  procedure Receive_Packet  (Packet : out
      Packet_Type_Manager.Packets);

  procedure Transmit_Packet (Packet : in
      Packet_Type_Manager.Packets);
end PMC_Interface_Handler;
```

Comments

- The with Packet_Type_Manager shows the dependency of this module on Packet_Type_Manager. In Ada, the use of modules (packages), encapsulating the type definitions and providing services to manipulate the type, is strongly encouraged. We will expect to see an arrow on the updated SAD corresponding to this dependency. The PDL is shown among the following helper modules.

Transmission_Protocol_Manager package specification PDL

```
with Packet_Type_Manager;
package Transmission_Protocol_Manager is
  procedure Acknowledge_Data (Temperature_Data_Ack : in
      Packet_Type_Manager.Temperature_Data_Acks);
end Transmission_Protocol_Manager;
```

Fuel_Reduction_Handler package specification PDL

```
package Fuel_Reduction_Handler is
  procedure Evaluate_Temperatures;
end Fuel_Reduction_Handler;
```

Temperature_Manager package specification PDL

```
with DTS_Handler;
package Temperature_Manager is
  Min_Temperature : constant := 900;
  Max_Temperature : constant := 3700;

  type Temperature_Range is range Min_Temperature .. Max_Temperature;

  type Temperature_Data is
    record
      Thermometer_Number : DTS_Handler.Thermometer_Numbers;
      Temperature        : Temperature_Range;
    end record;
```

```
type Temperatures is array (DTS_Handler.Thermometer_Numbers)
   of Temperature_Range;

procedure Store_Temperature (Thermometer_Temperature : in
   Temperature_Data);

procedure Get_Temperatures
      (Current_Temperatures : out Temperatures);
end Temperature_Manager;
```

Temperature_Data_Buffer package specification PDL

```
with Temperature_Manager;
package Temperature_Data_Buffer is
  procedure Enqueue (Thermometer_Temperature : in
     Temperature_Manager.Temperature_Data);

  procedure Dequeue (Thermometer_Temperature : out
     Temperature_Manager.Temperature_Data);
end Temperature_Data_Buffer;
```

Monitor_Command_Type_Manager package specification PDL

```
with DTS_Handler;
with Schedule_Manager;
package Monitor_Command_Type_Manager is
  type Monitor_Commands     is private;
  type Validity_Indications is (Valid, Invalid);

  subtype Monitor_Frequency_Fields  is String (1..3);
  subtype Thermometer_Number_Fields is String (1..2);

  type Monitor_Command_Types is
      (Temperature_Request, Scheduling_Info);
  type Valid_Monitor_Commands (Command_Type :
     Monitor_Command_Types := Temperature_Request) is
    record
      Thermometer_Number_Field :
          DTS_Handler.Thermometer_Numbers;

      case Command_Type is
        when  Scheduling_Info   =>
          Monitor_Frequency_Field :
              Schedule_Manager.Monitor_Frequencies;
        when Temperature_Request =>
          null;
        end case;
      end record;

  function Thermometer_Number_Field_of (Monitor_Command : in
     Monitor_Commands) return Thermometer_Number_Fields;

  function Frequency_Field_of (Monitor_Command : in
     Monitor_Commands) return Monitor_Frequency_Fields;
```

```
function Type_of (Monitor_Command : in Monitor_Commands) return
    Monitor_Command_Types;
private
  type Monitor_Commands is new String (1..8);
end Monitor_Command_Type_Manager;
```

Packet_Type_Manager package specification PDL

```
with Monitor_Command_Type_Manager;
package Packet_Type_Manager is
  type Packets is private;
  type Packet_Classifications is
     (Furnace_Monitor_Packet, Acknowledgement);

  subtype Monitor_Command_Acks  is Character;
  subtype Temperature_Data_Acks is Character;

  Invalid_Packet_Input : exception;
  Packet_Overflow : exception;

  procedure Initialize_New_Packet (Packet : out Packets);

  procedure Initialize_Packet_Reading (Packet : in out Packets);

  procedure Get_Packet_Character (Packet : in out Packets;
      Packet_Character : out Character);

  procedure Store_Character_In_Packet (Packet_Character : in
      Character; Packet : in out Packets);

  function Classification_of (Packet : in
      Packets) return Packet_Classifications;

  function Furnace_Monitor_Conversion (Furnace_Monitor_Packet :
      Packets) return Monitor_Command_Type_Manager.Monitor_Commands;

  function Monitor_Ack_Conversion (Monitor_Command_Ack :
      Monitor_Command_Acks ) return Packets;

  function Temp_Ack_Conversion (Acknowledgement :
      Packets) return Temperature_Data_Acks;

private
  Max_Packet_Chars : constant := 9;  -- includes STX and ETX
  type Packet_Lengths is range 0 .. Max_Packet_Chars;
  type Packet_Strings is new String (1 .. Max_Packet_Chars);

  type Packets is
    record
      Packet_String : Packet_Strings;
      Packet_Length : Packet_Lengths;
      Char_Reading  : Packet_Lengths;
    end record;
end Packet_Type_Manager;
```

7.5.5 Step 5: Decompose Tasks

The following tasks are not very complex, in that the FFD contains only one process. As such, we will not decompose them until detailed design.

- PMC_Data_Receiver
- Temperature_Monitor
- Scheduled_Reading_Controller
- PMC_Data_Transmitter
- Fuel_Reduction_Controller

That leaves:

- Packet_Analyzer
- Scheduler (because it encapsulates the data store SCHEDULE)
- Transmission_Protocol

We will show structure charts for each of these latter tasks. For Packet_Analyzer, we will show the intermediate steps taken to perform some of the analysis. The others will have the final chart only. Section 7.5.8 contains a description of the data and control flows shown on the structure charts. If this were the actual Ada implementation, we would show additional PDL (for task bodies) at this time in addition to the structure charts.

7.5.5.1 Packet_Analyzer   The transform analysis proceeds as follows.

Draw DFD/CFD: Figure 7-23 shows the excerpt from the FFD for Packet_Analyzer task. We have included the names of the module services (in highlighted letters) with which the Packet_Analyzer interfaces.

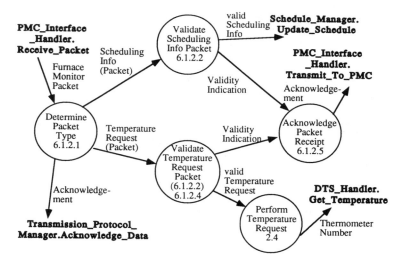

Figure 7-23   FFD Excerpt for Packet_Analyzer

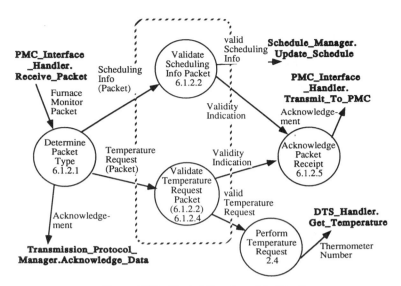

Figure 7-24 Central Transform Identification

Identify the central transform: The central transform is outlined in Figure 7-24. The rationale is as follows:

- Trace afferent stream: In this case the afferent stream ends with the individual packet coming into "Validate Scheduling Info Packet" or "Validate Temperature Request Packet."
- Trace efferent streams: The ACKNOWLEDGEMENT and valid SCHEDULING INFO or TEMPERATURE REQUEST are outputs.
- That means that "Validate Scheduling Info Packet" and "Validate Temperature Request Packet" form our central transform (connect the arcs). In some cases, you may find that only one process remains in the central transform area. This is OK—the strategy covers how to handle this case.

Convert the DFD/CFD into a first-cut structure chart: We have two choices to do this:

- Promote a boss: Which of the two processes could you promote? In actuality, they are both the same type of processing, but neither seems to fit as "the boss."
- Hire a boss: We could invent a subprogram above these to control the calling of one or the other, but there is no clear function that the new "boss" subprogram is to perform.

It may be at this point that we realize that this was not a good candidate for transform analysis; rather, "Determine Packet Type" is a transaction center. So we'll draw a structure chart based on this knowledge. See Figure 7-25.

Comments

- Remember steps 1, 2, and 3 from the guidelines for what a transaction center does (Section 7.3.5). The Packet_Analyzer

    1. receives incoming data (PMC_Interface_Handler.Receive_Packet)
    2. analyzes each transaction—packet—to determine type (Determine_Packet_Type)
    3. selects a process path based on transaction type ("Process Packet" and its subordinates)

- Under each packet we see the validation, routing, and acknowledgement.

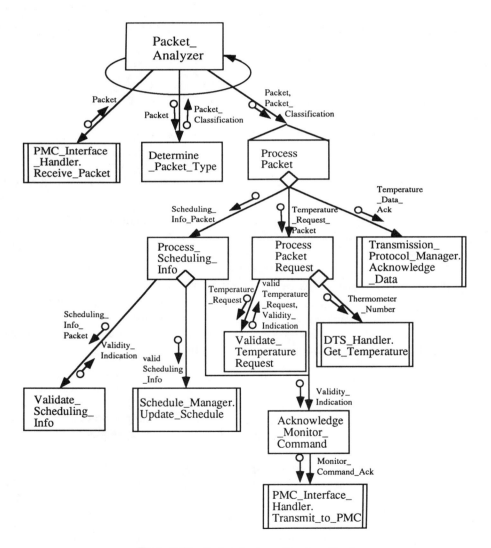

Figure 7-25 Packet_Analyzer Structure Chart

- Acknowledge_Monitor_Command is an example of *fan-in* (multiple use of a subprogram). More on this topic will be found in Chapter 8.

7.5.5.2 Scheduler Figure 7-26 shows the structure chart for the Scheduler task.

Comments

- Although the *methodology* for performing transform analysis is language-independent, the actual *design* is very much dependent on the model of concurrency or real-time executive used. For example, this could be the processing for a called task in an Ada program. It needs to be able to accept a request to update the schedule, provide scheduled reading, update a reading, or update a hot furnace indication. We see lexicals used to keep the selections separate. Alternatively, there could be a task waiting for any one of four events to occur (in some real-time executive), with a call to one of four mailboxes, depending on which event occurred. These issues need to be addressed on each project.

- Here we see the access to the data store Schedule. This task has actually encapsulated the store and provides any necessary services to other tasks to read or update Schedule. This is noted by the "accept" lexicals. Notice that in addition to the services (Update_Schedule and Update_Hot_Furnace) that were listed for the module in which this task resides, two new services have been added to allow the Scheduled_Reading_Controller to Request_Reading and Update_Reading_Time.

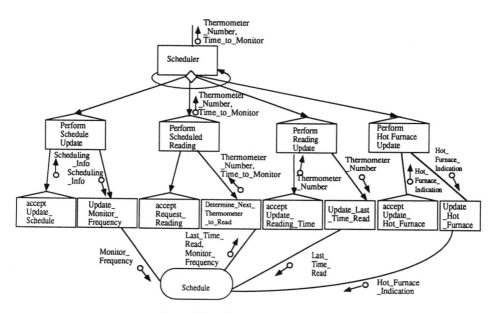

Figure 7-26 Schedules Structure Chart

7.5.5.3 *Transmission_Protocol* The structure chart for Transmission_Protocol is shown in Figure 7-27.

Comments

- The "accept Acknowledge_Data" or "wait for time-out" could be a selective wait on a rendezvous accept in Ada. There could also be a call to a mailbox for the Acknowledge_Data with a time constraint for the time-out.
- We have added a subprogram to perform the construction of the Furnace_Temperature_Packet. This involves getting the next Temperature_Data and converting the fields from integer to ASCII format for the packet. The decision on calling Construct_Furnace_Temperature_Packet is that it needs to be called once to initialize a packet to send, and then whenever a positive Temperature_Data_Ack has been received or the old packet has been sent 3 times.
- We also see some clarification here within the promoted boss (Transmission_Protocol). The actual performance of the protocol has been called out with the lexicals "Perform Protocol" and "accept Acknowledge_Data." "Wait for time-out" has been made a lexical as well, since it is only a delay statement.

7.5.6 Step 6: Finalize Top-Level Software Architecture

Figure 7-28 shows the interaction between all of the modules of the CSCI as identified for top-level design. A module uses or has visibility to the modules its arrows point to. For example, PMC_Interface_Handler makes use of Transmission_Protocol_Manager and Packet_Type_Manager. The

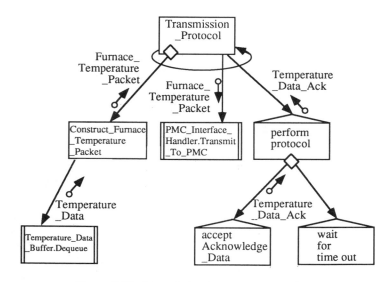

Figure 7-27   Transmission_Protocol Structure Chart

PMC_Input_Analyzer does not provide any services itself, so no other module is shown using (pointing to) it.

7.5.7 Step 7: Document Traceability

Figure 7-29 shows an example of traceability: The software requirements have been allocated to application and helper modules. Depending on your corporate or customer style and standards, you may wish to trace down to the task or individual subprogram level.

7.6 KEYS TO UNDERSTANDING

- Top-level design establishes the overall architecture of the software, including tasks, modules, and interfaces.
- It begins with the identification of tasks based on the requirements expressed in a flattened data flow diagram. All tasks are identified during top-level design.
- Modules are identified based on information hiding principles. A useful distinction is between *application* modules, which do the main work of the system, and *helper* modules, which are (generally passive) data abstractions that encapsulate and defer complex details to simplify the application modules.

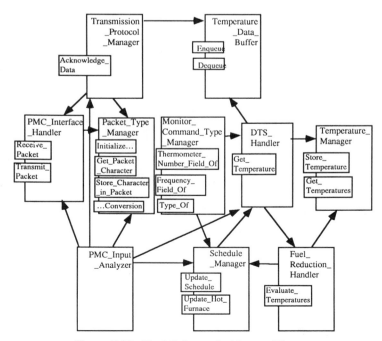

Figure 7-28 Final Software Architecture Diagram

Software Requirement	PMC_ Interface_ Handler	PMC_ Input_ Analyzer	Schedule_ Manager	Fuel_ Reduction _Handler	DTS_ Handler	Trans- mission_ Protocol_ Manager	Temp- erature_ Manager	Temp- erature _Data_ Buffer	Packet_ Type_ Manager	Monitor_ Command _Type_ Manager
1 Schedule Temperature Reading										
1.1 Maintain Schedule			X							
1.2 Initiate Scheduled Temperature Reading			X							
2 Monitor Furnace Temperature										
2.1 Initiate Periodic Temperature Reading			X							
2.2 Get Temperature					X		X	X		
2.3 Evaluate Temperatures				X			X			
2.4 Perform Temperature Request		X								
6 Interface with PMC										
6.1 Receive Data from PMC	X									
6.1.1 Receive Packet									X	
6.1.2 Analyze Packet		X								X
6.2 Send Data to PMC										
6.2.1 Handle Data Transmission Protocol						X		X		
6.2.2 Transmit to PMC	X									

Figure 7-29 Requirements Traceability Matrix

- It is useful and important to view the modules in layers of abstraction.
- Structured design principles are used to develop the top levels of structure charts for the most complex tasks.
- Module definition (information hiding) and structured design (functional decomposition) are used hand in hand to develop the design, using the principles of modular structured design (MSD) presented in Appendix A, "Software Design Concepts."

CHAPTER 8

Detailed Design

Objective: to provide a set of graphical notations, guidelines, and a step-by-step process for the detailed design of a CSCI

The purpose of this chapter is to describe the methods to be used during the detailed design phase of the development cycle. It includes the continuing aspects of modular structured design (MSD), first introduced in Chapter 7. Figure 8-1 illustrates the phases of the development cycle. This chapter covers the phase that is highlighted.

Detailed design is the determination of the low-level architecture of the CSCI and the specification, in a pseudocode format, of algorithms in each callable software component.

This is the final phase of software design prior to the actual implementation of the CSCI. The input to this phase is the top-level software architecture, determined during software top-level design.

To accomplish the methodology definition, the following items are covered:

- Transition from top-level design to detailed design
- Graphics
- Guidelines
- Methodology—step by step
- Example

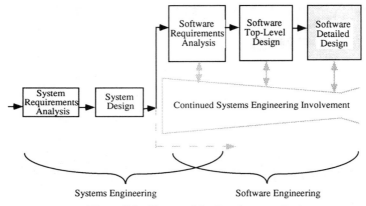

Figure 8-1 Phases of the Development Cycle

8.1 TRANSITION FROM TOP-LEVEL DESIGN TO DETAILED DESIGN

This "transition" is straightforward, being simply the continued refinement of the top-level design, involving refinement of algorithmic detail with additional modularization. The detailed design methodology balances functional decomposition and data abstraction in such a way as to take advantage of the best of both approaches. There are correspondingly two graphical representations of the design (the same ones used for preliminary design): structure charts for the step-by-step processing of functional decomposition and a software architecture diagram (SAD) to show the modularization using information hiding and data abstraction. In addition, there is a pseudocode representation of the design that expresses details of both the modularization and the step-by-step processing.

Keep in mind the objectives of a good design while performing this transition and in completing the actual design:

- Traceability
- Modularity
- Understandability
- Implementability
- Testability
- Maintainability
- Reliability
- Reusability

Refine the modules into subprograms that show a straightforward logical structure and correctness.

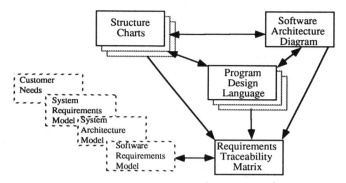

Figure 8-2 Detailed Design Structure Components

8.2 GRAPHICS

This section describes the graphics that are used for the methodology. The graphics in this section are not intended to tell the whole story of the methodology and are not necessarily tightly related; they are only intended to introduce the *form* of the notation. The final section of the chapter, "FMS Example," will use these graphics, the guidelines of the next section, and the step-by-step methodology to present an integrated picture. Recommended conventions are also listed. We will cover the following graphics and associated data, with relationships as illustrated in Figure 8-2.

- Structure chart
- Software architecture diagram (SAD)
- Program design language (PDL)
- Requirements traceability matrix (RTM)

It is important to note that traceability in the RTM (during detailed design) is related to the individual callable subprograms of the structure chart and PDL, not only to the modules of the SAD.

The majority of these graphics are the same ones that are used during top-level design to represent the software. This provides for continuity of the design as well as its representation. Because of this similarity, we will provide detailed discussion here only for new information, either new graphics or a different focus on graphics discussed earlier for preliminary design.

8.2.1 Structure Chart

The structure chart describes the data and control flow of a set of subprograms that are executed sequentially, and it shows the hierarchical organization of these

```
BEGIN Packet_Analyzer                          task body Packet_Analyzer is
DOFOREVER                                       • • •
 CALL PMC_Interface_Handler.Receive_Packet     begin
 to get the next packet to analyze             loop
                                                 PMC_Interface_Handler.Receive_Packet (Packet);
 CALL Analyze_Packet to determine the type
 of packet                                       Analyze_Packet (Packet, Packet_Classification);

 IF the packet is a Furnace_Monitor_Packet       if Packet_Classification = Furnace_Monitor_Packet
 THEN                                             then
  CALL Process_Monitor_Command to                 Process_Monitor_Command (Monitor_Commands
  validate and route the valid command            (Packet));
 ELSE                                             else
  CALL Transmission_Protocol_Manager.             Transmission_Protocol_Manager.
  Acknowledge_Data to route acknowledgement       Acknowledge_Data (Monitor_Command_Acks
       received                                   (Packet));
 ENDIF                                            endif;

 ENDDO                                           end loop;
END Packet_Analyzer                             end Packet_Analyzer;

        a. Structured English PDL                        b. Ada PDL
```

Figure 8-3 PDL Example for Detailed Design (*a*) Structured English PDL; (*b*) Ada PDL

subprograms. Thus, it illustrates the architecture within each task or module identified for the CSCI. In detailed design, requirements are allocated to and traced from the subprograms identified. A detailed description of structure charts is given in Section 7.2.4.

8.2.2 Software Architecture Diagram (SAD)

The SAD is discussed in Section 7.2.3.

8.2.3 Program Design Language (PDL)

PDL is described in Section 7.2.6. Figure 8-3 shows an example of some PDL for detailed design. Examples of structured English PDL and Ada PDL are shown side by side to illustrate both ways of using PDL.

8.2.4 Requirements Traceability Matrix (RTM)

The graphic notation for the RTM is the same as that described in Section 4.1.7. The difference between top-level and detailed design representations with respect to the RTM is that for detailed design, the requirements must be allocated to and traced from the individual subprograms within a module in addition to the module as a whole.

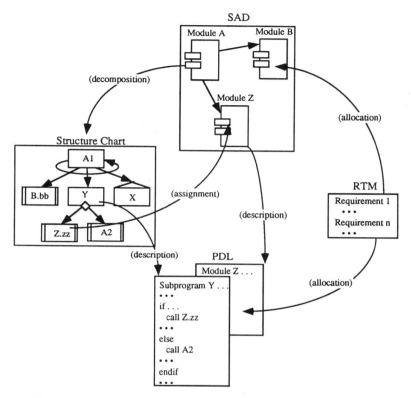

Figure 8-4   Relationship between Detailed Design Structure Components

8.2.5 Graphics Summary

Now that we've seen all of the graphics individually, we will summarize with how the major components interact with each other. Figure 8-4 is an illustration of the ways in which the SAD, structure chart, PDL, and RTM relate to each other to demonstrate the integrated details of the design of the CSCI. Beginning with the SAD from preliminary design, each module is further decomposed using SSEM/MSD into individual subprograms that will be coded. PDL is used to describe each subprogram and module identified. The RTM is used to allocate the software requirements to the modules in the SAD and to each individual subprogram within the modules.

8.3 GUIDELINES

This section introduces several sets of guidelines for use in the methodology steps. The application of these rules will be indicated at the appropriate steps in the

Coupling criteria \ type	Data	Stamp	Control	Common	Content
Direct reference between the subprograms	N	N	N	N	Y*
Subprograms are packaged together	N	N	N	N	Y*
Some interface data is external or global	N	N	N	Y	
Some interface data is control information	N	N	Y		
Some interface data is in a data structure	N	Y			

* either one of these or both

Figure 8-5   Coupling Level Determination

methodology. The guidelines include:

- Coupling and cohesion measurements
- Factoring
- Structured design criteria
- Design for error handling and testability

8.3.1   Coupling and Cohesion Quality

Coupling is the degree to which two subprograms are interconnected, and conversely, the degree to which they are independent. As already mentioned in Section 7.3.6, the types of coupling from best to worst (loose to tight) are:

Data coupling by passing elementary parameters (primitive variables)

Stamp coupling by composite parameters (structure or records) where not all elements of a parameter are needed

Control coupling by parameters used explicitly to control the behavior of the recipient subprogram

Global or *common* coupling via a globally accessible data area

Content or *pathological* coupling by direct connection between the internals of the subprograms

Myers [MYE75] offers guidance for determining the type of coupling involved, as illustrated in Figure 8-5. Blanks indicate "don't care" condition.

Cohesion is the degree to which an individual subprogram's components are working together to accomplish the same function. High cohesion (single, clearly understood individual function) is desirable for a good design. In sequence from best to worst (high to low), the levels of cohesion are:

Functional cohesion: Elements contribute to a single, problem-related activity.

Informational cohesion: Elements perform multiple functions, where the functions, represented as entry points in the module, deal with a single data structure.

Sequential cohesion: Activities within the module are connected in that the output from one serves as the input to another.

Cohesion criteria \ type	Func-tional	Informa-tional	Sequen-tial	Commun-icational	Temp-oral	Logical	Coinci-dental
Difficult to describe module /Subprogram function(s)	N	N	N	N	N	N	Y/N*
Module/Subprogram per-forms more than 1 function	N	Y	Y	Y	Y	Y	
Only one function performed per invocation		Y	N	N	N	Y	
Each function has an entry point		Y	N				N
Module/Subprogram performs related class of functions						Y	N*
Functions are related to problem's procedure			Y	Y	Y		
All of the functions use the same data		Y		Y	N		

* either Y here or N in both

Figure 8-6 Cohesion Level Determination

Communicational cohesion: Activities share the same input or output, but order is not important.

Temporal cohesion: Activities can be carried out at the same time.

Logical cohesion: Activities appear to belong to the same general category.

Coincidental cohesion: Activities have no relationship to one another.

Myers [MYE75] offers guidance for determining the type of cohesion involved, as illustrated in Figure 8-6. Blanks indicate "don't care" condition.

Proper use of balancing functional decomposition and information hiding should lead to a design exhibiting high cohesion and low coupling. However, there may be conflict between this and the mapping of the requirements model to the design model. The quality (for example, good modularity) of the software design is to be favored over traceability, because requirements traceability will be achieved through the generation of an RTM.

8.3.2 Factoring

Factoring is discussed in Section 7.3.7.

8.3.3 Structured Design Criteria

The following is a list of structured design criteria to consider in addition to coupling, cohesion, and factoring as you decompose the software into subprograms. These criteria are adapted from Myers [MYE75] and Page-Jones [PAG88].

1. *Predictable subprograms*: A predictable, or well-behaved, subprogram is one that, when given identical inputs, operates identically each time it is called. It also operates independently of its environment.

2. *Decision structure*: Wherever possible (without weakening a subprogram's cohesiveness), it is desirable to arrange subprograms and decisions in those subprograms in such a way that modules directly affected by a decision are subordinate (beneath) the subprogram containing the decision. This is an attempt to hide the results of a decision in a subprogram from the calling subprogram. This also tends to keep decisions affecting program control at a high level in the program structure.

3. *Data access*: Minimize the amount of data that any subprogram can reference. This is related to the coupling principles.

4. *Input/output isolation*: Isolating a program's input/output operations into a small number of subprograms is a desirable goal. This strategy enhances the portability and extensibility of a program.

5. *Fan-out*: The fan-out from a subprogram is the number of immediate subordinates to that subprogram. Try to limit the fan-out from a subprogram to no more than about seven, applying the 7 ± 2 principle [MIL56]. A subprogram with too many subordinates can be cured by the remedy of factoring each subfunction into a subprogram of its own.

6. *Fan-in*: The fan-in of a subprogram is the number of immediate bosses it has. High fan-in is the reward for intelligent factoring and the removal of restrictive subprograms. Having one function called by several bosses avoids the need to code practically the same function in several places and also avoids redundancy at maintenance time.

7. *Recursion*: Recursion is the most natural method of solving certain problems, such as tree searching or following paths through a network. Although any recursive subprogram can be coded as a nonrecursive subprogram, recursion can simplify the logic of a subprogram and also make efficient use of storage.

8. *Subprogram size*: Subprogram size is related to subprogram independence, clarity (or understandability), and the ease with which a program can be tested. As a general guideline, the average subprogram should contain 100 executable high-level language statements.

9. *Match of program structure to data structure*: The design of many subprograms is made easier if the structure of the program follows the structure of the data. Modular structured design (MSD) uses data modules to encapsulate the data structures.

10. *Simplicity*: Everything else being equal, the simplest solution, design, or interface is best.

11. *Initialization and termination*: Initialize (and clean up) within the subprogram for which the initialization and termination is being done. To look at it another way, perform initialization and termination processing as far down in the structure as possible, but not to a depth that would create an unpredictable subprogram.

12. *Restrictive subprograms*: A restrictive subprogram is a subprogram whose general use has been needlessly restricted in either its documentation or

its code. The use of restrictive subprograms should be avoided. Since a restrictive subprogram is one whose function is actually broader than it is documented to be, one that could be more flexible by changing wired-in values to input parameters, or one that makes assumptions about its caller, correcting the subprogram in one of these categories does not contradict the ideas of simplicity.

13. *Internal subprograms*: An internal subprogram is a called piece of code that physically resides in the calling subprogram. In terms of composite design, an internal subprogram is not a subprogram, although it has many of the characteristics of a subprogram. Internal subprograms should be avoided. In general, if an internal subprogram seems justified, don't do it; make it another subprogram.

14. *Redundancy*: Minimization of redundancy is an important principle in the design of flexible, maintainable systems.

8.3.4 Design for Error Handling and Testability

It is very important to design the software in such a way as to be able to handle the errors that may arise. The error handling should not *drive* the design, but it should complement it and be coordinated with it.

The way in which error conditions are treated within the design of a subprogram is related to the characteristic of predictability. Error flags are a form of control coupling and, hence, increase coupling (remember that low coupling is better design). The system will be simpler if subprograms can be designed to eliminate the need for error flags. This implies that the subprograms, if possible, should handle their own error detections and correction [JEN79].

Nielsen [NIE88, Chapter 18] offers the following list of errors that need to be considered during the design of software systems.

1. *Anticipated conditions*: This category applies to situations that are expected to occur during the normal processing of the system.

2. *General-purpose software*: Since one cannot guarantee that the user of a reusable software component will use it properly, the software must protect itself by identifying when a misuse has occurred. For example, a queue manager must not allow the user to attempt to retrieve an item from an empty queue or place an item into a full one. Although the general-purpose software must recognize that an error has occurred, the user of the component must handle the error (such as by handling an Ada exception or by checking an error flag on return).

3. *Hardware failures*: The hardware devices with which the software interfaces are expected to fail at some point in time. Those failures should not affect the entire system. As such, we would like to be able to detect the failures and attempt to recover and continue execution.

4. *Invalid input data*: The program needs to analyze input data from the environment to determine that the input is valid and can be used. If it is determined

that the input is invalid, error handling needs to occur. Exactly what this handling is depends on the system. Can the input simply be ignored, going on to the next input? Does the error need to be reported (either to some console or file or back to the originator of the data)?

5. *Unanticipated errors (bugs)*. The detection of unanticipated bugs is important in any software system. For real-time processing, we would always like to recover from the exceptional condition and continue normal execution. For some bugs, however, there is no way to continue, so it is best to report where the error was detected and allow that error to be fixed during maintenance.

8.4   METHODOLOGY—STEP BY STEP

This section goes through the details of the methodology in a step-by-step style to give an understanding for the issues that come up. The guidelines introduced above are discussed at the appropriate step of the methodology.

The following lists the steps in the general order that they occur. In practice, most will probably be worked on in parallel and iteratively.

1. Decompose the application and helper module(s).
   1.1   Draw a next-layer structure chart.
   1.2   Decompose according to type.
   1.3   Write PDL.
2. Design the data module(s).
3. Represent detailed software architecture.
4. Document traceability
5. When am I done?

Step 1   Decompose the application and helper module(s).   For each application or helper module identified during preliminary design, decompose the module or individual task into subprograms with the following substeps. Remember, the general philosophy is that of MSD, as explained in Appendix A.

Step 1.1   Draw a next-layer structure chart.   Draw the (next) layer on the structure chart. Each level is represented as a set of subprogram calls, perhaps with some simple logical connections: a `loop`, an `if...then...else`,or a `case` statement. Coupling, cohesion, factoring, and other structured design criteria are used here while considering the decomposition of the problem.

Step 1.2   Decompose according to type.   For each subprogram identified, determine whether it is an algorithmic step in the processing (a virtual machine) or an operation on some data structure.

- If the subprogram is an operation on a data structure (object), do not refine the instruction at this time. Instead, write the description of the rest of the object (the rest of the operations on the data structure). This operation may be part of an information-hiding (data) module that has already been identified, or it could be a part of a new module. Notions of information hiding, deferral of detail, and abstract data types are all important in this effort. It is likely that you will not immediately identify all needed operations, but as you refine the structure, you will find need for additional operations on it.

- If the instruction is algorithmic in nature, refine it by starting at Step 1.1.

Step 1.3   Write PDL.   Write PDL for each subprogram identified for this module. The PDL should first be written for the normal flow of processing in the subprogram; then add error processing necessary to make the design robust. Use the guidelines for error handling and testability here. This step may be done as each subprogram is identified.

Step 2   Design the data module(s).   The data modules are those modules that encapsulate a data structure, providing operations as services to other modules that need the data. Write PDL for each operation provided by the module. The PDL should be first written for the normal flow of processing in the subprogram; then add error processing necessary to make the design robust.

For complex algorithms involving data structures, it will be necessary to accomplish the implementation by starting at Step 1.1 and following the steps to decompose the subprograms further. This may involve lower-level data modules that are hidden from higher levels.

Step 3   Represent detailed software architecture.   Update the SAD to reflect the changes to existing (preliminary design) modules and the addition of modules identified during detailed design.

Step 4   Document traceability.   Draw a requirements traceability matrix (RTM) depicting the allocation of the software requirements to each of the modules identified in the SAD and to each of the subprograms within the modules.

Step 5   When am I done?   Detailed design is considered complete when the following questions can be answered in the affirmative.

1. Have all subprograms been identified to perform the processing necessary for each module or task?
2. Have all subprograms' interfaces been defined?
3. Have all subprograms and algorithms been designed through PDL?
4. Do all subprograms exist within the structure charts and their module on the SAD?
5. Does each subprogram trace back to a CSCI requirement?
6. Have all CSCI requirements been allocated to modules and subprograms?

8.5   FMS DETAILED DESIGN EXAMPLE

This section provides an example of the detailed design methodology, essentially solving the following problem. If you wish to test your knowledge of the methods presented, you may wish to solve the problem yourself, before looking at the solution.

Assignment: Perform detailed design for the FMC prototype for which the top-level design was developed in Chapter 7.

What follows is a completed detailed design, including answers to the questions you asked yourself (or should have asked yourself).

8.5.1   Step 1: Decompose the Application and Helper Module(s)

The following is a list of the application and helper modules identified during top-level design. We will show the detailed design for each of these as well as any additional modules that we may identify during the decomposition. For PMC_Interface_Handler (PMC_Data_Receiver task), we will show each intermediate step taken (that is, Step 1.1 to 1.3). The others will have only the final (complete) structure chart and PDL.

Application modules:

- PMC_Interface_Handler
- PMC_Input_Analyzer
- Schedule_Manager
- DTS_Handler
- Transmission_Protocol_Manager
- Fuel_Reduction_Handler

Helper modules:

- Temperature_Data_Buffer
- Monitor_Command_Type_Manager
- Packet_Type_Manager

Data modules:

- Temperature_Manager

More helper modules can (and usually will) be "discovered" as the detailed design progresses. We will mention and define them when they come up (Step 1.2). PDL will be given at the end of the helper module section (not in the middle of the discussion of another module).

8.5.1.1   *PMC_Interface_Handler*   During preliminary design, we have identified the following tasks within PMC_Interface_Handler that may run concurrently. Each needs to be decomposed individually.

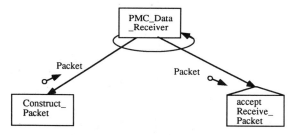

Figure 8-7   PMC_Data_Receiver: First-Layer Structure Chart

- PMC_Data_Receiver
- PMC_Data_Transmitter

The detailed steps are as follows for the *PMC_Data_Receiver* task.

Step 1.1: Draw a next-layer structure chart: Figure 8-7 is the first-layer structure chart for PMC_Data_Receiver task.

Comments

- Recall from the flattened flow diagram (FFD) grouping in Section 7.5.1 that this task was allocated only the processing shown in Figure 8-8.
- To solve the problem of data reception, we look at the protocol for this interface. We need to construct a packet one character at a time and then buffer it. At the top level, we don't need to worry about the details of how to construct a packet — just that it will be done.
- Notice the loop to allow the task to receive (construct) another packet after completing one. It is assumed that this task runs "forever".

Step 1.2: Decompose according to type:

- Construct_Packet is algorithmic, so we will refine it further.
- "accept Receive_Packet" is a simple copy of the packet received, so it needs no further refinement here.

Step 1.1, layer 2: The decomposition of Construct_Packet is shown in Figure 8-9.

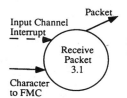

Figure 8-8   PMC_Data_Receiver
FFD Excerpt

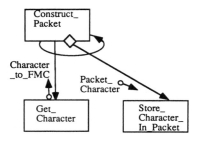

Figure 8-9 Layer 2: Construct_Packet Structure Chart

Comments

- Carrying the process down another layer, we see that to construct a packet, we must loop to get a character and make a decision to store that character into a packet. Exactly what the decision making involves is not shown on this chart. The constraints of the loop are also not shown. We will see them both in the PDL.

Step 1.2, layer 2:

- Get_Character is algorithmic, so we will refine it further.
- Store_Character_In_Packet—In thinking about Store_Character_In_Packet, we have decided to make a helper module that knows all about Packets: Packet_Type_Manager. The definition(s) for what a Packet is and how to construct one or convert one to a specific instance (such as Monitor_Command) will be included there. Because of this decision, we add a call to another service within this new module to initialize the packet (Initialize_New_Packet). An updated structure chart segment is given in Figure 8-10. The details of this module are discussed at the end of Step 1 after the modules identified during top-level design.

Step 1.1, layer 3: Figure 8-11 is the structure chart for Get_Character.

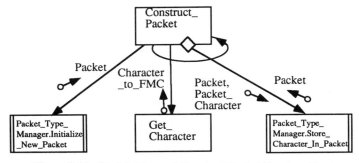

Figure 8-10 Updated Layer 2 Construct_Packet Structure Chart

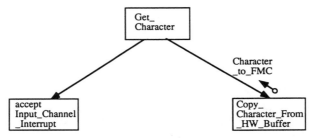

Figure 8-11 Layer 3 Get_Character Structure Chart

Comments

- Here we see the actual interrupt being accepted to get the character and the character being removed from the hardware buffer.
- In many languages, each of the boxes on the structure chart could indeed become an individual subprogram. Other languages place restrictions on where in a program an interrupt can actually be accepted. The "final" structure chart for the entire task PMC_Data_Receiver, given in Figure 8-12, shows an example

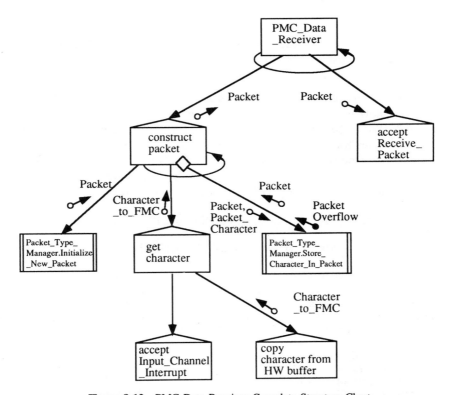

Figure 8-12 PMC_Data_Receiver Complete Structure Chart

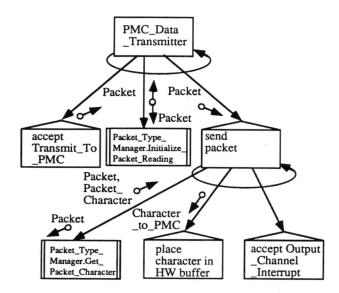

Figure 8-13 PMC_Data_Transmitter Structure Chart

where, because of language restrictions (in this case the Ada tasking model), the interrupt must be performed within the task body. This causes several of the boxes to become lexical within the task body.

Indeed, some of the breakdown of this structure chart is too low-level for a large system. We show it here to illustrate the organization of abstraction into levels.

Step 1.3: Write PDL: We will show the PDL for this entire module after we give the structure chart for the other task in this module (package).

Figure 8-13 is the structure chart for the PMC_Data_Transmitter task. Since this example is using Ada as PDL, we will first set the context for the tasks by giving the PDL for the module (Ada package) that encapsulates them.

PMC_Interface_Handler package specification PDL (see Section 7.5.4)

PMC_Interface_Handler package body PDL

```
package body PMC_Interface_Handler is
  Input_Channel_Address  : constant := 16#00A0#;
  Input_Buffer_Address   : constant := 16#00A2#;
  Output_Channel_Address : constant := 16#00A4#;
  Output_Buffer_Address  : constant := 16#00A6#;

  task PMC_Data_Receiver is
    entry Receive_Packet (Packet : out Packet_Type_Manager.Packets);
    entry Input_Channel_Interrupt;
      for Input_Channel_Interrupt use at Input_Channel_Address;
  end PMC_Data_Receiver;
```

```
task PMC_Data_Transmitter is
  entry Transmit_Packet (Packet : in Packet_Type_Manager.Packets);
  entry Output_Channel_Interrupt;
    for Output_Channel_Interrupt use at Output_Channel_Address;
end PMC_Data_Transmitter;

task body PMC_Data_Receiver is separate;
task body PMC_Data_Transmitter is separate;
procedure Receive_Packet (Packet : out
    Packet_Type_Manager.Packets) is
begin
  PMC_Data_Receiver.Receive_Packet (Packet);
end Receive_Packet;

procedure Transmit_Packet (Packet : in
    Packet_Type_Manager.Packets) is
begin
  PMC_Data_Transmitter.Transmit_Packet (Packet);
end Transmit_Packet;
end PMC_Interface_Handler;
```

Comments

- The actual hardware addresses for this interface are defined here as named constants, so that if they are changed, there is only one place to modify.

- Encapsulated in this package (module) we see the declaration of the two tasks identified during top-level design (PMC_Data_Receiver and PMC_Data_Transmitter). Notice the declarations for the hardware interrupts (for example, Input_Channel_Interrupt). The task bodies are declared `separate` for definition later during the design.

- The `entry` is a mechanism for task communication in Ada. It is called by other tasks or subprograms, with data being passed via the parameter list.

PMC_Data_Receiver PDL

```
separate (PMC_Interface_Handler)
task body PMC_Data_Receiver is

  Input_Packet    : Packet_Type_Manager.Packets;
  Input_Character : Character;
    for Input_Character use at Input_Buffer_Address;
begin
  loop
  begin
    Packet_Type_Manager.Initialize_New_Packet (Input_Packet);
    accept Input_Channel_Interrupt;

    if Input_Character = ASCII.STX then
      while Input_Character /= ASCII.ETX loop
      -- Construct Packet, using characters received
          with each interrupt.
        Packet_Type_Manager.Store_Character_In_Packet
            (Input_Character, Input_Packet);
```

```
          accept Input_Channel_Interrupt;
       end loop;

    Packet_Type_Manager.Store_Character_In_Packet
          (Input_Character, Input_Packet);

    accept Receive_Packet (Packet : out
          Packet_Type_Manager.Packets) do
       Packet := Input_Packet;
    end Receive_Packet;
  end if;
exception
  when Packet_Type_Manager.Packet_Overflow => null;
  -- Discard characters as garbage
end;
end loop;
end PMC_Data_Receiver;
```

Comments

- This shows the actual logic required for this task, including the hardware interrupt (Input_Channel_Interrupt) and the hardware buffer (Input_Character, which is the character located at Input_Buffer_Address).
- The accept is the active counterpart to the entry. A task that has reached an accept waits ("sleeping") until the entry is called by another task or a corresponding interrupt occurs.

PMC_Data_Transmitter PDL

```
separate (PMC_Interface_Handler)
task body PMC_Data_Transmitter is
  Output_Packet    : Packet_Type_Manager.Packets;
  Local_Character  : Character;
  Output_Character : Character;
    for Output_Character use at Output_Buffer_Address;
begin
  loop

    accept Transmit_To_PMC (Packet : in
        Packet_Type_Manager.Packets) do
       Output_Packet := Packet;
    end Transmit_To_PMC;

    Packet_Type_Manager.Initialize_Packet_Reading (Output_Packet);

    Packet_Type_Manager.Get_Packet_Character
        (Output_Packet, Local_Character);

    while Local_Character /= ASCII.ETX loop

      Output_Character := Local_Character;

      accept Output_Channel_Interrupt;
```

```
Packet_Type_Manager.Get_Packet_Character
    (Output_Packet, Local_Character);
end loop;

Output_Character := Local_Character;
accept Output_Channel_Interrupt;

  end loop;
end PMC_Data_Transmitter;
```

8.5.1.2 PMC_Input_Analyzer Within PMC_Input_Analyzer, we have identified only one task during top-level design: Packet_Analyzer. Figure 8-14 shows the structure chart for the Packet_Analyzer.

Comments

- This is the structure chart that was initially created during top-level design.
- We have updated it, because the services provided by Packet_Type_Manager include the functionality of Analyze_Packet. Note that this implies that we will have to change the requirements traceability to the new module or subprogram.
- Notice the factoring that has taken place in Validate_Scheduling_Info and Validate_Temperature_Request, ASCII_To_Integer has been identified as a generally useful subprogram that may be used elsewhere in this program as well as reused for others. It will show up as part of a new helper module (ASCII_Integer_Conversions, see Section 8.5.1.8).

PMC_Input_Analyzer package specification PDL

```
package PMC_Input_Analyzer is
end PMC_Input_Analyzer;
```

Comments

- Remember from the SAD that this module does not provide any services but uses the services of others. Thus, the specification is "empty": there is no need for other modules to see anything within this package (module). The package body that follows contains the task declaration and the declaration of the subprograms that that task alone will use. These had been identified during top-level design.

PMC_Input_Analyzer package body PDL

```
with Monitor_Command_Type_Manager;
package body PMC_Input_Analyzer is
  task Packet_Analyzer;

  procedure Acknowledge_Monitor_Command (Validity_Indication : in
    Monitor_Command_Type_Manager.Validity_Indications) is separate;
```

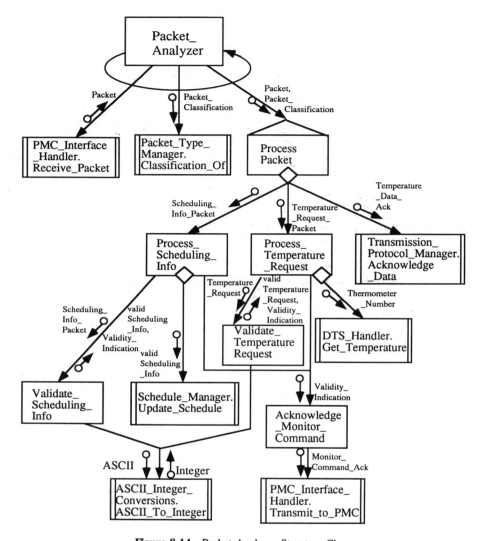

Figure 8-14 Packet_Analyzer Structure Chart

```
procedure Validate_Scheduling_Info
   (Monitor_Command    : in
       Monitor_Command_Type_Manager.Monitor_Commands;
    Valid_Monitor_Command : out
       Monitor_Command_Type_Manager.Valid_Monitor_Commands;
    Validity_Indication   : out
       Monitor_Command_Type_Manager.Validity_Indications)
          is separate;
```

```
procedure Validate_Temperature_Request
  (Monitor_Command        : in
      Monitor_Command_Type_Manager.Monitor_Commands;
   Valid_Monitor_Command  : out
      Monitor_Command_Type_Manager.Valid_Monitor_Commands;
   Validity_Indication    : out
      Monitor_Command_Type_Manager.Validity_Indications)
         is separate;

procedure Process_Scheduling_Info (Monitor_Command : in
   Monitor_Command_Type_Manager.Monitor_Commands) is separate;

procedure Process_Temperature_Request (Monitor_Command : in
   Monitor_Command_Type_Manager.Monitor_Commands) is separate;

task body Packet_Analyzer is separate;
end PMC_Input_Analyzer;
```

Packet_Analyzer PDL

```
with Packet_Type_Manager;
use Packet_Type_Manager;  — —  provides visibility for comparison
with PMC_Interface_Handler;
with Transmission_Protocol_Manager;
separate (PMC_Input_Analyzer)
task body Packet_Analyzer is
  Packet              : Packet_Type_Manager.Packets;
  Monitor_Command     : Monitor_Command_Type_Manager.Monitor_Commands;
  Temperature_Data_Ack : Packet_Type_Manager.Temperature_Data_Acks;

begin
  loop
    PMC_Interface_Handler.Receive_Packet (Packet);

    case Packet_Type_Manager.Classification_of (Packet) is

      when Packet_Type_Manager.Furnace_Monitor_Packet =>
        Monitor_Command :=
            Packet_Type_Manager.Furnace_Monitor_Conversion (Packet);

        case Monitor_Command_Type_Manager.Type_Of
           (Monitor_Command) is
          when Monitor_Command_Type_Manager.Scheduling_Info =>
            Process_Scheduling_Info (Monitor_Command);

          when Monitor_Command_Type_Manager.Temperature_Request =>
            Process_Temperature_Request (Monitor_Command);

        end case;
      when Packet_Type_Manager.Acknowledgement =>
        Temperature_Data_Ack :=
            Packet_Type_Manager.Temp_Ack_Conversion (Packet);
```

```
Transmission_Protocol_Manager.Acknowledge_Data
        (Temperature_Data_Ack);
    end case;
  end loop;
end Packet_Analyzer;
```

Comments

- This task shows an example of design for extensibility. Currently there are only two types of packets that can be received. Rather than using a simple `if...else...endif` construct, we have used the `case` statement to allow for easy expansion when other packet types are added. A `case` statement is preferable in situations such as this. Remember that this is currently the design for only a portion (prototype) of the FMC. There are other packets that will need to be added for the complete system.

8.5.1.3 Schedule_Manager   Within Schedule_Manager, during top-level design we have identified the following tasks that may run concurrently. Each needs to be decomposed individually.

- Scheduler
- Scheduled_Reading_Controller

The structure chart for the *Scheduler* task is shown in Figure 8-15.

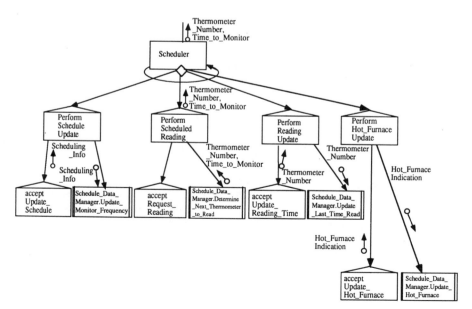

Figure 8-15   Scheduler Structure Chart

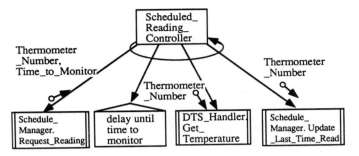

Figure 8-16 Scheduled_Reading_Controller Structure Chart

Comments:

- To make the SCHEDULE data store easier to reuse and maintain, we will break the store out of the Scheduler task and provide services as a lower-level helper module (Schedule_Data_Manager). This new data module will be discussed under Step 2.

The structure chart for the *Scheduled_Reading_Controller* task is given in Figure 8-16.

Comments:

- This task simply performs the timing necessary to monitor each temperature according to the schedule. The PDL also reflects this simple logic.

Schedule_Manager package specification PDL (see Section 7.5.4)

Schedule_Manager package body PDL

```
with Calendar;
package body Schedule_Manager is
   task Scheduler is
      entry Update_Hot_Furnace (Indicator : in
         Hot_Furnace_Indicators);
      entry Update_Schedule (Scheduling_Info : in
         Scheduling_Info_Type);
      entry Request_Reading (Thermometer_Number : out
         DTS_Handler.Thermometer_Numbers; Time_to_Monitor : out
         Calendar.Time);
      entry Update_Reading_Time (Thermometer_Number : in
         DTS_Handler.Thermometer_Numbers);
   end Scheduler;

   task Scheduled_Reading_Controller;

   task body Scheduler                    is separate;
   task body Scheduled_Reading_Controller is separate;
```

```
   procedure Update_Schedule (Scheduling_Info : in
      Scheduling_Info_Type) is
   begin
     Scheduler.Update_Schedule (Scheduling_Info);
   end Update_Schedule;

   procedure Update_Hot_Furnace (Indicator : in
      Hot_Furnace_Indicators) is
   begin
     Scheduler.Update_Hot_Furnace (Indicator);
   end Update_Hot_Furnace;
end Schedule_Manager;
```

Scheduler PDL

```
with Schedule_Data_Manager;
separate (Schedule_Manager)
task body Scheduler is
   Hot_Indicator    : Hot_Furnace_Indicators;
   Scheduling_Data  : Scheduling_Info_Type;
   Thermometer      : DTS_Handler.Thermometer_Numbers;

begin
  loop
    select
      accept Update_Schedule (Scheduling_Info : in
          Scheduling_Info_Type) do
        Scheduling_Data := Scheduling_Info;
      end Update_Schedule;
      Schedule_Data_Manager.Update_Monitor_Frequency
          (Scheduling_Data);

    or
      accept Update_Hot_Furnace (Indicator: in
          Hot_Furnace_indicators) do
        Hot_Indicator := Indicator;
      end Update_Hot_Furnace;
      Schedule_Data_Manager.Update_Hot_Furnace (Hot_Indicator);

    or
      accept Request_Reading (Thermometer_Number : out
          DTS_Handler.Thermometer_Numbers; Time_to_Monitor  : out
          Calendar.Time) do
        Schedule_Data_Manager.Determine_Next_Thermometer_To_Read
            (Thermometer_Number, Time_to_Monitor);
      end Request_Reading;

    or
      accept Update_Reading_Time (Thermometer_Number : in
          DTS_Handler.Thermometer_Numbers) do
        Thermometer := Thermometer_Number;
      end Update_Reading_Time;
      Schedule_Data_Manager.Update_Last_Time_Read (Thermometer);
```

```
      end select;
    end loop;
end Scheduler;
```

Comments

- Notice how simple and straightforward the task bodies have been. It is easy to see the logic of the entire task, because the details are abstracted and deferred to lower-level subprograms and helper modules.
- The construct `select...or...or...end select` means that this task will "wake up" if *any one* of the entries corresponding to one of the `accept` statements is called.

Scheduled_Reading_Controller PDL

```
separate (Schedule_Manager)
task body Scheduled_Reading_Controller is
   Thermometer      : DTS_Handler.Thermometer_Numbers;
   Time_to_Monitor : Calendar.Time;

   use Calendar;
begin
   loop
   Scheduler.Request_Reading (Thermometer, Time_to_Monitor);

      delay Time_To_Monitor - Calendar.Clock;

      DTS_Handler.Get_Temperature (Thermometer);

      Scheduler.Update_Reading_Time (Thermometer);
   end loop;
end Scheduled_Reading_Controller;
```

8.5.1.4 DTS_Handler Within DTS_Handler, we have identified the following task during top-level design:

- Temperature_Monitor

The structure chart for the *Temperature_Monitor* task is shown in Figure 8-17.

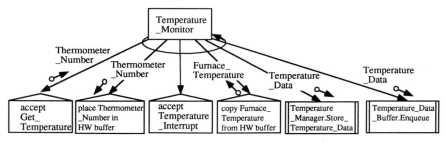

Figure 8-17 Temperature_Monitor Structure Chart

Comments

- This structure chart is needed to show the calls to Temperature_Manager and Temperature_Data_Buffer modules. The processing of the task itself is simple.

DTS_Handler package specification PDL (see Section 7.5.4)

DTS_Handler package body PDL

```
package body DTS_Handler is
   DTS_Interrupt_Address    : constant := 16#00B0#;
   DTS_Thermometer_Address  : constant := 16#00B2#;
   DTS_Temperature_Address  : constant := 16#00B4#;

   task Temperature_Monitor is
      entry DTS_Interrupt;
         for DTS_Interrupt use at DTS_Interrupt_Address;

      entry Get_Temperature (Thermometer_Number : in
          Thermometer_Numbers);
   end Temperature_Monitor;

   task body Temperature_Monitor is separate;
   procedure Get_Temperature (Thermometer_Number : in
       Thermometer_Numbers) is
   begin
      Temperature_Monitor.Get_Temperature (Thermometer_Number);
   end Get_Temperature;
end DTS_Handler;
```

Temperature_Monitor PDL

```
with Temperature_Data_Buffer;
with Temperature_Manager;
separate (DTS_Handler)
task body Temperature_Monitor is
   DTS_Temperature_Data : Temperature_Data_Manager.Temperature_Data;
   DTS_Thermometer_Number : Thermometer_Numbers;
      for DTS_Thermometer_Number use at DTS_Thermometer_Address;
   DTS_Temperature : Temperature_Data_Manager.Temperature_Range;
      for DTS_Temperature use at DTS_Temperature_Address;

   Max_DTS_Response_Time : constant Duration := 0.5;
   No_Response_From_DTS  : exception;
begin
   loop
      begin
         accept Get_Temperature (Thermometer_Number : in
             Thermometer_Numbers) do
            DTS_Thermometer_Number := Thermometer_Number;
         end Get_Temperature;
         select
            accept DTS_Interrupt;
```

```
      DTS_Temperature_Data.Thermometer_Number :=
         DTS_Thermometer_Number;
      DTS_Temperature_Data.Temperature          := DTS_Temperature;
      Temperature_Manager.Store_Temperature (DTS_Temperature_Data);
      Temperature_Data_Buffer.Enqueue (DTS_Temperature_Data);

   or
      delay Max_DTS_Response_Time;
      raise No_Response_From_DTS;
   end select;
   exception
   when No_Response_From_DTS =>
      null;
      -- currently there is no requirement to try again
      -- or report this error.
   end;
  end loop;
end Temperature_Monitor;
```

8.5.1.5 *Transmission_Protocol_Manager*   We have identified the following
task within Transmission_Protocol_Manager, during preliminary design:

- Transmission_Protocol

Figure 8-18 is the structure chart for the *Transmission_Protocol* task. It has been
updated from the one in top-level design to include a call to the new helper module
ASCII_Integer_Conversions (Integer_To_ASCII).

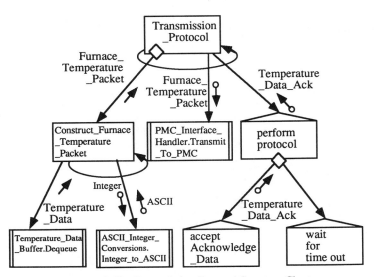

Figure 8-18   Transmission_Protocol Structure Chart

Transmission_Protocol_Manager package specification PDL (see Section 7.5.4)

Transmission_Protocol_Manager package body PDL

```
package body Transmission_Protocol_Manager is
   Max_Transmissions : constant := 3;
   type Transmission_Count is range 0..Max_Transmissions;

   procedure Construct_Furnace_Temperature_Packet
      (Furnace_Temperature_Packet : out Packet_Type_Manager.Packets)
      is separate;
   task Transmission_Protocol is
      entry Acknowledge_Data (Temperature_Data_Ack : in
         Packet_Type_Manager.Temperature_Data_Acks );
   end Transmission_Protocol;
   task body Transmission_Protocol is separate;

   procedure Acknowledge_Data (Temperature_Data_Ack : in
         Packet_Type_Manager.Temperature_Data_Acks) is
   begin
      Transmission_Protocol.Acknowledge_Data (Temperature_Data_Ack);
   end Acknowledge_Data;
end Transmission_Protocol_Manager;
```

Transmission_Protocol PDL

```
with PMC_Interface_Handler;
separate (Transmission_Protocol_Manager)
task body Transmission_Protocol is

   Packet_Transmit_Delay         : constant Duration := 2.0;
   Number_of_Transmissions       : Transmission_Count;
   Furnace_Temperature_Packet    : Packet_Type_Manager.Packets;
   Temperature_Data_Acknowledge :
         Packet_Type_Manager.Temperature_Data_Acks;
begin
   loop
      Construct_Furnace_Temperature_Packet
         (Furnace_Temperature_Packet);

      Temperature_Data_Acknowledge := ASCII.NAK;
      Number_of_Transmissions       := 0;

      Transmit_Furnace_Temp_Packet:
      loop

         PMC_Interface_Handler.Transmit_Packet
            (Furnace_Temperature_Packet);

         Number_of_Transmissions := Number_of_Transmissions + 1;

         select
            accept Acknowledge_Data (Temperature_Data_Ack : in
               Packet_Type_Manager.Temperature_Data_Acks) do
```

```
            Temperature_Data_Acknowledge := Temperature_Data_Ack;
         end Acknowledge_Data;
       or
         delay Packet_Transmit_Delay;
       end select;
       exit Transmit_Furnace_Temp_Packet when
           ((Temperature_Data_Acknowledge = ASCII.ACK) or
           (Number_of_Transmissions = Max_Transmissions));
     end loop Transmit_Furnace_Temp_Packet;
   end loop;
end Transmission_Protocol;
```

Comments

- The construct `select accept ...or delay ...end select` means that the task will wait for an `entry` call only a limited amount of time (Packet_Transmit_Delay) before "waking" and continuing execution.

8.5.1.6. Fuel_Reduction_Handler   Within Fuel_Reduction_Handler, we have identified only one task during preliminary design: Fuel_Reduction_Controller. Since this is a simple task in which all the processing will be done in the task body, no structure chart is given.

Fuel_Reduction_Handler package specification PDL (see Section 7.5.4)

Fuel_Reduction_Handler package body PDL

```
package body Fuel_Reduction_Handler is
  task Fuel_Reduction_Controller is
    entry Evaluate_Temperatures;
  end Fuel_Reduction_Controller;
  task body Fuel_Reduction_Controller is separate;
  procedure Evaluate_Temperatures is
  begin
    Fuel_Reduction_Controller.Evaluate_Temperatures;
  end Evaluate_Temperatures;
end Fuel_Reduction_Handler;
```

Fuel_Reduction_Controller PDL

```
with DTS_Handler;
with Schedule_Manager; use Schedule_Manager;
with Temperature_Manager; use Temperature_Manager;
separate (Fuel_Reduction_Handler)
task body Fuel_Reduction_Controller is
  Hot_Average : constant
    Temperature_Manager.Temperature_Range := 3500;
```

```
Hot_Spot      : constant
   Temperature_Manager.Temperature_Range   := 3600;

Saved_Hot_indicator  : Schedule_Manager.Hot_Furnace_Indicators :=
                       Schedule_Manager.Normal;
New_Hot_indicator    : Schedule_Manager.Hot_Furnace_Indicators;

Current_Temperature  : Temperature_Manager.Temperatures;

begin
  loop
  accept Evaluate_Temperatures;

  Temperature_Manager.Get_Temperatures (Current_Temperature);

  New_Hot_Indicator := Schedule_Manager.Normal;
  for I in DTS_Handler.Thermometer_Numbers loop
    if Current_Temperature (I) ) Hot_Spot then
      New_Hot_Indicator := Schedule_Manager.Hot;
      - - reduce fuel by 20%
      exit;
    end if;

    - -     compute average temperature
  end loop;

  - - if the average temperature is over Hot_Average then
     New_Hot_Indicator := Schedule_Manager.Hot;
  - -    reduce fuel by 10%
  - - end if;

  if New_Hot_Indicator /= Saved_Hot_Indicator then
    Schedule_Manager.Update_Hot_Furnace (New_Hot_Indicator);
      Saved_Hot_Indicator := New_Hot_Indicator;
    end if;
  end loop;
end Fuel_Reduction_Controller;
```

Comments

- The -- indicate comments. The comment lines here indicate the additional processing (both function and control logic) that must be added during the coding phase of development.

8.5.1.7 Temperature_Data_Buffer Note that access to this data must include a mechanism for mutual exclusion so that the tasks using it are not reading or writing at the same time. The following Ada task provides for this.

In other languages, the access would be done within a critical region (such as with semaphores). This difference in methods of data access is an example of why the actual design may be programming language– and run-time system–dependent.

Temperature_Data_Buffer package specification PDL (see Section 7.5.4)

Temperature_Data_Buffer package body PDL

```
package body Temperature_Data_Buffer is

  task Buffer is
    entry Enqueue (Thermometer_Temperature : in
        Temperature_Manager.Temperature_Data);
    entry Dequeue (Thermometer_Temperature : out
        Temperature_Manager.Temperature_Data);
  end Buffer;                             .

  procedure Enqueue (Thermometer_Temperature : in
      Temperature_Manager.Temperature_Data) is
  begin
    Buffer.Enqueue    (Thermometer_Temperature);
  end Enqueue;

  procedure Dequeue (Thermometer_Temperature : out
      Temperature_Manager.Temperature_Data) is
  begin
    Buffer.Dequeue    (Thermometer_Temperature);
  end Dequeue;

  task body Buffer is separate;
end Temperature_Data_Buffer;
```

Comments

- Since the task Buffer is simple and may be reused from another project we will not show the decomposition here.

8.5.1.8 ASCII_Integer_Conversions The ASCII_Integer_Conversions module contains simple functions to convert between ASCII and integer values. As such, no structure chart is needed. This is a new helper package identified during detailed design. Since each of the functions (services) provided by this module is straightforward, the actual coding of them has been left for the implementation phase.

ASCII_Integer_Conversions package specification PDL

```
package ASCII_Integer_Conversions is
  function ASCII_To_Integer (A : String)   return Integer;

  function Integer_To_ASCII (I : Integer) return String;

  Invalid_String_Input  : exception;
  Invalid_Integer_Input : exception;
end ASCII_Integer_Conversions;
```

8.5.1.9 Monitor_Command_Type_Manager See Section 7.5.1 for this Monitor_Command_Type_Manager package specification PDL. Since each of the functions (services) provided by this module is straightforward, the actual coding of them has been left for the implementation phase.

8.5.1.10 Packet_Type_Manager For the Packet_Type_Manager package specification PDL, see Section 7.5.4. Since each of the functions (services) provided by this module is straightforward, the actual coding of them has been left for the implementation phase.

8.5.2 Step 2: Design the Data Module(s)

8.5.2.1 Temperature_Manager Temperature_Manager encapsulates the TEMPERATURES data store and provides simple (disjoint) services to access the data. A task is used to ensure mutual exclusion in accessing the data.

Temperature_Manager package specification PDL (see Section 7.5.4)

Temperature_Manager package body PDL

```
package body Temperature_Manager is
  task Temperature_Protection is
    entry Store_Temperature (Thermometer_Temperature : in
        Temperature_Data);
    entry Get_Temperatures  (Current_Temperatures    : out
        Temperatures);
  end Temperature_Protection;

  task body Temperature_Protection is separate;
  procedure Store_Temperature (Thermometer_Temperature : in
      Temperature_Data) is
  begin
    Temperature_Protection.Store_Temperature
        (Thermometer_Temperature);
  end Store_Temperature;

  procedure Get_Temperatures (Current_Temperatures : out
      Temperatures) is
  begin
    Temperature_Protection.Get_Temperatures (Current_Temperatures);
  end Get_Temperatures;
end Temperature_Manager;
```

Temperature_Protection task PDL

```
separate (Temperature_Manager)
task body Temperature_Protection is
  The_Temperatures : Temperatures;
```

```
begin
  loop
    select
      accept Store_Temperature (Thermometer_Temperature : in
          Temperature_Data) do
        The_Temperatures
          (Thermometer_Temperature.Thermometer_Number) :=
          Thermometer_Temperature.Temperature;
      end Store_Temperature;

    or
      accept Get_Temperatures (Current_Temperatures : out
          Temperatures) do
        Current_Temperatures := The_Temperatures;
      end Get_Temperatures;
    end select;
  end loop;
end Temperature_Protection;
```

8.5.2.2 *Schedule_Data_Manager* Schedule_Data_Manager now encapsulates the SCHEDULE data store and provides simple (disjoint) services to access it. The services are:

- Update_Monitor_Frequency, when new scheduling info has been received from the PMC.
- Determine_Next_Thermometer_To_Read, to perform the scheduled reading
- Update_Last_Time_Read, when the thermometer has been read
- Update_Hot_Furnace, when Furnace changes between Hot and Normal

The structure chart in Figure 8-19 is simply the piece that was cut out of the Scheduler structure chart from top-level design.

Comments

- The Schedule_Data_Manager provides four distinct services with no interface between them other than the access of Schedule.
- Only Scheduler will use this module to access the data. Thus, no mutual exclusion needs to be provided here; the Scheduler task itself provides it.

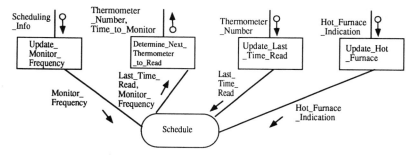

Figure 8-19   Schedule_Data_Manager Structure Chart

- Normally, a structure chart would not be drawn for simple services of a data module such as this; it is only needed for complex algorithmic services that can be decomposed into several subprograms.

Schedule_Data_Manager package specification PDL

```
with Calendar;
with DTS_Handler;
with Schedule_Manager;
package Schedule_Data_Manager is
  procedure Update_Monitor_Frequency
      (Scheduling_Info : in Schedule_Manager.Scheduling_Info_Type);

  procedure Determine_Next_Thermometer_To_Read
      (Thermometer_Number : out DTS_Handler.Thermometer_Numbers;
       Time_to_Monitor    : out Calendar.Time);

  procedure Update_Last_Time_Read
      (Thermometer_Number : in DTS_Handler.Thermometer_Numbers);

  procedure Update_Hot_Furnace
      (Indicator : in Schedule_Manager.Hot_Furnace_indicators);
end Schedule_Data_Manager;
```

Schedule_Data_Manager package body PDL

```
package body Schedule_Data_Manager is
  type Reading_Link is access DTS_Handler.Thermometer_Numbers;

  type Schedule is
    record
      Last_Time_Read        : Calendar.Time;
      Time_To_Read          : Calendar.Time;
      Monitor_Frequency     : Schedule_Manager.Monitor_Frequencies;
      Next_Scheduled_Reading : Reading_Link;
    end record;

  type Schedule_Orders is array
      (DTS_Handler.Thermometer_Numbers) of Schedule;

  Schedule_Order : Schedule_Orders;
  Next_Reading   : Reading_Link := null;
  Hot_Furnace    : Schedule_Manager.Hot_Furnace_Indicators;
  procedure Update_Monitor_Frequency (Scheduling_Info : in
      Schedule_Manager.Scheduling_Info_Type) is separate;

  procedure Determine_Next_Thermometer_To_Read
      (Thermometer_Number : out DTS_Handler.Thermometer_Numbers;
       Time_to_Monitor    : out Calendar.Time) is separate;
```

```
procedure Update_Last_Time_Read (Thermometer_Number : in
    DTS_Handler.Thermometer_Numbers) is separate;

procedure Update_Hot_Furnace (Indicator : in
    Schedule_Manager.Hot_Furnace_Indicators) is separate;
begin
  null;   — —*
  — —  Initialize the Schedule_Order —
  — —  there are currently no thermometers to read
end Schedule_Data_Manager;
```

8.5.3. Step 3: Represent Detailed Software Architecture

Figure 8-20 shows the updated SAD of the completed software architecture. Notice that all of the modules now appear.

8.5.4 Step 4: Document Traceability

Sometimes, a project demands the tracing of requirements down to the subprogram level. For large systems, the matrix described in Section 8.2.4 can become unwieldy. Another possible method of demonstrating the traceability is by means

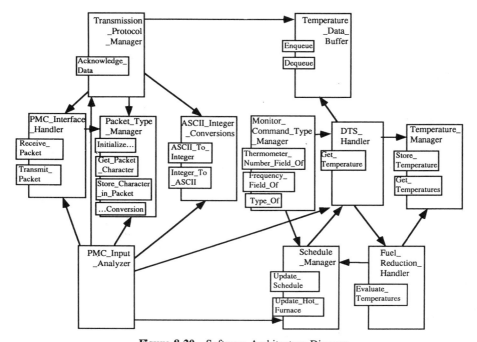

Figure 8-20 Software Architecture Diagram

Software Requirement	Software Component
1 Schedule Temperature Reading	---
1.1 Maintain Schedule	Schedule_Manager.Scheduler Schedule_Data_Manager.Update_Monitor_Frequency
1.2 Initiate Scheduled Temperature Reading	Schedule_Manager.Scheduler Schedule_Manager.Scheduled_Reading_Controller Schedule_Data_Manager.Determine_Next_Thermometer_to_Read Schedule_Data_Manager.Update_Last_Time_Read
...	...

Figure 8-21   Detailed Requirements Traceability Excerpt

of a table with two columns. The first column contains the requirements, while the second lists the modules and subprograms that satisfy each requirement. A segment of this type of requirements traceability to the subprogram level is shown in Figure 8-21. We will not be showing the entire list in the text.

8.6   KEYS TO UNDERSTANDING

- Detailed design is the continued refinement of the program begun during top-level design.
- It builds on the graphics used during top-level design and adds PDL.
- There is a balance between algorithmic refinement and information hiding, in the style of modular structured design (MSD) of Appendix A.
- Detailed design addresses all issues except the lowest-level coding details. All modules and subprograms are identified (as well as any tasks needed as corrections to the top-level design), and all difficult data structure, interface, and algorithmic problems have been solved.

Software Design Concepts

This Appendix addresses a number of software design concepts and issues that are vital to the use of SSEM but are best summarized or introduced separately from the main line of discussion and the FMS example. The topics addressed are:

A.1 Software design approach

A.2 Information hiding and data abstraction

A.3 Object-oriented design

A.4 Modular real-time design

A.5 Modular structured design

The Appendix is, first of all, intended to provide background information on two major approaches to software decomposition and design—functional, or step-by-step, decomposition and modular, or information-hiding (or object-oriented), decomposition—and their distinct differences. The Appendix then shows how the two different viewpoints can be usefully combined into an integrated approach to software design. At the point where the design techniques are sufficiently detailed to need a specific programming language, or when reference is made to actual projects using the methods, Ada is used for illustration (with necessary explanations for Ada-specific constructs).

A.1 introduces general notions of software design and lays some additional groundwork for the following sections. A.2 introduces information hiding ideas, while A.3 discusses the specific form of information hiding now popularly called "object-oriented" design. A.4 shows how real-time issues are dealt with and related to the earlier ideas, with a focus on top-level design. A.5 integrates the ideas of functional decomposition and information hiding and gives additional ideas to augment and complete, through detailed design, the approach given for real-time systems.

A.1 SOFTWARE DESIGN

The purpose of software design is to establish the architectural framework of a body of code. The design partitions the software into smaller pieces in a "divide and conquer" approach and hence provides a representation of the software in terms of a number of components. The components may equivalently be thought of as work units, assigned (either actually or potentially) to teams for further development.

The philosophy used for the partitioning, and the nature of the resulting components, is the fundamental choice of software design methodology. Broadly speaking, there are two choices: functionally driven decomposition or data-driven decomposition. Of course, either of these approaches incorporates some of the other, somewhat like the yin and yang of Oriental philosophies, but the distinction is useful. In practice, and in the literature, the distinction is certainly made, sometimes in hard and fast terms. The driving software design philosophy of this book is to blend the two approaches in a way that takes advantage of the best of each.

A.1.1 Functional Decomposition

Functionally driven decomposition results in components or work assignments that are named and callable pieces of software; we call these components *subprograms*. These subprograms may be aggregated into larger units for convenience, but nonetheless they retain their nature as representing the structure or framework for the code. The interface to each subprogram primarily consists of the input and output parameters that have effect when the subprogram is called. The subprograms typically have further important interaction via access to data that are shared among subprograms, which must all know the internal structure of the data. The subprograms represent the functions of the software: the step-by-step processing that it accomplishes.

A.1.2 Data-Driven Decomposition

Data-driven decomposition results in components or work assignments that are named pieces of software that *encapsulate*—hide while providing controlled access to—data structures; we call these components *modules*. The interface to each module primarily consists of a closely-related group of subprograms that provide access to the data structure, including complex functions associated with the data structure. The module itself is not callable; the subprograms are. The modules represent the building blocks of the software—the capabilities necessary to accomplish the software's functions. Typically, the actual step-by-step processing is hidden in one or another of the modules or is distributed among the various modules.

Much of the rest of this Appendix (Sections A.2, A.3, and portions of A.4 and A.5) deals with approaches toward data-driven decomposition; the techniques are not as well known as the older and more widely used—often called "traditional"—methods of functionally driven decomposition. The most common name and set of techniques for the functional approach is *structured design*. Although structured design is well known, we will set the stage for the remaining sections of the Appendix by discussing it here.

A.1.3 Structured Design

We will briefly define structured design, distinguish its principles and resulting software decomposition from a major form of data-driven design (information hiding, as explained in Section A.2), and anticipate how it is combined with information hiding in the discipline known as *modular structured design* (MSD). We view structured design as primarily dealing with sequential systems or with those aspects of real-time or concurrent systems that do not deal with parallel processing or task interactions; such real-time issues are dealt with at length in the main body of the book and are addressed in Section A.4.

Structured design is the discipline concerned with the decomposition of software into callable code segments (subprograms, subroutines, and other names; we will refer to them as subprograms) in a hierarchical structure. These code segments are sometimes called modules, but we are reserving that name for components derived using information hiding principles; such modules are the components shown on software architecture diagrams (SAD), and they typically encapsulate some data structure along with more than one callable subcomponent. The subprograms are derived using principles of coupling and cohesion described generally in Section 4.2.2 and in Chapter 7 (especially Section 7.3.6) specifically for software design. The phrase and the techniques associated with structured design are most closely associated with Yourdon and Constantine [YOU79]. The subprograms generally have the capability to access a wide variety of visible data structures.

The net effect of the application of cohesion (especially the strong emphasis on *functional* cohesion) leads to a design that has an emphasis on functional decomposition—on the step-by-step processing that accomplishes some function. Structured design typically does not take into account the ideas of information hiding advanced by Parnas [PAR72b] and explained in Section A.2, although it certainly allows some influence of those ideas, especially as expressed by Myers [MYE75] in terms of modules with *informational strength* cohesion. The design is expressed most practically as a structure chart that illustrates the calling hierarchy of the subprograms in the system. In this form, it usefully expresses what the software does and how it does it. Unfortunately, there are significant weaknesses—primarily related to difficulty of modification—to such a structure when it is used as the primary organizational approach for the software. Parnas, in the same paper noted above [PAR72b], criticized software organization based on the step-by-step processing and called for an alternate approach to modularization—namely, information hiding.

The alternate approach proposed by Parnas, and by now rather widely accepted in many circles, calls for software to be organized in modules that hide design decisions—most commonly related to data structures. A key aspect of this modularization is that the modules have quite different characteristics from the subprograms of structured design. The components derived from information hiding principles hide a design decision, such as the specific data structure used to implement a stack or the methods for accomplishing access to some external device. On the other hand, the components derived from structured design principles encapsulate steps in the processing, such as gathering data, calculating some intermediate results, or accessing a shared data structure. Information hiding is explained in Section A.2; the main point to be made here is that it is quite different from structured design.

A.1.4 Modular Structured Design

The fact that information hiding is different from structured design does not mean that the two approaches are incompatible; it is an important aspect of the design methods of this book that it is most useful to have two different viewpoints of the design. The primary structuring aspect is that of information hiding, while the techniques of structured design are used to understand better how the software does its job and to determine the best set of capabilities to be provided by the information-hiding modules.

Consistent with the combination of the two approaches, there are two primary sets of graphic representation of the designs. An architecture diagram shows the modules in the software and represents its primary structure, that is, the representation of components that would be used as work assignments. The structure chart (or a set of individual structure charts) is a secondary representation that shows the calling relationships of the subprograms. The structure chart is related to the architecture diagram in that the majority of the callable subprograms are those subprograms exported by the modules and that all the subprograms exported by the modules will be somewhere represented on a structure chart, or at least logically could be so represented.

The use of these graphics, and general methods for accomplishing design in an integrated data/functional manner, are provided in Section A.5.

A.1.5 Summary

Some design approaches make a distinct choice between functionally driven and data-driven decomposition—essentially treating them as incompatible. The best known methods that take such an approach are structured design and object-oriented design.

The approach of this book is to integrate the two approaches into an integrated method that takes advantage of the best of each and uses each viewpoint to enhance the other.

A.2   INFORMATION HIDING AND DATA ABSTRACTION

The purpose of this part of the Appendix (which is adapted from [SHU90]) is to introduce and explain the notions of information hiding and data abstraction. The ideas are language-independent, but in order to be concrete in illustrating general principles, some examples in Ada are provided.

The basic issue is that you cannot design software systems effectively without understanding the basic principles of data abstraction and information hiding. These principles are used to determine what modules should be created in order to establish the overall software architecture.

The next sections present the notion of data abstraction and discuss why the use of data abstraction is important to software design. We'll start with a little of the history of data abstraction and some quotes about its importance, followed by some illustrations of the meaning and effect of data abstraction, including a short Ada-specific example. Then we'll illustrate some principles of how data abstraction is important in software design.

A.2.1   History

One of the early important commentators on the importance of data abstraction was C. A. R. Hoare. In "Notes on Data Structuring" in [DAH72], (originally written in 1970), he wrote, "In the development of our understanding of complex phenomena, the most powerful tool available to the human intellect is abstraction." He also noted that "the benefits of using high-level languages instead of machine code may be largely due to their incorporation of successful abstractions, particularly for data."

In general, abstraction is simply concentration on aspects of the problem that are important, while ignoring the aspects of the problem that are unimportant for what we are attempting to achieve at any one time. Wegner [WEG83] states, "Abstraction is concerned with specifying relevant attributes of a class of objects, situations, or processes and ignoring (hiding) irrelevant attributes."

By *data abstraction* we mean the exclusive focus on the *contents* of a data structure and the *operations* that may manipulate a data structure, without regard to the programming details of the data structure's implementation. We'll make this more specific in the next section.

In a more modern context, Liskov & Guttag have written a book about how to do program decomposition based on abstraction. They write [LIS86], "It is data abstraction that most often provides the primary organizational tool in the programming process."

However, the author whose work we will follow most closely in terms of applying notions of data abstraction to software design is Parnas, who published two very important papers in 1972. The first [PAR72a] deals with the notion that a component of a software system ought to be usable through knowledge only of its specification, independent of its implementation. The second paper [PAR72b] deals with determining the modules of a system; that is, its software architecture.

The two papers are closely related. The first says, "The specification must provide to the intended user *all* the information that he will need to use the program correctly, *and nothing more*." The second, usually referenced as introducing the phrase "information hiding," says, "One begins with a list of difficult design decisions which are likely to change. Each module is then designed to hide such a decision from the others." The relationship is that the specification provides all the information necessary to use a module, while the hidden design decision is the "and nothing more" of the first paper. Parnas goes even further to say that to modularize otherwise (for example, in accordance with the steps in the processing) is wrong ("almost always incorrect").

Parnas also relates these ideas to other aspects of building large systems. For example, in [PAR85] he shows how to supplement "the software design technique known as information hiding, or abstraction" with a specific set of documentation. This actually transcends the basic notion of data abstraction to have broad implications for software design.

We will now narrow in on specific issues related to data abstraction and abstract data types.

A.2.2   Meaning and Effect of Data Abstraction

"Data abstraction" can refer both to the concept defined in the preceding section and to a software module that specifies a data structure in terms of its use rather than its implementation. The latter use of "data abstraction" is essentially synonymous with *abstract data type* (ADT). The basic difference is that the phrase "abstract data type" usually implies the ability to create instances of a type definition, whereas the general notion of data abstraction (or information hiding) is important even in languages that are not strongly typed. We will use the definition that a data abstraction specifies the allowable contents of a data structure and the operations that allow manipulation of the data structure.

For example, let's consider a *stack*: a last-in, first-out data structure similar to a stack of plates in a cafeteria. You can take a plate only from the top of the stack. Similarly, you can add a plate only to the top of the stack. Under no legitimate circumstance can you add plates to or take plates from the middle of the stack. We say that adding a plate is a "push" on the stack, while taking a plate is a "pop" from the stack. A data abstraction representing the stack provides the operations Push and Pop; the implementation is hidden from the user.

Figure A-1 illustrates the idea behind a stack implemented as a data abstraction. The left-hand side of the figure represents more-or-less traditional programming, in which each programmer can "see" the representation of the data structures. The other side of the figure represents the situation in which the data structure is encapsulated. You can think of the module encapsulating (or hiding information about) the stack as a *server,* or *manager* of the data structure, while the module making use of the stack is the *client.*

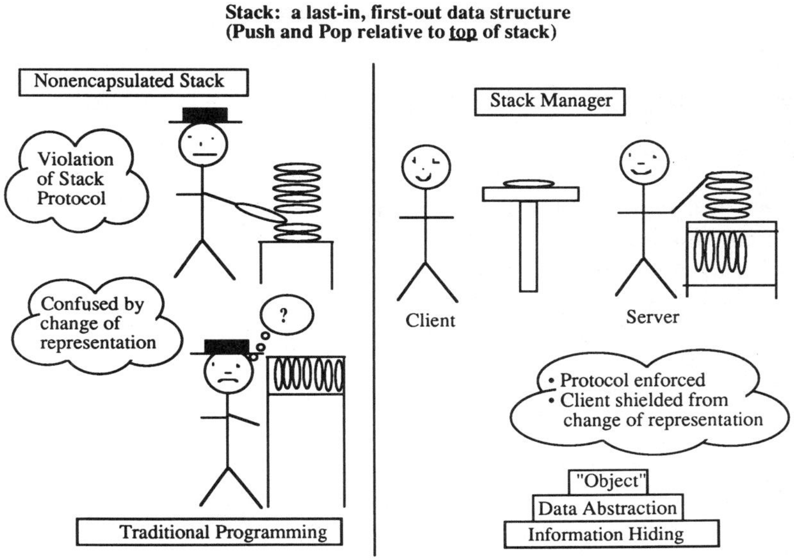

Stack: a last-in, first-out data structure
(Push and Pop relative to top of stack)

Figure A-1   Stack Implementation

In the nonencapsulated case (no data abstraction), the using programmer or using module has access to the data structure, perhaps an array. The programmer can therefore remove or replace items in the middle of the stack or incorrectly modify the stack pointer, thus violating the abstract concept of the stack. Furthermore, a later decision to change the representation of the data structure (perhaps to a linked list) causes the using module to become invalid. Note that it is not really the *programmer* that is confused by the change in representation—the *code* written by the programmer is "confused." That code must be revised when the representation changes.

In the encapsulated case, the server (the encapsulating module) provides the operations to manipulate the data structure while hiding its implementation. The user, and the user's code, is unaffected by a change in representation.

The stack is represented abstractly, illustrating the notion of information hiding. Such an encapsulation of a data structure is often called an "object."

Let's see a simple example of how this looks in Ada.

A.2.3   An Example of Data Abstraction

We will only illustrate the simplest form of data abstraction, with all information about the stack hidden by the specification of the operations on the stack. First, we will show how abstraction can be introduced without a package (module).

In order to allow clients to use the the stack in an abstract manner, we can define some push and pop operations for a stack of integers (or anything else) as:

```
...  definition of the stack data structure ...
procedure Push (Item :  in  Integer) is ...   end Push;
procedure Pop  (Item : out Integer) is ...   end Pop;
```

Many languages, for example Pascal, allow this level of abstraction, although any module with visibility to these procedures would also have visibility to the actual data structure. Pascal does not *enforce* the encapsulation shown by the "Stack Manager" in Figure A.1, so a programming team can get most of the benefits of the encapsulation only by *agreement* among the programming staff and careful management control.

The way to get the encapsulation offered by Ada is to place the procedure specifications in a package specification.

```
package Stack is
   procedure Push (Item :  in  Integer);
   procedure Pop  (Item : out Integer);
end Stack;
```

The module is used by the clients of the stack, which make use of (call) its abstract representation to store and retrieve. The actual declarations of the structure of the stack, and the stack object itself, are in the body of the module—not visible to the clients.

This is exactly an implementation of the ideas of Parnas, and an illustration of the "Stack Manager" in Figure A-1. The design decision that is difficult and likely to change is the representation of the stack, which is hidden. The specification of the stack provides the operations to push and pop, nothing more. (A more complete representation of the stack might have more operations, but it still would not reveal the details of implementation of the stack object.) Next, we will discuss these issues from the viewpoint of a large programming project, continuing to use the short and simple example of the stack.

A.2.4 Data Abstraction in Software System Design

Let's look at an example of how these ideas affect software system design. In order to be concise, we will use an abstract example of design. Specific examples, in a case study format, are given in [SHU89].

Parnas says that we should not determine the modules of a system based on the step-by-step processing. Instead, we should focus on important design decisions, encapsulating the decisions in modules. The following example addresses the design of a large software system but uses the single example of the stack data abstraction to illustrate the overall principle. You will have to imagine how the single illustration of the stack really represents the dozens of complicated data structure decisions one must make to build large systems.

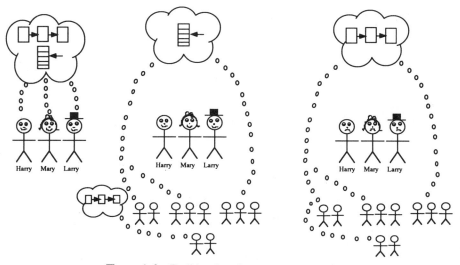

Figure A-2   Traditional or Step-By-Step Architecture

Harry, Mary, and Larry are three task leaders in a programming project. Suppose they first define a functional partitioning of the programming task in accordance with the steps in the processing, with responsibilities—the modules of the system—being input, processing, and output. Figure A-2 illustrates this situation, the approach of traditional structured design. Their next job, illustrated on the left side of the figure, is to define the data structures that specify the interfaces between their separate parts of the project. For simplicity of exposition, we will assume that their only decision is what data structure to use for a stack. In reality, this is a very complex and time-consuming process, taking up a good portion of the design time and effort.

In the middle of the figure, Harry, Mary, and Larry have settled on an array implementation, have assembled their programming staffs, and are deeply involved in implementation. All members of the programming team have knowledge of the data structure decision. Indeed, this decision, and the actual stack, is the major interface between the different parts of the program. Then one of the programmers encounters a good reason for needing the stack to be implemented as a linked list.

In the right part of the figure, Harry, Mary, and Larry have changed the decision—to a linked list—about the implementation of the stack. All members of the programming team must now change their code, leading to rework, delays, and so on. This is why the establishment of the overall architecture in accordance with the steps in the processing is wrong. The key, and changeable, design decision was visible throughout the programming team. There was no use of information hiding. You can see how unhappy Harry, Mary, and Larry are—they have to tell the program manager about the six-month slip!

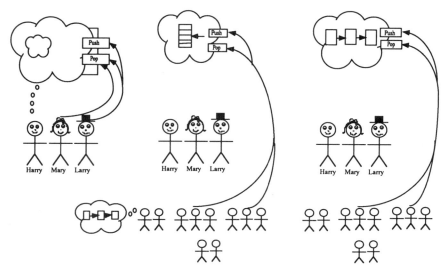

Figure A-3   Encapsulated Object-Oriented, ADT, information-Hiding Architecture

Suppose instead that Harry, Mary, and Larry were to follow the precepts of Parnas in terms of modularizing and of careful specification of the modules, hiding information that was not needed for effective use of the module. This is illustrated in Figure A-3.

They might first decide that Harry is responsible for the data abstraction that implements the stack, while Mary and Larry are responsible for the rest of the system. This situation is shown in the left part of the figure. Specification of the interface between the different parts of the system is now easier and faster, since only the abstract representation of the stack need be defined, rather than all the specific details of the data structure.

Harry, Mary, and Larry can now form the programming teams earlier, beginning parallel work on the system at an earlier time. This is illustrated in the middle of the figure, with most of the programmers only concerned about the abstract representation (Push and Pop), while only Harry's team is concerned with the details. Someone on Harry's team is about to convince Harry to change from an array to a linked list. How will this affect the project?

The right part of the figure illustrates that changes to the data structure are limited to Harry's team, mitigating the effects of change and the negative consequences earlier shown in Figure A-2.

A.2.5   There's More to This Issue

We have only discussed some basic principles of data abstraction—enough for you to understand that something fundamental is going on with this approach to software design. The actual data abstractions in large systems will be more complex than simple data structures such as stacks and queues, although such data structures will *also* be in the software design. Large systems may have abstractions of large data stores, such as track files, dictionaries, images to be sent to a printer, or entire databases. There will also be system- or problem-related abstractions, such as ships, airplanes, factories, or operator consoles; these are often called *objects* and are pertinent to methods called object-oriented design.

Another aspect of this issue is that although we must not establish the overall software architecture based on the step-by-step processing—a functional partitioning of the system—the functional viewpoint is still important. There are methods that combine the object-oriented and the functional viewpoint in a balanced way.

These larger issues—object-orientation, functional partitioning, and their combination—are addressed in the later parts of this Appendix.

A.2.6 Summary

Understanding data abstraction is a prerequisite to being an effective software designer. The mechanism for implementing data abstraction is the *module,* with the implementation of a module being language-specific. A practical synonym for designing with data abstraction is using the principles of information hiding as defined and established by Parnas. Object-oriented design is a closely related topic.

A.3 OBJECT-ORIENTED DESIGN

The purpose of this part of the Appendix is to introduce and explain *object-oriented design*, a concept closely related to and derivative of the notions of information hiding and data abstraction that we discussed in Section A.2. We will differentiate it from functional decomposition, show how it can help in the identification of modules, and set the stage for later presentation (in Section A.5) of a design approach that balances functional decomposition and object-oriented design.

For our purposes, object-oriented design (OOD), is a method of determination of a software architecture that identifies modules and their interactions by establishing a correspondence with entities (objects) in the "real world" (the problem space). That is, it is a method of decomposition of the software into modules. It turns out that modules identified in this way always encapsulate some data structure and export operations that (among other things) manipulate the data structure.

We will see in Section A.4 that an important aspect of SSEM is the decomposition of the software into tasks. How does OOD interact with such a decomposition? There are two aspects:

- OOD notions can provide guidance for how the tasks are aggregated into modules. This is also addressed in Chapter 7.
- OOD can help in the further decomposition of complex tasks into modules (addressed in Chapter 8 and Section A.5).

The next sections present the basic definition of object-oriented design, a small problem to be solved, and both traditional function- and object-oriented design decomposition to solve the problem.

A.3.1 Definition

Object-oriented design has many different aspects, viewpoints, and definitions. Although highly useful as a concept, it is by no means a mature, well agreed-upon methodology. For the form of OOD with which we will be concerned, the most important innovator and popularizer is Booch, who defines *objects* and *object-oriented development* ("development" means "design" for our purposes) as [BOO87, page 12]:

> Simply stated, *object-oriented development* is an approach to software design and implementation in which the decomposition of a system is based upon the concept of an object. An *object* is an entity whose behavior is characterized by the operations that it suffers and that it requires of other objects. By *suffers* an operation, we mean that the given operation can legally be performed upon the object.

The sorts of objects that Booch is talking about here in relation to software design are entities or things that are visible in the system intended to incorporate the software being developed. In other words, objects represent ships, planes, airports, cars, trucks, missiles, furnaces, people, and so on that are part of the problem space of the system to be constructed. The idea is that the architecture of the software should be partially dictated by the important entities or objects that are recognizable by nonsoftware users of the system.

He goes on to assert:

> Object-oriented development is fundamentally different from traditional functional methods, for which the primary criteria for decomposition is that each module in the system represents a major step in the overall process.

Then he states the fundamental criterion for decomposing a system using object-oriented techniques [BOO87, page 16]:

> Each module in the system denotes an object or class of objects from the problem space.

We might consider this a subset—or perhaps additional guidance—to the Parnas criterion we stated in Section A.2.1, in which the modules were designed to hide design decisions. The OOD viewpoint can be considered to be that the key design decisions have to do with objects.

Let's take a look at an example of OOD and contrast it with more traditional structured design.

A.3.2 A Software Requirement

We will illustrate the ideas of OOD by using a small example adapted and simplified from Booch [BOO87, pages 13–15]. The problem is that of a cruise control system

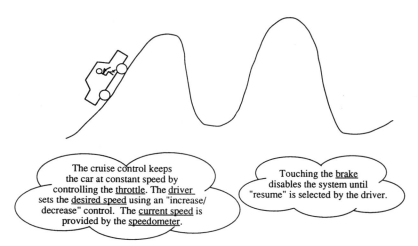

Figure A-4 Simple Cruise Control (SCC) Concept

intended to maintain a constant speed for an automobile, even over varying terrain. Figure A-4 illustrates the basic idea.

Figure A-5 is a context diagram showing the inputs and outputs of the cruise control software. We won't go into explanations of each of the data elements, instead relying on your general understanding of automobiles. Figure A-6 is a simplified data flow diagram further defining the problem. Of particular interest are the terminators (driver, brake, wheel, and so on) and the data stores (current speed, desired speed, and brake state). The terminators are the *objects* in the system, while the data stores can be considered as a sort of internal object. Certainly the data stores represent data structures that will involve software design decisions of the sort indicated by Parnas that need to be hidden.

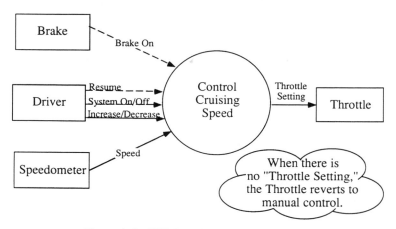

Figure A-5 SCC Data/Control Context Diagram

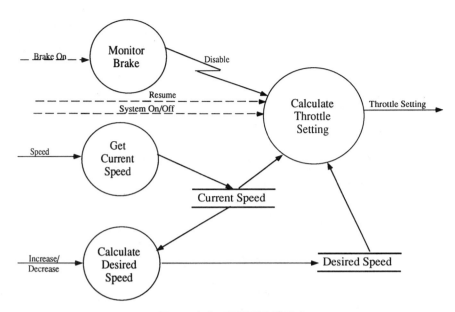

Figure A-6   SCC DFD/CFD 0

A.3.3   A Traditional Design

It is likely that a traditional "structured" design, or functional decomposition, would look something like the simplified structure chart in Figure A-7. Each of the major modules are steps in the process or functions to be performed. They are interconnected by access to common data structures not shown on the diagram.

In the sense of Section A.2, these are the modules that would be assigned to Harry, Mary, Larry, and their programming teams. Of course, this is also the decomposition that Parnas said was "almost always incorrect" and that we discussed at length in the earlier section. Nonetheless, there is considerable merit in such a representation of the solution, since it is clear that, in fact, the problem is being

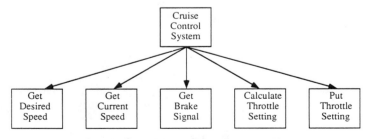

Figure A-7   SCC Functional Decomposition

solved. That is, it is clear that the system will calculate and output the throttle setting based on the input data.

Let's contrast this to the design resulting from a focus on the objects in the system.

A.3.4 An Object-Oriented Design

Figure A-8, following Booch, shows the modules and relationships resulting from a modularization based on focus on the objects. The arrows indicate *visibility to* (ability to make use of) other objects. For example, "Brake" is visible to "Driver" and "Throttle." This modularization is a clear application of the notions of information hiding and, since the object (module) will invariably be encapsulating data structures, an application of data abstraction or abstract data types. How were these modules identified? We feel that the easiest way to identify modules is from the terminators and data stores of a DFD. Booch has also suggested using the nouns in a simplified statement of requirements (such as the underlined words in Figure A-4). This is somewhat simplistic for large, complex problems, but may be a useful guideline in certain instances.

The top-level design components are now the modules that would be assigned to the three teams in Figure A-3 in the previous section to solve the problems of change in data structure discussed earlier in this section. An additional advantage of such a design is that it is clear at this top-level viewpoint, and clear to an interested customer reviewing the design, that the major components of the actual system are being dealt with in an organized manner.

However, a potential problem with such a representation of the design is that it is not clear at this top-level viewpoint, or to an interested customer reviewing the design, that the throttle setting is, in fact, calculated and output.

A.3.5 Summary and Analysis

What should be clear is that Booch is correct when he says that OOD "is fundamentally different from traditional functional methods." There is a close relationship between the ideas of OOD and information hiding.

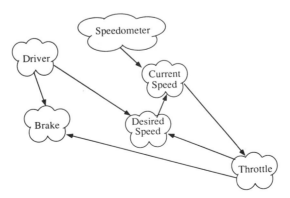

Figure A-8 SCC Object-Oriented Decomposition

What about the advantages and disadvantages *vis à vis* a functional decomposition? The functional decomposition had the advantage of showing the steps in the process but the disadvantage of likely problems resulting from change in data structure. The object-oriented decomposition had the advantage of likely robustness in the face of change but the disadvantage of not showing the steps in the process.

Is it possible to combine the approaches to take advantage of the strong characteristics of each while avoiding the problems? Section A.5 will show how we can use object-oriented decomposition to establish the major software organization but still use structured design ideas (and the resulting structure chart) to enhance and balance the object-oriented or information hiding approach and to show the processing involved in meeting the software requirement. First, having established the important ideas related to object orientation, let's turn, in the next part of the Appendix, to real-time issues.

A.4 MODULAR REAL-TIME DESIGN

A.4.1 Overview

This part of the Appendix (adapted from [SHU91]) deals with modular real-time design, a design approach that accomplishes the transition from requirements analysis to a real-time design encapsulated in modules. It uses the language of Ada, but addresses the issues in a language-independent manner. It specifically addresses some important issues related to object-oriented design and analysis.

Some form or other of object-oriented design has become common, even standard, for the design of Ada programs. Some form or other of structured analysis is and has long been standard for the specification of software requirements. Recent discussions in the software development community advocate object-oriented analysis as being preferable to structured analysis, especially for Ada software development; such discussions further assert that structured analysis and object-oriented design are incompatible. Others have argued for the effectiveness of combined use of the two methods. The topic has become controversial.

The thesis of this Appendix is that structured analysis is a desirable way to specify software requirements and that structured analysis and object-oriented design are compatible and work effectively together.

The following sections provide some general background and state the basis for the controversy. Structured analysis is then advanced as an effective method for the specification of requirements, particularly when one considers large hardware/software systems developments and not just software-only projects. Some approaches to making the requirements-to-design transition are summarized, and a specific method is presented in somewhat more detail, including the rationale for identifying tasks before modules (Ada packages). The specific topics covered are:

- Background
- What's the controversy?

- Structured analysis is right for requirements.
- Some approaches to transition
- Real-time design method
- Why concurrency first?
- Conclusion

A.4.2 Background

We take it as given that object-oriented design (OOD) is desirable for Ada software development. For Ada, OOD incorporates ideas of data abstraction and information hiding, and separation of specification and implementation, largely associated with the work of Parnas [PAR72a, PAR72b]; he calls this—and the name has become common—*information hiding*. The additional emphasis on entities in the problem space has been concisely stated by Booch [BOO86]. Parnas notes the equivalence of many similar methods [PAR90, page 642–643].

> Modern software engineering standards call for software to be organized in accordance with a principle known variously as "Information Hiding,""Object-Oriented Programming," "Separation of Concerns," "Encapsulation," "Data Abstraction," etc. This principle is designed to increase the cohesion of the modules while reducing the "coupling" between modules.

In order to avoid some compound phrase, such as "an information hiding/object-oriented/encapsulated design using data abstraction," the remainder of this Appendix will occasionally use the term *modular design* as the form or sort of object-oriented design (explicitly excluding inheritance) with which we will be concerned. The use of information hiding is the most important aspect of such designs.

A.4.3 What's the Controversy?

The published literature only partially indicates the amount of discussion going on in the community about perceived problems in making a transition from a functionally-oriented requirements specification to an object-oriented or modular design. There is a strongly vocal school of thought that this transition is somewhere between awkward and near-impossible. There are some widely available writings that surface the issue. For example, Bailin asserts [BAI89] that "Proceeding from a structured analysis to an object-oriented design can be awkward." Coad makes an even stronger assertion that the transition problem "plagues those who have tried to follow structured analysis with object-oriented design; this trouble seems especially popular with those wrestling with Ada-oriented methods," and even that the transition is an "untenable problem" [COA90, page 26].

An important theme of the arguments against functional requirements specification is that there must be a paradigm change to a focus on objects during design and that the use of some form of object-oriented analysis will allow a project to avoid the shift. Coad even asserts that "Design should consist solely of expanding the requirements model to account for the complexities introduced in selecting a particular implementation." [COA90, page 27].

A.4.4 Structured Analysis Is Right for Requirements

The popularity of functional methods for the specification of system and software requirements almost speaks for itself. The use of data flow diagrams and associated methods are ubiquitous in both the United States and Europe and are widely accepted and successful. (There are literally dozens of references in this area; one of the most popular is Hatley & Pirbhai [HAT87]. It is useful to augment those methods with entity-relationship diagrams [CHE76] and event-response methods [MCM84]. Such a combined approach gives a balanced data and functional viewpoint of the system. We will continue to call such methods *functional,* emphasizing the *strong functional cohesion* of the data transforms. One could equivalently emphasize the beneficial *weak coupling* between transforms, as a consequence of grouping around common data stores; strong cohesion and weak coupling go hand in hand. One of the reasons functional methods are popular for *software* requirements specification is that they are in virtually universal use for *systems* requirements specification.

As discussed in Chapter 2 (see especially Figure 2.5), Davis [DAV90] makes the useful distinction between "software only" and "systems" (that is, software and hardware) developments. He shows the hardware specification and design phases that occur in parallel, and are later integrated, with the software development. The discipline that oversees the entire process, explicitly concerned with system design and both system and software requirements, is *systems engineering.*

The system design phase itself is concerned with the establishment of the overall system design as hardware and software subsystems and the allocation to hardware and software of the system requirements defined during the earlier phase. The software requirements analysis phase addresses the software subsystems on a subsystem-by-subsystem basis to further define what is to be done—what problem is to be solved—by the software of each subsystem.

The reason we show this entire process is that it is vital that any consideration of the proper specification of software requirements and the transition to a software top-level design take systems engineering considerations into account. This is a key aspect of this section. What is important to understand is that the software requirements—at least for the sort of systems we are discussing—are not developed independently; they are derived from the system requirements and system design.

An important guideline document for the conduct of systems engineering states [DOA79, page 2–5], "The first step in the system engineering process is function analysis." A more tutorial document, also providing guidance for U. S. Government systems engineering, defines functional analysis as follows [DSM86, page 6–1]: "Functional analysis is a method for analyzing performance requirements and dividing them into discrete tasks or activities. It involves the identification and decomposition of the primary system functions into subfunctions at ever-increasing levels of detail." A standard systems engineering text also stresses the importance of this process [BLA90, page 55]: "An essential element of preliminary design is the employment of a functional approach as a basis for the identification of design requirements for each hierarchical level of the system." The approach of Hatley & Pirbhai, virtually the only text referenced in the structured analysis/OOD controversy that really deals with systems issues, is also based on functional approaches for specification of requirements.

The point of this discussion has been that the functional approach is (and long has been) the foundation of systems engineering and, hence, the basis for the software requirements for large system developments. Systems engineers and system users are highly satisfied with this approach and are unlikely to change. It is important that the software portion of the system development process take this into consideration and be prepared to make the transition from functional to information hiding/object-oriented representations.

Not only are we going to be *required* to make a functional-to-object paradigm shift, but it is not all bad to do so. Requirements and design have different purposes and serve different masters; it should not be surprising to see different modes of expression. Looking for analogy once again to systems engineering, the primary form of requirements specification is the functional flow block diagram (which has some similarity to data flow diagrams), while the mode of expression of the design is the schematic block diagram (roughly analogous to software architecture diagrams showing the major modules in a system).

A final powerful argument for structured analysis is its strong educational foundation: textbooks, courses, and the widespread availability of automated tools to support the methods. This is likely to make structured analysis continue to be the method of choice for the specification of requirements, mandating some mechanism for the transition to object-oriented (or modular) design.

A.4.5   Some Approaches to Transition

So what's the approach for the transition from requirements to design? A number of schemes have been either explicitly proposed or demonstrated by example. The general strategy is to use the products of structured analysis, including context diagrams, data flow diagrams, state transition diagrams, and entity-relationship diagrams, to identify objects; an alternative is to identify first tasks and then objects.

Booch's well-known paper [BOO86] has an introductory example that derives objects from terminators on a context diagram and data stores on a data flow diagram. Gray [GRA88] does the same, adding additional rules (and attributing some of the ideas to Bullman).

Ward [WAR89] chooses to extend structured analysis slightly but concludes, "There is no fundamental opposition between real-time structured analysis/structured design and object-oriented design." Although not explicitly addressing the transition, Section A.5 makes the related argument for the fundamental compatibility of *structured design* and OOD, using them together to balance functional decomposition and information hiding.

Kennedy & Carter [KEN88] feel no need to extend structured analysis in the Ward style, and they provide a detailed set of guidelines and a step-by-step procedure to demonstrate "that there need be no discontinuity between the use of [real-time structured analysis] for requirements modeling and OOD for design of Ada software."

Seidewitz & Stark define a process called "abstraction analysis" to begin the transition from a data flow diagram to an object-oriented design. The guidance is [SEI87] "to find a *central entity*. This is the entity that represents the best abstraction for what the system does or models." To find the central entity, they "look for a set of *processes* and *data stores* that are most abstract." They provide additional rules for finding entities, which then form the basis for objects, illustrated in the paper by Ada packages.

The methods discussed address tasking and concurrency issues either not at all or only slightly, as an issue of detail to be dealt with as internal to the design of the objects. There are some authors who address the tasking and concurrency issues as fundamental to the transition and the preliminary phases of design.

Nielsen & Shumate [NIE88] incorporate many of the ideas discussed up to now, but they also explicitly provide a set of guidelines for identifying modules (packages) based on a number of additional criteria and a taxonomy of packages. The Nielsen & Shumate work differs from some other methods, since its initial focus is concurrency, using the guidelines to aggregate tasks into packages. Many of the ideas are built upon language-independent real-time experience and on early work by Gomaa [GOM84]. Gomaa, in turn, has later Ada-related work [GOM89] continuing the notion of specifying tasks before packages, then aggregating according to guidelines, many of which trace to continuing work by Parnas [PAR89]. The method is called "Adarts." Krell similarly addresses tasks before objects [KRE90], feeling strongly that it is important to avoid a premature decomposition and consequent isolation of tasks in separate components.

Although not as strongly oriented toward an initial transition from data flows to tasks as the Nielsen–Shumate–Gomaa–Krell approaches discussed above, the *hierarchical object-oriented design* (HOOD) method [ESA89] does significantly differentiate between objects that do and do not represent concurrent execution. HOOD is important, and growing in importance, in Europe and is likely to influence thoughts on design in the United States. One of the HOOD "basic design steps" as illustrated by Heitz [HEI90] is a mapping from data flow diagrams to objects.

What we see then, are a large number of approaches and ideas for the requirements-to-design transition. The transition may not be "seamless," but, then again, it likely should not be, given the different nature of requirements and design. Not all the ideas are mature or tested, but some are and have been based on successful development projects. The specific method discussed in the following section draws on all the previous experience, both published literature and successful project use.

A.4.6   Real-Time Design Method

This section provides a brief overview of a specific method for making the requirements-to-design transition. It is essentially an elaboration of the approach of Nielsen & Shumate referenced above (and hence of Gomaa). The basic idea is the transition from context, data flow, and control flow diagrams, first to a representation of concurrency (Ada tasks) and then to a grouping of tasks into packages that represent modular components, or objects. It is exactly the method presented in a language-independent manner in Chapter 7 of this book.

The elaboration of the earlier methods lies in integrating a number of additional guidelines for task and package identification and generally tying the method to the specification scheme of Hatley & Pirbhai, with a corollary emphasis on control flows and state transition diagrams. The techniques are closely tied to the phases of the system development life cycle.

These methods have been applied on several real projects. One such project, on which both authors worked, involved a U.S. Navy command and control application. It was a "shadow" project, to accomplish in Ada the same functionality being implemented in another language (in this case CMS-2) as part of a major combat system. This project was reported in [BRI90], which indicated that the method resulted in a design that eased maintenance of the software.

The transition begins with a set of "flattened" data flow diagrams (FFDs). This works in terms of size of the problem, since there is a significant amount of software decomposition accomplished during the *system* design phase. In addition, it may not be necessary actually to go to the lowest level; the designer may recognize that all lower-level data transforms (circles or "bubbles") definitely represent sequential processing and will be part of the same task. There should be no more than about a hundred or so bubbles to do the aggregation into tasks; this is a tractable number.

The next step is the aggregation into tasks. There are a large number of guidelines for doing this, such as grouping around hardware devices, by temporal considerations including periodic actions, time-criticality, or functional cohesion. Actually, the full method does this in several steps: language-independent processes; process interconnection and coupling; Ada tasks including intermediary, communication, and uncoupling tasks; and then explicit consideration of caller/called decisions, involving consideration of which tasks have entries and how data are passed. The task communication graph (TCG) reflects these decisions.

It is important to note at this point the way in which this method eases traceability from the design back to the requirements, often a sticking point with other approaches. Since the task identification and allocation of requirements occur simultaneously, the traceability is easy to describe—nearly trivial.

The discussion has been in terms of a flattened data flow diagram, made feasible for large systems as a consequence of partitioning into reasonably sized pieces of software during the system design process. If you are dealing with a large system that has not undergone such partitioning, you may wish to start looking for tasks at the higher levels of the data flow diagrams, identifying tasks exactly with the higher-level transforms, and looking at lower levels only when it is likely that a high-level transform contains necessary or desirable concurrent activity. However, this approach may suffer from allowing the design to be overly driven by the statement of requirements. This is potentially harmful, since the requirements statement has a different purpose: the statement of *what* is to be accomplished, as opposed to a description of *how* to create the software to meet the requirement.

The next step is the aggregation into objects. There are once again a number of guidelines, some of them similar to those summarized in the previous section: objects as terminators, data stores, data abstractions for flowing data, and so on. In addition, there is explicit consideration of objects existing as entities in the problem space (the primary OOD criterion), reuse, and recompilation issues. A major additional factor is the consideration of a set of guidelines and module hierarchy introduced by Parnas [PAR89]. Packaging decisions relevant to distributed systems are made at this time. The software architecture diagram (SAD) illustrates the module (task/object) interactions. There are alternate and additional design representations that may be useful for continuing the design, but we will not address them, since at this point the *transition* is essentially complete. Of course, there may be iteration, changes, and so on as part of the continuing design process.

Do we *always* identify tasks before objects? Well, almost. There are certain classes of data-intensive systems for which it is useful to identify objects and their operations (based on terminators, data stores, and transforms of the data flow diagram) either before or at the same time as task identification. In addition, simply as a matter of style, some designers may wish to identify objects early in order to help them make decisions about the major concurrent elements and their interfaces. Such effort and analysis may help simplify the remaining problem and clarify the remaining design. Objects identified at this point in the design are basically passive data abstractions; they *do not* contain tasks, except perhaps for the sole purpose of enforcing mutual exclusion. In the package taxonomy of [NIE88], they are *helper* packages (of the data manager category), rather than *application* packages that do the primary work of the system.

Let's look at what has just happened. The movement from an FFD to the TCG and SAD *is the transition* we have been discussing. The FFD is a description of the problem, the software requirements; the TCG and SAD actually describe software components. Indeed, at this point for an Ada project they can, and should, be further described in PDL and compiled into the program library.

What is the next step? The remaining design has to do with the partitioning of the tasks and packages into lower-level components. This involves the definition of additional packages, but not tasks. (If a need for additional concurrency is discovered at this point, it is a reflection of an incomplete initial design phase; the initial design phase is revisited to incorporate additional tasks as necessary. In practice, this does not typically happen.) For large tasks, this further design may involve more work with data flow diagrams, including object and module identification using some of the ideas summarized in the previous section. The use of traditional structured design ideas are also appropriate, balancing object orientation and functional decomposition in the sense described in Section A.5. Both the aggregation of tasks into objects and the further decomposition benefit from the straightforward allocation of requirements resulting from the data flow diagram-to-task transition.

What if there are no tasks? Then the problem simplifies directly into essentially one task; all the ideas above, with the exception of concurrent elements, are still applicable.

A.4.7 Why Concurrency First?

Why do we address tasks before objects? For real-time systems, it is necessary to have an overall view of the concurrent architecture of the system; this is essentially a "flat" view, showing the designers the task interactions and the specific model (rendezvous? mailboxes? semaphores?) of real-time communication and synchronization that will be used for implementation. It is at the tasking level that the most difficult problems reside, and they must be dealt with "up front." (Yes, it is often wise to defer difficult design problems; this is not one of them.) A premature hierarchical decomposition (into packages) at this point makes it difficult to assess the overall impact of design decisions. This factor influences not only initial design but also the later integration and maintenance. Further, early consideration of tasks clarifies package interactions. For example, if two packages exchange data, it is not always clear which package should export an operation and which package should have a call to the operation. Consideration of tasking at the same time as caller/called decisions, coupling, and so on makes the situation more clear.

In addition to the technical reasons above, there are some hard-nosed practical reasons for taking this approach. One is that much of the real-time community has a relatively long (and pre-Ada) history of doing task identification in this manner. It is a technique known to work. Then, once tasks are identified, it is easier to identify objects with a set of guidelines, hints, and heuristics.

History is similarly at work in that noncomputer customers and users of systems are used to seeing their requirements (let's emphasize, *their* requirements) specified in functional terms, that is, *what the system does*. This must not be dismissed as näiveté; there are good reasons for such a representation of the system to explain how the user's needs or operational requirements are satisfied. Similarly, it is useful for the user to see how the design *functions* (what it *does* or *accomplishes,* not just its static representation) to satisfy the requirements. A closely related issue is the traceability between requirements and design, made easier by initially relating requirements to active entities—tasks. There are additional practical considerations having to do with timing and sizing analysis, management of projects, and so on, but there is no need to go on.

Many of the reasons are not 100 percent related to the concurrency-first approach but are important to the general notion of using structured analysis and making the functional-to-object transition. The concurrency-first approach enhances many of the reasons, particularly those related to demonstrating how the design accomplishes what is required and the associated requirements traceability.

Finally, it seems as though the concurrency-first scheme can never result in a design inferior to an object-first scheme. This is because the concurrency-first scheme always takes the object criteria into account when aggregating into packages; the object-first scheme, on the other hand, depends on decomposition, presumably never going back to address all the tasks at the same time in a "flat" manner. (The object-oriented literature certainly does not advocate such a step; indeed, the literature has little guidance on concurrency issues at all.) Actually, with good designers making good design decisions, it is likely that—in terms of the package architecture—quite similar designs will result from the two schemes. Nonetheless, the concurrency-first approach is more explicit in what is going on, provides more guidelines for making decisions, and is more likely to address the real-time aspects of the design correctly.

The concurrency-first notion is not intrinsic to the compatibility of structured analysis and object-oriented design, but it is a powerful reason to use such a combined approach and takes effective advantage of the work done during the analysis phase.

A.4.8   Conclusion

It is OK to have different representations of software requirements and software design. Requirements and design have two different purposes. Looking to systems engineering, we see a similar difference in representation, with requirements being functional in nature and design expressed in schematic block diagrams.

The functional approach to the specification of requirements is effective and is here to stay. If we wish to have object-oriented software designs, there must be a paradigm shift.

There's nothing wrong with that paradigm shift; the transition is neither difficult nor discontinuous. There is a great deal of guidance on how to do it effectively. A particularly effective way to make the transition, and to provide a solid foundation for continued design, is to address concurrency issues first, then object or package issues. In fact, there are a large number of aerospace companies in both the United States and Europe who are now successfully doing exactly what is described in this Appendix; using structured analysis for requirements specification and effectively making the transition to object-oriented design. Some of them are using the Hatley & Pirbhai model of requirements referenced earlier [HAT87] and the transition to design described by Nielsen & Shumate [NIE88].

Note that none of the conclusions in this section, or elsewhere in this Appendix, say that structured analysis, or functional analysis for systems requirements, could not be improved by paying greater attention to data relationship issues earlier in the development process; such additions to traditional structured analysis *can be* beneficial. Further, nothing here says that object-oriented analysis is flawed or ineffective; it may well prove to be important in the future. But object-oriented analysis and specification methods need to stand on their own merits, not on the loose sand of assertions that structured analysis is incompatible with OOD.

A.4.9   Summary

Structured analysis is effective for requirements specification, OOD is effective for design, and the requirements-to-design transition can be accomplished effectively by an intial focus on determination of tasks. Structured analysis and object-oriented design are compatible; the compatibility is the basis for the modular real-time design methods of this book.

A.5 MODULAR STRUCTURED DESIGN

A.5.1 Overview

Designing software systems calls for a parallel concern with algorithms and data structures; it is useful to view this process in terms of constructing virtual machines and objects.

Modular structured design (MSD) is a software design method that stresses a balance between data abstraction and functional decomposition. The data abstraction concepts fully embrace the notion of information hiding and object-oriented design.

Data abstraction is the guiding principle for the determination of modules that establish the overall architecture of the system. Inasmuch as the notion of object identification plays an important role in MSD, the method may be said to be object-oriented.

Functional decomposition is the guiding principle for the determination of the step-by-step processing of the program that satisfies a software requirements specification. Functional decomposition is secondary to data abstraction in terms of overall software architecture, but is vital in understanding what the system does and how it accomplishes its requirement. In addition, functional or step-by-step considerations are important in helping define the exact partitioning in data abstraction terms.

Graphics are used to portray both the architecture and the step-by-step processing.

The model for thinking about data abstraction is the *object,* an encapsulated data structure. The model for thinking about functional decomposition is the *virtual machine,* an imaginary computer with a powerful, problem-oriented instruction set.

This part of the Appendix (based on [SHU88]) describes how to design software using virtual machines and objects. It discusses recent literature and important historical papers, presents the general ideas of the method, and then shows a small case study as a concrete example.

A.5.2 Introduction

Constructing complex computer programs involves a parallel concern with algorithms and data structures.

In order to devise the steps of a program to solve a problem, it is advantageous to envision a "virtual machine" that simplifies the algorithm. This viewpoint of a virtual machine is simply an extension of the virtual machines represented by assembly language and high-level languages. This is illustrated in Figure A-9.

It is advantageous to encapsulate data structures in such a way that only the operations on a data structure are available, and the details of the actual data

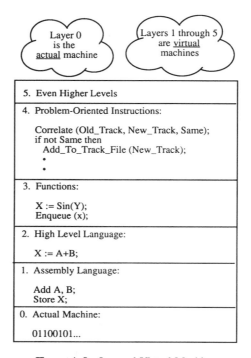

Figure A-9   Layered Virtual Machines

structure are hidden. Such encapsulated data structures are called objects and are represented by software components called modules. Although the representation is that of a module (in Ada, a package), logically the component is an *object,* the phrase we will most often use. The objects not only provide the operations on a data structure; they also make use of operations on other objects. This is illustrated in Figure A-10. The figure illustrates that the data structure of the object is hidden. It may be an array, or a linked list, or anything else. Both the visible operations and internal subprograms may operate on other objects.

Both the virtual machines and the objects are *layered,* in the sense that they each may depend upon both lower-level virtual machines and objects for their implementation. MSD integrates these notions into a design methodology that balances data abstraction and functional decomposition in such a way that each viewpoint enhances the other. The design method is not unique to Ada, although Ada facilitates and encourages its use. Structure charts are used to graphically portray the virtual machines, while architecture diagrams are used to portray objects. Simplified forms of these graphics, and their relationship to virtual machines and objects, are shown in Figure A-11.

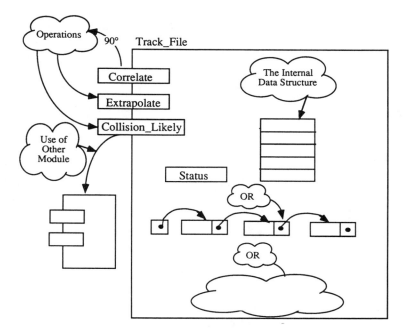

Figure A-10   Encapsulated Object

The balanced consideration of algorithms and data structures has a long history. Dijkstra [DIJ68] introduced the notion of a software structure composed of a set of layers, a strict hierarchical discipline with each layer depending only on the next lower level. In [DIJ72], an important basis for MSD, he refers to building software in layers of virtual machines, where his use of "virtual machines" incorporates the notion of objects. An important aspect of his discussion is its balance between refinement of algorithms and refinement of data structures. A similar balance is shown by Wirth in [WIR71] and in other writings.

A.5.3   Foundations of MSD

Six important concepts provide the foundation for MSD. They are, in the order in which we discuss them:

1. Information hiding
2. Data abstraction
3. Object-oriented development
4. Structured design
5. Stepwise refinement
6. Structured programming

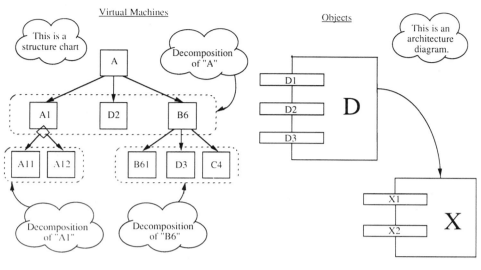

Figure A-11 Virtual Machines and Objects

Information Hiding Parnas [PAR72b] introduced the concept of "information hiding," the idea that we should decompose a system into modules such that each is "characterized by its knowledge of a design decision which it hides from all others." The design decision might relate to either an algorithm or a data structure.

Data Abstraction The idea of abstract data types has been discussed in the literature for many years. Liskov & Guttag [LIS86] recently integrated and clarified the construction and use of abstract data types. They define a data abstraction as "a set of objects and a set of operations characterizing the behavior of the objects." Their book largely concerns concepts of design: "how to do program decomposition based on abstraction."

Object-Oriented Development Object-oriented development has been popularized by Booch [BOO86]. He draws on earlier design literature, including work of Liskov, Guttag, and Parnas. The method involves designing software around abstractions of "objects" in some real-world problem. It "lets us map solutions directly to our view of the problem." It seeks a balanced treatment of objects and operations, allowing software objects to both provide operations and use the operations provided by other objects. The operations are visible as subprograms exported by packages.

Booch [BOO86] also introduced an important graphic aid to visualizing program components and their interactions: the *architecture diagram*. It shows the objects in a system and their relationship to one another.

Structured Design   Structured design, popularized by Yourdon & Constantine [YOU79], places an emphasis on designing a system of small, independent "black boxes" (in our terms, subprograms) that are related to the application. Its focus is on functional decomposition—*what* is being accomplished. The decomposition principle is based on keeping highly related parts of the system together, "highly related" being measured in terms of functional cohesiveness.

An important graphic tool for structured design is the structure chart. It shows the partitioning of the software into subprograms that accomplish specific functions and the data flows between the subprograms. The decomposition is shown in terms of the processing steps, each step further decomposed (in layers) into lower-level steps.

Stepwise Refinement   Wirth [WIR71] considers programming, what we call "design," to be "a sequence of design decisions concerning the decomposition of tasks into subtasks and of data into data structures." The process proceeds as "stepwise refinement" until the subtasks and data structures are expressible in some programming language. Wirth has also expressed this idea as "algorithms + data structures = programs." (Note that "algorithm" does not imply concern with detailed processing, but rather is an abstract statement of the steps to solve a problem using subprograms.)

The important point that Wirth makes is "Refinement of the description of program and data structures should proceed in parallel."

Structured Programming   Dijkstra, in "Notes on Structured Programming" [DIJ72], wants to view a program as being executed by its own (virtual) machine, one that has just those instructions and variables necessary for the problem to be easily solved. After the problem is "solved" using the virtual machine, the remaining (simpler) problem is to implement each of the instructions of the virtual machine. The new problem is solved by inventing a lower-level virtual machine.

He emphasizes that "as little as possible" should be accomplished at each step and that decisions should be postponed for as long as possible. This is especially true in the case of data; the style is to operate as long as possible on abstract notions of data.

Dijkstra uses the term "stepwise program composition" to describe the process. He also uses the phrases "layered hierarchy of machines" and "virtual machines." He is explicit about dealing with stepwise decomposition of both algorithms and data.

About algorithms he says, "I want my program text to reflect somewhere the fact that the computation has been decomposed into a time-succession of the actions."

About data: "We treat the structural refinement of a data type on a footing very similar to the algorithmic refinements."

About both algorithms and data, he goes on to say that the decomposition relative to actions is "only half of what we are trying to do, as we are trying to apply a similar technique to data structures as well." He also points out that at various steps in the design process we must choose next either to refine an algorithm or to refine a data structure.

About design in general he says, "The point is that we try to associate with each level a separate design decision."

Summary of Foundations Many important concepts in software engineering deal with data abstraction: how data should be used in the design of large programs. This is the major domain of discourse for Liskov & Guttag and generally for Parnas as well. Booch builds on their notions and on other data structuring concepts.

Yourdon & Constantine's structured design deals with functional decompositions: It emphasizes the abstract algorithms, the processing steps that solve the problem. The method is quite well defined and has become a popular approach for software design in many languages.

Wirth, although writing earlier than the others, essentially integrates the two approaches of data abstraction and functional decomposition. He emphasized stepwise refinement on both abstract algorithms and data. He references early Dijkstra work.

Dijkstra's concepts of structured programming inspired disciplined thinking on how to construct programs. His work provided the foundation for much of what came after; it still captures the essential characteristics of how a programmer should think about designing software.

MSD builds on, integrates, and attempts to make more intuitive, the ideas in the six approaches discussed. Its primary source of inspiration is Dijkstra's "Notes on Structured Programming" [DIJ72].

Figure A-12 illustrates the relationship of the ideas discussed in this section to MSD. It indicates that object-oriented development draws primarily on ideas related to data abstraction, whereas structured design draws primarily on ideas related to algorithms. It also illustrates that a shorthand way of thinking about MSD is that it combines elements of structured design and object-oriented development (information hiding, data abstraction, and the form of object-oriented design discussed earlier in the Appendix).

A.5.4 The Method of MSD

The general scheme of MSD is that of Dijkstra: Keep the problem as simple as possible at each step by using the capabilities of a computer with a powerful, application-oriented instruction set. The problem is thereby simplified—reduced to the creation of that abstract computer, or virtual machine. As part of the deferral

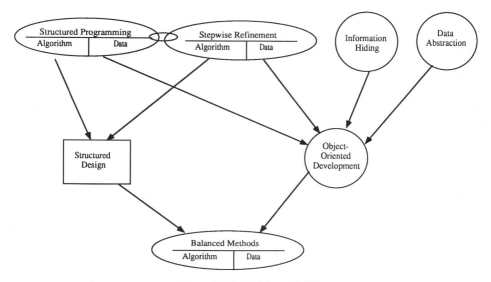

Figure A-12   Origins of MSD

of detail, information about data structures is encapsulated in modules, allowing abstract specification and manipulation of the data.

The virtual machines and objects hide the information contained within them, describing their relationship to other software components through abstract interfaces that provide only the minimum information needed to use the machine or object.

This section presents a detailed discussion of objects, virtual machines, the distinction between them, machine–object interaction, and the design process of MSD.

Objects   Objects, or modules, encapsulate data structures. They export (make available to clients) abstract operations on a data structure. The operations are the only way to change the state of the data structure. Therefore, we say that the operations characterize the behavior of the object. Objects are expressed as modules, with the operations being the visible subprograms of the module.

The operations are determined by the application, although certain data structures always have some general-purpose operations. For example, a track file may have a Correlate operation (application-specific), while a stack will always have Push and Pop operations (general-purpose). The operations are visible; the data structure is hidden. Objects allow virtual machines to operate on abstract data, thereby narrowing attention to the problem to be solved.

Objects are identified and constructed by a process of composing related data elements into structures, and the definition of operations necessary to abstractly manipulate the data. Considerations of information hiding, abstract data types, and deferral of detail all come into play in identifying good objects for a specific application. Objects may also be identified as software models of real-world entities in the application problem space.

The implementation of the operations on the object may be very complex. If so, the implementation is accomplished by a recursive application of MSD. Hence, the object may make use of virtual machines and lower-level objects. In the frequent case that an object makes use of lower-level objects, we have a layering of abstractions—a layering of data structures encapsulated in objects. This is an important point made by both Dijkstra and Wirth: stepwise refinement is as applicable to data structures as it is to algorithms. The complexity of use of lower-level objects or virtual machines is hidden from the user of the object.

Virtual Machines   Virtual machines are abstract computers: They describe algorithms, the steps taken to solve a problem. These steps can be considered to be the "instructions" of the abstract computer. The instructions consist of two sorts of operations: lower-level machines and the operations exported by objects. Virtual machines provide the functionality of the program that is commonly referred to as the "application."

The instruction set of the virtual machine is very powerful and application-oriented. The processing steps are closely related to the problem to be solved. This makes it easy to invent a solution to the problem.

For example, in an air traffic control application, we might think of steps such as:

- Determine number of aircraft in this sector.
- Correlate two tracks (compare to see whether they are actually the same track—that is, aircraft).
- Correlate a potential new track with all existing tracks.
- Determine new course to avoid collision.

These are abstractions of the processing; they ignore or defer the details of how much the abstract steps are to be implemented. If we had a machine that could directly execute such instructions, our problem would be easy to solve!

We do not have such a machine, however, so our task is to create it. The instructions of such a first level virtual machine may be very complex. Therefore, in the implementation of the individual instructions of the virtual machine, we reapply MSD, inventing a lower-level virtual machine. For example, to create the instruction "Correlate a potential new track," we might invent a lower-level virtual machine with instructions such as:

- Obtain the next track from the track file.
- Correlate two tracks.
- Place the new track into the track file as a separate entry.

The track file is the storage for the location, velocity, and identification of all aircraft being controlled.

This illustrates that what is an *instruction* from one point of view may be a *virtual machine* from its own point of view. We would, as necessary, reapply the same notion to construct yet lower-level virtual machines. Hence, we construct *layered* virtual machines.

Some of the instructions of the virtual machine that we are considering have a special characteristic: They are abstract operations on a data structure. For example, the instructions "Obtain the next track from the track file" and "Place the new track into the track file as a separate entry" operate on the "track file" data structure.

To allow the virtual machine to deal with abstract data, it is important to hide the actual implementation of the methods for storing the track file, exporting only the operations on the track file. This is accomplished by encapsulating the data structure (the track file) together with the operation (the "instructions" noted above) that manipulate the data structure. This composition creates a track file object. The details of how the object manipulates the data structure are hidden from the virtual machine.

The creation of the virtual machine makes use of the operations on the object. In fact, it is often the needs of the various virtual machines in a system that dictate the operations that will be defined on the object. It is this interaction between virtual machines and objects that leads to a *parallel concern* with the two viewpoints of design.

Figure A-13 illustrates the components of a virtual machine. The small rectangles are subprograms. Some of them are on the side of larger boxes that represent modules. Two of the modules represent objects.

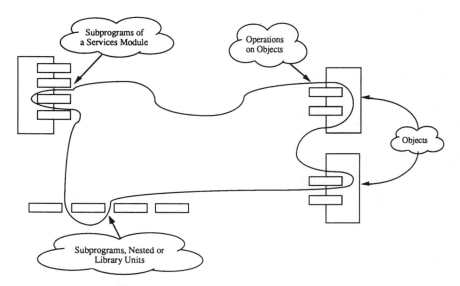

Figure A.13   Components of a Virtual Machine

Distinction Between Virtual Machines and Objects   We distinguish two uses for subprograms: as operations on objects and as virtual machines. Each of these may be thought of as primitive operation, extending the instruction set of an (abstract) computer, or virtual machine. Here are some distinctions between virtual machines and operations on objects.

Operations on objects: An object encapsulates a data structure; it is a module that provides subprograms to manipulate the abstract data structure. The subprograms are the operations on the object. They are *bound together* by the fact that they provide operations on the data structure.

Each operation on an object operates *directly* on a persistent data structure. They are primitive operations on the data.

The operations on a single object do not, typically, provide all the operations of a virtual machine. The set of primitive operations on an object typically do not provide any particular *function* other than the manipulation of the encapsulated data structure. Furthermore, we typically choose not to group together in a single module (package) all the operations of a virtual machine that we have devised.

Virtual machines: A virtual machine consists of a set of abstract instructions that solve some problem. The instructions are of two sorts: operations on objects and lower-level virtual machines. A virtual machine is not (necessarily) a module. It is a set of subprograms, some of which may be components of modules. Others may be library units, and still others may be nested in the higher-level virtual machine.

How are these subprograms bound? They are *logically* bound by the step-by-step processing that they accomplish.

A virtual machine does not operate on any persistent data structure except by invoking an operation on an object. It accomplishes some function, not directly related to a data structure.

A virtual machine is an abstract computer that has a powerful instruction set ideally suited to the problem we are trying to solve. In fact, we say that the instructions *are* the virtual machine. Once we devise or invent the virtual machine, the problem is reduced to the implementation of each of the instructions. This is simpler than the original problem. If an instruction is complex, we apply MSD to its implementation. If an instruction is simple (can be coded directly in the base programming language without virtual machines), we do not reapply MSD. When all the instructions are simple, we are done with design.

Virtual Machine and Object Interactions   Design involves a parallel concern with algorithms and data structures. In one sense, the design of the virtual machines and objects are largely independent.

When we are concerned with the functional processing of the system, we should not be concerned with the details of data structures. We should be concerned with the steps taken to satisfy a software requirement.

When we design data structures and operations, we need not be concerned with how they will be used. We instead should be concerned with localization of operations on the data and the completeness and consistency of the set of operations.

However, there is an important way in which the virtual machines and the objects are intimately linked: The needs of the virtual machine often dictate operations on the object. In fact, this is a major motivation for an emphasis on virtual machines; as we consider the needs of the virtual machines, we better understand the objects and their required operations.

Design Process of MSD Figure A-14 illustrates the process of designing with MSD. The steps are:

1. Invent a machine that will solve the problem. Always think of data abstractly. This is the top-level virtual machine. Inventing the machine should be easy, because we have as powerful an instruction set as we require. The machine is represented in a programming language as a set of subprogram calls, perhaps with some simple logical connections: a `loop`, an `if...then...else`, or a `case` statement. The machine is represented graphically with a structure chart.
2. For each instruction of the virtual machine, decide whether the instruction is a lower-level virtual machine or an operation on an object.

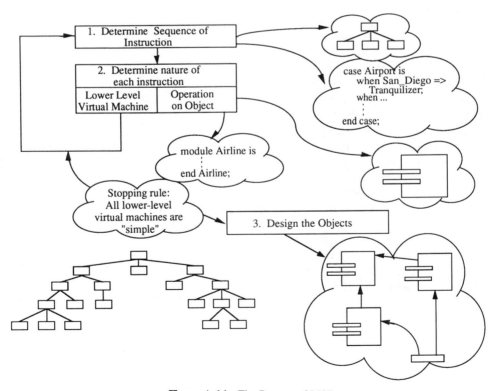

Figure A-14 The Process of MSD

- If the instruction is an operation on an object, do not refine the instruction at this time. Instead, write the description of the rest of the object; the rest of the operations on the data structure. This is not easy.
- If the instruction is a virtual machine, refine the instruction by starting at Step 1.

3. Design the objects. For complex algorithms, it will be necessary to accomplish the implementation by starting at Step 1 and following the MSD process.* This aspect of the design process illustrates that levels of abstraction are important for objects as well as for virtual machines.

The substep "write the description of the rest of the object" is important, because it helps clarify what actions must be taken relative to the objects in the system. The problem specification can be used to help identify both objects and the operations on them. (This is the main criterion of object-oriented development.) Notions of information hiding, deferral of detail, and abstract data types are all important in this effort. It is likely that you will not immediately identify *all* needed operations, but that as you refine the virtual machines, you will find need for additional operations on the object.

Actually, it is possible to have a preliminary substep 0, in which you first attempt to identify all the objects in the system. There is, then, less object identification during the remainder of the process, but there is still likely to be considerable object refinement. If this approach is taken, MSD becomes closer in nature to object-oriented design as described in Section A.3.

As you continue the design, document it both in a program design language and with graphics, as illustrated in Figure A-14. When the remaining virtual machines are "simple," stop the virtual machine decomposition process. The meaning and determination of when "simple" machines have been reached is an engineering judgment, but it is typically at the point where the lowest-level virtual machines can be implemented with the "programming language virtual machine" and with some use of operations on objects that have been previously defined. The designer must be confident that all objects have been identified and defined.

The process need not be accomplished in exactly the order given. For example, it may be necessary to implement an object completely in order to appreciate timing characteristics. Reuse of existing software modules may provide for some of the needed objects or machines and will alter the sequence of events. It may be convenient to identify some or all of the objects before you begin to devise the top-level virtual machine. What is important is the parallel and balanced concern for virtual machines and objects.

In addition, particularly for a large programming project, many steps can proceed in parallel after the initial partitioning. The ability to initiate parallel development early in the design process is a consequence of decisions about data structures being buried *inside modules* rather than *in the module interfaces*. This is a major advantage of the design approach.

---

*This may involve lower-level objects that are hidden from higher levels.

The process described above results in a design that consists of two representations: code (PDL) and graphics. At several points along the way, typically called top-level design and detailed design, the program architecture and processing described by these materials should be reviewed. The review is important. It is a part of the design process, intended to improve the design; that is, make it clearer, easier to implement, easier to maintain—and correct. Correctness largely depends on satisfying the stated software requirement for which the program is being developed; traceability of design to requirements is vital.

Both traditional structured design and object-oriented development offer guidelines for design evaluation. Some important design principles are that the design should emphasize strong locality of function within modules and low coupling between modules. The interfaces between modules should be as narrow as possible, often consisting of nothing but parameterless subprogram calls. The instructions of the virtual machines should be clear, simple, and ideally suited to their purpose. Major data structures should be encapsulated in objects.

Graphic representations of the design should play an important role in the design review. Graphics are important, because people grasp overall structure and relationships more quickly from pictures than they do from text. You should be above to evaluate the quality of the design from the graphics, and you should be able to determine how the problem is being solved. Reflecting the two viewpoints of the designer, there are two forms of documentation.

1. Virtual machines are effectively represented by structure charts. (See Section 7.2.4.)

2. Objects and their interactions are effectively shown with architecture diagrams. (See Section 7.2.3.)

After the design reviews, continuing stepwise refinement of the design results in a fully coded system, ready to test and deliver.

A.5.5 An Example of the MSD Method

The following example is adapted from Dijkstra [DIJ72]. He presents a design in textual format. We will use Ada as our vehicle for presenting the text of the design, and we will add graphics.

This is the "Draw_Image" problem. We will present the example in case study format: a statement of the problem, essentially a software requirements specification, and then a solution. Although it is a simple problem, we will treat it as a much larger and difficult problem in order to illustrate the layering effect of MSD.

The problem involves drawing an image in a certain way, given a restricted set of facilities. The drawing facility (you may think of it as a simple printer) has two functions, invoked by two commands:

- NLCR (new line carriage return) moves the print position to the first position of the next line.
- Print_Symbol prints a symbol, given as an argument, at the current print position and moves the current print position immediately to the right.

The only two permitted print symbols are mark and space, where mark is some visible character (say an asterisk) and space is a blank.

The problem environment also consists of two integer functions of integer arguments that satisfy, for $0 <= I <= 999$:

- $0 <= FX(I) <= 99$
- $0 <= FY(I) <= 49$

Given this environment, the problem is to create a program that prints 50 lines, numbered from top to bottom by a Y coordinate running from 49 through 0. Each line is numbered from left to right by an X coordinate running from 0 through 99. (The X and Y coordinate numbers are not to be printed; the numbering is relative to the relationship given next.) There are, thus, 5000 print positions.

At the 1000 positions specified by the X and Y coordinates given by

$X = FX (I)$ and $Y = FY (I)$
for all I in 0 to 999,

a mark is to be printed; all other positions are to remain blank.

In other words, the printer prints a curve or other figure given by the functions of X and Y. We are using the simple printer as a digital plotter. The functions of X and Y are not specific to the problem; the solution must be valid for any FX and FY satisfying the preceding relationships.

Multiple marks at the same print location are permitted. When we say "1000" marks on the page, we are ignoring overstrikes. Figure A-15 illustrates the problem graphically.

Let us consider some important aspects of the problem, and how they will affect the solution. Since we must proceed from line to line, never backing up, and since we proceed from character to character (in each line), never backing up, the printing of the curve must be independent of the determination (with FX and FY) of where marks should be printed; FX and FY will return values in arbitrary order, inconsistent with the functioning of a printer. Therefore, we need to construct, in a random access storage, an *image* of what we wish to print.

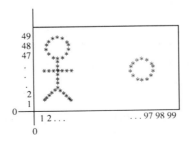

Figure A-15 Draw_Image Illustration

The way in which we store the image is the major decision in this program; it deals with the major data structure and the ways in which that data structure is to be manipulated. We will postpone, or defer, the decision of how to store and (in detail) manipulate the image for as long a time as possible. We will deal with an *abstract* version of the image.

Now we turn to the construction of the program that solves the stated problem. Our general approach is to take small (even tiny) steps at each stage of the problem. At every level we defer as much detail as possible in order to make our algorithms simple—as close to childishly simple and obviously correct as we can. By a process of stepwise refinement, we will add detail until the problem is solved. Along the way, we will see that what we are doing is building a sequence of virtual machines.

We begin the process of MSD by inventing a solution to the problem, using an "instruction set" that is suited to our application and is abstract—that is, it defers unnecessary detail. Here is our solution.

Step 1: Build the image

Step 2: Print the image

Now we must determine which instructions are virtual machines and which are operations on objects. Although "Build the image" clearly has something to do with the image, it also involves a large number of steps: looping for each value of I, evaluating FX and FY of I, and so on. We will consider it to be a virtual machine. "Print the image," however, is a primitive operation on the image. We will consider it to be an operation on an image object.

Now we choose to define the object that encapsulates the image, to construct the Ada package. To determine the remaining operations on the object, let's consider the characteristics of the image.

In addition to being able to *print* the image, let's suppose that we must be able to *clear* the image between its separate invocations. We certainly need the capability to note which of the positions (indicated by X and Y coordinates) are to have marks—we must be able to *mark positions* that are not blank.

In order to make this discussion more specific, we will show an implementation of the Draw_Image solution in the programming language Ada. The Ada "package"—which is nearly identical to the Chapter 7 notion of a module—will be used to implement the objects.

In Ada, the discussion above turns into the following package specification:

```
package Image is
   type X_Coordinate is range 0 .. 99;
   type Y_Coordinate is range 0 .. 49;

   procedure Clear;
   procedure Mark_Position (X : in X_Coordinate; Y : in Y_Coordinate);
   procedure Print;
end Image;
```

We have used Ada's ability to define new types to capture some aspects of the problem statement (the range of the X and Y coordinates). This will lead to a more readable program and also provide the advantages of strong typing in preventing inconsistent use of coordinates and other program variables.

Let's stop and think about the advantages of dealing with this abstract view of an image.

First, because we are dealing with an idealized version of the image, we can construct relatively simple, straightforward algorithms.

Second, we can separate algorithmic and data implementation issues. In the first part of program development, we deal with the simple algorithms for manipulating the idealized image, whereas later we confront the details of how to store and manipulate the data structure.

Third, as an alternative to first dealing with one issue and then the other, we can assign different programming teams to deal with the separate issues. Especially in a large programming project, it is advantageous to have several teams working on the same problem, with the interface between the teams being as narrow as possible. In this case, the interface will be merely the methods for the abstract manipulation of the image. This is a simpler interface than the complete definition of the image data structure. It would be easy to have one team working on the implementation of the image while another team designed and implemented the solution to the problem using the image.

Fourth, and last, the deferral of details of the data structure makes the part of the program that deals with the abstract image independent of the actual image structure. This eases maintenance (in truth, it also eases program development and testing) in two ways:

1. The mechanisms for manipulating the image data structure may be changed without causing changes in the rest of the program.
2. Any changes to the part of the program that deal with the concrete image are *positively bound* to that part of the program. We are guaranteed that errors introduced in making changes cannot "ripple" and cause errors in some other part of the program.

Now we return to the development of the program to solve the Draw_Image problem. Before we treat the step "Build the image" as a virtual machine, let's implement the top-level machine in Ada. This is a vivid illustration of an important advantage of Ada; it allows us to express our design in such a way that it is compilable (which allows us to check interfaces), is potentially executable (with stubs to allow us to demonstrate partial completion of a program), and is a product that will exist unchanged into the coding phase. Here is the top-level machine in Ada:

```
with Image;
procedure Draw_Image is
   procedure Build_Image is separate;
```

```
begin
   Build_Image;
   Image.Print;
end Draw_Image;
```

We build the image (somehow—the details are deferred), and then use the capabilities of the image abstraction to print the image.

Draw_Image is a virtual machine. Its instruction set is Build_Image and Image.Print.

We should note at this point that an alternative design is available. Both operations, building the image and printing the image, could be in a single package. This package might be viewed as an image object, providing all capabilities needed to manipulate the image, or as a virtual machine encapsulated in a package. We prefer the design shown, since we prefer to view the operations on objects as being "close" to the object, or as "primitive" operation. In addition, we see no need to encapsulate a virtual machine in a package. It is an abstract concept, not an Ada component.

Our next level of refinement will focus on Build_Image. The implementation of Build_Image is dependent upon a lower-level notion, that of *setting marks*. Setting marks is an algorithmic function. We will make use of procedural abstraction to reduce the process of setting marks to the invocation of a machine. Here is its specification:

```
procedure Set_Marks;
```

The function of Set_Marks is to place marks in the image in accordance with FX and FY.

Now we can devise the algorithm for Build_Image.

```
with Set_Marks;
separate (Draw_Image)

procedure Build_Image is
begin
   Image.Clear;
   Set_Marks;
end Build_Image;
```

Build_Image is a virtual machine. Its instruction set is Image.Clear and Set_Marks. As we develop our algorithm, we clarify the notion of the abstract operations on the image object; we may even discover additional needed operations, emphasizing the interaction and parallel nature of the concern with virtual machines and objects.

We have shown the Set_Marks procedure as a library unit to illustrate that it is one way of getting operations for virtual machines. However, in a system larger than Draw_Image, it will typically be the case that there are a number of procedures that perform closely related functions. These can be grouped in a package, providing services to the application-driven software that needs to be treated abstractly. Seidewitz & Stark [SEI87] refer to such a package as an object of the form "Action Abstraction."

Now we turn our attention to the algorithm for setting marks. Setting marks in the image involves two issues. The first is iteration through the 1000 values of the Index given in the problem statement, and the second is adding marks to the image. We will again separate those concerns by envisioning a separate machine instruction for adding marks.

```
procedure Set_Marks is
   type Mark_Range is range 0 .. 999;

   procedure Addmark (Mark : in Mark_Range) is separate;
begin
   for Index in Mark_Range loop
      Addmark (Index);
   end loop;
end Set_Marks;
```

Set_Marks is a virtual machine. Its instruction set consists of an Ada construct and a still lower-level virtual machine. All values of the Index (in the appropriate range as indicated by the type mark) are used to add marks to the image. The "value added" of this procedure is to satisfy the requirement that Index is to iterate over some range, with each value being used one time only to add a mark to the image. *It makes no further commitment!* That is the point of the style of programming that we are illustrating. At each point, we do as little as possible, making as little commitment as possible, and deferring as much as possible. (In a larger problem, the virtual machines would not really be this small. We are treating this small problem in such a manner as to illustrate the nature of layering of virtual machines.)

The next refinement, which follows from Set_Marks and also minimizes our commitment to a data structure, is to explain the instruction "Addmark." The function of Addmark is, for a given value of its input, to compute FX and FY of the input and to mark the corresponding position in the image:

```
with Image;
separate (Set_Marks)
procedure Addmark (Mark : in Mark_Range) is
   function FX (Mark : Mark_Range) return Image.X_Coordinate
      is separate;
   function FY (Mark : Mark_Range) return Image.Y_Coordinate
      is separate;
begin
   Image.Mark_Position (FX (Mark), FY(Mark));
end Addmark;
```

We introduce the function FX and FY here, deferring their implementation until later.

At this point we have essentially completed the program at a high level of abstraction. Figure A-16 is an architecture diagram of this program. The lines indicate dependency relationships. In the Image object, the ellipses represent type

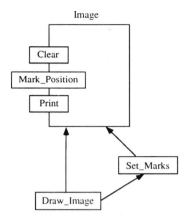

Figure A-16   Draw_Image Architecture Diagram

definitions and the small rectangles represent visible subprograms. Figure A-17 is a structure chart of the program so far. It does not show the internals of the image abstraction, treating it as a primitive concept.

If we were to explain the design to someone, we would start with these graphics. In the design of a large system, the engineering process must involve design reviews. The presentation of the design should involve use of graphics to help the reviewers understand the nature and interaction of the virtual machines and objects. The reviewers must be able to both assess the quality of the design and

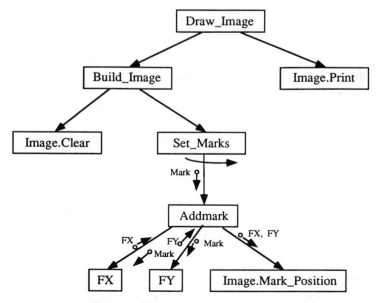

Figure A-17   Draw_Image Structure Chart

determine whether it satisfies the software requirements specification. This sort of review improves the design, and is an integral part of the software development process.

It is of some significance that we have been able to construct so much of the program without being concerned with the details of the image. We are using our powers of abstraction. The image abstraction can be constructed in a number of different (correct) ways without affecting what we have done so far.

Now we are ready to begin the design of the image abstraction. We can proceed no further without committing to a specific data structure. However, let's continue to apply the principle of minimal commitment. We will decide that the image is to be made up of an array of lines, but there is no need yet to decide upon the structure of a line.

Thus far, we have been discussing single objects. However, since there will be multiple lines, it is convenient to introduce a new sort of object.

The Image package encapsulates a single object, with exported operations to change the state of the hidden data structure. It is useful to think of the operations as "managing" the data structure. We then call such an encapsulation of a data structure an *object manager*.

A different sort of package encapsulates a *definition* of a data structure (a type). It exports an abstract type definition, which includes operations on instances of the type. The specific instances of the type (variables, the actual objects) are created by the users of this sort of package. The operations "manage" the encapsulated data structure definition. This sort of encapsulation of a data structure is called a *type manager*.

We will specify an abstraction of the notion of "line". For now, we won't worry about the length of a line. Since there may be many lines, created by one or more users of the package, we want a type manager, with the specific line to be operated on passed as a parameter to each operation. To accomplish this, we provide an abstract type definition of Lines as `limited private,` restricting the user of the package to only the operations exported by the package. The only possible operations on objects of type Lines are to clear, mark in a specified position, and print.

These characteristics of the line manager are captured by the package specification below, assuming that the type definition for Line_Length is visible at this point. (We will explain the Ada-specific construct `type lines is limited private` later. For now, just assume it defines a type that is not explained at this point, much as if we had written `type Lines is . . . .`

```
package Line_Manager is
   type Lines is limited private;
   procedure Clear_Line (Line: in out Lines);
   procedure Mark_Line  (Position: in Line_Length;
                         Line: in out Lines);
   procedure Print_Line (Line: in Lines);
private
   . . .  - - some missing Ada code
   - - This is the ''private part'' of the package specification.
end Line_Manager;
```

We will not show the private part here, but will provide it later. The user of the package cannot use the information in this part of the package specification in any event.

We say that the type Lines is an *abstract data type* and that it is *exported*. It is available for use by other modules as a type definition, but the other modules, called clients, do not need to know the complete definition. That is, they will create variables, called objects in this context, of the type Lines, but they will not manipulate the components of the object, instead relying on the module Line_Manager to perform all the operations on the object. The module Line_Manager is sometimes called a type manager, since it "manages" objects of the type. Programming in this style has important implications for robustness in the face of change, as we will see later in this example.

Now we are ready to develop the image abstraction, based on the Lines abstraction. We then use the exported abstract type to create a type Images as an array of abstract lines. The array will be indexed by the Y coordinate of our image, as illustrated in the problem specification. Then we create the actual variable, the object, that is encapsulated and managed by the package. Last, we provide the implementation of the operations exported by the Image package specification.

```
with Line_Manager;
package body Image is
   type Images is array (Y_Coordinate) of Line_Manager.Lines;
   Image_Of_Lines : Images;
   - - this is the object being managed

   procedure Clear is
   begin
     for A_Line in Y_Coordinate loop
       Line_Manager.Create_Line (Image_Of_Lines (A_Line));
     end loop;
   end Clear;
   procedure Mark_Position (X : in X_Coordinate;
                            Y : in Y_Coordinate) is
   begin
     Line_Manager.Mark_Line (X, Image_Of_Lines (Y));
   end Mark_Position;

   procedure Print is
   begin
     for A_Line in reverse Y_Coordinate loop
         Line_Manager.Print_Line (Image_Of_Lines (A_Line));
     end loop;
   end Print;
end Image;
```

The phrase "with Line_Manager" allows the client (Image) to see, or have visibility to, the server (Line_Manager). The_Image_Of_Lines is the "object" being managed by this package. It is the array of abstract lines.

An important point to recognize is that we still have not committed to a representation for a line. We have deferred that decision in order to focus on the manipulation of the lines in the image. We therefore simplify the manipulation of the image. In addition, we could have a parallel programming effort to implement the Line_Manager while we are implementing the Image package.

There are some additional observations to be made at this point. Heretofore, we have been refining the algorithms used to solve the problem. At this level, we are refining the *data structures* used to solve the problem. This example illustrates most vividly the separation of concerns between algorithm and data structure. Another important point is that the definition of data structure does not occur all at once: It involves the same sort of refinement as does the development of the algorithms.

We have also repeatedly made the point that modules (in Ada, packages) should be used to hide *design decisions*. The earlier levels were hiding, or abstracting, design decisions about algorithms. The Image package, however, also hides a design decision about a data structure. It is therefore an "object" in the sense of object-oriented development.

We are finally ready to consider implementation of the line abstraction. First we show the private part of the package. A first attempt might assume an array of lines. Here is the private part of the package specification, with the full definition of the type of Lines.

```
type Print_Symbols is (Mark, Space);
type Lines is array (Line_Length) of Print_Symbols;
```

The constant value Line_Length defines the length of the line and is assumed to be visible at this point in the program. The importance of the private part and the associated business of `type Lines is limited private` is that the client of the package has no visibility to the actual definition, in the private part, of the abstract data type Lines. The definition can change to anything whatsoever without the client being affected. Except for assignment and comparison for equality, the client can perform no operations on data elements of the type except those exported by the package that defines the type. Of course, the creator of the package is responsible for ensuring that the operations still make sense if the type definition is changed. We'll see an example of a change in the type definition immediately below.

We could implement and use the package with the above private part in an operating Draw_Image solution.

An important aspect of the use of abstraction in programming is that programs are easy to change; this eases maintenance and encourages reuse. We can change the implementation of the abstract line without causing any change in higher-level machines. For example, if we choose to maintain the position of the last mark in a line explicitly (this makes some of the line algorithms more efficient), we could define a line in the private part as:

```
type Print_Symbols is (Mark, Space);
type Lineimage is array (Line_Length) of Print_Symbols;
type Lines is
   record
     Last   : Line_Length;
     Symbol : Lineimage;
   end record;
```

This change, and corresponding changes to the body of the Line-Manager, will have no effect on higher-level machines.

The implementation of the Line-Manager depends upon yet a lower-level object, the printer. The printer object encapsulates the print capabilities described in the problem specification and is needed only by the Print-Line procedure of the Line-Manager. Ada gives us the capability to limit visibility to only that procedure.

We will not complete the implementation of the problem, but we will show the specification of the printer object here:

```
package Printer is
    procedure Mark;
    procedure Space;
    procedure Next-Line;
end Printer;
```

The Printer package encapsulates the basic capabilities needed to manipulate the physical printer device. This package is then used by the Line-Manager in order to do the printing.

This is as far as we will go with the problem for this Appendix. Notice that we have not extended the structure chart to include the additional operations on lines or the printer. We are treating the exported operations of the Image object exactly as though they were part of our language's basic instruction set. At some later point (or earlier or in parallel) we convince ourselves of the correctness of the Image abstraction — perhaps using additional structure charts and architecture diagrams. The advantage of this is that we can deal with the image as a separate problem; it is both easier than the original problem and can be solved without confounding its solution with the rules for drawing the image (I in 0 .. 999, use of FX and FY, and so on). However, there may be certain sorts of problems for which a complete structure chart, showing the lower-level operations on an object, is desirable. Even more often, we may wish to see the complete architecture diagram.

The use of MSD has achieved several important objectives. First of all, the step-by-step processing is easy to understand, since it is at a high level of abstraction, using the abstract operations on the image. Second, it is easy to change. A change in the internal representation of the image will not affect the virtual machines using the image. A change in the representation of the line does not affect the image. A change of printers will not affect the rest of the program. Further, a change in the algorithm to *construct* the image will not cause change in the *representation* of the image. This holds true whether the change is only in FX and FY (this change being hidden in those virtual machines), or is a complete change in the notion of how images are created.

The latter point brings us to the final objective that has been achieved. The Image and Line-Manager abstractions are reusable software components. They are indifferent to the methods that are used to construct images; they can be used in many different contexts.

Dijkstra [DIJ72] describes the virtual machines and (what we call) objects as "pearls" and says that programs are constructed by creating pearls and stringing them together. In discussing the system architecture, he states, "We have described the program in terms of levels and each level contained 'refinements' of entities that were assumed available in higher levels. These refinements were either dynamic refinements (algorithms) or static refinements (data structures) to be understood by an appropriate machine. I use the term 'pearl' for such a machine, refinements included."

In regard to the understandability and adaptability of programs with this structure, he says, "The larger the number of pearls independent of the particular representation, the more adaptable one's program and the more easily understandable — because that set of pearls can be understood at a higher level of abstraction."

Although the case study is based on a simple problem, it has illustrated the important ideas of MSD and suggested why these ideas are important to the construction of large, long-lived software systems.

A.5.6 Rationale for the Method

Why is MSD an effective design method? Reflecting the balance between data abstraction and functional decomposition, the answer has several components.

Why Object-Oriented Design?   Object-oriented design focuses on "objects as the primary agents involved in a computation; hence, the architecture of a system is organized around collections of objects — not algorithmic abstractions." [BOO86]. We believe that this is the proper way to organize the architecture of a system. Further, we agree with Brooks [BRO87a] in holding out "more hope for object-oriented programming than for any of the other technical fads of the day." Object-oriented design captures, and goes beyond, the essential characteristics of information hiding and design with abstract data types; it can be an important component of effective design.

Why Layered Virtual Machines?   In any software system, there must be, somewhere, the step-by-step processing by which the work of the program gets done. However, as Parnas says, "It is almost always incorrect to begin the decomposition of a system into components on the basis of a flowchart i.e, the steps in the processing" [PAR72b]. We agree that modularization should not be done on this basis. However, we do not feel that the step-by-step processing should be either ignored or hidden. It is this step-by-step processing that actually accomplishes the purpose of the software system. Further, the step-by-step processing, the virtual machine, is a major contributor to determining the necessary objects. In the creation of virtual machines and objects, neither comes before the other; the refinement occurs in parallel.

We feel that the balance between data abstraction and functional decomposition must be represented in the graphics used to describe the design. Hence, we use both architecture diagrams and structure charts. This allows the reviewer of the design not only to understand the system architecture, but also to understand the steps in the processing representing the functionality of the system. Since we feel that design reviews are an integral part of the engineering process, the ability to communicate the design graphically is a direct contribution to the quality of the design.

In addition to the issue of the design itself and its representation, there is the need to *teach the design method*, to provide guidance to designers. Brophy, Agresti, and Basili [BRO87b] feel that object-oriented design "did not provide enough guidelines in its representations." Using the needs of the virtual machines to determine operations on objects provides additional guidance to the designers.

Why Both? Object-oriented development alone, without the notion of layered virtual machines, would have provided a solution of the Draw_Image problem that had essentially the same characteristics of modifiability, software reuse, and so on that we discussed at the conclusion of the case study. In fact, all three Ada objects (the image, the line, and the printer) represent objects in the problem space, explicit in the problem specification. That congruence with the real world is often a characteristic of good Ada objects. MSD uses modeling the real world as one guideline for determining objects, but it also allows other ways of discovering or designing objects, perhaps reaching the same destination as object-oriented development, but by a different path. Then the question, "Why both LVM and OOD?"

The parallel concern with virtual machines and objects provides a convenient mechanism for teaching design and for providing guidance to designers. Convenience is important: It makes programmers better designers in less time. The explicit notions of information hiding, deferral of detail, abstract data types, and so on also give designers additional guidance for creating effective abstractions.

In addition, the *expression* of the design is different in MSD, particularly the use of structure charts to express the steps in the processing. This has significant potential to enhance the design through the engineering review process and to explain the design to customers for whom the system is being created.

Summarizing the need for a parallel concern for algorithms and data structures, we again quote Wirth [WIR71]: "Refinement of the description of program and data structures should proceed in parallel." Dijkstra [DIJ72] also wants either dynamic refinements (algorithms) or static refinements (data structures) to be understood by an appropriate machine."

A.5.7 MSD and Concurrent Systems

The idea of designing with virtual machines and objects is applicable to real-time systems. In concurrent systems, the virtual machines operate in parallel, and the objects often must provide for mutual exclusion. The virtual machines become cooperating sequential processes. The foundation abstraction becomes *process abstraction*, addressed as a design model by Cherry [CHE86] and Shumate [SHU88]. Nielsen & Shumate [NIE88] provide a set of explicit process selection rules for cooperating sequential processes, then use MSD as a decomposition method for the design of large individual tasks.

A.5.8 Summary

The modular structured design methods presented here illustrate how separation of concerns, deferral of detail, layering of abstraction, and a parallel focus on algorithms and data structures can be the basis for the design of software systems. The method is strongly object-oriented but uses the virtual machine concept to retain a sense of the *steps* needed to solve the problem. It uses a graphical notation that captures both the objects representing the system architecture and the virtual machines representing the step-by-step processing of the system. This allows a reviewer to understand readily what the software does, thus enhancing the engineering process and allowing a determination of whether the design satisfies a software requirements specification.

ACD (architecture context diagram): The ACD is the top-level diagram for the system architecture model. Like the DCD and CCD, it contains information showing the system's place in its environment.

Action: The set of activities that must be performed in response to an external event.

ADC: Analog-to-digital converter (case study acronym).

ADT (abstract data type): A software module that specifies a data structure in terms of its use rather than its implementation. See *Data abstraction*.

AFD (architecture flow diagram): A network representation of a system configuration. Similar in content to SBD.

Afferent stream: A string of processes on a DFD whose chief function is to collect or transport data from its physical source or to refine input data from the form provided by its source to a form suitable for the major functions of the CSCI.

AID (architecture interconnect diagram): This graphic represents the physical means by which information travels from one architecture module to another.

AIS (architecture interconnect specification): The AIS establishes the characteristics of the physical media connecting the architecture modules.

Analysis: The creative activity involved in understanding a problem, associated constraints, and methods of overcoming constraints and in determining how to organize the mass of information being gathered.

Application module: A module that contains the subprograms (and concurrent tasks) that accomplish the main processing of the CSCI.

ASC: ACME Steel Corporation (case study acronym).

Balancing: Checking for consistency of flows between levels of DFDs or CFDs.

CASE: Computer-aided software engineering.

CCD (control context diagram): The CCD establishes the control boundary between the CSCI under study and the environment. It is used to show communication between the CSCI and the environment and the entities in the environment with which the CSCI communicates.

Central transform: The portion(s) of a DFD that remains when the afferent and efferent streams have been removed; the major data-transforming functions of the CSCI.

CFD (control flow diagram): A CFD mirrors the processes and stores from the DFD, but shows control flows instead of data flows. It is constructed simply to constrain the control signals to flow along the same paths as data signals may flow.

Child DFD: Lower-level breakdown of a process (parent) on a DFD.

CI: Configuration Item.

Client: The user of information or services; (a module that makes calls to get data or accomplish its work. See *Server*.

Cohesion: The characteristic of a process that indicates the degree to which its components are working together to accomplish the same function. High cohesion (single, clearly understood individual function) is desirable. See *Coupling*.

Concurrency: The concept of two or more processes (tasks) operating simultaneously.

Control action: The control response to an internal event.

Control flow: Pipeline through which control information of known composition flows. It may consist of a single element or a group of elements.

Control signal: The control represented by a control flow. It may be a control action or a process activator.

COTS: Commercial, off the shelf.

Coupling: The characteristic of a number of processes that indicates the degree to which they are interconnected and, conversely, the degree to which they are independent. Loose coupling (little interconnection) is best. See *Cohesion*.

CSCI: Computer software configuration item.

CSpec (Control Specification): A CSpec converts input control signals into output control signals or into process activators. It shows the control processing for the associated CFD.

CSpec bar: Symbol used on a CFD to indicate the interface between the CFD and its CSpec.

Customer need: The operational requirement given to the contractor to begin analysis and development of the system.

Data abstraction: The use of data structures abstractly by referring to operations on the data rather than to the elements of a data structure directly. The focus is on the *contents* of a data structure and the *operations* that may manipulate a data structure without regard to the programming details of the data structure's implementation.

Data dictionary: An ordered list of data flow, control flow, and data store names, each with a definition in terms of its components and structure. Each data flow, control flow, and data store on the flow diagrams must be defined in the dictionary down to its primitive elements.

Data flow: Pipeline through which data of known composition flows. It may consist of a single element or a group of elements.

Data module: A module that encapsulates a data structure and provides operations (subprograms) to manipulate it.

DCC: Data concentrator computer (case study acronym).

DCD (data context diagram): The DCD establishes the data boundary between the CSCI under study and the environment. It is used to show the communications between the CSCI and the environment and the entities in the environment with which the CSCI communicates.

Decision table: Table used in CSpec to show control signal processing; it creates a mapping of input control signals into output control signals.

DemVal: Demonstration and validation.

Derived requirement: A requirement not directly stated by the system requirements but necessary to satisfy the system design. See *essential requirement*.

Detailed Design: The determination of the low-level architecture of the system and the specification in pseudocode format of algorithms in each callable software component.

DFD (data flow diagram): A DFD is a network representation of a system's functional requirements. It portrays the requirements in terms of their functional component parts, with all interfaces among the parts indicated.

DTS: Digital temperature sensor (case study acronym).

EAD (event–action diagram): "DFD" showing all of the actions in the system with their inputs, outputs, and interactions. The interactions between actions must be through data store(s).

EFD (enhanced flow diagram): "DFD" showing all system-level requirements (including the derived ones) allocated to a CSCI.

Efferent stream: A string of processes on a DFD whose chief function is to transport or dispatch data to its physical destination or to format output data from the form produced by the major functions of the CSCI to a form suitable for output.

ER: Entity relationship.

ERD (entity relationship diagram): A form of diagram that views a system as an abstract collection of components of the system (entities) and their relationships; it does not pay attention to processes or inputs and outputs.

Essential requirement: A requirement necessary to fulfill the purpose of the system—satisfying a customer's operational needs—regardless of *how* the system is implemented. Essential requirements are stated by the system requirements phase. See *derived requirement*.

Event: An external or internal stimulus. The EAD is used to represent the responses to external events. The STD or SEM is used for internal events.

FAO: Furnace Administrative Office (case study acronym).

FAOC: Furnace Administrative Office computer (case study acronym).

FFBD (functional flow block diagram): Functional breakdown of system requirements showing what needs to be accomplished by each function and the flow of information between functions. See also *DFD*.

FFD (flattened flow diagram). "DFD" that captures all the software requirements for a CSCI and provides for aggregation of these processes to identify concurrency.

FMC: Furnace Monitor Computer (case study acronym).

FMS: Furnace Monitoring System (case study acronym).

Function: An action, job, or set of steps that provide the capability to accomplish some specific requirement. For a process on a DFD, this is a transform of data from one form to another. For a subprogram, it is what occurs upon invocation. Examples: control fuel flow; validate message; monitor communication channel; report all temperatures.

Helper module: A module used to support the application modules. These include those that are used to encapsulate data structures (data modules) and types as well as those (such as conversion modules) that provide services.

HWCI: Hardware configuration item.

Implementability: The ease with which a design can be turned into code.

Information hiding: The idea of decomposing software into modules that "hide knowledge of a design decision" from all other modules.

LVM: Layered virtual machine.

Maintainability: The ease with which a system can be kept in operating condition.

Methodology: A set of procedures, graphics, and guidelines that explains how to accomplish the task at hand.

MNS: Mission needs statement. See *Customer need*.

MO: Maintenance Office (case study acronym).

MOC: Maintenance Office computer (case study acronym).

Modularity: The ability of a system to be expanded or changed with minimal difficulty.

Module: A collection of software components that interact closely together to perform functions necessary to satisfy the requirements. In SSEM, the primary form of module is that based on data abstraction and principles of information hiding. See *Application module, Helper module*.

MSD (modular structured design): Methodology for late stages of top-level design, carrying into detailed design and resulting code. It integrates the notions of structured design with information hiding, data abstraction, or OOD, calling for a balanced approach between functional decomposition ("structured design" part) and information hiding ("modular" part).

MSpec (architecture module specification): Describes the information and processing of each architecture module.

MTBF: Mean time between failure.

MTTR: Mean time to repair.

Object: An encapsulated data structure.

OOA: Object-oriented analysis.

OOD (Object-oriented design or object-oriented development): The method involving the design of software around abstractions of "objects" in some real world problem.

OORA: Object-oriented requirements analysis.

Parent process: Next higher-level process on DFD or CFD network.

PAT (process activation table): A subset of decision tables. It maps control signals into process activators that shows which process(es) should be activated based on the control signal input.

PDL: Program design language.

PMC: Plant Management Computer (case study acronym).

Process: (1) The set of steps that must be accomplished to complete a task. (2) On a DFD, process indicates the transformation of incoming data flow(s) into outgoing data flow(s). It is also used to map the paths along which control signals flow and may be activated or deactivated by a process activator.

Process activator: Control action that activates or deactivates a process. It can be shown as a lightning bolt on the DFD/CFD or described within a CSpec (usually in a PAT).

PSpec (Process specification): The specification of a primitive process, describing how the output data and control signals are generated from the input data of the process being documented. It may generate control signals, including process activators.

RAS (requirements allocation sheet): This systems engineering graphic shows the relationship between requirements and the components of the system design. See *RTM*.

Reliability: The degree to which a system can be depended on to work correctly.

Requirement: Feature or capability that a system must possess to satisfy its purpose; an action necessary to be accomplished to satisfy a customer's operational need. See *Essential requirement* and *Derived requirement*.

Requirements model: Description of those things that a system must do to be successful, regardless of the technology chosen to implement it.

Reusability: The degree to which a program or program component can be used again within the same project or on other projects without changing it.

ROC (required operational capability): See *Customer need*.

RTA (response time allocation): The allocation of response times from the systems requirements model to components within the systems architecture model.

RTD (real-time design): The methodology approach for making the transition from software requirements to software design, ending with a complete top-level design or architecture of the software system.

RTM (requirements traceability matrix): A table that shows traceability of each portion of the model to the requirements that it satisfies.

RTS (response time specification): A list of system input events and their resulting system output events, both expressed in terms of the system input and output signals that represent them. The timing relationships are listed for each input-to-output event pair.

RTSA (real-time structured analysis): The methodology approach toward structured analysis that incorporates those elements needed for real-time software design.

SAD (software architecture diagram): This graphic identifies the major modules (ones that hide design decisions) in the CSCI.

SBD (schematic block diagram): This systems engineering graphic shows the actual system (hardware and software) components and the characteristics of their interconnections. See *AFD*.

Server: Manager of data or operations, a module called by clients, which need the information or work performed. See *Client*.

Software design: The product, or documentation, resulting from the software design phases (top-level and detailed design).

Software engineering: The establishment and use of sound engineering principles in order to obtain, economically, software that is reliable and works efficiently on real machines.

Software requirements analysis: The detailed specification of the necessary functionality of each CSCI and the interfaces among all CSCIs and HWCIs.

Software requirements model: The set of graphics and associated textual explanation that describe the capabilities and performance requirements of the CSCI and associated interfaces to be built to satisfy the allocated and derived requirements. The requirements are *allocated* to the software components during software design and are *traced back* to the system requirements model and system architecture model to ensure that all requirements have been satisfied. (See *Requirements model*).

Software specification: The product, or documentation, resulting from the software requirements analysis phase.

SSEM (systems software engineering methodology): The collective methodology for development of systems software. The components of SSEM are RTSA, RTD, and MSD.

STD (state transition diagram): This graphic illustrates the states (or modes) of a system and the transitions (changes) between states.

Store: A data or control flow frozen in time. The data or control information it contains may be used any time after that information is stored and in any order.

Structure chart: A graphic tool for depicting the partitioning of a CSCI into subprograms, the hierarchy and organization of those subprograms, and the communication interfaces between the subprograms.

STT (state transition table): See *STD*.

System architecture model: The set of graphics and associated textual explanation that describe the physical components and characteristics (including the software components) of the system to be built to satisfy the customer's operations requirements or essential needs. The requirements are *allocated* to the system components during system design and are *traced back* to the system requirements model to ensure that all requirements have been satisfied.

System design: The determination of the overall system architecture consisting of a set of physical processing components—hardware, software, people, and the communication among them—that will satisfy the system's essential requirements.

System engineering: The process used to transform an operational need into a working system that satisfies the requirement.

System requirements analysis: The transformation of the customer's operational needs into a set of capabilities and performance requirements suitable for the interactive and parallel determination of a system design and allocation of requirements to components of the design.

System requirements model: The set of graphics and associated textual explanation that describe the capabilities and performance requirements of the system to be built to satisfy the customer's operations requirements and essential needs. See *Requirements Model*.

Systems software: Software that is developed in accordance with and to satisfy the needs of overall systems development, as distinct from software that is created as a software- only development on existing or purchased hardware.

Task: Concurrent component of a CSCI.

TCG (task communication graph): This graphic identifies software tasks and their interactions.

Terminator: Represents an entity outside the context of the system that is a net transmitter or receiver of system data (also called a source, sink, or external).

Testability: The ease with which a system can be evaluated in order to determine if any errors exist.

Thread: All the processing (literally, all the instructions) necessary to respond to an event.

Time line sheets: Systems engineering graphic depicting the activities that occur at given times and how long the activities take.

Timing thread: The ordered set of tasks and task interactions that must execute to transform an external input signal or event into the required external output signal or event. There is a timing thread for each external input signal in the RTS (from software requirements analysis).

Top-level design: The determination and description of the overall software architecture and of the interfaces between the major modules within that architecture.

Traceability: The ease with which system (or software) components can be mapped back to the requirements that they satisfy.

Transaction analysis: A design strategy in which the structure of a CSCI (or portion thereof) is derived from a study of the portions of the DFD where there is parallel flow of similar data items by type.

Transform analysis or transform-centered design: A design strategy in which the structure of a CSCI (or portion thereof) is derived from a study of the flow of data through the CSCI and of the transformations to that data.

Understandability: The degree to which a system or component can be clearly understood by another person.

Virtual machine: An abstract computer with a powerful, problem-oriented instruction set ideally suited to the problem being solved.

[BAI89]: Bailin, Sidney C., "An Object-Oriented Requirements Specification Method," *Communications of the ACM,* Vol. 32, No. 5, May 1989, pp. 608–623.

[BLA90]: Blanchard, B. S., and W. J. Fabrycky, *Systems Engineering and Analysis*, 2nd Ed., Englewood Cliffs, NJ: Prenctice Hall, 1990.

[BOE88]: Boehm, Barry W., "A Spiral Model of Software Development and Enhancement," *IEEE Computer,* May 1988, pp. 61–72.

[BOO86]: Booch, G., "Object-Oriented Development," *IEEE Transactions on Software Engineering,* Vol. SE-12, No. 2, February 1986, pp. 211–221.

[BOO87]: Booch, G., *Software Engineering with Ada,* 2nd edition, Menlo Park, CA: Benjamin/Cummings, 1987.

[BRI90]: Brintzenhoff, A. L., K. Nielsen, and K. Shumate, "C2P Ada Shadow Program: Design, Prototype Development and Implementation of Command and Control Software," *Ada: Experiences and Prospects— Proceedings of the Ada-Europe International Conference,* Dublin, 12–14 June 1990, Cambridge University Press, pp. 56–67.

[BRO87a]: Brooks, Frederick P. Jr., "No Silver Bullet: Essence and Accidents of Software Engineering," *IEEE Software,* April 1987, pp. 10–19.

[BRO87b]: Brophy, C.E., W.W. Agresti, and V.R. Basili, "Lessons Learned in Ada-Oriented Design Methods," *Proceedings of the Joint Ada Conference,* Washington, DC, March 16–19, 1987, pp. 231–236.

[CHE76]: Chen, P., "The Entity-Relationship Model—Toward a Unified View of Data," *ACM Transactions on Database Systems,* Vol. 1, No. 1, March 1976.

[CHE86]: Cherry, G.W., *The PAMELA Designer's Handbook,* Vols. I and II, Reston, VA: Thought**Tools, 1986.

[CHE90]: Chen, P., "Entity-Relationship Approach to Data Modeling," in Thayer, R. H., and M. Dorfman, eds. *System and Software Requirements Engineering,* IEEE Computer Society, 1990, pp. 238–243.

[COA90]: Coad, Peter, and Edward Yourdon, *Object-Oriented Analysis,* Englewood Cliffs, NJ: Yourdon Press/Prentice Hall, 1990.

[DAV90]: Davis, Alan M., *Software Requirements: Analysis and Specification,* Englewood Cliffs, NJ: Prentice Hall, 1990.

[DEM78]: DeMarco, T., *Structured Analysis and System Specification,* New York: Yourdon, Inc., 1978.

[DIJ68]: Dijkstra, E. W., "The Structure of 'THE' Multiprogramming System," *Communications of the ACM,* Vol. 11, No. 4, May 1968, pp. 341–346.

[DIJ72]: Dijkstra, E.W., "Notes on Structured Programming," in O. J. Dahl, E. W. Dijkstra, and C.A. R. Hoare, eds., *Structured Programming,* New York: Academic Press, 1972, pp. 1–82.

[DOA79]: Department of the Army, *System Engineering, FM 770-78,* Washington, DC, April 1979.

[DOD87]: *Defense Science Board Task Force Report on Military Software,* Washington, DC: Office of the Undersecretary of Defense for Acquisition, September 1987.

[DOR90]: Dorfman, M, and R. H. Thayer, eds., *System and Software Requirements Engineering,* Los Alamitos, CA: IEEE Computer Society, 1990.

[DSM86]: Defense Systems Management College, *Systems Engineering Management Guide,* Fort Belvoir, VA, October 1986.

[ESA89]: European Space Agency (ESA), *HOOD User Manual,* Issue 3.0, WME/89-353/JB, Noordwijk, The Netherlands: ESA Research and Technology Centre, 1989.

[FIS71]: Fisher, *Cost Considerations in Systems Analysis,* New York: American Elsevier, 1971.

[FLA81]: Flavin, Matt, *Fundamental Concepts of Information Modeling,* New York: Yourdon Press, 1981.

[GOM84]: Gomaa, H., "A Software Design Method for Real-Time Systems," *Communications of the ACM,* Vol. 27, No. 9, September 1984, pp. 938–949.

[GOM89]: Gomaa, H., "A Software Design Method for Ada Based Real-Time Systems," *Proceedings of the Sixth Washington Ada Symposium,* June 26–29, 1989, Washington, DC.

[GRA88]: Gray, Lewis, "Transitioning From Structured Analysis to Object-Oriented Design," *Proceeding of the Fifth Washington Ada Symposium,* June 27–30, 1988, ACM, Washington, DC.

[HAT87]: Hatley, D. J., and I. A. Pirbhai, *Strategies for Real-Time System Specification,* New York: Dorset House, 1987.

[HEI90]: Heitz, Maurice, "Practical Issues of Using HOOD," *Ada UK Tutorials, Ada UK International Conference,* Brighton, England, 23 October 1990.

[HUM89]: Humphrey, Watts S., *Managing the Software Process,* New York: Addison-Wesley, 1989.

[JEN79]: Jensen, Randall and Charles Tonies, *Software Engineering,* Englewood Cliffs, NJ: Prentice Hall, 1979.

[KEN88] Kennedy, Allan and Colin Carter, "Real Time Structured Analysis and Ada—A Pragmatic Object-Oriented Approach," *Ada User,* December 1988, pp. 77–84.

[KRE90]: Krell, Bruce E., "Ada Software Development Methodology with Case Study," *Tutorials of Tri-Ada 1990,* Baltimore, Maryland, December 3, 1990.

[LIS86]: Liskov, G., and J. Guttag, *Abstraction and Specification in Program Development,* Cambridge, MA: MIT Press, 1986.

[MCM84]: McMenamin, S. M., and J. F. Palmer, *Essential Systems Analysis,* Englewood Cliffs, NJ: Yourdon Press, 1984.

[MIL56]: Miller, G. A., "The Magical Number Seven, Plus or Minus Two: Some Limits on Our Capacity for Processing Information," *Physiological Review,* Vol. 63, March 1956, pp. 81–87.

[MYE75]: Myers, Glenford J., *Reliable Software through Composite Design,* New York: Petrocilli/Charter, 1975.

[NIE88]: Nielsen, Kjell, and Ken Shumate, *Designing Large Real-Time Systems with Ada,* New York: McGraw-Hill, 1988.

[PAG88]: Page-Jones, M., *The Practical Guide to Structured Systems Design,* 2nd ed., New York: Yourdon Press, 1988.

[PAR72a]: Parnas, D. L., "A Technique for Software Module Specification with Examples," *Communications of the ACM,* Vol. 15, No. 5, May 1972, pp. 330–336.

[PAR72b]: Parnas, D. L., "On the Criteria to be Used in Decomposing Systems into Modules," *Communications of the ACM,* Vol. 15, No. 12, December 1972, pp. 1053–1058.

[PAR85]: Parnas, D. L., Paul C. Clements, and David M. Weiss, "The Modular Structure of Large Systems." *IEEE Transactions on Software Engineering,* Vol. SE-11, No. 3, March 1985.

[PAR86]: Parnas, D. L., and P. C. Clements, "A Rational Design Process: How and Why to Fake It," *IEEE Transactions on Software Engineering,* Vol. SE-12, No. 2, February 1986, pp. 252–257.

[PAR89]: Parnas, D. L., P. C. Clements, and D. M. Weiss, "Enhancing Reusability with Information Hiding," in Biggerstaff, T. J. and A. J. Perlis, eds., *Software Reusability: Concepts and Models,* Reading, MA: Addison-Wesley, 1989.

[PAR90]: Parnas, D. L., et al., "Evaluation of Safety Critical Software," *Communications of the ACM,* Vol. 33, No. 6, June 1990, pp. 636–648.

[PRE87]: Pressman, Roger S., *Software Engineering: A Practitioner's Approach,* 2nd Ed., New York: McGraw-Hill, 1987.

[QUA68]: Quade, E. S., and W. I, Boucher, *Systems Analysis and Policy Planning: Applications in Defense,* New York: American Elsevier, 1968.

[ROY70]: Royce, Winston W., "Managing the Development of Large Software Systems," *Proceedings of IEEE WESCON,* IEEE, 1970, pp. 1–9.

[RUM91]: Rumbaugh, James, et al., *Object-Oriented Modeling and Design,* Englewood Cliffs, NJ: Prentice Hall, 1991.

[SAN89a]: Sanden, B. "An Entity-Life Modeling Approach to the Design of Concurrent Software," *Communications of the ACM,* Vol. 32, No. 3, March 1989, pp. 330–343.

[SAN89b]: Sanden, B. "Entity-Life Modeling and Structured Analysis in Real-Time Software Design—A Comparison," *Communications of the ACM,* Vol. 32, No. 12, December 1989, pp. 1458–1466.

[SEI87]: Seidewitz, Ed, and Mike Stark, "Towards a General Object-Oriented Software Development Methodology," *Ada Letters,* ACM/SIGAda, July/August 1987.

[SHA90]: Sha, Lui, and John B. Goodenough, "Real-Time Scheduling Theory and Ada," *IEEE Computer,* April 1990, pp. 53–62.

[SHI67]: Shinners, Stanley M., *Techniques of System Engineering,* New York: McGraw-Hill, 1967.

[SHU88]: Shumate, Ken, "Layered Virtual Machine/Object-Oriented Design (LVM/OOD)," *Proceedings of the Fifth Washington Ada Symposium,* ACM, June 27–30, 1988, Washington, DC, pp. 177–190.

[SHU89]: Shumate, Ken, *Understanding Ada: with Abstract Data Types,* 2nd ed., New York: John Wiley & Sons, 1989.

[SHU90]: Shumate, Ken, "Establish Overall Software System Architecture Using Data Abstraction," *Journal of Pascal, Ada, and Modula-2,* Jan./Feb. 1990.

[SHU91]: Shumate, Ken, "Structured Analysis and Object-Oriented Design Are Compatible," *Ada Letters,* May/June 1991, pp. 78-90.

[TRU77]: Trueman, Richard E. *Quantitative Methods for Decision Making,* New York: Holt, Rinehart and Winston, 1977.

[WAR85]: Ward, P., and S. Mellor, *Structured Development for Real-Time Systems,* Vols. 1-3, New York: Yourdon Press, 1985.

[WAR89]: Ward, Paul T., "How To Integrate Object Orientation with Structured Analysis and Design," *IEEE Software,* March 1989.

[WEG83]: Wegner, Peter, "On the Unification of Data and Program Abstraction in Ada," *Proceedings of the 10th Annual ACM Symposium on Principles of Programming Languages,* 1983.

[WIR71]: Wirth, N., "Program Development by Stepwise Refinement," *Communications of the ACM,* Vol. 14, No. 4, April 1971, pp. 221–227.

[YOU79]: Yourdon, E., and L. L. Constantine, *Structured Design: Fundamentals of a Discipline of Computer Program and Systems Design,* Englewood Cliffs, NJ: Prentice Hall, 1979.